CAVE DIVING

The Cave Diving Group Manual

Compiling editors:
F. G. Balcombe, J. N. Cordingley,
R. J. Palmer, R. A. Stevenson

Publishing editor:
Bruce Bedford

Published & Printed by:
Mendip Publishing,
Castle Cary Press,
Castle Cary, Somerset,
England

Typeset by: Creative Types, Glastonbury, Somerset

ISBN: 0 905903 14 5

© 1990, Cave Diving Group, CDG Publications,

This book is dedicated to

F. Graham Balcombe

and

Dr. Oliver Cromwell Lloyd

For setting up, nurturing and stirring when required.

The Cave Diving Group would like to thank the following for their contributions to this publication:

Jim Abbott, John Adams, Paul Atkinson, Richard Bartrop, George Bee, Mike Boon, Simon Brooks, John Cooper, John Cordingley, Geoff Crossley, Dani Danilewicz, Martyn Farr, Peter Glanvill, Axel Gnadinger, Julian Griffiths, Bob Grimes, Jim Hanwell, Chris Howes, Rob James, Mike Jeanmaire, Chris and Annie Milne, Dave Morris, Gavin Newman, Rob Palmer, Phil Pappard, Steve Pickersgill, Graham Proudlove, Pete Riley, Jonny Shaw, Rupert Skorupka, Brian Smith, Richard Stevenson, Barry Sudell, Steve Tucker, Julian Walker, Clive Westlake, Fred Winstanley, Mark Wright, Paul Whybro, Geoff Yeadon.

This is the second Manual to be produced by the British Cave Diving Group. It replaces that produced by Dr. Oliver Lloyd in 1975. For those readers who might wish to take up cave diving, this book must be referred to *only* in conjunction with the official training course of the Cave Diving Group. It must *not* be regarded as an instructional work in its own right. Cave diving is recognised as being potentially an extremely dangerous activity, and must not be undertaken lightly. The standard training and qualifications provided by open-water diving organisations are an inappropriate preparation for the demands of cave diving.

The Cave Diving Group, contributors, editors and publishers of this book do not accept responsibility for any accident or misadventure arising from use of the material contained within this book.

CONTENTS

Page

Chapter 1: INTRODUCTION
The development of cave diving in Britain 5
Selection & training 10
The effects of stress 13

Chapter 2: EQUIPMENT
Wetsuits 20
Drysuits & underclothing 22
Fins & footwear 28
Instrumentation 31
Masks 39
The demand valve 41
Cylinders, taps & fittings 52
Harnesses & weightbelts 58
Helmets 60
Lighting 61
Compressors 63

Chapter 3: MOVEMENT & TECHNIQUE
Carrying diving equipment 65
Buoyancy control & equipment 70
Visibility in underwater caves 75
Line laying & following 79
Air margins 102
Stage diving 105
Tight sumps 109
Free-diving 112
Long-distance sump diving 115

Chapter 4: SAFETY & RESCUE
Diving accidents 119
Caving beyond sumps 123
Solo caving & self-rescue 134
First Aid beyond long sumps 137
Therapeutic recompression 141

Chapter 5: THE EFFECTS OF PRESSURE
Deep diving problems 145
Diving at altitude 149
Air decompression 150
Oxygen decompression 158
Dive computers 160

Page

Chapter 6: MIXED GAS DIVING
Nitrox 168
Heliox 172
Trimix 176
Rebreathers 178

Chapter 7: ADVANCED TECHNIQUES
Underwater cave photography 185
Underwater cave surveying 191
Underwater digging 197
Diver propulsion vehicles 201
Submarine cave diving 204
Expedition cave diving 209
Scientific cave diving 215

Chapter 8: RESEARCHING & RECORDING
Information about sumps 218
International cave diving bodies 221
Cave diving and the HSE 225

Chapter 9: TRAINING & TESTS
Development of the CDG training programme 229
CDG training schedule & qualifying tests 234

Chapter 10: REFERENCE SECTION
CDG constitution 238
Telephone numbers & physical laws 243
Decompression tables 245
Bibliography 255
Glossary 262
Index 265

Chapter 1: Introduction

THE DEVELOPMENT OF CAVE DIVING IN BRITAIN

CAVE diving in the United Kingdom did not originate or develop in isolation from caving. Cavers learnt to dive; cave divers did not become cavers. It was regarded simply as another technique to further cave exploration. Being underground and underwater doubled the skills to be mastered by the pioneers. But, because the whole exceeded the sum of both its parts, the dangers confronting the first cave divers were incalculable. Submerged cave passages, then pointedly known as traps rather than as sumps, would not be places in which to lose one's nerve or have an equipment failure. No manuals were available to get things going and no organised cave rescue teams existed at the time should anything go wrong. Those involved were on their own; true explorers have to be.

The early history of cave diving reveals the independent outlook needed by those involved; by modern standards, their progress was slow but sure. Every step forward, however, measured up to any advance achieved today. In France, the Fontaine de Vaucluse was reconnoitred by a diver on an air line in 1878 and Norbert Casteret made his now celebrated free-dive through a sump in Montespan in 1922. But the moment cave diving was really conceived came when cavers carried a respirator underground and succeeded in breathing underwater to explore a virgin sump.

Those principally concerned were F G Balcombe and J A Sheppard, the cave was Swildon's Hole on Mendip, and their objective was to push the sump that had held up exploration of the streamway since its discovery in 1921. The dive took place on 17th February 1934, and the lightweight respirator was home-made from parts of a bicycle! At the time, the Swildon's Sump was the deepest point reached in any British cave and the "Bicycle Respirator" had to be carefully portered over 610m along a potholed streamway that included two wet pitches. Whilst they did not pass the sump for another two years, they had sown the seeds of cave diving that day.

Although it was not known for sure until January 1967, the Swildon's stream feeds the subterranean River Axe that rises from under Mendip at Wookey Hole Caves. These well-known caves were lit and opened to the public by the owner Gerard Hodgkinson in the late 'twenties. In 1932, they attracted over 38,000 visitors, paying one shilling each. Three chambers with lakes could be seen and the water entering the show cave was noted for its clarity. By releasing the 1852 dam at the resurgence, it was possible to lower the lakes and open an airspace between the Third and Fourth Chambers. The way on upstream was unknown, though earlier water tracing had shown that stream sinks at Eastwater Cavern and from the Priddy Minery (now St Cuthbert's Swallet) were sources of the Axe. Both swallets are in similar geological locations to Swildon's Hole.

After the Swildon's dive in 1934, Graham Balcombe approached the long established diving company Siebe Gorman for assistance. This firm was in the forefront of designing and building respirators for use in mines with bad air, in flooded tunnels, and at sea for submariners in particular. Sir Robert Henry Davis, who started work for Siebe Gorman in 1882 and had been its managing director since 1904, responded favourably. Jack Sheppard visited him and, grateful for any equipment to further cave diving, accepted Sir Robert's generous offer of standard helmets and diving dress fed by air lines from hand pumps. Sir Robert also agreed to provide an experienced diver to train those wanting to learn, and the pools at Priddy Mineries were chosen as "base camp".

The sheer bulk of all the helmet diving gear forced the pioneers to focus attention on the roomy and easily accessible Wookey Hole Caves throughout 1935. It was an accident that resulted in a success story. The excitement and rewards of that summer are best gleaned from *The Log of the Wookey Hole Expedition, 1935*, by The Divers. This now classic book of cave diving history was largely written and produced by Graham Balcombe during the following months. From a diving base in the Third Chamber his team progressed beyond the already known Fourth Chamber and entered new Fifth, Sixth and Seventh Chambers. Being restrained by base fed air lines and weighted for bottom walking, they were restricted and unable to go more than 61m. But the way on was tantalisingly wide open. Cave diving had a promising future.

Wookey Hole Caves are thus regarded as the birthplace of cave diving. In the years following the Second World War, the River Axe became the cradle of the Cave Diving Group. The 1935 expedition and the nature of Wookey Hole's commodious sumps set the standards for years to come: safe-water training, kit testing, meticulous log keeping, good lighting, line laying, navigating, surveying and the accurate recording of every dive became rules. Porters (or sherpas), dressers, photographers and, of course, a controller were needed. Bottom walking ruled, too, for the need to swim, let alone the opportunity, had simply not arisen.

Another aspect of the early days at Wookey Hole that considerably influenced later cave diving was the need to fit in with the owner's requirements since the cave was, after all, a major tourist attraction. In fair return, Captain Hodgkinson expected full media coverage of any discoveries. Some cave divers learnt to perfect the art of publicity themselves, and it is basic to the larger expeditions of today. But the preferred outlook that still appeals to many cave explorers is the unsung pushing of a streamway in the independent manner shown by Balcombe and Sheppard down Swildon's Hole.

The prize for the first ever cave dive that led to further exploration of a streamway fell to Jack Sheppard on 4th October 1936. Having learnt the hard way that it was necessary to have a pressurised supply of gas underwater, he made up a lightweight drysuit with a hood for the dive and breathed from air pumped to it through a long hosepipe. Using this, he passed Sump One and found another 274m of Swildons. Shortly afterwards, on 22nd November 1936, Graham Balcombe made the next crucial step. He connected a handheld oxygen cylinder to the old "Bicycle Respirator", cracked it open when he wanted to breathe and turned it off to exhale. Without any waterproofs, he thus dived about 12m through Sump Two to surface in the Bell Chambers. Apart from a lifeline, he was on his own - the first self-contained cave diver. Again, the option of swimming had not even been considered. It would have been inappropriate given the lighting available and the size of Swildon's sumps let alone the unfamiliarity of such a venture. The potential for cave diving was proven. Only the threat and arrival of the Second World War held up further exploration.

During the early 'forties, on a posting to Yorkshire, Balcombe found time to experiment with a war-surplus oxygen rebreathing respirator. He probed the risings at Keld Held several times, climbed down a ladder underwater at the bottom of Alum Pot, and pushed the sumps in Goyden Pot. As a solo diver, all his pre-war training and experiences on Mendip were strictly followed; this included bottom walking and carefully recording every moment, whether good or bad. It marked a period of gestation that led directly to the formation of the Cave Diving Group.

At the end of the war during Easter 1946, Graham Balcombe and Jack Sheppard held court at Ogof Ffynnon Ddu in South Wales and, although failing to discover the great cave of OFD that lay waiting upstream, they succeeded in converting several cavers to the cause. Most came from the Bristol area, and so Wookey Hole Caves became the main focus of attention for

Fig. 1: A North Florida sign warns sport divers of the dangers of untrained cave diving.

the rest of the decade. Peak Cavern played a similar role in Derbyshire. Thus, the CDG was co-ordinated on a regional basis with Somerset, Welsh and Derbyshire sections. "HQ" was at Balcombe's home in London.

The availability of surplus War Department diving gear was a boon in the austerity years. Ex-WD equipment shaped all aspects of caving until the arrival of the 'sixties. National Service had a big impact upon cavers and cave diving in particular. Transport was difficult and time-consuming. The support of Sir Robert Davis and Gerard Hodgkinson, who had reached the rank of Wing Commander during the War, underwrote the strong links fostered between the CDG and Royal Navy. The 'Wing Co' encouraged the divers and provided them with a substantial wooden hut in the cave's car park which became known as Crooks' Rest. It soon filled with diving gear.

By 1949, the CDG had explored the subterranean Axe to the majestic Ninth Chamber and pushed beyond to the submerged Eleventh. Here the river welled up a steep slope which went well below the depth limit of 9.1m for oxygen rebreathers. It marked the end of Graham Balcombe's era, though his influence remained strong through his authoritative chapter on cave diving in *British Caving* edited by Cecil Cullingford (1953).

Swimming with fins in the manner of wartime frogmen and French divers was first considered in 1949. It was likely to be faster yet stir up less mud. The steep descent in the Eleventh Chamber of Wookey Hole Caves would probably be best attempted in this way. A highly experienced naval diver, Gordon Ingram-Marriott, was invited to demonstrate the technique. After visits to Wookey Hole and Peak Cavern in March, the dive to Eleven was arranged on the evening of 9th April. All the leading divers of the CDG were there. Somehow, on the return journey from the Tenth Chamber ahead of Robert E Davis, Marriott went missing in poor visibility. His body was subsequently found by Donald Coase just upstream of the Sixth Chamber. Desperate attempts to resuscitate him on the nearby diving platform in Six failed. He had run out of oxygen and inexplicably lost his reserve cylinder. Wookey Hole Caves had claimed the first cave diving tragedy. It was a traumatic event for the CDG, and Graham Balcombe in particular.

The inquest concluded that a faulty test pressure gauge must have been responsible, but the divers were not so sure. Their uncertainty reinforced the old rule that aspiring cave divers should be cavers first and that the trusted routines, which included bottom walking, were intrinsically safer. A lull in pushing dives followed into the early 'fifties.

When Bob Davies became lost beyond the Eleventh Chamber whilst finning with an aqualung on 10th December 1955, and returned to tell of a remarkable escape from a Thirteenth Chamber that he had luckily chanced upon, the dice seemed loaded against swimming and breathing air in cave diving. For the rest of the 'fifties, the divers, led by John Buxton and Oliver Wells, perfected the use of P-Party oxygen/nitrogen mixture rebreathers to go deep. They preferred bottom walking. The longer duration of the rebreathers compensated for the necessarily slower but traditionally surer navigation on foot. Good progress was made to record depths of 21m in Wookey Hole Caves; the Swildon's streamway was broken into beyond Sump Three, and Sumps Four and Five were passed. The latter involved several mammoth expeditions, still some of the largest manned and most complex diving operations ever undertaken in Britain.

The large scale approach began to slim down in the early 'sixties as a direct result of tackling the very constricted Sump Six in Swildon's Hole and Sump Two in Stoke Lane Slocker. Diving was also coming into its own in every caving region as more sumps were found by cavers. Changes in the availability and pricing of diving equipment occurred as the commercial markets expanded. A new and freer phase in our social history helped. Cave divers slimmed down their gear and immediately met with success in passing tight sumps. In underwater squeezes the question of walking or swimming simply did not arise. Divers became virtually self-supporting and capable of pushing farther ahead. Ingenious modifications were made to the smallest oxygen rebreathers available by Steve Wynne-Roberts and Fred Davies, whilst Mike Boon opted to use air and tiny "tadpole" cylinders. On 7th July 1961, Mike succeeded in passing Sump Six in Swildons; the first of many successes using air sets. The following year on 9th June 1962 he forced his way through the very tight Sump Seven by removing his kit and feeding it ahead by hand. It was a daring technique that had been carefully rehearsed in a swimming pool. During this period there were few thoughts about pushing the 21m-deep sump in Wookey Hole whilst short and shallow ones were "going" elsewhere on most weekends.

It was a great shock and setback when E J Waddon died whilst practising with a newly modified oxygen rebreather in the Priddy Minery pool on Saturday 3rd November 1962. Jack had encouraged and helped train the younger divers of the day, and in their eyes he embodied the traditions of the CDG. Naval experts blamed the equipment at the inquest; but, yet again, other factors seemed just as likely to those who used the very same set before and after the incident. Once more, uncertainty clouded CDG affairs. There were critical moments when its regional framework might have collapsed but for a strengthening of the constitution, training procedures and tests under Michael Thompson's leadership and Dan Hasell's commonsense presidency. Cave divers in the regions rallied to the overhauled CDG.

Whilst all this was going on, three students from Bristol University set about training themselves during the Autumn of 1964 and formed the self-styled Independent Cave Diving Group by Christmas. Mike Wooding, Dave Savage and Dave Drew adopted Mike Boon's approach: they bought a couple of Scubair regulators and bottles and got on with it. Cylinders were slung from waistbelts, weights were kept to a minimum, only wetsuits were worn, a single Nife lamp on an ordinary helmet sufficed and they carried fins for swimming the longer sumps. It was a logical reduction of the old view that ordinary cavers with the bare minimum of diving equipment could get results. Solo caving and diving were the ultimate developments, of course.

By the beginning of March 1965, the ICDG trio had pushed the Swildon's streamway to Sump Twelve and Stoke Lane Slocker to a final choke beyond Sump Seven. Neither have been passed since - a remarkable legacy and vindication of their work. Later in March they joined the Cave Diving Group. Dr Oliver C Lloyd (OCL) also submitted himself for tests with them. He was 54 years of age and became the oldest active cave diver to qualify. OCL had taken on the task of running the CDG the previous Easter in 1965 after Alan Clegg drowned because of tangled lines in the Master Cave Sump of Lancaster Hole.

The next twenty years of the CDG, into the mid 'eighties, were dominated by OCL in many ways. He ran Friday night training sessions for the Somerset Section and all-comers in the Students' Union swimming baths at Bristol

University. The Severn Bridge and M4 to South Wales ensured close links with the Welsh Section. He organised and held most of the equipment at his home in Westbury-On-Trym. Editing the CDG *Newsletter* and other publications was one of his great pleasures for it kept him in touch with everyone, and in control. His distinctive editorials and comments were very influential far afield, and he was a good correspondent for active divers around the world. The modern phase of cave diving bears his stamp, a phase which has seen rapid advances in equipment and techniques with record long and deep dives in every caving region of Britain and in other countries. The pages that follow contain much that is attributable to OCL.

Oliver Lloyd died after going to Priddy on Mendip on the weekend of 18th-19th May 1985 to show the film he made down Swildon's Hole in 1960 about sump rescue for the Mendip Rescue Organisation. So, sadly he missed the fiftieth anniversary celebrations of cave diving and reunion of cave divers who represented the full 50 years, held in the Third Chamber of Wookey Hole Caves on 4th October. The recollections of those involved in pioneering and pushing sumps under Mendip have been compiled into a commemorative volume. This will provide a much fuller history than is briefly summarised here.

In this, the introduction to a manual on cave diving, it is appropriate to conclude with the comments of the first cave diver to pass a sump and explore beyond. In the first *Report* of the CDG (1946), Jack Sheppard wrote:

"A dive, or job of underwater exploration is abandoned when the total of all difficulties and danger becomes equal to the diver's determination to complete the job. To push any job to its limit it is therefore necessary to eliminate every possible weakness or imperfection in the apparatus used, so there remains nothing to over come except the natural hazards of the cave..."

SELECTION & TRAINING

CAVE diving fatalities have occurred and careful selection of personnel is clearly vital. The Cave Diving Group requirements are that trainees should be medically sound and physically fit, reasonable swimmers, experienced cavers, reliable and elected by regional fellow members. These requirements determine an obvious minimum, and a trainee who does not meet high standards of competence in caving and diving must be firmly rejected.

Individual Attitude

Cave diving calls for complete self-reliance and independence of judgement, which does not imply ignoring the experience of others as embodied in codes of practice, etc. Nevertheless, the trained diver's responsibility for his own safety is his and his alone. If he delegates responsibility for any part of the operation which affects his own safety, he does so at his own risk. The trainee would do well to examine the whole question of danger in relation to caving and cave diving and should consider carefully the following ways of reducing the risks of this extremely hazardous technique of cave exploration.

(1) Examining his motives for cave diving. Does he wish to dive to further the exploration of specific systems, or because it attracts him as a branch of

underground exploration? How does he assess his own temperament in relation to these motives? What are the relative proportions of boldness and caution in his make-up in relation to diving? How easily does he panic? How susceptible is he to outside pressures - will he be persuaded to dive when he feels he should not?

(2) Ensuring that his attitude to diving is thorough. Cave diving requires much time and thought. The diver must always be in good diving and caving practice before a dive. A short lay-off from diving may leave an experienced diver almost as nervous as a beginner. Likewise, the cave diver's links with conventional caving cannot be close enough. He must also be a perfectionist with regard to equipment which his life is absolutely dependent on. This is easy to state, easy to agree to and very hard to adhere to in practice. Nevertheless it must be adhered to. If a diver's equipment is not exactly as he would wish it the dive must be postponed.

The diver will also make good use of experience, both his own and that of others in the scattered but considerable volume of literature on diving and especially cave-diving. This may help him to interpret the merits of different techniques in various circumstances. He must, to a great extent, live cave-diving as well as practice it.

(3) Limiting the number of dives strictly to projects where the chances of discovering new passages justify the hazards involved, or where the personal reward of passing a previously explored sump justifies the risk. Sumps engender enthusiasm which is often misplaced and a careful assessment of the chances of a successful dive should be made. This is a hard doctrine for an enthusiastic recruit to accept, nevertheless it is doctrine of experience.

TRAINING

The intention of training should be to enable the diver to operate with confidence and competence in all conditions met underground, including being lost and being entangled with lines, and to realise the full potential of the kit. The training period will also be used as an invaluable opportunity to test the suitability of the recruit.

Basic aqualung training has been comprehensively investigated by the British Sub-Aqua Club, who have devised a series of progressively more difficult tests for the beginner which act as a training schedule. These tests are designed to build up confidence, and usually achieve this end. Tests include fitting the kit on the bottom of the pool, flooding and clearing the mask, breathing from a snorkel tube with the nose exposed to the water, sharing a kit with another swimmer and so on. All these exercises are useful, but most vital of all is that a diver should be able to breathe quietly and normally with his nose exposed to water.

The BSAC tests are excellent for the early stages of training, but much more is required for the training of a cave diver, particularly as the bright shallow waters of the swimming pool encourage confidence. Under the CDG system, each trainee joins a section, which is responsible for his training. Training can then be adapted to the aptitudes and requirements of the individual. Such a training programme will include preliminary experience in open water conditions; dives in bad visibility and at night; dives to depths greater than 15m; searches for objects in muddy conditions and tasks underwater. The trainer will try to simulate conditions where panic might arise underground, eg being lost, or entangled in lines. The trainee will be encouraged to broaden his experience by using a variety of makes of diving equipment.

A log-book of dives should be kept, to be written up by the trainee and signed by the trainer.

Fig. 2: Stress, a potent factor to be recognised - and coped with.

THE EFFECTS OF STRESS

AS can be seen from the bulk of this manual, safe cave diving relies on a wide range of highly sophisticated and often expensive equipment. However, one of the most important items of equipment is without doubt the well-trained cave diver's brain. This cannot be bought in a dive shop or borrowed from a friend! One of the main functions of training is therefore to adapt the mind to the demands of what is potentially a very hazardous activity. Unfortunately, little research has been done into exactly what psychological attributes are necessary to make a good cave diver. What is clear is that unfavourable responses to various kinds of stress have been closely related to many diving accidents (1). One study on behalf of the Australian Navy revealed that successful divers tend to be "intelligent, physically fit, emotionally stable and usually self-sufficient. They usually possess a low level of neuroticism, i.e. they are not anxiety prone." (2)

Even though the Cave Diving Group is a relatively small organisation, there is amongst its members a wide range of personality types. Many may admit to having experienced mild symptoms of common psychological disturbances early in their diving careers, such as agoraphobia, claustrophobia, loneliness, fears of dark water, etc. Most novices learn to cope with these through training, or they soon give up diving. It goes without saying that anyone who has tranquillisers or anti-depressants prescribed in connection with any such disorders should not dive at all. Furthermore, any individuals who habitually use to excess any substance which may affect their personality in the long term (eg. alcohol, drugs) should not consider becoming a diver. They are more susceptible to periods of emotional instability and often do not recognise related symptoms which are likely to affect their judgement or reaction to stress under water.

In "normal" individuals there is no way of knowing who will become a safe cave diver or who will be a liability. Good cave divers are not simply born, they must be trained, and in the past some unlikely characters have eventually become accomplished divers. Therefore individuals must take their first faltering steps in cave diving under the watchful eye of more experienced practitioners and accept fully that for reasons beyond their control they may eventually prove not to be suited to the activity.

In the early days, when development of the sport was relatively slow, cave divers were able to improve their equipment and adapt mentally more or less at similar rates. The novice of today already has the knowledge of impressive achievements of others, and what equipment was needed for their explorations. Nowadays, a keen person can buy, borrow and make all the items needed for long, deep or difficult dives in a relatively short time. Thus a large gap can exist between equipment acquisition and psychological preparation. Unfortunately the simple mistakes made while "learning by doing" can easily prove fatal. All cave divers, novice or expert, need to be aware of the factors which may influence judgement and to prepare mentally for their occurrence.

BEFORE THE DIVE

It is a useful exercise to try and identify one's own motives for going cave diving. There is probably a wide variety of reasons amongst cave divers, depending on their personal attitudes. It is generally accepted that, under British conditions at least, the best motive for cave diving is the desire to explore caves, rather than simply as an extension of one's conventional diving interests. There is a need to develop honesty and self-awareness in this area, as certain motives create dangerous situations. They can dim one's judgement of the risks involved, and perhaps cause individuals to behave in ways different from those under normal circumstances. The so-called thrill-seeker, or those with a hero-syndrome, may easily fall into these traps. For these divers, danger equals excitement, but deliberately encountering danger blindly, without adequate preparation, generates little respect from other cavers or cave divers. Being able to operate safely in a potentially very dangerous environment is for many one of the greatest exhilarations in cave diving. Those with undesirable motives will never experience such satisfaction, which comes only after extensive training and adaptation to the demands of cave diving. It is more likely that their cave diving career will quickly reach a premature end.

A diver's awareness of risks may also be dimmed if a lot is being expected of him by others. This may arise, for example, if he is diving at the request of another caving club, or on a rescue, or even just as one of a pair (not wanting to let one's buddy down). The experienced and psychologically well-adapted diver will be able to judge the likely effect of certain important factors on his performance (such as not enough sleep, not properly fed, too much alcohol recently consumed, poor physical condition, not enough build-up dives, and so on). The poorly trained individual has no objective way of assessing such factors, and is therefore more likely to take foolish risks.

Another important factor, which affects one's psychological well-being once underwater, is how well the equipment has been prepared prior to the dive. The knowledge that all items have been carefully chosen, are familiar to the diver and are well maintained is very important in building confidence. If back-up systems have been incorporated, so that several alternatives are available if things go wrong, then trivial problems are far less likely to develop into major disasters. This increases psychological security. Remember, however, that even the safest equipment can prove problematic if the diver is not familiar with its use in practice. The need to switch to one's back-up equipment in an emergency is always a possibility, and if one is properly prepared should not generate undue anxiety. In fact the more one is aware of what may go wrong, the less effect it has psychologically if things actually do go wrong. This is because the mind is more prepared to cope with such events if they have been anticipated. This mental preparation before diving will naturally develop out of appropriate training and experience.

Finally, it should be noted that most individuals feel at least some apprehension just before a dive, especially if the intended dive comes close to the diver's perceived limits of his own ability. Moderate apprehension is quite normal and does not in itself indicate any lack of the necessary ability for competent cave diving. In fact, it is useful in helping to keep the diver from making mistakes through complacency. However, if such anxieties grow to the extent that they affect the diver's performance so that his safety in the water is in question, then this is a different matter. Often, the cause of a serious lack of confidence lies in some previous short cut in the diver's training.

If any individual feels unduly apprehensive about cave diving, they should give it up. They will not lose the respect of any other cave diver worth knowing!

STRESS

Most psychologists agree that we experience stress all of the time and that, within certain limits, some stress is actually necessary in maintaining good health. The problem with cave diving is that the stresses encountered may be very great and therefore potentially very dangerous to individuals who are not properly prepared.

There are two broad categories of stress which affect cave divers: psychological and physiological. Although there will inevitably be some interaction between these, it is useful to consider them separately. It is important to anticipate specific sources of stress, as this helps the diver to modify his approach to particular dives in ways which decrease his susceptibility to the expected stressors (a stressor is a particular source of stress). Physical stress can, for example, arise from temperature extremes, weightlessness, over-exertion (hard carries), inert gas narcosis, and so on, and such factors are dealt with elsewhere in this manual.

Examples of stressors which can affect cave divers psychologically are:

1) Darkness: This, along with the lack of direct access to free air (due to the presence of a roof or even the need for decompression stops) can cause feelings of claustrophobia. In large caves, where walls may not be visible in the range of the diver's torches, agoraphobia can be another related stress source. Some individuals are actually afraid of darkness itself.

2) Poor visibility: Normally, man relies considerably on the sense of sight to gain information about his surroundings. Underwater, if vision is restricted, the diver must rely on his sense of touch. This sensory deprivation is stressful to untrained individuals.

3) Other divers: Some individuals find that the presence of other divers is stressful on what they would prefer to be solo dives. Cave divers must be totally independent, and cannot rely on any real or imagined security arising from the presence of another diver. Part of their attention is inevitably directed towards any other diver present, making it impossible to concentrate totally on their own dive.

4) Panic: This is not experienced by all divers, and usually results from inadequate mental acceptance of previous experience or training. For example, if a hose bursts, it creates a problem that can be solved by controlled breathing and an immediate return to base. It cannot be rectified underwater. However, the noise and rapid and dramatic air loss, which might surround the diver in a cloud of bubbles, reduce visibility and physically batter him can stress the inexperienced diver to the degree that he becomes confused and unable to respond at all adequately to the situation. This then makes the problem worse... And so on.

5) Difficulties in orientation and navigation: This is directly related to darkness and loss of visibility. The aware diver will consistently be monitoring

information such as compass bearings, line tag numbers, depth readings, current direction, orientation of scallop markings or sand ripples, etc. Most divers on returning though complex sumps in bad visibility have experienced subtle doubts as to whether they are still on the right line. The severe effect of stress associated with being lost in a sump is easily explained, in that most divers realise that this has been the main cause of deaths in cave diving. This kind of stress assumes great and additional importance if the diver suddenly realises that he has lost contact with the line.

6) Time Pressure: This arises from a knowledge that the air supply being carried has a limited duration. The diver knows what will happen if the air runs out before the entrance can be regained. Every obstacle on the return will take time to negotiate, especially if poor visibility, adverse currents or physical restriction compound the difficulty of the exit. Any diver who has been second in the queue to pass a constriction when the person in front has been stuck for several minutes will be familiar with this kind of stress.

7) Distance: One of the most obvious obstacles in an underwater cave is the distance between the diver and the entrance. Long dives will be physically tiring, if only in view of the extra drag created by the amount of equipment worn, and the sheer effort of maintaining an efficient finning speed over long durations. If the diver begins to tire whilst still a long way from the entrance on the return swim, this creates a form of time pressure stress, especially if he is aware of an increase in air consumption.

8) Depth: Problems which arise at depth are always worse than if they occur in shallow water. Physical stresses are more important (eg greater heat loss at depth due to suit compression, or exertion due to buoyancy loss), and stress can seriously affect air consumption and decompression schedules. This is exacerbated if the diver is aware that he is diving towards or beyond the limits of his experience, or is in danger of developing, or actually under the influence of, narcosis. In extreme cases, high stress levels at depth can cause depth blackout, due largely to hyperventilation under pressure, or can cause the diver to "beat the lung" if the demand valve is not fully adequate for use at depth.

9) Dependence on equipment: A further source of stress is the knowledge that one's survival is totally reliant on the equipment used. If equipment has been poorly maintained, ill-treated during transport, or subject to physical abuse in harsh underwater passages, this can be worrying even in very short sumps.

10) Loss of control: The extreme stress caused by problems beyond the diver's capability may cause a loss of control over the immediate situation. Often the problems may be relatively minor (like slight difficulties with buoyancy control, or abrupt changes in passage conditions) but if they begin to occur collectively they can produce a more serious situation. Open water divers sometimes refer to this as "falling into the incident pit". Experience has shown that serious cave diving accidents often arise when a number of apparently trivial problems arise at or near the same time (3).

11) Physical stress: An awareness of worsening or unacceptable levels of physical stress can produce anxiety even in experienced divers. The diver should learn from his experience and find ways of removing such stress (or should avoid physical tasks which may exceed his ability).

A DIVER'S RESPONSE TO STRESS

Generally speaking, stress beyond a certain limit impairs judgement and affects behaviour. It therefore poses a real threat to a diver's safety. Although the types of stress encountered in cave diving are many and varied, the responses shown by the stressed individual usually follow a general pattern. This range of responses generally begins with slight anxiety, which, if unchecked, can rapidly lead to blind panic. Panic occurs when the amount of stress becomes so high that the diver really feels threatened, thinks that the situation cannot be remedied, and loses psychological control. If the diver succumbs to total panic he will be unable to function, and is likely to die.

In a stressful situation, as fear grows stronger, the nervous system automatically triggers physiological adaptations in the body. Perhaps the most important of these is the release of a hormone called adrenalin into the bloodstream. This causes many effects, including an increase in the pulse rate and in the rate and depth of breathing. These and other associated effects would normally be beneficial to man if danger were encountered, as they prepare the body for sudden activity, such as escape from, or fighting off, an attacker. However, in cave diving, they lead to more rapid air consumption (time pressure!) and thereafter even greater releases of adrenalin into the blood. The diver may begin to feel that his demand valve is not supplying enough air. So more adrenalin is released... There may come a point when the demand valve actually cannot supply enough air to cope with the vastly increased rate of breathing, especially at depth. If the diver cannot control this chain of events, he may die from nothing more than his own fear. This might explain the deaths of some cave divers who have been found with air still in their bottles.

The deeper breathing associated with the adrenalin response may also be linked to another cause of cave diving deaths, which has been called syncope of ascent. The abnormally-expanded lungs press on and restrict blood flow to the major arteries close to the heart. A brief interruption to the flow of oxygenated blood to the brain causes a temporary loss of consciousness, which leads to drowning if the mouthpiece falls out. There will also be a danger of embolism on an uncontrolled panic ascent.

Clearly, the only safeguard against these events is to prevent them from happening in the first place through adequate training and equipment, good dive planning, knowing when to turn back, and by rectifying any minor problems at the earliest opportunity. Divers also have a responsibility to watch out for signs of stress in their companions, both before and during a dive (5). These can include being unusually quiet, being preoccupied with some trivial problem, forgetting certain basic pre-dive procedures, a reluctance to communicate verbally or by underwater signals, nervous behaviour, erratic movements underwater, wide staring eyes and so on. Be aware that the other diver's ego may cause him deliberately to mask the early symptoms of stress until it is too late and the situation becomes out of control. It should always be remembered that if any diver is genuinely unhappy before or during a dive for any reason (even if the cause cannot be pin-pointed), then the dive must be abandoned.

COPING WITH STRESS

The best approach is to anticipate potential stressors before the dive as a result of adequate training and experience, and to learn from mistakes made by yourself and others, so that stress levels may be reduced for future dives. Examples of specific ways in which this can be done are given in the table in this section. In general, dives should be undertaken only under ideal circumstances. This requires a diver to be honest with himself, even if a dive has taken a long time to prepare, and others have worked hard to transport the gear underground. Never be pressurised by other people into taking undue risks on a dive!

It is useful to discuss mistakes, or decisions made, with other divers later. Here there is also a need to be absolutely honest about one's own failures. Mistakes do happen and there is no reason at all to be ashamed - except of course if the same mistakes are happening again and again!

All problems which arise must be sorted out as soon as is practical. In this way, a series of problems should rarely need to be dealt with at the same time. Make your progress through the cave slow and deliberate; there are several advantages to this approach, including:
- more time to collect navigational information
- less effort is needed, promoting better air consumption
- problems are likely to be noticed sooner
- fewer problems are likely to occur simultaneously
- decisions can be taken in a relaxed manner
- equipment damage may be reduced
- less chance of becoming jammed in tight sections

The best way to stop panic is not to get into it in the first place. All divers should be able to estimate how far they can comfortably swim into a flooded cave before turning round. Yet despite this, panic is always a possibility, and the first reaction is the urge to escape. This must be suppressed, and the initial cause of the problem established and, if possible, resolved. It is vital to control the breathing rate by relaxing, and only when this is achieved should any retreat begin. The diver should then consciously try to direct all his attention to making the journey out safe, leaving no room in his thoughts for panic. It is better to turn round within your limits and enjoy the swim out, than to press on beyond and risk your life.

Finally, remember that "Safety results only when there is an intimate relationship between the diver, his self-awareness, skills, equipment and the environment" (6).

WAYS OF COPING WITH STRESS

Stress source	Remedy
Darkness	Practise night diving in open water. Improve lighting system.
Poor visibility	Wait for good conditions. Improve finning technique. Dive solo for minimum disturbance. Mount torch in hand or on forearm.

Other divers	Dive solo. Practise buddy diving in open water. Choose partners you can trust.
Negative imagination	Improve general diving ability and confidence in open water. Practise emergency procedures frequently.
Navigation/Orientation	Study surveys and other information before dive. Make sure line properly belayed. Check all available directional information underwater. Mark all junctions with "out" tags. Get to know cave gradually by tourist dives before pushing end. Carry and practise using a search reel.
Time pressure	Maintain adequate air margins within the "thirds rule". Be aware of and avoid situations which increase air consumption. Practise emergency procedures.
Distance	Ensure equipment is comfortable. Over-kill on air, lighting, etc. Do adequate build-up dives. Use a DPV or stage extra air cylinders as required.
Depth	Ways to remove stress or improve tolerance. Be physically fit. Do build-up. Do not go deep in caves until all other skills are second nature. Practise deep diving in open water.
Equipment dependence	Devise a set-up of your own with which you feel happy. Do not blindly copy others, but place advice in context. Familiarise gear by open water training. Maintain equipment well. Pack equipment properly for cave transport. Incorporate back-up systems and ensure pre-dive checks are made.
Loss of control	Practise all cave diving skills in open water. Don't cut corners in training. Learn to sort out problems methodically, and not to try too much at once. Gain experience at a sensible rate, with the help of experienced cave divers.
Physical stress	Keep within your physical limits, and those of your equipment. Mend wetsuits. Take more sherpas. Develop fitness.

Chapter 2: Equipment

WETSUITS

THE introduction of neoprene wetsuits in the early 1960s revolutionised caving in Britain. Though this fashion of dress has been changing recently, with more specialised materials available for dry cave exploration, most cave divers continue to use foam (or expanded) neoprene wetsuits for cave diving. Wetsuits work on the principle that a layer of water will enter beneath the fabric of the suit on entering the water, but the close fit of the suit will ensure minimal ensuing circulation, allowing the trapped water to warm through contact with the body, and be additionally insulated from the colder outside water by the gas-filled neoprene material of the suit.

From the start, it must be stressed that the traditional caver's wetsuit, complete with broken zip and gaping holes in knees, elbows and crutch, is totally inadequate for cave diving. Cavers who do short swims or free dives know that even a good wetsuit is scarcely warm enough, whilst wetsuit-clad open-water divers commonly give up diving in winter, when sea water temperatures may still be higher than those in sumps.

The precise style and thickness of wetsuit required depends on the type of sump to be dived. For fairly short dives, a well-maintained and close-fitting caving suit of 4-5mm neoprene, with the addition of gloves, neoprene hood and a neoprene vest or waistcoat over the top, will suffice. For longer, deeper dives, especially in colder water, a suit of 6-7mm neoprene, comprising neoprene long-johns and hood-attached jacket (or hood-attached vest and one-piece long-armed long-john) is more suitable. Many cave divers have two wetsuits, or even a selection of neoprene garments to choose the appropriate outfit from depending on the dive to be undertaken. The advent of wet/dry suits, a halfway stage to full drysuits, has seen an increase in the number of high-quality commercially-made suits suitable for long dives in the coldest waters, and these are worth considering for the longest and coldest of dives. They work on the principle of minimal water admittance, and are constructed with wrist, ankle and neck seals to ensure ingress of water is slight. For all suits, good fit is important, the fewer air spaces and points of water admittance in a suit, the better its insulation value.

It is worth remembering that too great a thickness of neoprene can cause severe overheating during a long caving trip to reach the dive site, and it is advisable to pack some of the suit (eg. vest, hood, hood-attached jacket) and carry it with the other diving equipment to the dive-site. In extreme cases, where excess sweating is unavoidable, divers have found that electrolytic drinks of the kind used by runners and cyclists are beneficial.

Wetsuits and neoprene vary in quality and suitability for cave diving. Cup-stitched ("Stroebel"-stitching, where the needle does not fully penetrate the neoprene) are more watertight than Mauser stitched (where the needle penetrates fully, stitching each piece to a fabric tape which holds the joint together). Double-lined neoprene is often regarded as being less warm than

Fig. 3: A diver prepares to dive, clad in a neoprene drysuit - just one choice from the protective clothing available.

single-lined, due to slower evaporation of water from its fabric surface, but it is stronger, and more readily available. A good overlap between trousers and socks, arms and gloves, and helmet and hood all help reduce the circulation of water. Neoprene flaps over zips have a similar effect, and prolong the life of the zips by protecting them from abrasive materials present in the cave.

If boots are not worn or carried through the sump, it is worth considering the use of wet-suit sock with hard soles to minimise the effect of abrasion on the soft neoprene material when caving on the far side of a sump, though the use of proper boots is far preferable.

Wetsuit gloves should be worn, five-finger gloves allowing more dexterity than mitten-type, but having less insulation value.

All wetsuits are prone to damage during underground exploration, both above and below water, and the use of knee-pads, and perhaps elbow pads, will prolong the life of a suit considerably. If such pads are used, they should not be of a type to allow line entanglement, and pads with buckles are not to be recommended.

When not in use, wetsuits should be rinsed in clean freshwater, dried carefully, repaired if necessary, and stored the right way round on a hanger in a dry, cool place. Crumpling them in a corner, dirty and wet, or stuffing them in a container, or leaving them covered in mud, seawater or oil in the sunshine, only ensures the regular need for a new suit. The occasional use of a fabric conditioner will make the suit more comfortable to wear in strenuous caves.

Trainee cave divers would do well to ask the advice of their trainers and other experienced cave divers before purchasing a diving wetsuit. The comfort and ultimately the safety of cave diving is affected by the quality of wetsuit worn. However, beyond a certain length, depth and temperature, a change to the use of a dry-suit becomes essential.

DRYSUITS & UNDERCLOTHING

WITH the advent in the late 1970s of techniques for deeper and longer cave diving the drysuit became re-adopted, replacing the wetsuit which had gained popularity in the 1960s.

Basic Description of a Drysuit

The drysuit of today is made of a fully waterproof material. It has seals at the neck and wrist (and at the ankles unless feet are fitted) to prevent the entry of water. It has a zip which is proof against water under pressure and a means for inflation and deflation. Thus the diver is able to wear insulating clothing underneath it. Some drysuits have a waterproof hood whereas a wet hood is worn with others. In a well chosen suit there is enough room for sufficient clothing to keep the diver warm for the duration of his dive.

Material

There are four basic types of material used in the construction of drysuits. These are:
1) Foam neoprene
2) Rubber (or rubber laminate)
3) Nylon laminate
4) Crushed neoprene.

Foam neoprene drysuits of 6-8 mm thickness are perhaps the most popular drysuits used in modern cave diving. The main advantage over the other two types of suits is the inherent insulation property of the neoprene at shallow depths. This means that the diver does not have to wear so much insulating underclothing if the dive is shallow. Underclothing should be borne in mind when planning the dive; in some instances if the diver is doing a lot or work (eg hard finning) it is possible to overheat. This can also occur when such drysuits are worn in warm climates.

This type of drysuit has reasonable abrasion resistance. The suit can be scuffed and sometimes even nicked without developing a leak. The seals are usually of smooth-skin foam neoprene, generally more robust than thin latex.

The main disadvantage of the foam neoprene drysuit is its buoyancy at shallow depth - everything has a price. A considerable quantity of lead must be worn to achieve neutral buoyancy - some divers need 10 kg or even more! This may cause problems during a decompression dive - the diver can end up being very overweight at depth and still too buoyant during decompression. Staging weights may be useful on some dives with foam neoprene suits.

Rubber laminate drysuits come in two main types: the Viking suit, and the ex-Navy Avon suit. Viking suits tend to be as expensive as foam neoprene drysuits, whereas ex-Navy Avon suits can often be obtained very cheaply.

Rubber suits provide less insulation than neoprene so more, or better insulating undergarments need to be worn to keep warm. If the suit is punctured and floods, the diver would lose both body heat and air, and become very negatively buoyant. Underclothing must be warm enough and of a sufficient standard to take flooding into account. The effect of flooding might not be so bad if the diver were wearing a foam neoprene drysuit.

The third type of drysuit can be made from one of a number of different nylon laminate materials. A popular material in use today is that in which PTFE is sandwiched between two layers of woven nylon; this was originally developed for the inflatable life-raft industry. This type of suit is the least expensive of the three. When it originally came on the market in the early 1980s it was manufactured from a rather thin material and had flimsy latex seals so the diver had to take great care with his suit. It was hardly appropriate for use in a cave. A number of manufacturers were troubled by delamination resulting in permeability. The problem has since been solved and this type of suit has been widely adopted by open-water divers owing to its low cost, light weight and relative comfort.

There are a number of independent manufacturers now producing suits from three different weights of material and with three different thicknesses of seals. This enables a diver to choose a suit for his individual needs. The comments about the buoyancy of rubber drysuits apply more or less equally to nylon laminate drysuits.

Crushed neoprene suits (eg DUI, Northern Diver) are probably the toughest of all. They are marginally warmer than laminates and offer less of a variable buoyancy problem than foam neoprene. They must be worn with underclothing, and, because of the low-stretch of crushed neoprene, are often a slightly looser fit. A well-fitting suit is an advantage! Their high cost, a problem for some divers, is offset to some degree by excellent durability.

USE OF DRYSUITS

Dressing

Since the neoprene drysuit is currently the most popular used in cave diving, this section relates mainly to that type. However, many of the principles can be applied equally to other types of suit.

All drysuits are one-piece; many have the entry-zip across the shoulders, some have it diagonally across the body or from the middle of the back to the middle of the chest via the crutch. With this last it is inherently awkward for a diver to dress or undress unaided.

When dressing, it is important to open the zip fully to avoid placing excessive stress on it. Prior to dressing, the zip should be lubricated with beeswax or a proprietary liquid lubricant if necessary - but *never* with a mineral based oil such as WD40.

When the diver has put on his underclothing he should check that nothing such as grass or thistles has become attached to them. With the shoulder-entry suit the diver puts his feet into the suit and pulls it up to his waist, checking that there are no ruckles in either the suit or his underclothes. Once the suit is round his waist he can, if necessary, apply some talcum powder or dermatological cream (eg. E45) to the wrist and neck seals. The suit is then pulled up around his body until he can put his arms into the sleeves. Once again he should ensure the sleeves of his underclothes are comfortable. The rest of the suit is then pulled up until he can put his head through the neck seal - this is often the most troublesome part of the whole procedure. When the diver has his head through the seal, the seal should be turned in so that the smooth side of the neoprene is next to the skin. It should be checked to ensure it is close-fitting and, if necessary, an assistant can adjust the seal. Note that too tight a neck seal can be extremely dangerous; excess pressure on the neck can trigger unconsciousness.

It is best if the diver at this stage stretches and squats alternately to get the suit and underclothing to settle down. Now, with assistance, the suit can be zipped up, though some divers can manage this themselves by performing various contortions or by using home-made devices.

Once the suit has been zipped up it should be vented. This is often best done by pulling the neck seal away from the neck whilst squatting down, thus expelling a lot of the air. When most of the air has been expelled, the seal is released and the diver can stand up again. He can now put on the rest of the equipment and, as the straps are tightened, he will not, or should not, look like a knotted balloon. Finally, some divers like to wear knee and elbow pads over their suits and these can be used to carry other items of equipment (eg snoopy loops can be tucked behind them). It is a good idea to wear a tight-fitting ankle strap to lessen the potential for air migration to the feet if inverted (see below).

During the Dive

The diver should carry enough weights to make him about 4kg negative at the surface when all air is expelled from the suit. (NB The degree of negative buoyancy should take into account the full and empty weights of the cylinders used on the dive).

When the diver is underwater, the principle for buoyancy adjustment is simple:
- Inflate the suit if you are sinking
- Deflate the suit if you are too buoyant.

Owing to the frequent changes of depth involved in cave diving the practice is not so simple. In open-water, the profile of a dive usually consists of vertical descents and ascents with repeated stops at the same depth. Diving profiles in caves are obviously determined by the passages and involve many more and irregular changes in depth than in an open-water dive. Also, cave divers often have to descend steeply head first which, in a drysuit, creates buoyancy problems: the air in the suit will migrate to the high points, the legs and feet. This can cause loss of one or both fins, and the diver may suffer from buoyancy inversion in which he may become suspended upside-down in the water. To prevent this occurring it is best to choose a drysuit with closely fitting legs, or to use ankle straps to restrict airflow to the feet, and to make a point of descending feet first whenever possible.

If a diver does become inverted owing to air shifting to the feet of his suit the best method of correction is this:

1) Bend the legs and pull the knees towards the chin so that the thighs are flat against the chest.

2) Using a suitable solid object (such as the passage roof or wall or projection) for leverage, rotate the body until in an upright position.

3) When in an upright position straighten the legs so that once again the air returns to the top of the suit, and adjust buoyancy if necessary.

4) If the procedure fails, as a last resort the diver can pierce the feet of his suit to release the air; this will, of course, allow water to enter the suit and will, more than likely, make him very negatively buoyant as well as wet and cold.

A further buoyancy-related problem is the sticking of inflation or dump valves. If an inflation valve jams open the suit will inflate continuously until the diver has to let go of the diving line and floats up to the roof. This can be very disorienting and dangerous (eg in a decompression schedule). There are two remedies. One is to disconnect the hose from the inflation valve, thus removing the supply of air, but this is not possible with all valves and, further, some valves would then let water into the suit. Neither of these types of valve should be used for cave diving. The alternative is to turn off the tap of the cylinder which is supplying air to the suit. This alternative should not be taken without due regard to the consequences. If a dump valves jams shut, then obviously, the diver can dump air from his suit through the wrist and neck seals.

Most buoyancy problems with drysuits can be anticipated. The diver should dump some air before starting to ascend. He should always dump air before dumping becomes a necessity, and he should inflate, when descending, before he becomes too negatively buoyant. Usually, when diving in caves, it is best to be a little negatively buoyant.

One further point about diving in a drysuit is that any quick or awkward movement of the head or wrist, or the lifting of a heavy weight may cause leakage at a seal. Note that in sumps with steep ascents or descents the diver should not solely rely on buoyancy provided by the drysuit; an adjustable buoyancy device should also be worn.

Care and Maintenance

After the dive the drysuit should be washed in clean, fresh water and allowed to dry. It should be checked for cuts and abrasions and, when dry and clean, repairs made to it if necessary. These can range from simply applying a little glue to a cut to patching entire areas. The most awkward leaks to repair are those that occur on a seam and it is worth checking, when selecting a suit, whether seams in stress areas, eg the crutch and the armpits, are reinforced.

A drysuit can be checked for leaks either by observations while diving or when the suit is immersed. To test in a bath the sleeves and neck must be plugged (eg with balls or plastic bottles), the inflated suit can then be rolled in, or brushed with a solution of washing-up liquid, and pushed underwater, but be sure all leaks are positively identified before rinsing off.

Inflation and dump valves need to be dismantled, cleaned and lightly greased with silicone grease if there has been any risk of grit having entered them. The zip of the drysuit should also be washed free of any mud or grit and later lubricated with beeswax or other proprietary lubricant - not with silicon spray or grease.

ACCESSORIES AND UNDERCLOTHING

Most British divers wear wet gloves with their drysuit. For long dives many divers wear mitts. Dry gloves are now becoming available; these are a heavy-duty type of washing-up glove with an elongated wrist and a small entry-hole for the hand. The entry forms the seal. It is recommended that for warmth the diver should wear some form of fabric glove underneath, wool being best.

Many drysuits do not have any form of hood. A simple wet hood is often the best way of protecting the head against cold. Similarly, some drysuits do not have built-in bootees and wetsuit socks have to be worn with them.

There is now a wide variety of thermal underclothing for use under a drysuit. In the past divers have worn woolly jumpers and tracksuit bottoms or suchlike; now there are furry suits, thermal underwear and a large number of undersuits made from synthetic fabrics, (eg Thinsulate, open cell foam, pelt fabrics).

Important properties required in underclothing are:
1) Good thermal insulation (even when wet or damp);
2) Ability to absorb a certain amount of water (this makes for greater comfort if the diver is sweating or the suit is slightly leaking);
3) Light weight.

For some long dives, often involving decompression during which the diver is not moving and consequently his body is not generating much heat, to keep warm a diver may choose to wear several layers of thermally insulating clothing.

All drysuits have an inflation valve and there is a bewildering number of valves on the market. The best valves allow the inflation hose to be detached completely from the valve by a simple and secure mechanism, but the hose on some valves can only be detached by removing a part of the valve. Most valves have the desirable feature of not letting in water when the hose is removed. To inflate the suit some valves have a push button and others have a tap. It is important that the valve should not inflate the suit accidentally by, for example, contact with the floor in a low section of passage. An inflation button that does not protude is a good idea, it cannot then be accidentally knocked on.

Divers can dump air from their suits either through the wrist, the neck seal or through a dump valve. Dumping through the seals is difficult when the seals are covered by equipment, gloves or the hood, and is not recommended. It can also damage thin latex seals. There are two types of dump valve, manual and automatic. To dump air from the manual kind, a button is pushed or a string is pulled. An automatic dump valve allows air to vent through the valve when the air in the suit reaches a preset pressure. On some valves this pressure is adjustable. Some valves can dump either manually or automatically. The advantage of the automatic valve is that the diver does not think about it and it does not need a spare hand. The disadvantage is that deflation is not entirely in the divers control, and control needs careful practise.

The positioning of the valves is important. They must be located where they can function properly, be accessible, not be exposed to knocks and not interfere with the harness. Most divers locate their inflation valve on the chest. The dump valve can be fitted nearby or on the upper arm or wrist. Some divers put it behind their head, the highest point where air collects, and operate it by a cord running over their shoulder to the chest. This can, however, be affected by striking the passage roof, or by back-mounted cylinders.

ADAPTATIONS OF DRYSUITS FOR CAVE DIVING

Over the years various adaptations have been made by individual divers to their suits to improve their usefulness for cave diving. Drysuits can now be obtained with an extra buoyancy compartment in the chest inflated by an independent valve. Such a compartment reduces air migration within the suit and, should the suit have a major leak, the diver retains a certain degree of control over his buoyancy. It also allows inflation from either cylinder.

Suits are available which have two seals on the wrists, so, if the diver chooses to wear dry gloves, the gloves can be fitted between the two seals. Alternatively, gloves may be glued directly to cuffs.

Since the weight a cave diver carries is suspended about his waist and his buoyancy acts predominantly around his chest and near his feet, he tends to assume a sagging posture when swimming and after long dives this can cause acute back pain. Beware also of too much weight around the waist ponding air below the neck seal and choking the diver. Some divers have countered this by adopting a lead breastplate (cast in an old frying pan) and small ankle weights thus redistributing the load to better advantage. Since a cave diver does not want to remove his weight belt (indeed, to do so could be dangerous) some divers wear their lead breastplates under their drysuits; this also has a major advantage in that it removes straps from an already cluttered area.

Finally, make sure that drysuit seals are not too tight. Excessively tight seals can restrict blood flow to both brain and hands, and it is possible that one death has already occurred in British caves through neck compression.

FINS & FOOTWEAR

THE majority of sumps require the use of fins for propulsion, although the option exists, when sumps are short and narrow, of wearing normal caving boots. Here the various types of fin are examined, and attention is given to the types of footwear preferable where cave diving is involved.

FINS

There are two basic forms of fin, the shoe-type, and the heel strap fin.

Shoe Type

This form of fin is worn over a neoprene sock and must be a close and comfortable fit - if too restrictive, cramp may develop. Fin retainers, available commercially or made from car inner tube, help hold these in place, and may be worn throughout the caving trip to avoid being lost. The shoe section may have a drain hole at the end of the shoe, which also forms a useful point of attachment for a sling to help transport them through dry cave to the sump. With shoe-type fins, normal caving boots cannot be worn through the sump and must be carried.

Heel Strap Fins

These are the choice of most cave divers, and can be worn over boots or hard-soled neoprene socks, the fin being retained by means of an adjustable heel strap at the back of the cut-off shoe section. They are particularly suitable for wearing with drysuits that have a moulded foot or boot. They can be used with neoprene socks, but may require an insert in the shoe pocket to prevent slippage. These may come with the fins, or can be made from neoprene or flexible plastic sheeting.

The buckles on the heel strap must be robust, with a strong permanent attachment to the fin. Some makes have buckles which are attached by a moulded fitting which, when not loaded, can fall off. Once adjusted for a specific fit, insulating tape should be wrapped round the buckles and strap to reduce the possibility of the diving line catching on the fin underwater. A sling threaded through the heel straps provides an adequate means of transport if necessary.

Fig. 4: Vapour shrouds a diver just emerged from a sump. Ordinary caving boots will now replace fins for the way forward.

With both types of fin, the rubber construction must be supple enough to be comfortable, but strong enough to prevent them from splitting in the harsh environment of a cave. Most modern fins are of composite construction; soft rubber for the shoe and harder rubber, plastic or fibreglass for the blade. Flaps or slots are sometimes built into the blade, and such fins are colloquially known as jet-fins. The concept behind such designs is to generate lift by increased water flow and reduce effort on the downward stroke. Some work, some don't, and with modern aerodynamically designed smooth blades, a similar performance can be obtained. Extremely long bladed fins, used for speed racing, should be avoided in cave diving. They make manoeuvrability difficult, and increase the risk of silt disturbance behind the diver. Fins suitable for cave diving should allow a good degree of lateral control as well as forward motion, and trial and error (and practise in technique) will eventually decide which style is best suitable for you. Some divers have several types of fin (eg one set for distance diving, another for delicate control).

To prevent fins from becoming lost on a dive, a short length of cord can be attached through a hole drilled near the ankle of the fin, the other end of which is fixed to a loop of rubber inner tube worn around the ankle. This also allows fins to be removed and retained on leaving the water by sliding the rubber loop up to knee height and letting the fins dangle beside the shins.

FOOTWEAR

The majority of cave dives involve a carry to the sump, and often dry caving on the far side. There is a need for divers to adapt their standard footwear to cope with these requirements.

The most suitable footwear to be worn with the heelstrap fin is a moulded rubber boot. There are makes of lace-up rubber ankle boots with a robust sole available, but the most commonly used and inexpensive form of footwear is the standard wellington boot. These can restrict ankle movement and create a certain amount of drag underwater, and are not recommended on very long dives. Reducing their length to just above the ankle can help to alleviate this problem. On no account should boots that have lace hooks be used on cave dives, these provide a real danger of entanglement with diving line.

If the shoe fin is used, or if steel-toecap boots are preferred, then footwear will have to be carried through the sump. Great care should be taken to ensure boots do not drag in floor sediments, or become detached, and it is best to carry a small tackle bag for such through-sump transport. Some divers thread wire through lace holes and attach this to the harness, or fix boots to tanks with "snoopy loops", but such techniques can result in entanglement. Footwear can be left beyond a sump if visits are regular.

An alternative to boots, if shoe fins are worn, are hard-soled neoprene bootees. These can fit in the larger sizes of shoe fin, but offer problems with grip and foot support if much caving is envisaged beyond a sump. For long dives, where no surfacing is envisaged, or where brief exploratory probes may be made to surface, they are entirely suitable.

INSTRUMENTATION

THE equipment described in this section is a fundamental part of the cave diver's kit. Whilst in some cases, such as when passing through a known sump, much of may not be necessary, its presence in an emergency may mean the difference between life and death. The cave diver can never know exactly what is going to be encountered on a dive, and should be prepared for all eventualities. Therefore, the equipment described here, whether necessary on every dive or not, should be regarded as essential.

DEPTH GAUGES

The maximum depth of any dive, along with the duration of the dive, must be known to enable the diver to ascend before the "no-stop" time is exceeded, or to ensure the correct decompression procedure is completed at the end of an extended dive. Therefore as accurate a depth gauge as possible is required for safe cave diving. Several types are available:

1) Capillary gauge (or bathymeter): The capillary gauge is simply a bathymeter in convenient packaging (figure 5). It consists of a rigid transparent tube, closed at one end, and full of air at atmospheric pressure.

It relies on Boyle's Law, which states that "the volume of a gas is inversely proportional to the pressure at a constant temperature". Put simply, this means that if the pressure doubles, then the gas will be compressed to half of its original volume. Water will enter the tube as the depth and pressure increases, and the interface between water and air is the indicating point on a graduated scale of depth readings. The bore of the tube is not important, as long as it exceeds 2mm in diameter (3mm is normal). The accuracy of tube marking is critical, as the compression factor decreases with increasing depth. If a 90mm long tube is used, the volume of air within will have been compressed to half its original length at 10m (when the pressure has doubled), and the 10m mark will be 45mm along the tube. At 20m depth, the air column will have compressed again by 50%, but the reading will now only be 15mm further along the tube, while at 30m it will only have moved another 7.5mm.

No matter what length the tube is, the air column will contract to:
At 10m (2 bar absolute): half its original length.
At 20m (3 bar absolute): one third original length.
At 30m (4 bar absolute): one quarter original length.
At 40m (5 bar absolute): one fifth original length.

The main advantages of the capillary gauge are: its cheapness; its accuracy at shallow depths; its comparative accuracy at altitude in reading comparative depths (see section on *Diving at altitude*). Its disadvantages are: due to its logarithmic scale it is rendered virtually unreadable beyond only shallow depths and so is worthy of little consideration except perhaps for accurate decompression stops; also there is a tendency for the tube to become obstructed by silt particles from cave sediments, rendering it inaccurate.

2) Bourdon Tube Gauges: The majority of mechanical depth gauges use a Bourdon Tube, which consists of a curved metal tube which, when pressure

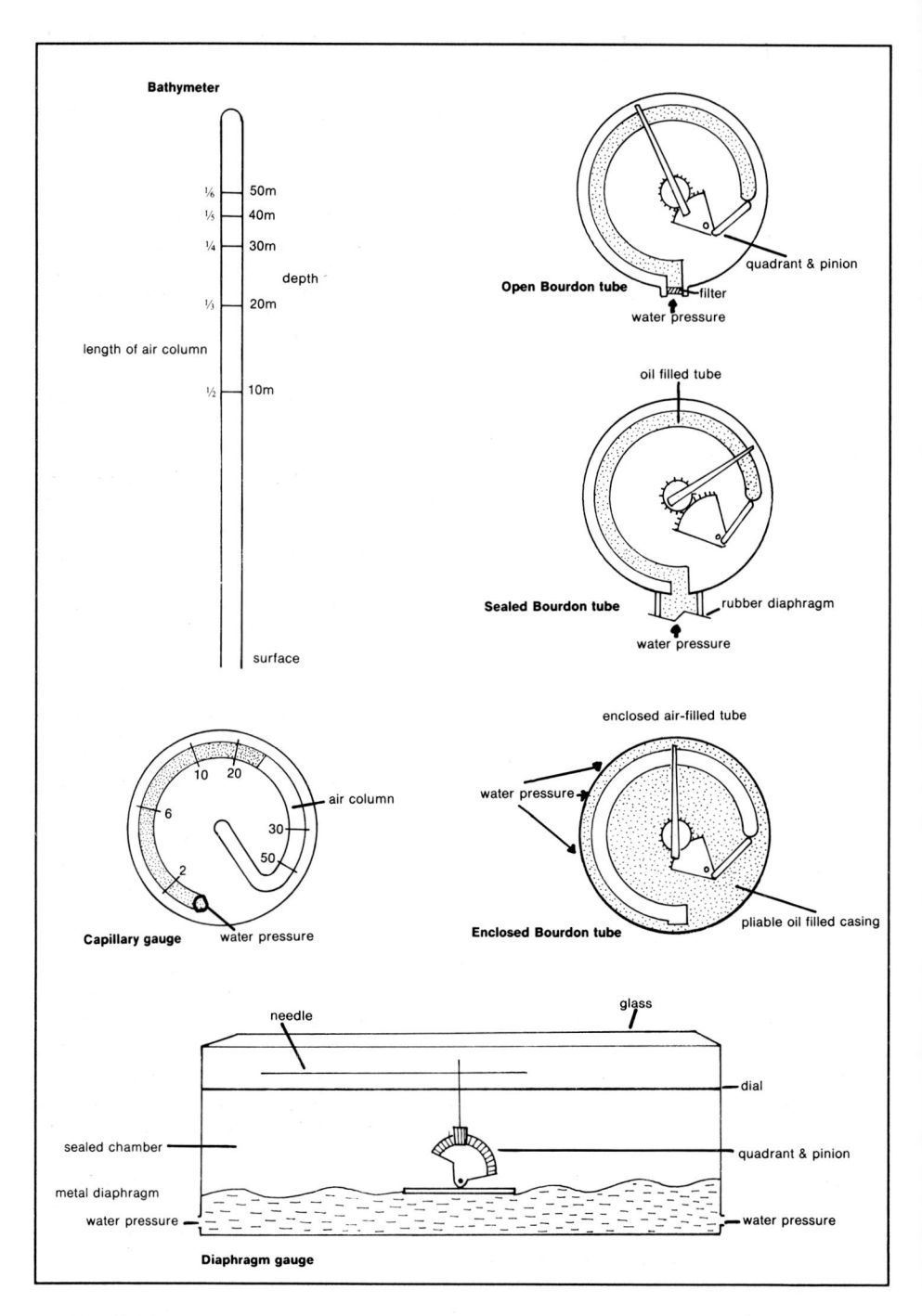

Fig. 5: Various depth gauges - bathymeter, capillary, Bourdon and diaphragm.

32 **Equipment**

is applied to its cavity, attempts to straighten out. A linkage attached to the closed end of the tube moves with it and operates a simple quadrant and pinion mechanism, so turning the needle and indicating the depth attained on the pressure calibrated dial. There are three types of Bourdon Tube, open, sealed and enclosed (figure 5).

The open Bourdon Tube is open to the water at one end via a simple filter. Water floods the tube and the increased pressure acts against the sealed airspace in the casing, which is at atmospheric pressure, and the curved tube attempts to straighten, moving the needle. This type of gauge is particularly subject to silt and corrosion inside the tube, preventing water access and so causing inaccuracies. Due to these problems, the open Bourdon Tube has been largely superseded by more reliable gauges.

The sealed Bourdon Tube works on the same principle as the open tube, but overcomes the problems of silt and corrosion by having an oil-filled tube, separated from the water by a rubber diaphragm. The pressure acting on the diaphragm is transferred to the oil in the tube, and thus to the needle.

The enclosed Bourdon Tube is sealed at both ends and contains only air at atmospheric pressure. The gauge casing is completely filled with oil. As pressure increases, it acts on the pliable casing and is transmitted to the oil which in turn acts against the air in the tube. As this gauge is filled with oil, changes in temperature can cause a change in the volume of oil and hence in the pressure within the gauge, causing it to read inaccurately. However, being filled with oil the gauge is fairly resilient to knocks and the mechanism is self-lubricating.

3) The Diaphragm Gauge: This gauge has a corrugated metal diaphragm which is hermetically sealed onto the base of the gauge (figure 5). Beneath this, water floods a small chamber and the increasing pressure acts on the diaphragm and causes the diaphragm itself to operate a quadrant and pinion mechanism, so moving the needle. This is by far the most accurate of the mechanical gauges, but also the most expensive.

4) Electronic depth gauges: These gauges operate by pressure-sensitive electronic sensors and are generally the most accurate of all, if perhaps the least robust. Most electronic decompression meters (see separate section) contain an electronic depth gauge with an accuracy of 0.5m or better, as well as a maximum depth readout.

On purchasing a depth gauge, you should ensure that it has an easily read scale. Divisions should ideally be in 1m increments, but a minimum of 2m increments is necessary to comply with RNPL or USN decompression tables. Capillary gauges are practically useless for all but the shallowest of decompression stops. Bourdon and diaphragm gauges can develop inaccuracies, and should be regularly calibrated against a tagged shotline, or against a gauge of known accuracy. None of these gauges have a guaranteed accuracy of better than 1m in every 50m. Electronic depth gauges are generally more precise, reading to 0.5m, and can occasionally be obtained with illuminated displays. Bourdon and diaphragm gauges for underground use should have a luminous display allowing depth to be read even if lights fail.

A useful extra, and one that is generally found on electronic gauges, is a maximum depth indicator. Often the circumstances of a dive and the complications of its profile make the deepest point easy to miss, and some way of recording it without constant observation is advisable. Several models of gauge have some method of altitude compensation, allowing gauges to be reset at altitude. This is essential if high altitude diving is to be undertaken. Most electronic gauges in decompression meters have some facility for automatic altitude compensation, though this should be checked when buying the gauge. Uncompensated gauges may be irretrievably damaged at high altitude, or during air travel (even in pressurised compartments the pressure is held at approximately 2000m of altitude equivalent). In such cases, transport in a pressure-sealed container is essential.

Most gauges are calibrated for seawater, and due to the differing densities of saline and freshwater, it is usually taken that 9m depth of seawater is equivalent to 10m of fresh. Most electronic guages or decompression meters are, however, calibrated for freshwater. Most electronic guages in decompression meters are, however, calibrated for fresh water.

COMPASS

The compass is an essential piece of equipment for the cave diver, not only as a survey tool, but also as a survival aid. When diving any submerged cave passage, the diver should have a knowledge of the general direction in which the passage is heading so that in the event of the diver losing the line he will not become totally disorientated. This is only possible if a compass is worn and the bearing of the passage known. On recovering the line, it is essential to know which of the two possible directions lead to safety. A note of the bearing can be made on the diver's slate (see below).

The degree of accuracy of diving compasses is not likely to be better than ±5°. It must of course be waterproof and able to withstand pressure. Most are damped by being oil filled. The compass should have divisions of at most 5° and have a rotatable bezel with an attached cursor. The bezel can be rotated to a set bearing so that if the needle is kept within the limits of the cursor line the direction can be predetermined. Right handed divers should wear it on the left wrist, and vice versa.

The compass should be held well in front of the line of vision with the forearm at right angles to the direction of travel, and the compass must be level so that the needle tilt does not affect the reading (figure 6). Failure to do this will give a false reading. As with any compass, ferrous metals (ie knife, steel air cylinders and possibly other gauges) may affect readings, and must be kept as far as possible from the compass. Beware also of magnetic fields created by bright diving lamps. The bezels of compasses are particularly susceptible to silt and grit, making rotation difficult. They should be regularly stripped and cleaned.

For accurate survey work, a compass mounted on a hand-held survey slate may provide more accurate measurements.

SLATES

A writing slate, though possibly not essential, is certainly advisable, and serves several functions. It is either worn on the arm, or carried separately (eg in a buoyancy compensator pocket), the latter being more convenient when

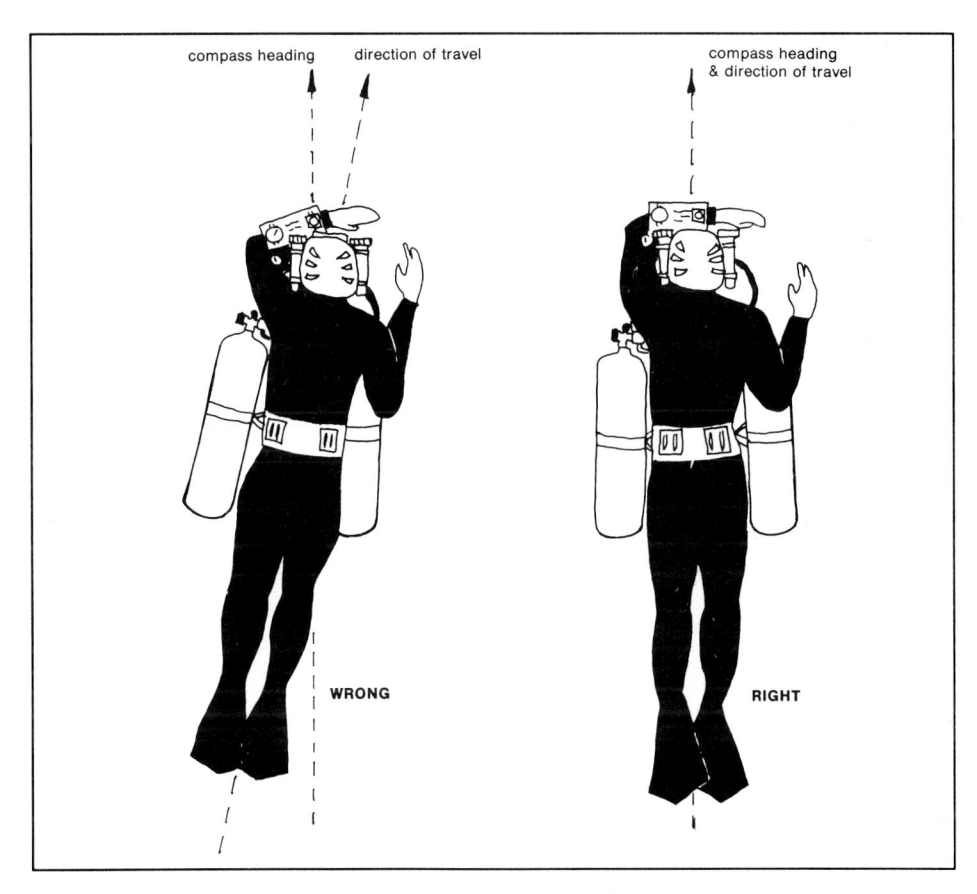

Fig. 6: Position of compass for reading underwater.

divers have to communicate with each other in writing.

It is certainly essential if a diver intends carrying out even the simplest of surveys, and is used in this context with depth gauge and compass to record depth, direction and distance along a tagged line (see chapter on *Surveying*). Many divers attach their depth gauge, compass, and perhaps watch, to their slate to minimise the number of separate straps worn on arms, and make survey reading simpler (figure 7).

Slates can also record information for use in the dive (eg cylinder contents at start, decompression information, passage directions, dive start time, greatest depth, etc.) It also allows divers to communicate in writing.

Slates can be constructed from white Formica or light coloured PVC tube, bent into shape by heating in water. The surface should be roughened slightly with fine sandpaper to make writing easier, and a pencil attached by a short lanyard. A plastic self-propelling pencil is better than a wooden one, being easier to sharpen underwater and less affected by the wet. After the dive, the slate can be cleaned with washing-up liquid or a slightly abrasive cleaning material such as toothpaste or Vim.

Equipment 35

Fig. 7: Arm-mounted slate with compass, pencil and knife.

Alternatively, waterproof writing paper can be made up into a notepad, thus allowing a greater degree of note-taking or communication than with a slate. Such pads can be clipped to a wrist, a shoulder harness, in a small pouch strapped to the diver, or in a buoyancy compensator pocket. A pencil should be attached in some manner to the pad.

WATCHES AND DIVE TIMERS

There are many makes of diving watch on the market, but the basic requirements for cave diving are that it be waterproof to the maximum depth the diver intends to operate at, shockproof, and capable of measuring the maximum duration of the dive.

An analog watch should be equipped with a rotary bezel by which dive time can be measured. These have the disadvantage of being able to be knocked out of position. Some modern analog watches have bezels which can only be rotated anti-clockwise thus allowing a mistake to err on the side of safety.

The digital dive watches available are both cheap and effective, though care must be taken with some of the cheaper 50 and 100m rated, so-called sports watches, for if the buttons are pressed underwater the watches can flood. The 200m models are still relatively cheap, and offer several functions that can be used underwater at the touch of a button, such as stop-watch and alarm facilities. Time alarms can be preset to warn of impending no-stop time at a planned depth, though in practice few alarms are loud enough to be easily heard through a wetsuit hood while on the move. The possibility of pressing the wrong button accidentally in stop-watch mode can affect timing of the dive, and a note should still be made of the actual start of diving time on the diver's slate.

Bottom timers can be mechanical or electronic and usually operate automatically when immersed in water. These have the advantage that if the diver forgets to note the time at the beginning of a dive the timer switches itself on and begins to register elapsed dive time. Advanced models may also register the surface interval between repeat dives while still logging the duration of the previous dive, essential information if multiple divers are planned which might involve decompression.

KNIVES

A knife is one of the most important pieces of equipment carried by the diver. A cave diver should never dive without at least one, and preferably two, knives. In the event of entanglement, it is all he has to cut himself free.

The knife should ideally be of a size to be worn on the upper arm or forearm, while not hindering movement of the arm. This allows it to be easily reached in emergency. It should be kept sharp and be attached to the sheath by a length of cord to avoid loss if it is dropped. The cord can be tucked under the straps when not in use to avoid entanglement and snagging while on the move. Larger knives, as worn on the leg by sports divers, are rarely of use in a cave, save as tools for specific tasks. They cannot easily be worn on the arm, and simply offer potential for entanglement if worn on the leg. It might also be impossible to reach in confined passages. Some divers use a small kitchen knife as a second knife, often attached to the slate. This should be kept in a sheath to avoid laceration of the arm.

Where there is any possibility of entanglement in stainless steel guide-line, a pair of wire-cutters is also mandatory.

EQUIPMENT DISTRIBUTION

Most of the cave diver's ancillary equipment is worn on the arms, where it is within vision even in confined spaces, and is always readily accessible. It is worth deciding on particular places for particular items and sticking to them so that you know instinctively where to look. As mentioned above, it is possible to combine some items on one piece of equipment, such as depth gauge and compass forming party of a console on the slate. The knife should be worn well away from the compass to avoid affecting it. Knife straps are often used to mount a small search reel (see *Line laying* chapter). If the diver is right-handed, the slate and its relevant meters are usually mounted on the left forearm, and decompression meters and other gauges on the right. The knife can be worn inverted on the upper left arm without interfering with the slate. It is common practise to loop pressure gauges to wrists or elbows. A small ancillary item of great use in low visibility waters is a small clear perspex tube,

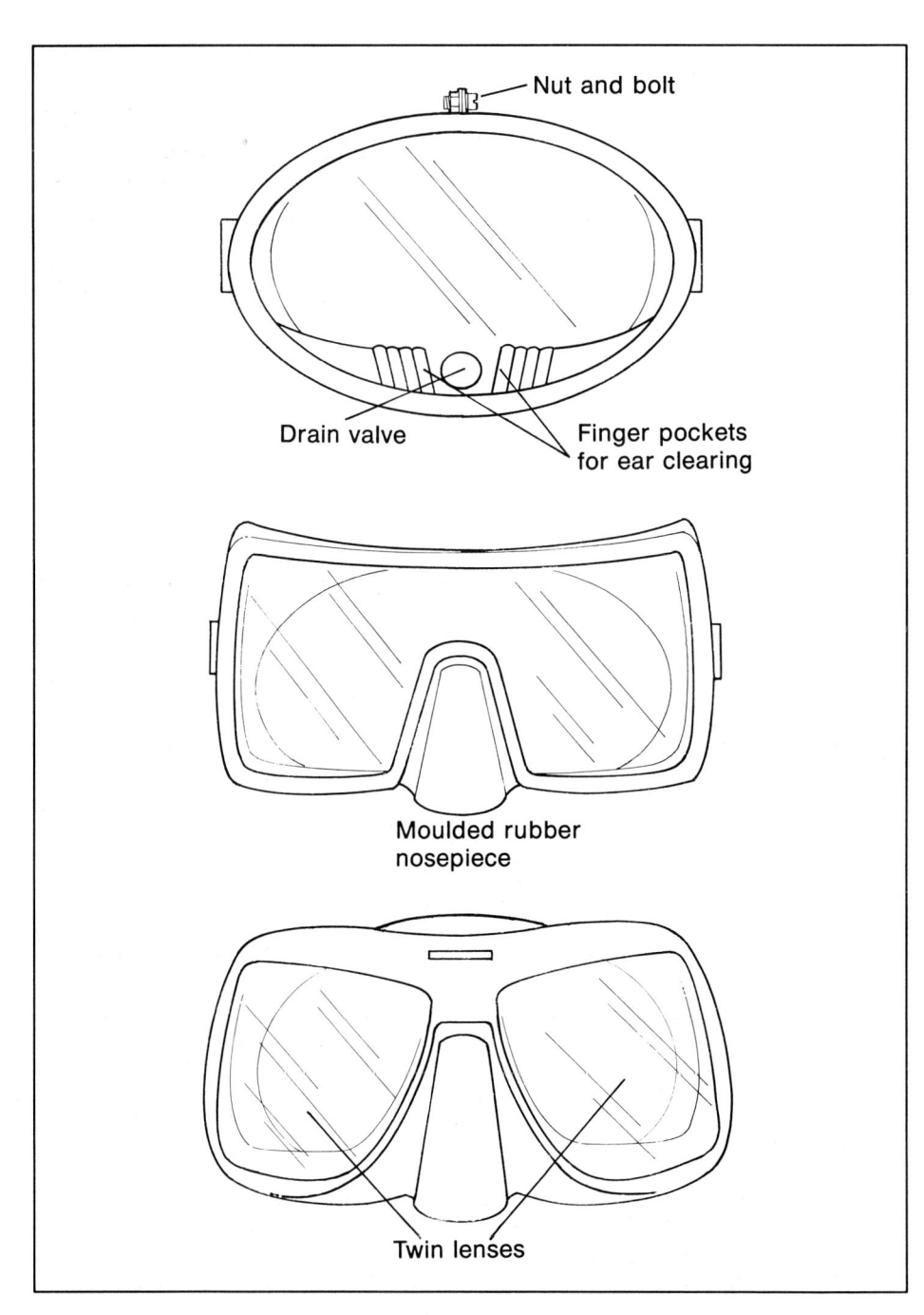

Fig. 8: Types of masks - (from top) single faceplate; single faceplate and moulded nosepiece; low-volume semi-goggle.

filled with clean water, through which gauges can be read by placing it to the eye and shining light through the side.

As with all diving equipment, all the items of ancillary equipment should be carefully cleaned and serviced after use. Depth gauges should be calibrated at least annually, depending on use. Straps should be checked for wear and replaced when necessary. As with all items on which your life depends, retire them when they get old. Don't hang onto old friends for sentiment's sake.

MASKS

WHEN a diver is underwater, his eyes can only focus properly if there is an airspace immediately in front of them. The diver's mask provides this necessary airspace, and in addition protects much of the face from the effects of cold water.

The diver's nose must be enclosed within the mask for three main reasons:

1) As the diver descends the water forces the mask against his face, resulting in the unpleasant condition of mask squeeze. To avoid this the diver needs only to exhale gently into the mask to restore equilibrium with the outside pressure.

2) Most divers find that ear-clearing (ie restoring pressure equilibrium within the ear and sinuses) is simpler if the nose is closed by pinching it. Masks which enclose the nose usually have recesses on either side of the nose, or some other suitably-shaped access for fingers to pinch through.

3) The diver may have to expel water from a flooding mask; this he does by exhaling air through the nose into the mask.

TYPES OF MASKS

The range of masks on the market should offer something to meet any individual's needs (see figure 8). Each face shape is different, and every diver may have to try several masks before finding one which is suitable for his use. The faceplate should be tempered or toughened glass. Untreated glass can easily shatter (with imaginable consequences!). Plastic faceplates are prone to scratching and misting up. The faceplate must be firmly fixed so that it neither leaks nor can be easily dislodged. Apart from the immediate embarrassment, a faceplate dropped in water becomes virtually invisible, and is extremely difficult to find. The fixing is usually done by clamping the faceplate in position by a plastic or metal band tightened by a screw. In some later masks, the band is snapped firmly in position by a number of tabs which locate in slots in the body of the mask. If a faceplate is lost, or breaks, it is often possible to replace it without purchasing a new mask.

1) *Masks with a single faceplate*: The simplest form of mask has one large faceplate and has finger pockets for ear-clearing. It gives good all-round vision but is more cumbersome than more modern low-volume masks. Ear-clearing is a little more awkward with finger pockets than with a moulded nosepiece

(see below). Because of the larger volume of air enclosed by this mask, it takes longer to clear it should it flood. More positive clearing can be achieved if a drain-plug is fitted near the bottom of the mask, often a mushroom valve fitted in the faceplate itself. Valves have the obvious disadvantage that grit can lodge in them and cause leaks, or that the valve could become lost, leaving the fixing hole open, but the advantages generally outweigh this.

2) *Masks with a single faceplate and moulded nosepiece*: These masks are usually lower in volume because the nosepiece allows the faceplate to be brought closer to the eyes. The smaller airspace allows for easier mask-clearing and access is easy for nose-pinching.

3) *Low-volume semi-goggle masks*: The ultra-low-volume mask has a plastic frame attached to the rubber of the mask, and the frame has a small separate glass for each eye. It encloses the nose, is close-fitting, and is the smallest type of mask available. Since the eyes almost touch the glass, the mask gives an excellent wide view. It is very easily cleared if flooded, the small glasses are less prone to breakage, nose-pinching is simple, and its smaller size eases packing and transport. It does have some disadvantages, in that there is less latitude for individual face-matching, especially in divers with prominent noses, and, being very close-fitting, the mask may allow the eyelashes to touch the glass, causing considerable irritation on a long dive. It is, however, probably the best type of mask for cave diving.

OTHER MASKS

A type of mask *not* recommended for cave work is that designed to give a specially-wide field of vision, either by having a wrap-round lens, or by the inclusion of side windows. All windows introduce distortion underwater, but curved and multiple windows have their own characteristic pattern of distortion. They also may give a sense of tunnel vision. Both types tend to be bulky, which not only makes them less easy to transport, but they may be more prone to dislodgement underwater in a collision with another object, be it rock wall or diver's fins.

Some masks have a small inner flange, a secondary seal. This can be effective, especially for faces with difficult contours, but normally it is unnecessary. For spectacle wearers, prescription lenses are available, either by purchasing masks with pre-ground prescription lenses, or by obtaining prescription lenses that can be glued to the inside of the faceplate. In some larger masks, a spectacle frame may be fitted.

Full facemasks, which also cover the mouth, are for specialised activities such as decompression or rescue. They may have a considerable respiratory dead-space, and ear-clearing may be very difficult.

CHOOSING A MASK

A wrongly-chosen mask will be the source of many niggling problems, so it is important to choose correctly first time. The mask must be comfortable and watertight. To check this, place it in position on the face, without using the retaining strap, and inhale. It should remain in place and show no sign of leakage. Note that facial hair may affect a seal underwater. Check that nose-pinching can be effected both with and without gloves. Check that the retaining strap is well-proportioned and has sound fixings and fittings - avoid any mask that has even a hint of flimsiness. Ensure that the glass is toughened and is firmly held, but is removable for cleaning or replacing; this is a considerable advantage. An upper seal which fits snugly under a neoprene hood will have a considerable thermal advantage during long cold dives; a mask which leaves a large gap between hood and mask is not to be recommended. (Essentially, the more of your face it covers, the warmer you will be). Look for wide peripheral vision and low volume.

USING A MASK

The mask should be carried to the diving site in a robust container (eg ammunition box, BDH or rocket tube). Once at the site, treat the mask with care. It helps to have a brightly-coloured mask, or to mark it with luminous paint or tape to prevent accidents and assist recover if it is lost in the sump pool. Always carry a spare mask strap, perhaps taped inside the helmet. The strap is most likely to break while the mask is being put on or taken off, quite possibly at the far side of the sump. Some cave divers in countries other than Britain carry a complete spare mask taped to their forearm or worn back to front behind the neck.

Misting of the glass often occurs, due to the warm, moist breath inside the mask causing condensation on the cold glass. No remedy is completely effective, though rubbing saliva into it immediately before diving and rinsing it off is as good as using raw potato, French chalk, methylated spirit or a proprietary demisting agent. Where a mask is badly scratched, this will be virtually un-noticeable underwater, as the water entering the scratches will restore much of the optical quality to the lens. Rubbing carefully with a clean tissue and toothpaste will restore some of the clarity for surface use.

Masks should be dismantled occasionally to remove all grit and dirt, and to check for deterioration. Ensure that reassembly is correctly done, then test for leaks as described above.

THE DEMAND VALVE

EARLY experiments with hosepipes at Swildon's Hole highlighted the limitations of the human lungs to suck air from the surface more than about 30cm above one's head. If surface air is going to be used then it must be pressurised to somewhere near ambient pressure, ie the pressure on the lungs due to atmospheric and water pressure.

At Swildon's, Sheppard and Balcombe experimented with a simple hand pump, but soon had to turn to commercial diving equipment, the standard diving wear. This type of equipment is only suitable for the shortest sumps. Free-swimming self-contained equipment was needed.

In the 1940s, oxygen rebreathing equipment became available. As explained elsewhere, oxygen becomes toxic at relatively shallow depths and the equipment at the time was unreliable in inexperienced hands and was prone to numerous malfunctions. About this time SCUBA diving equipment started to become available, and it was the use of compressed air and the demand valve that revolutionised cave diving in the late 1960s. This has continued to be by far the main apparatus in use, even for recent deep dives which used alternative gas mixtures from air.

The demand valve (or regulator) is a device that reduces air at cylinder pressures to ambient pressure so that the diver can breathe it without harm. Early demand valves worked through a single stage pressure reducer, usually mounted on the cylinder tap. From this a dual hose led to and from the diver's mouth, bringing fresh air in and removing exhaled breath. This was not suitable for side-mounted cylinders, and the CDG have always preferred the use of double stage regulators, where air is reduced to several bars above surface pressure by the first stage on the cylinder valve and then finally to ambient pressure at the second stage, which contains the mouthpiece. There are various designs of double stage demand valves, some more suitable than others for the environmental problems encountered in underwater caves.

VALVE CONFIGURATION & PERFORMANCE

In this section we will look at some of the styles of demand valve available, and how their construction affects their performance in cave diving.

Orientation

All demand valves work in the normal swimming position, ie face down, with the body upright or horizontal. The cave diver may get in a position where he may have to work on his back, side, or head down, for extended periods. A cave diver needs a valve that will work effectively in all these positions. Some demand valves may not.

One of the functions of the exhaust valve is to allow any water out of the valve. If all is operating correctly no water should enter the valve. But fluid can enter from a poorly fitting gag, saliva from the diver's mouth, or from a minor malfunction on the valve (a hole in or poorly fitting main or exhaust diaphragm are the commonest examples). During normal diving this fluid may be no problem, but if allowed to build up it can become at the least an annoyance.

For the second stage to drain the fluid away, the exhaust valve needs to be lower than the mouth. This allows water to drain to the lower part of the breathing chamber where it is exhausted on the next breath out. If you look at most second stages you will see that the exhaust port has been located at the bottom front of the main air chamber. If the valve is used upside down (ie diver is head down or upside down) this draining cannot occur until there is sufficient fluid in the valve for some of it to be blown out of the exhaust. Before this becomes effective the diver will be aware of the build up, as some of the fluid will enter the mouth on each breath, and you have to do a lot of swallowing! What is more dangerous is if a diver is working hard and suddenly turns so that an amount of water is breathed in unexpectedly; this can cause him to gag or choke.

This orientation problem depends on the type of valve. The early ones with large air chambers were worst; most modern valves behave reasonably well. Those with exhausts at the side probably perform the best as they work just as well when the diver is upside down, because there is no upside down for them. But even these valves will give problems if used on the side with the diaphragm uppermost. If you are using side-exhaust valves and are working on your side, you may experience this problem. You can swap to your second valve which will operate with its diaphragm down to overcome the problem, but if you cannot use the first valve in this position your safety margin is gone!

Handedness

Cave divers in Britain use side mounted cylinders, and this requires the second stages to come to the mouth from each side. Most valves are "handed", ie they only have the air inlet on one side, with the exhaust valve below (figure 9). If two left hand valves are used, your air hose will have to be twisted through 180° to reach the mouth. This should be avoided.

There are two solutions to this problem. You can use only demand valves that are not handed and can therefore be inserted from either the left or right side (ie side-exhaust valves such as the Poseidon or Manta range). The alternative is to have one valve of each handedness, a right and a left air inlet valve. A lot of manufacturers will supply both right and left valves and different models of valve may be opposite handed. You can, of course, use one side-exhaust valve together with any other valve to overcome the problem.

DIN (Screw) or A-Fitting

The majority of cave divers have favoured the DIN (5/8ins BSP screw) fitting against the A-clamp type used by sports divers (figure 10). This preference is because A-clamps are felt to be more susceptible to being dislodged by knocks during the dive. The modern type of A-clamp is probably

Fig. 9: A 'handed' demand valve (left) and a 'non-handed' type.

as reliable as the screw fitting to pressures of 210 bar once fitted correctly, but the screw type is probably more robust in use. The DIN valve will work with higher pressures than the A-clamp (ie over 210 bar) though longer first stage screw-threads are needed for high-pressure tanks (250 bar and over).

The demand valves for sale in this country usually have A-clamp fittings but several types are fitted with interchangeable mountings. It is possible to screw a Poseidon DIN/A-yoke adapter into a DIN fitting and to convert it to A-clamp. If you are going to use cylinders with DIN fittings it is better to use a DIN valve as opposed to an A-clamp converter, and to fit such a yoke to your valve if you want to use it with A-clamp cylinders at some time. If ordered, most valves can be supplied with DIN fittings.

Adjustable Second Stage

Some valves have an adjustable second stage that allows you to adjust the pressure relief setting a little while in use. Thus if set up correctly you can make it a little more difficult to breath or make it easier, but free flow may result if adjusted too far.

The device is used to adjust for difference in intermediate pressure with an unbalanced first stage and to open it up to free flow when sharing during an ascent or if very out of breath. The adjustment screw is another thing that can go wrong. It nearly caused a fatality to one cave diver when, due to a setting-up error, the adjustment would only allow less air to be obtained at depth. Even the most open position would not supply enough air. Most cave divers have little use for such a device. A well set up modern valve should perform well enough to eliminate the need for any adjustment during a dive.

Fig. 10: An A-clamp first stage fitting (left) and a DIN fitting.

44 **Equipment**

MAINTENANCE AND REPAIRS

For most sports divers maintenance and repair is of secondary importance. They probably rely on the local diving supplier to maintain their equipment. Cave divers need to carry out emergency adjustment and repairs and be able at least to strip down the main components for cleaning. Cave diving, certainly in Britain, is dirty. Grit and dirt get into the valves mechanism and must be cleaned out and the valve checked regularly. As you will often be out of reach of a diving shop at these times you should be able to carry out simple tasks yourself. The choice of valve is thus important.

You may need to lubricate O-rings, etc. Only use silicon grease as recommended by the manufacturers. Do not use hydrocarbon-based greases (eg WD40) as mineral grease can become explosive under high pressures and can affect some rubber components. Do not use silicon grease on any silicon rubber components, as silicon grease causes the silicon rubber to deteriorate. Especially, do not allow such grease to come into contact with the diaphragm.

First Stage

Of the two main types of first stage, diaphragm and piston, the diaphragm needs the least day to day maintenance. The diaphragm seals the main moving parts from ingress of water and dirt, and thus once set up it should not deteriorate due to use in adverse conditions. The diaphragm and main spring are exposed to water and grit. This should cause no problems, as long as the water chamber is cleaned out after a dive, with clean water, unless you have an environmentally-sealed first stage. Although there is less need to dismantle a diaphragm first stage, you may have to if you plan to dive in areas remote from a diving supplier. Check that your choice of valve can be dismantled easily. After any dismantling the delivery pressure must be checked and adjusted (see below).

A piston first stage allows water, and hence dirt, to one side of the moving piston. In time, dirt can pass the sealing O-ring and enter the intermediate chamber or stop the "O" ring from sealing. This is not a major problem as long as the piston is cleaned after every dive in dirty water, ie in a cave. At least one cave diver has had a piston first stage pack up due to dirt ingress. When stripped down later the intermediate chamber was found to be full of water! Check how easy it is to strip down the valve to the piston; on a lot of modern valves this can be done by hand, unscrewing the main body. As the intermediate pressure is usually determined by the geometry of the piston, there is no need for any adjustment on reassembly of the valve. But check that your piston valve is not one of the few that do have an adjustment screw.

There are a number of makes of environmentally-sealed first stages on the market. Though these offer considerable advantages for the cave diver diving in very dirty waters, as no foreign matter can enter the first stage, they are more difficult to service, generally being oil-filled, and often requiring special service tools. Their claimed performance as anti-freeze units is suspect in extremely cold weather.

Main Points to Check

1) *Piston first stage*: O-rings, piston and cylinder bore are clean and free from grit. The O-rings should be checked for cracking and elasticity. Replace

them if in any doubt and lightly lubricate them with silicon grease.

2) *Diaphragm first stage*: Cleaning the water chamber by rinsing with water is about all that is routinely needed, but be careful not to let any water into the valve through the air inlet, which can result in damage to the pressure guage. Occasionally the diaphragm might need to be checked, but this will require the valve being set-up again. Only check the first stage diaphragm if you are competent and have the equipment to service the valve. The diaphragm is usually screwed down in place and is fairly easy to dismantle. It should be checked for any signs of deterioration, delamination of the rubber fabric or cracking. It should be replaced on a routine basis every year or so. While the valve is stripped down check the condition of the main spring. Check that it is free from corrosion and not cracked. Clean parts before assembly, taking special care not to get any dirt in the intermediate chamber.

Under no circumstances use silicon grease on a silicon rubber diaphragm.

If a full service is being undertaken you will also need to check the valve piston. This piston is located by a small spring and requires checking that it is free from corrosion and defects. The O-rings should be checked as for the rings in the piston valve. Take care not to damage the valve surface (knife edge).

3) *Filter*: The filter should be changed at a service. Between services it should need no attention unless the valve has been used with very dirty air. Check that the air flow from the first stage is correct. To do this properly you need to use a flow meter and follow the manufacturer's recommendations. But if when you take deep breaths from the valve the high pressure gauge fluctuates, it indicates that some restriction is present. A blocked filter is the most likely cause. Replace it, do not try to clean it.

4) *Valve Seat*: These are usually made from nylon, plastic or PTFE. If doing a service, check that it is not cut or cracked and that it is free from distortion. Some types, usually in diaphragm valves, must be accurately seated. Great care must be taken to locate the seat down correctly. Even the wrong grade of grease can inhibit the location of the valve seat.

5) *O-rings*: All O-rings that form part of moving seals (eg on a piston) should be replaced at a service. Other O-rings should be checked for wear, damage and elasticity. If in any doubt, replace them. When replacing them they should be *lightly* lubricated with silicon grease.

6) *Delivery pressure and flow rate*: After dismantling or adjusting a diaphragm or adjustable piston first stage, you must check the delivery pressure. To do this you will need a medium pressure gauge (0-18 bar) to fit to a low-pressure port. It is important to get the first stage working correctly to specification. Then if the whole valve is not correct you know it is the second stage that is wrong. With some types of valves it is impossible to set up the second stage unless the first is correctly set up. With some downstream second stages, it is possible to set up the pressure roughly by adjusting it so the second stage *just* stops short of blowing off. Remember to set up the valve at the manufacturer's recommended feed pressures.

The flow rate should also be checked after a service, but you are unlikely to have the equipment available. Have your valve checked by a service agent occasionally.

Second Stage

When rinsing out the second stage with clean water, take care not to press the purge button while immersed. If you do, water can enter the intermediate pressure hose and chamber. Normally the only internal part that may need to be checked between services is the exhaust diaphragm. Make sure you can get to the exhaust port easily without tools. Occasionally something may jam in the exhaust port jamming it open. A filter over the mouthpiece will help to stop this problem, and some valves tend not to be seriously affected by this problem.

On most second stages, all the maintenance that a valve seat will need is regular and careful cleaning of any O-rings and an occasional replacing of the seat itself if it shows signs of wear. No adjustment should be made to the spring, which should be replaced if defective. As a temporary measure in the field, some improvement in performance or stopping of leaks may be gained by removing the rubber seat with great care and reversing it.

If your valve is serviced regularly there should be no need to strip it down to check the main component parts. All that should be needed is a good visual check of accessible components and that it is functioning correctly.

Cave diving puts a lot of wear and tear on equipment, and the second stage is subject to the most abuse. You will need to have your valve serviced regularly or carry out a service check yourself. In the writer's experience the second stages of most valves can be stripped down and reassembled by a careful diver, and all qualified cave divers should be capable of at least stripping down and checking his second stage diaphragm, exhaust valve and lever action on his second stage valve. As long as the first stage is correctly set up the second stage can be adjusted easily. Check that your chosen valve is easy to work on and that you know the correct procedures.

Hoses

High- and low-pressure hoses are easily damaged in the cave environment, and it may be worth considering the use of hose protectors at all junctions with first and second stages. Some divers use wraps of insulating tape, or coiled plastic wrapping, but whichever form of protection is used it should be regularly removed to check for leaks or damage. If hoses are badly nicked, worn, or have slight pressure leaks then they should be replaced immediately. Divers should ensure that low-pressure hoses are *never* connected to high-pressure outlets, this is dangerous, will cause the hose to burst, and may injure someone.

Corrosion and Accumulative Deposits

All valves may suffer some slight corrosion whilst in use, especially in seawater. Washing regularly in freshwater, and ensuring they dry properly, will minimise this. An occasional soaking in warm water will remove salt deposits, and a soaking overnight in a weak acid solution such as vinegar will remove any corrosion of brass components. Stubborn corrosion deposits are best removed by an ultrasonic cleaning tank (often this can be done by your diving shop).

Leaks

Demand valve should be tested for leaks, both in the cave immediately before a dive and during servicing. Major leaks from high-pressure junctions can often be identified by touch, or heard as a high-pitched hiss. High-pressure leaks are the most dangerous, and the most likely to end in rapid air loss, and should be treated immediately. Low-pressure leaks might not be obvious until the pressurised valve is placed in water. They may not result in catastrophic air loss, but they should be repaired at the earliest opportunity, and it is not advisable to use such valves underwater until repaired. Minor leaks may be caused by grit jamming open the second stage lever, or by a small lump of grit entering the second stage valve seat. These can often be repaired in the field by careful use of a simple tool set. Leaks from first stages will probably be the result of O-ring failure.

Water entering the second stage whilst in use may be the result of a leak in the exhaust diaphragm, and this will then probably need replacing. The valve should not be used until this is done, or the leak otherwise corrected.

Air Flow

Air flow in the demand system depends not only on the fine tuning of the valve pressure, but also on filters present in the first stage to stop extraneous material entering the valve, either from the tank or from the outside environment. The filter can be seen by removing the dust-cap from the first stage before fitting it to a tank. This should be regularly checked and, if it shows signs of corrosion (metal filter) or is excessively discoloured or clogged, then it should be replaced. Reddish discoloration may mean rust in the cylinder, so the cylinder should be internally inspected as well. On many valves, filter replacement is a simple job, involving the removal of a small circlip or other retaining device. Care should be taken, however, and if the filter appears to be firmly stuck, it should be taken in to a dealer for service and replacement.

Minor Maintenance

1) *Tools*: Most diver-servicing can be done with the aid of a small adjustable wrench, a set of allen keys (metric or imperial depending on make of valve), a 13mm or 1/2ins open-ended spanner, a flat-head and a Phillips screwdriver, a tube of silicone grease, clean soft tissues and a few cotton buds on sticks. Anything requiring more elaborate tools is probably best left to a qualified repairer. The work surface should be scrupulously clean, and a small container should be placed by the valve to take parts that might be easily lost. If the diver is inexperienced, a pencil and piece of paper will be useful to record the position of parts as the valve is stripped.

2) *Spares*: A basic spares kit for a demand valve would include a full set of O-rings, tube of silicone grease, exhaust diaphragm, blanking-off bolts for pressure outlets (with O-rings), valve piston and second stage lever seats, filters and circlips. For remote-location diving (ie expedition work, a more sophisticated kit might include springs, mouthpiece, hoses (low- and high-pressure), screws, dust-cap, and all seatings.

PRESSURE GAUGES

All regulators should have a pressure gauge capable of registering 25% higher than the planned cylinder pressure. The pressure gauge tells how much pressure is in the cylinder, not simply its contents, and this pressure might vary considerably in changing temperatures. It also indicates the contents of the cylinder to the diver above and below water, and is vital for maintaining the relevant air reserves during the course of a dive. ON NO ACCOUNT should the Continental-style reserve lever be used for cave diving. It is dangerous, and utterly irrelevant to proper air monitoring. Cylinders obtained with a reserve lever should have the cylinder valve replaced with a non-reserve valve before use in a cave.

Pressure gauges can be mounted on the elbows or wrists by the attachment of a small elasticated loop (eg cut inner tube) to the top of the hose, taking care not to compromise the integrity of the hose by doing so. High-pressure hoses should not be unduly kinked, and this should be borne in mind when attaching them to the diver. Pressure gauges should never be left to dangle below the diver, as they can be damaged by catching in crevices, creating a high-pressure leak.

DEMAND VALVE ATTACHMENT

Demand valves are usually attached to the cave diver in a way that allows him to reach them immediately in an emergency. This may be by the use of neck straps made from nylon cord or tape, or elastic shock-cord. Both valves can be mounted on a single cord if required, and most divers have their own idiosyncratic way of wearing them. If diving formally in pairs, where each diver is depending on the other for assistance in an emergency, then at least one of the valves must be instantly removable to offer in such an incident. In pre-dive planning consider the orientation of this valve. American and some Continental cave divers mount this second demand valve on a 2m low-pressure hose to enable the divers to swim together and pass restrictions more easily. These long-hose demand valves are usally wrapped once round the diver's neck once all other equipment is donned, and allowed to hang slightly loose.

Fig. 11: Another sump to pass, and the final checking.

MOUTH PIECES & FILTERS

Demand valve mouthpieces come in two basic types. One is a simple rubber gag to be held in the mouth; the other, slightly more expensive type, has moulded insets on the toothgrips which can be softened in warm water and then bitten hard between the teeth to give a unique contoured fit. Some people like using these, and feel it gives a more secure and less tiresome grip when in the mouth.

If it is planned to dive in very silty water, or in low sumps where much gravel is present, it may be worth considering the use of a nylon filter across the mouthpiece of the second stages. This can be made by cutting up an old nylon stocking (male divers, pick your girlfriends carefully) and stretching a section around the outside of the mouthpiece, securing it in place with a stout rubber band or an electrician's small pull-tie. Alternatively, the mouthpiece can be removed and the nylon stretched across the valve orifice, to be held in place by the mouthpiece when it is refixed. In shallow water, this will not affect the performance of a demand valve to any significant degree unless several thicknesses of nylon are used.

FULL FACE MASKS

To date, these have been little used in cave diving, other than as last-resort cave rescue equipment. Their use makes it difficult to change demand valves, although it might be possible to use snap-connectors on the low-pressure hoses from each first stage (see the section on *Air margins*) to change cylinders in an emergency. Full-face masks may have an application in extremely polluted waters, in cave rescue, and where voice communications are essential. They do not form part of standard cave diving equipment.

POINTS TO CONSIDER WHEN CHOOSING A REGULATOR

1. Cost
2. Performance
3. DIN or A-clamp availability
4. Ease of maintenance.
5. Maximum operating pressure
6. Abuse tolerance
7. Handedness
8. Enough outlets.
9. Freezing resistance
10. Spares availability (long term)

TROUBLE SHOOTING GUIDE

Air Purging from Second Stage

1) *In bursts*: First stage problem, usually resulting in gradual build-up of pressure in low-pressure hose that pushes past second stage filter when pressure becomes too great. Causes could be too high a tank pressure, badly adjusted first stage, or failure of the first stage valve seating, allowing slow leakage of HP air into the low-pressure compartment. Improper tuning of the second stage can also produce an erratic air flow in some cases.

2) *Slow and steady*: This suggests improper internal adjustment or a damaged valve seat in second stage. When in use, it can mean foreign matter jamming open the purge valve. Purging the valve in brief bursts may dislodge any contaminating material, but the valve should be stripped and cleaned. If the leak persists beyond basic servicing, consult an authorised repair dealer.

3) *Slow air supply*: Excessive inhalation resistance can be caused by low tank pressure, by a clogged or damaged sintered filter, or by improper internal pressures within the regulator (usually caused by damaged or maladjusted internal components). If the valve has been used in the sea, salt particles may be encrusting the inside. Check filters, clean first stage or send for service.

No Air

First, check the cylinder is turned on. If so, and the cylinder is pressurised and still no air is emerging from the second stage, then either there is a blockage in the system or the second stage tilt lever is not engaging the purge diaphragm on inhalation. Check that the lever is properly oriented to the diaphragm, and that the second stage adjustment is correct. If this does not solve it, see whether it is a first stage problem by removing the second stage from the low-pressure hose and turning the valve on, keeping a firm hold of the low-pressure hose (which may otherwise flail about a bit). If air is emerging from the hose in apparently normal quantities, it is probably not a first stage problem. If it isn't, check the first stage for blockages or internal damage.

Wet Air

Water coming in with the air is usually an indication of a damaged exhaust valve or a damaged second stage diaphragm. Alternatively, the mouthpiece may be loose or damaged. Dismantle the second stage, check all rubber parts for signs of wear, damage or bad seating, and replace if necessary. Check the tightness of the second stage outer retaining clamp or circlip on reassembly. Do not grease the diaphragm or exhaust valve or this may cause them to distort on their seating when the clamp is tightened. If leakage persists, consult an appointed repair dealer.

Air Leaks

If air is leaking from any part of the valve, try and pinpoint the approximate source in a bucket of water with the valve under pressure. Strip the offending part, check O-rings and seals for wear, damage or foreign contamination, clean and lightly coat with silicon grease, or replace if necessary. If the leak persists, consult an authorised repair agent. Leaks in hoses at end swages or along the hose itself are a sign that the hose should be immediately replaced.

MAJOR SERVICING

Major servicing usually requires specialist tools and an intermediate pressure gauge. Unless you are competent to do so, and have a full service manual for the make and model of valve concerned, take your valves into an authorised service agent for major overhauls. Check that the dealer you take them to has been on a service course for your valve, and is authorised by the manufacturer to repair it.

CYLINDERS, TAPS & FITTINGS

THERE are stringent rules regarding the transport of pressure vessels for use underwater which have virtually outlawed any cylinder for breathing equipment which has not been manufactured and held to a prescribed standard. New and second-hand diving cylinders, complete with the appropriate test certificate, are available without restriction through retail outlets and privately. These are the only cylinders that should be used for diving. Safety must take priority over every other consideration.

The most popular size of cylinder used for cave diving in Great Britain is between 4.9 and 6.25l water capacity. It makes good sense for the trainee to acquire a pair of such cylinders, plus a "mini" usually holding between 2l and 4l. This combination should see the trainee through all his training dives and many of the exploratory dives he is likely to undertake.

To bring CDG into line with standard metric nomenclature for diving tank capacity, the following system is used. This corresponds to the sizes of diving tank in current use at approximately 3000psi (200 bar) and is a record of the water volume necessary to fill an empty tank.

If tanks are slightly overblown for particular dives (a practice not to be recommended for tanks if in other than in perfect condition), then volumetric content can be calculated by using the equation: 1l = 0.1225 cu ft.

The following table gives the metric and imperial equivalents for some of the more standard tanks used in British cave diving.

Cubic Feet	Litres	Cubic Feet	Litres
15	1.84	60	7.35
28	3.43	75	9.2
30	3.7	80	9.8
40	4.9	94	11.5
45	5.5	100	12.25
50	6.25	122	15.0
55	6.7		

Dives can only be planned according to the available cylinders, so, the greater the number and the sizes available to the diver, the greater the variety of sumps that can be attempted. Although it is true that cylinders can be twinned or staged to bring long and deep sumps within the diver's reach, it is also true that the equipment should not be unnecessarily complicated, which means that the correct cylinders should be used for the intended dive.

Whether cylinders for use in Great Britain be 2 or 15l they must be manufactured to the specification approved in Great Britain; they must bear the appropriate manufacturing and capacity details; if not new, they must be stamped with their test details and be complete with a test certificate as proof that they have been tested to British Standard 5054 or 5430.

Equipment

Cylinder Materials

Owing to the hostile environment in which the cylinders will be used, steel is the preferred material for most British sumps. Steel cylinders are of two kinds, high-pressure and low-pressure. They differ in wall thickness and each will have its own buoyancy characteristics; high-pressure cylinders are usually smaller but both types will hold the same amount of air when filled to their correct pressure. Care should be taken to regularly check the inside of a steel cylinder for corrosion, and the outside should be protected from damage (including rust) as much as possible. It is not recommended that any diving cylinder, steel or aluminium, be left in a cave for an extended period of time.

Care of Cylinders

Cylinders, like explosives, should be treated with the greatest respect; the energy of a charged 3l cylinder at 1800psi is much the same as that of 0.4kg of 80% gelignite. Regular inspections should be made for deep surface scratches (which can precipitate failure), for pitting and rusting. All mud and residues should be washed off in clean fresh water - this is especially important after diving in sea caves for salt water is very corrosive to steel. If cylinders are to be stored for any length of time, they should not be left empty, or with the valve open, for changes in ambient pressure may result in internal condensation and rusting. Ideally, cylinders should be stored at constant temperature and upright, and they must not be exposed to sunlight or extreme cold if at full working pressure. They are best kept at about 10 bars pressure, using the driest air possible. Internal corrosion is very hard to detect without removing the valve, though sometimes traces of rust may be found on the demand valve filter. Always have cylinders filled by a reliable and competent source. Remember that cylinders failing their test are not usually returned in one piece.

Special precautions are necessary if gases other than air are to be put into cylinders (or other diving equipment).

Cylinder Markings

All the cylinder markings are to be found on the neck or shoulder of the cylinder; they should not be covered or obliterated in any way. Each manufacturer will have his own markings; the other information will be serial number, specification (eg HOS, HOT), date of manufacture (and, if not new, dates of testing), capacity (expressed as the weight of water it can contain), working pressure (WP) and test pressure (TP). Other markings may include the country of origin, if outside the British Isles.

Cylinder Test Criteria

An official requirement is that all cylinders designed to contain pressurised gas shall be inspected and tested on a regular basis according to the appropriate specification. Responsibility for having the cylinders tested at the prescribed intervals rests with the owner. Filling stations will not fill cylinders unless they have a current test certificate and have a current test date stamped on them. Periodical inspection will include both visual examination and hydraulic testing.

Cylinder Threads

Assuming the cylinders you buy are new, or have been subjected to the periodical tests, there should be no need to remove the pillar valve. Serious damage can result from trying to extract pillar valves without using the proper tools. All pillar valves can be serviced without the need to remove them from the cylinder, so removal is best left to the specialists.

The older types of steel cylinder will almost certainly have tapered threads, but on more recent ones parallel threading is used for ease of sealing. The thread is standardised in both cases, with the exception of Siebe Gorman cylinders, so take care if changing the pillar valve on that make. (NB Non-European cylinder threads may have different specifications.)

When a parallel thread is used there is an O-ring in the cylinder neck and the pillar valve has a shoulder which mates with it. The advantage of this design is two-fold: firstly, less torque is needed to achieve a good seal, thereby avoiding excessively straining the cylinder neck, and secondly, a larger hole can be used so giving better access for inspection. Taper threads have a sealing medium such as PTFE tape to effect a pressure-tight seal.

CYLINDER VALVES AND FITTINGS

It is generally accepted within the Cave Diving Group that demand valves are best screwed directly into the pillar valve (DIN-fitting) and not attached by an A-clamp (see previous chapter). Diving equipment tends to take quite a bashing in low and narrow passages and a screwed-in demand valve has less chance of being disturbed by a direct bump to the first stage.

When buying new cylinders, the buyer has the choice of pillar valve. Whichever is chosen no problems should arise as almost all pillar valves manufactured today are of the balanced type (see below) and should give years of dependable service. However, should second-hand cylinders be purchased the buyer has no choice but, if the valves have to be changed, the cost of the valve change should be borne in mind when negotiating the price!

New high-pressure tanks may have a much deeper first-stage female DIN attachment thread than standard 3000psi DIN taps. This is to provide greater security for the higher pressures involved. Most standard DIN first stages will not reach the O-ring seat on these, and divers using high-pressure DIN tanks should ensure their first stages are compatible.

Some valves are fitted with burst discs as standard. Their function is to rupture and empty the tank should the working pressure be exceeded, as by overfilling or leaving tanks exposed to heat (ie in direct sunlight). The discs can become brittle with age and rupture for no apparent reason; however, the disc can be removed and the hole blanked off, but *empty the tank first*. With screw-in valves the tap is usually on the side - this is called a cross-flow valve. With the A-clamp valves, three types exist - the unbalanced valve where the air pushes on the spindle rather like a domestic water tap, the glandless valve which, though still unbalanced, has improved features which result in less wear on the moving parts, and the balanced valve, which allows air to flow past the thread of the valve head so that pressure on both sides is equal (or "balanced"). Cross-flow valves are generally balanced. (See figure 12)

Note that valves for aluminium cylinders are made of aluminium alloy or chrome plated brass to prevent corrosion; steel valves must not be fitted.

All valves are fitted with anti-debris tubes which extend down into the cylinder from the base of the pillar valve; they are designed to prevent rust or other debris from entering the valve.

Fig. 12: A selection of valves - A-clamp, DIN cross-flow and Y-valve.

British cave divers generally side-mount their tanks, and attach a separate regulator to each tank. As stated previously, DIN-fitting taps on the tanks are felt to provide a greater degree of security where the taps may strike on the sump walls, roof or floor; A-clamps might be more likely to unseat and cause a high-pressure leak.

In many overseas cave diving groups, air supplies are back-mounted. This method allows tanks to be twinned together with a manifold. The Benjamin cross-over dual manifold (figure 13), common in North American cave diving allows each of two demand valves access to either cylinder, yet allows either to be isolated in the case of valve failure, without compromising access to the full remaining air supply. However rapid air loss from both tanks can occur through tank or manifold "O" ring failure. Again, DIN taps give a greater degree of security with this system.

Fig. 13: An American double backpack with Benjamin dual manifold and a long buddy-hose on one demand valve second stage.

Equipment 55

A Y-valve allows two separate demand valves to be fitted to a single cylinder, thus giving greater safety than an Octopus or single regulator system. However, it potentially shares the same disadvantages as the cross-over dual manifold.

The arguments for and against are many; it becomes a matter of personal choice. There are numerous items for kit construction on the market, but many of them are of doubtful utility. When, however, a new system is made up, always test it thoroughly in safe water before venturing into danger.

All tank valves have a tendency to gather mud and grit down caves if not protected by a covering. This pollution can be removed easily by a syringe and toothbrush, but an adequate covering (plastic tube, blanking off cap, etc) is advised to allow the regulator to seat properly on the O-ring, and not allow a high-pressure leak.

RECENT DEVELOPMENTS

Manufacturers of all sports equipment are constantly striving to improve their products; cylinder manufacturers are no exception. Apart from materials, very few changes can be made to cylinder design. Size seems to be the main criterion and manufacturers have managed to make cylinders progressively smaller over the years. However, as the size has gone down the pressure necessarily has gone up and cylinders for filling to 4,500psi are now available. To withstand the extra pressure the wall thickness has been increased and the cylinders are much heavier. Most commercial operators will only fill cylinders to 3,500 psi so, before buying these extra high-pressure cylinders, make sure that your filling station can fill them to capacity and that the demand valves you use are suitable.

THE FUTURE

Experiments have been going on for a long time with lightweight composite tanks but as yet, for reasons given below, retailers have not been keen to market them. Composite tanks consist of two parts, a metal liner and an external wrapping of Kevlar, E-Glass or S-Glass fibre, wrapped under tension and dipped in resin. To give the tanks different properties, two different construction processes are used, namely, hoop-wrapping and full over-wrapping. The hoop-wrapped tanks have metal liners with tops and bottoms of normal thickness, but with very thin side walls. Lateral bursting is prevented by hoop-wrapping with fibre; the liner is sufficiently strong to prevent the tank from failing lengthways. In the full over-wrapped version the metal liners are formed with thin top and bottom and with even thinner side walls. The tank is then wrapped from top to bottom with the fibre and then hoop-wrapped. The second method achieves the greatest saving in weight, which can be as much as 16kg for a typical 11l capacity cylinder.

Why then are the diving shops not full of composite tanks? Just some of the reasons: The tanks are very buoyant when full and become even more so as they empty; the fibres tend to break under high stress; the metal liner cannot be inspected for external corrosion; the highly technical processes required to produce them make them expensive; not least, they have a very high working pressure.

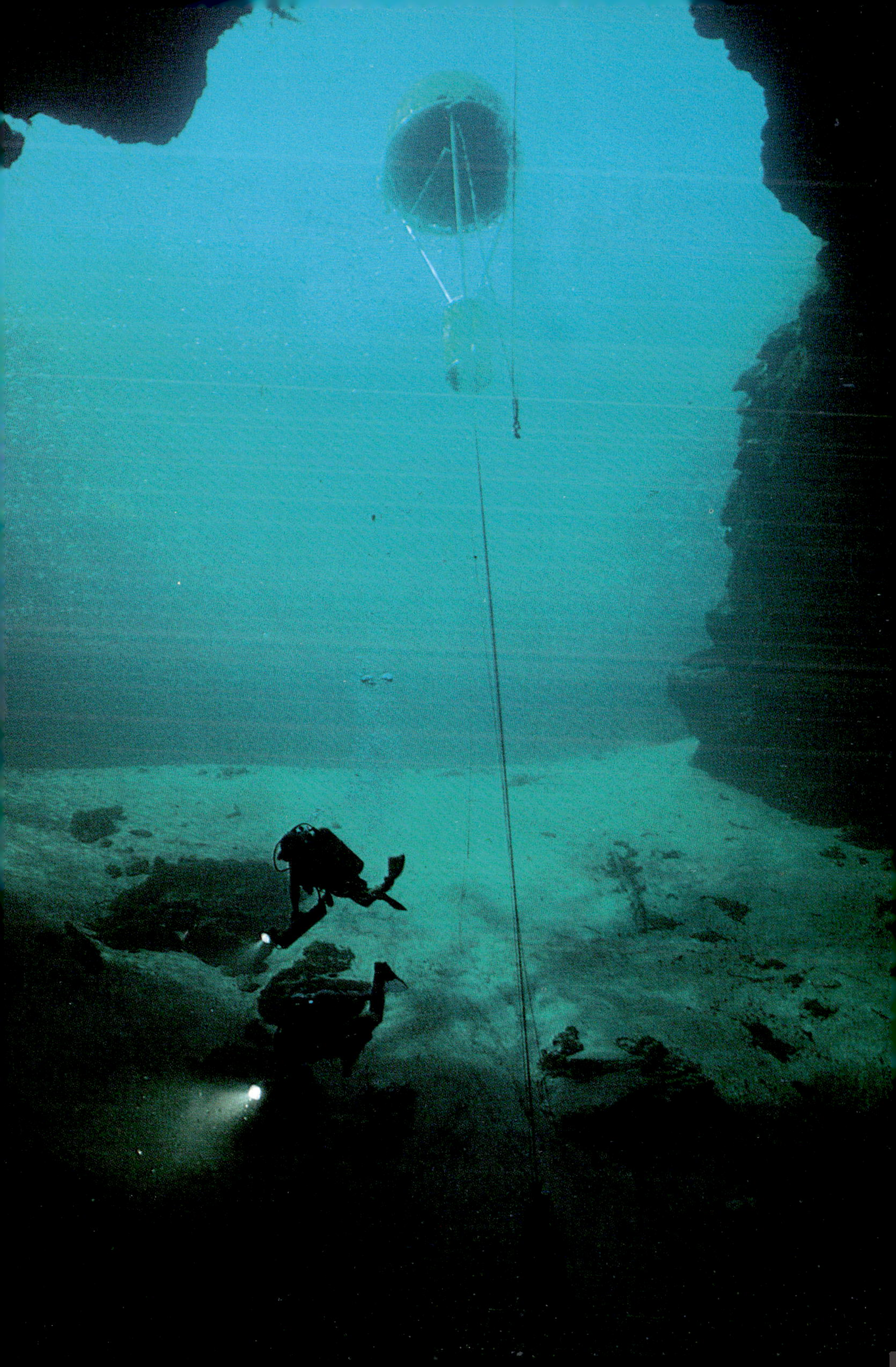

Preceding page: Two divers below the underwater decompression habitat used on the 1987 Wakulla Springs Project.

This page: (Top) Silt arises around a diver with a line reel in the submarine Urchin Cave, Eire. (Bottom) Plunging into the deep vertical chasm of Stargate Blue Hole, Bahamas.

Opposite: (Top) Diver with a mixed gas rebreather and separate composite construction stage cylinder. (Bottom) The splendour of the China Shop, Boreham Cave, discovered by diving in 1975.

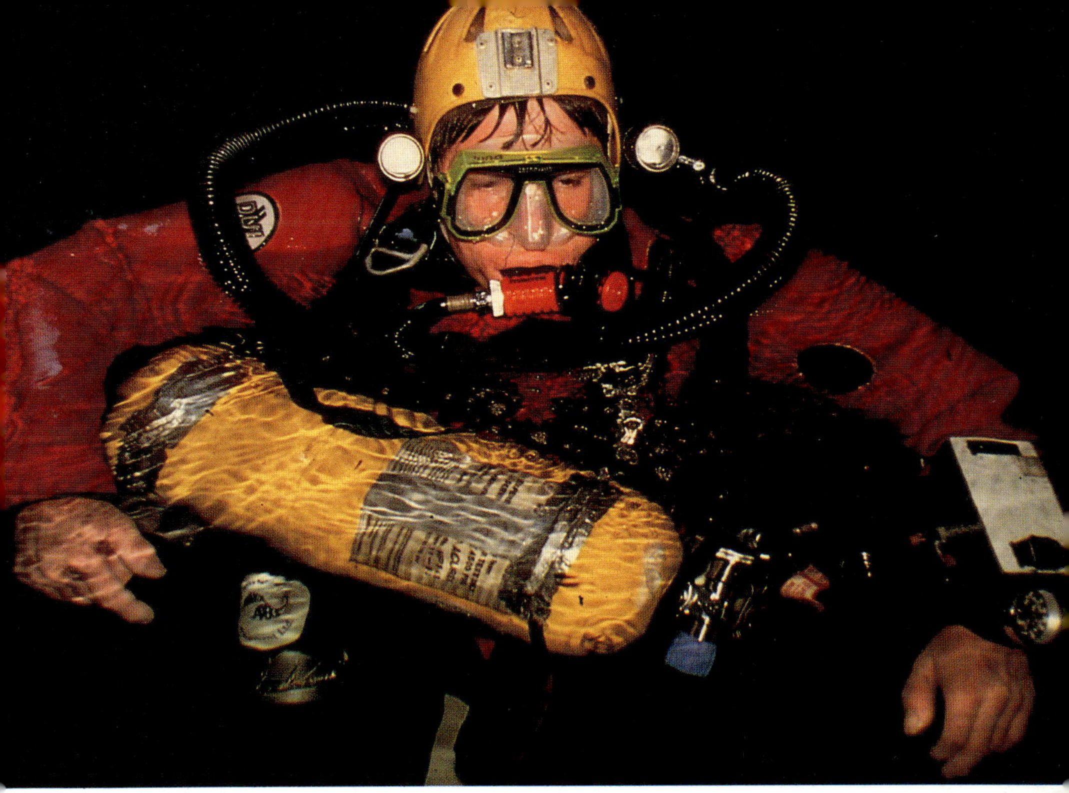

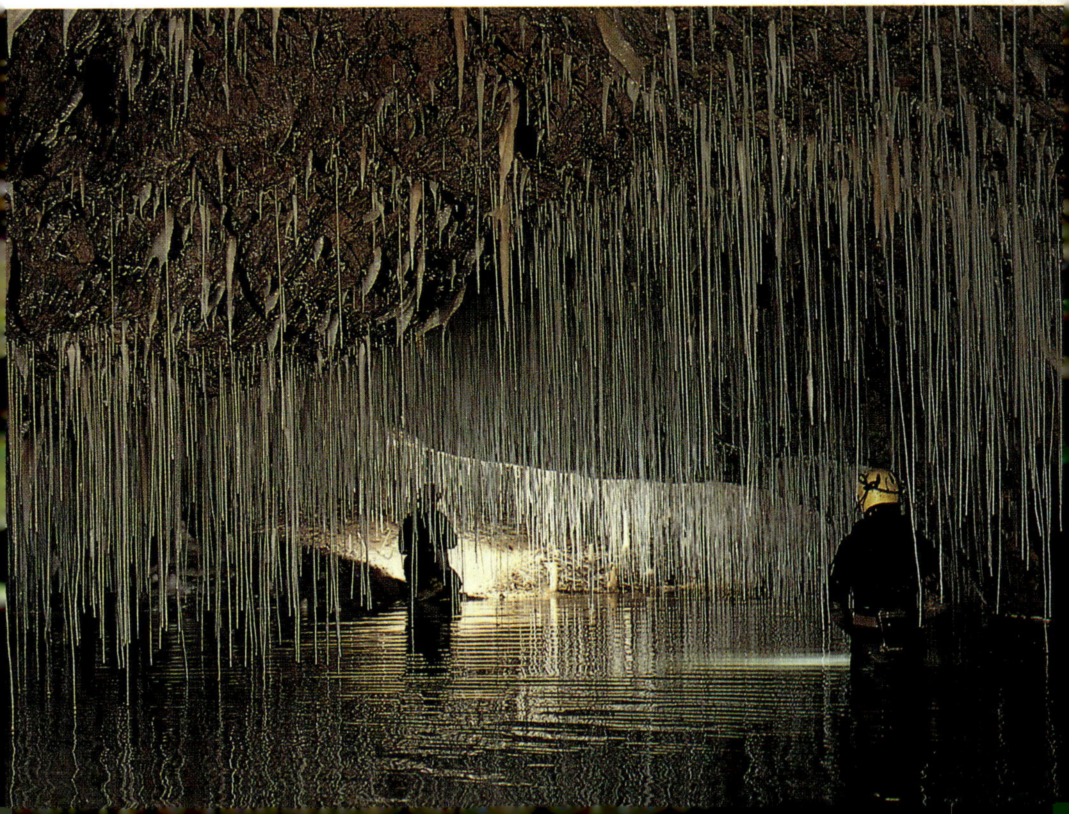

(Top) Following a taut and well-belayed line. Rippled floor sediments indicate a high current. (Bottom) Supported by independently-valved back-mounted cylinders, a diver fins into a Bahamian cave.

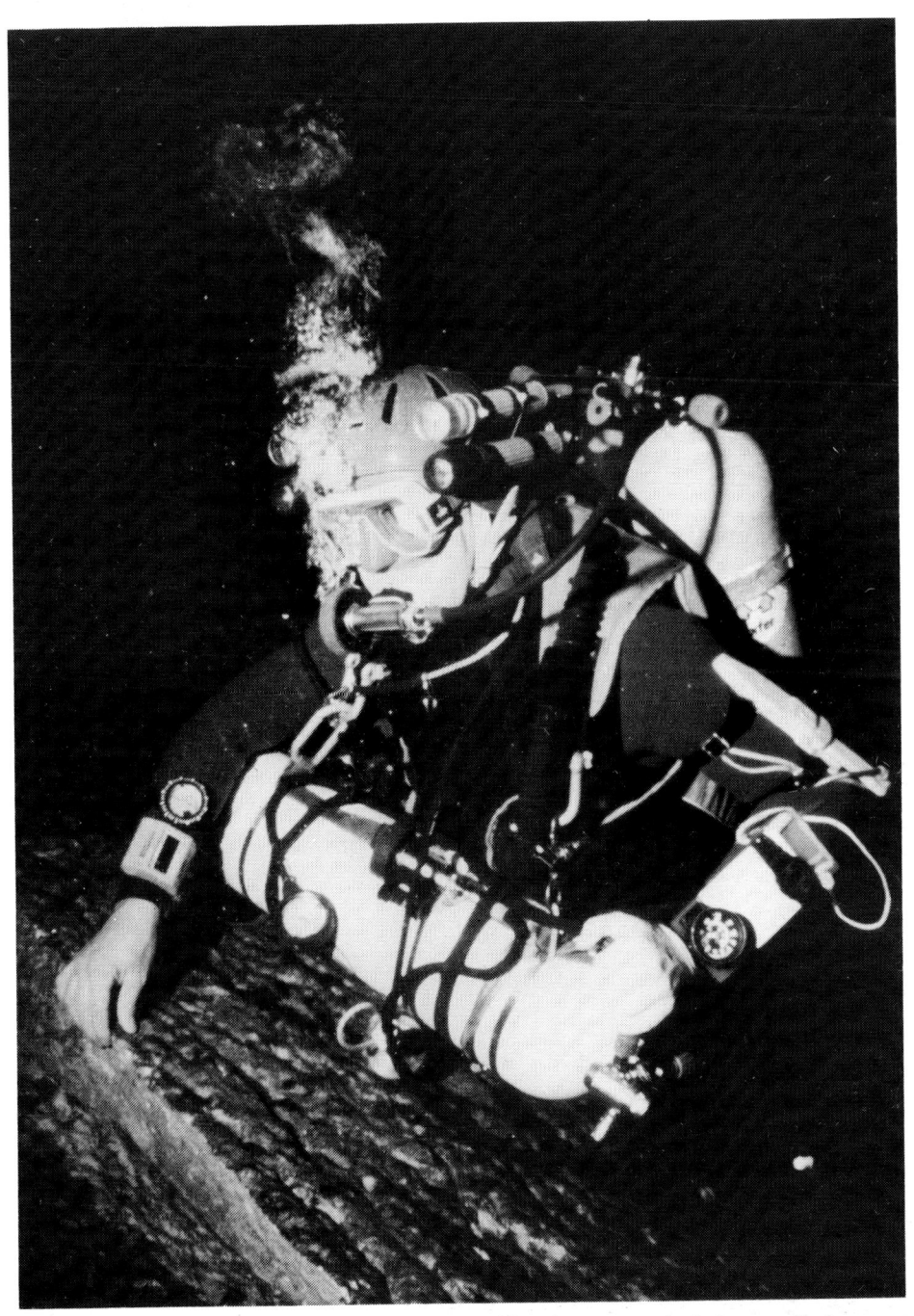

Fig. 14: Rigged for long-distance dive with a front-mounted stage cylinder

HARNESSES & WEIGHTBELTS

OVER the past few years, cave diving harness have evolved from a simple belt on which cylinder bands were looped to relatively sophisticated harnesses custom built for cave diving. The basic system is still the same, with two separate cylinders held in metal cylinder bands, usually tightened down with a screw, and strapped to the diver's sides.

CYLINDER BANDS

The cylinder bands should be constructed from mild or stainless steel of sufficient strength and durability to stand up to the harsh cave environment and should have some means of holding the cylinder firmly. A loose fitting cylinder can easily drop out in use, and it is fairly common practice to place a ring of rubber inner tube around the cylinder to afford a better grip for the band. Two welded belt loops on the side of the band allow a nylon harness or belt to be slipped through the band to attach it to the diver. Simple bands can be constructed from stainless steel jubilee clips of a diameter to match the size of cylinder being used, with two small metal cross-pieces to provide belt attachment (figure 15). Cylinders should be mounted on the harness in a manner that allows easy access to the cylinder taps in emergency. Mild steel cylinder bands will need to be painted frequently in order to combat corrosion.

HARNESSES

Each cylinder can be worn on a separate belt but this increases the number of buckles around the diver's waist and can cause confusion, especially when a weight belt is added. Most serious cave divers now use one of the custom harnesses designed specifically for cave diving (figure 16).

This type of harness allows two cylinders to be either mounted on secondary straps attached to a main belt of wide nylon webbing or to hold the cylinders firmly in place on an outer belt supported by vertical bands of webbing on a wide inner belt. These distribute the weight more evenly around the diver's waist. Where straps are used, cylinders can be replaced without removing the belt, though this can be awkward for the diver to do by himself.

Fig. 15: A standard cylinder band

Optional shoulder straps take some of the strain off the waist when out of the water, or with larger cylinders, and help keep unevenly weighted cylinders from sliding the whole belt unevenly around. Small D-rings on the bottom of the belt can offer attachment points for line reels, extra lights and other small items. Spare sections on the front and rear of the belt allow weights or larger light units to be mounted on the belt, keeping all equipment on one single belt. This has both advantages and disadvantages - it is easier to get in and out of the water, but very difficult to remove tanks, lights or weights underwater.

Modifications made to the shoulder harness allow lead weights to be shoulder-mounted to distribute weight more evenly, and Fastex clips attached to a shoulder harness can provide a greater variety of attachment points for contents gauges, small torches and decompression tables.

Fig. 16: An example of a harness - the Troll

Whichever harness system is used, it should fit the diver snugly and not allow undue movement of cylinders around the diver's waist. Buckles should be sturdy, secure and non-slip, and should allow simple adjustment underwater by touch alone. All fittings should be maintained in good condition, and renewed when they show undue signs of wear.

WEIGHTBELTS

Most diver's wear lead weights on a separate belt, though they can be mounted on the main harness. Weights should be distributed evenly but not in such a manner as to cause discomfort beneath cylinders. The use of lead shot in pouches is becoming more commonplace, and these shotbelts are more comfortable and simpler to adjust than traditional solid block block belts. The buckle on the weightbelt should fasten in the opposite direction to that of the harness, or should be of a different design to avoid confusion. Quick-release buckles are to be avoided as a positively buoyant diver would be unable to recover an accidentally-released belt.

The distribution of weight around the body can considerably ease discomfort on long dives. With most of the weight concentrated around the waist, backache is a real problem, and this can be lessened by wearing some of the weight on shoulder straps or in a breast-plate to help maintain a head-down position. Weight loops on the ankles (these must be less that 1kg each to avoid leg strain) can also help maintain position and spread the load, but may increase the possibility of line snagging the feet, and may cause leg cramps on long dives.

The diver should make a record of how much weight he needs with which ever variation of equipment configuration he uses in both fresh and salt water. This means he must just sink at the surface with an empty BC and empty tanks when correctly weighted, to ensure ascents can be made from depth without being positively buoyant at the end of a dive, especially where decompression is involved. This makes for more efficient diving and lessens the need for in situ adjustment in the cave.

HELMETS

THE two fundamental purposes of a cave diver's helmet are to protect his head and to provide a convenient mounting for one or more light sources.

Until the late 1970s, most cave divers used a normal caving helmet, sometimes drilled to provide an outlet for trapped air - a floating helmet can be most disconcerting. The move towards mounting additional torches on the helmet, and the inadequacy of many caving helmets for positive underwater attachment, has led to the use of alternative types - such as skateboarding, ice hockey or canoeing helmets. These attach more securely, and have preformed holes in them for the release of air, and through which elastic straps can be set to mount torches. Helmets with a deep profile at the back of the neck can interfere with head movement when back-mounted tanks are worn. Some modification of any helmet is probably necessary.

Any helmet used for cave diving may have to be used for dry caving as well, and must therefore be capable of withstanding the same impacts that a standard caving helmet can. The drilling of holes for mounting torches may weaken the integral structure of some helmets, and this should be borne in mind during the adapting of helmets specifically designed for caving or climbing. The chin-strap on a diving helmet must be substantial, and both it and the cradle should be easily adjustable to allow for the wearing of a neoprene hood and its subsequent removal on leaving the water. For extensive caving beyond a sump, where a non-caving helmet will be used for diving, it is probably worth taking (and perhaps leaving) a true caving helmet.

Fig. 17: Mounting torches on a helmet using elastic cord.

Torches can be mounted either by using elastic loops (shock-cord or inner tube are commonly used materials) or by cutting off a length of suitable-diameter PVC tubing and slitting it to make a clip-type mounting (figure 17). This can then be clipped or bolted to the side of the helmet.

A lightweight survival bag can be carried in the helmet between the cradle and the shell; just possibly, it may save your life one day.

60 **Equipment**

LIGHTING

CAVE divers, like all cavers, depend totally on an adequate light source. Moreover, unlike non-divers, cave divers are often alone and have to contend with the additional problems encountered underwater in a cave - for example, silt and depth (and hence pressure). Cave diving light units have to be as reliable and simple as possible, whilst being sturdy and of high quality. Each light should have a burn time in excess of twice the anticipated dive time, and at least three separate light sources should be carried. Note that lights can be conserved by not using them all at once, though burning two at a time when underwater is desirable. If dry caving is expected beyond the sump, that should be allowed for in the burn time of all lights. Spare bulbs and batteries should be carried at least as far as the dive site, and further if practicable.

Traditionally, cave divers employed the Nife, NiCad and Oldham cells used by non-cavers. Then, helmet-mounted waterproof torches were used. Even more recently, special light units with separate battery packs (which can be attached to waist or tank) and hand-held or helmet-mounted lamp-heads, have been adopted. Ordinary caving lamps are a constant source of trouble for divers, and they should only be used for dry caving to or beyond sumps. Their light is not really adequate for underwater work; the lamp-head is not waterproof and must be carefully dried after immersion, and only a few standard makes of battery packs will keep out water under pressure. Only these fully-sealed battery packs (eg Speleotechnics, Explorer) are suitable for underwater use, though the Oldham lamp case can be modified to take ex-WD NiCad batteries which are ideal for underwater use to medium depths.

Torches

There are several types of underwater torch available which take either disposable batteries or the rechargeable NiCad type (generally C or D cells). The favourite for many years was the now unavailable Aquaflash, but other makes like Q-Lites and Ikelites are proving almost equally popular. Many use expensive halogen bulbs with a limited burn life, and this should be borne in mind if they are to be used for caving beyond sumps. Most of those suitable for the rough usage of cave diving have a screw-down bezel to turn on the torch.

Such torches are generally mounted on the helmet to keep the hands free, and to allow the torches to follow the movements of the head, but wearing several torches in such a fashion can cause neck-ache on long dives, and the helmet becomes unwieldy in dry caves. Spare torches, when not in immediate use, can be clipped to the harness or belt by Fastex clips or small karabiners. Eastern European cave divers often mount a torch on each forearm which illuminates the hands and reduces backscatter where suspended particles are present.

Separate Battery/Lamp Units

For major dives, there is currently a move towards using a waist- or tank-mounted battery pack with hand- or helmet-mounted lamp unit. These units give longer duration than smaller helmet torches and they are particularly suitable for large, clear visibility sumps. Some lampheads offer the possibility of display-grade bulbs with built-in reflectors to be used. These have a considerably greater life-expectancy than the pre-stressed projector bulbs more commonly in use. Where pre-stressed tungsten/halogen bulbs are used, it is worth considering the incorporation of a warm-up circuit in the design to minimise the effect of power surges on initial turn-on. The best wattage for the bulb used depends on the clarity of the water ... silted water causes backscatter, which is considerably increased by high wattage torches, and the effect is even more troublesome if the lamp unit is helmet-mounted. In murky water, the farther away from the eyes the lamphead can be held, the better the visibility.

Maintenance

Any light unit should always be meticulously maintained. O-rings should be cleaned and greased between dives, lights should be checked for leaks immediately after diving (especially in salt water), and batteries should be freshly-charged after each use, if rechargeables are being used. Where non-rechargeables are being used, they should ideally be replaced before each

Fig. 18: Standard air compressor with Haskel booster pump filling composite gas cylinders to high pressure.

dive, or well before they become drained. The contacts within any light should be kept clean and corrosion-free; dirty contacts can reduce battery life.

Bulbs

Bulbs, especially halogen ones, should never be handled with bare fingers - clean gloves or a piece of tissue must always be used. Spare bulbs can be carried in a small film container strapped to the helmet, or in an empty torch case, along with a small tool and a first-aid kit (see section on *Solo caving & self-rescue*). Some bulbs, especially those with a small solder nipple as their base contact, can cause short-circuiting in the torch if pressure-wearing of the nipple after much use allows a circuit to be completed between the solder core and the bulb outer. This can be dangerous if rechargeable NiCads are being used, as the potential rapid discharge rate can cause considerable heat to be released, melting the outer casing of the torch, or causing a pressure explosion. The inherent resistance in non-rechargeable cells lessens the chance of this happening if such prime cells are used.

For emergency use, or for marking underwater junctions, stage tanks or other gear drops, or decompression points, Cyalumes (completely self-contained, one-use only, chemical light tubes) are ideal. They come in a variety of colours and burn rates, and the nature of use should dictate which is used for a particular task. Their use can help ease stress considerably.

COMPRESSORS

THERE are two types of compressor used for diving operations: low-pressure (LP) and high-pressure (HP). The low-pressure compressors are either the rotary vane or reciprocating piston type. Both usually have a maximum output pressure of 6-10 bar with a large volume output. They are suitable for surface supply only. The rotary vane compressors are only suitable for shallow-water work.

Owing to the nature of cave diving, surface supplies are rarely used, so the compressor with we which we are concerned is the high-pressure type used to charge diving cylinders.

A compressor has three basic constituents: the power source, the compressor and the filter units.

The Power Source

The power source can be one of three types: petrol engine, diesel engine or electric motor. The unit most commonly used for compressors up to 200l/min is a two- or four-stroke petrol engine; it has the advantage of being light, reliable and relatively cheap, so it is suitable for use on portable compressors at diving sites. Electric units are found in fixed installations; the larger compressors need a three-phase power supply. Electric units have the advantage of requiring little maintenance, have no exhaust fumes and are relatively quiet. Diesel engines are found on some portable compressors, usually those between 150 and 250 l/min, and on most fixed compressors above 200l/min. They are economical, reliable, and are durable owing to their normally lower speeds, but have the disadvantages of weight and cost.

The Compressor (HP)

A typical HP compressor will be a unit of three stages, each stage air or water cooled. The output, measured as the volume of free air, is directly related to the displacement of the first stage for further stages only increase the output pressure.

Piston-type compressor require lubrication to the bearings and the pistons as in a car engine. They require special non-toxic mineral-based lubricating oil as recommended by the manufacturer, for some oil (as mist or vapour) is bound to contaminate the compressed air.

Air is heated by compression, so cooling is arranged between each stage and after the final stage. The cooling may be by air or water; the former is usual on portable units.

Also, water-vapour is condensed by compression and further by cooling, so each cooler has a drain valve. After the final compression stage the air is filtered to remove solid particles and reduce the oil and water-vapour content.

Filter Unit

On a large compressor the filter would be two or three separate units before the outlet manifold; on a small compressor it would be a single unit. In the filter of a typical 200l/min compressor the air passes first through a felt pad (oil-mist and solid particle remover) into a bed of silica gel (vapour trap), through a second felt pad then through activated charcoal (more powerful vapour trap) and finally though a last felt pad to the manifold. On smaller compressors the silica gel stage is usually omitted. The charcoal in removing vapours also destroys the smells.

The filter unit must be carefully and regularly maintained; to neglect this is dangerous. Some filter units use replacement packs; in all cases follow the maker's instructions. Where replacement packs are not used, renew the felt pads and charcoal but the silica gel can be re-used after drying in a vapour-free oven.

Filter and accumulator fittings usually have fine threads; take care not to cross-thread or otherwise damage them, in particular avoid the use of pipe-wrenches and suchlike tools.

Air Intake

The air intake must be cleaned regularly. Absolute care must be taken to ensue that no exhaust fumes can pollute the air intake from petrol or diesel engines.

Relief Valves

Check that relief valve settings are not materially higher than the filling pressure of the cylinder being filled - ie do not charge 200 bar cylinders with a relief valve set for 300 bar.

Chapter 3: Movement & Technique

CARRYING DIVING EQUIPMENT

MANY diving sites are far from the surface, and owing to the relatively delicate nature of some diving equipment, due care must be given to the packaging and transport of such equipment to the dive site. Some equipment stands up to the rigours of the underworld better than other, but the main problem areas can be summarised as follows:

Air Cylinders

Cylinders filled with high-pressure air are potential bombs, and must be treated with respect. The weakest point is where the valve joins the neck of the cylinder. Protecting the valve is important, and can be achieved by several devices.

1) A tube or cup of plastic or metal with a securing screw.
2) A drilled wooden block which is a push-fit on the tap.
3) An inverted tank boot.
4) A rubber buffer as an integral part of the valve (for instance, the Normalair tap).
5) A complete cylinder protection tube (see below).

A blanking cap to protect the seating from grit particles is useful, and should be designed such that it does not become a projectile in case of inadvertent operation of the cylinder valve. It should either have a pressure release facility, or be plastic.

The cylinder body can be protected by the use of commercially available plastic mesh (not very robust), by car inner tube of suitable diameter (robust and inexpensive, but beware of corrosion if left on bare metal), by fire hose of suitable diameter, or by plastic piping. Special cylinder carrying containers can be made out of the latter material (sewer or heavy-duty drain pipe) or from glassfibre, and these can be adapted as backpacks for diving. Cylinders in tackle bags require caution; the bag will wear through quickly if dragged with a heavy cylinder inside. Weaknesses in base stitching and in hauling loops of tackle bags are likely to manifest themselves during hauling operations at pitches. Tanks should be hauled up pitches by attaching the rope directly to the tank as well as to the valve. Cross-flow taps are almost essential for tanks intended to be hauled up pitches.

Demand Valves & Accessories

A rigid box offers good protection for the more fragile accessories, such a demand valves, gauges, torches and the like. The traditional ammo box is good but heavy; one of the wide-mouth plastic containers currently available (BDH containers, rocket tubes) is probably better. Whatever is used, it must be big enough to accommodate valves so that the hoses are not bent so far that it could lead to premature failure. A watertight container is an added advantage.

Equipment can be packed in a tackle bag padded by spare neoprene suiting, fins, etc, but this should be treated with extra care. Regulators must be equipped with suitable first stage blanking-off caps, otherwise water may enter the pressure gauge when assembled for use. All gauges, especially electronic meters, must be wrapped in shock-absorbent material (foam rubber, sponge or neoprene) and treated with special care.

A drysuit with zip entry is best carried zipped up and in a separate bag. A small toothbrush and some liquid soap are useful for removing grit from the zip, and for removing grit or mud from cylinder valves.

Pressure-proof containers for carrying gear through sumps are best tested before use. Many varieties can be constructed, some are available commercially (rocket tubes will withstand up to 30m depth if in good order, BDH tubes are only water-resistant), but it is worth considering size and weight if caving between sumps is contemplated, and their buoyancy in the sump itself. Several small containers, spread amongst divers, are better than one large container that may need huge amounts of lead to sink it. In very deep sumps, it is possible to fit pressure compensating devices to waterproof containers - drysuit inlet and exhaust valves are obvious choices, though an automatic exhaust might be a preferable option to avoid the risk of explosion on ascent.

Carrying

If passage size allows, gear is best carried on the back, the cylinders having their valves properly protected. Carrying cylinders hip-mounted on a belt is possible, but becomes painful, and better weight distribution can be obtained by sliding a simple crossover strap through the band loops and over the opposite shoulder. In conjunction with the waistbelt, this helps prevent cylinders swivelling round the body during motion. A more sophisticated harness with shoulder-straps can accommodate twin cylinders, and can be used for diving.

Tools to fit any nuts and bolts used in the carrying system should be readily available on the carry to adjust tightness as necessary.

All loads should be packed to give balanced carrying, and where hauling is envisaged, it helps if each item has its own karabiner and haul loop. Marking otherwise identical tackle bags or tubes with a number or symbol can help identify the more fragile items which need special attention (lights, valves, decompression meters, cameras, etc).

A checklist of gear required is useful to prevent things being left behind, and labelling bags with their destination and/or diver's name prevents confusion if different sites in the same cave are being dived by different teams, or if loads are destined for beyond particular sumps.

Fig. 19: In roomy sumps, tacklebags can be worn on the back, if care is taken against entanglement with guidelines.

Sherpas

Carrying diving equipment through a tight and awkward cave passage is hard work, and the diver must beware of asking too much of his support team. The best sherpas are experienced cavers with an understanding of the delicacy of diving equipment. Heavier loads can be swapped within a party on a long trip, and loads for a single person should not be excessive.

People carrying cylinders should understand their potential destructive power and be quite clear on the operation of the valve. They should be warned of the possible dangerous effect of a compressed gas jet on the skin (contact embolism).

A party should stick together. This prevents equipment being abandoned en route, ensures everybody gets to the same place at the same time, and allows mutual assistance through awkward bits of passage. Chaining equipment through low or awkward sections of cave can make things much easier for everyone, and tends to ensure better treatment for the gear.

Sherpas must be equipped to prevent hypothermia whilst waiting for a diver to return through a sump. Taking a large polythene bag, some food and a simple brew kit is a good idea. Where a diver is undertaking a dive involving decompression, or could be forced into a situation requiring it, he should have a person at base who is briefed to assist in the event of an incident.

Fig. 20: Portering diving tanks through constricted passages is often best done without tacklebags.

Vertical Transport

Diving equipment can be transported vertically within a cave system in one of three ways:
1) As part of a Single Rope Technique system, slung below the sit harness
2) Carried up a ladder (always use a lifeline)
3) Hauled on a rope.

Whenever possible, cylinders should be lowered in a good-quality tackle bag, with the haul line attached to both bag and cylinder. Cylinders should be secured to a karabiner by a short haul loop of thin nylon climbing tape threaded beneath a cross-over valve (if fitted) and secured by a larks tail knot. Where a straight pillar valve is fitted, the cylinder should *always* be hauled in a tackle bag. If suitable, the cylinder bands can be incorporated in the hauling system, (though they should *never* form the only point of attachment) but the cylinder is less likely to snag if hauled vertically upright (figure 21). Other loads should all have their own karabiner and haul loops to ensure efficient hauling operations.

People should always be kept clear of the base of a pitch during hauling operations involving cylinders. Communication between top and bottom of the pitch should be good, and hauling teams kept aware of what loads they are raising.

A diver should always give due acknowledgement to sherpas in diving reports.

Fig. 21: Cylinder hauling in a tacklebag - (left) the correct way, (right) the wrong way.

Movement & technique

BUOYANCY CONTROL & EQUIPMENT

BUOYANCY can be defined as "the ability of an object to stay afloat". In the underwater cave environment, we are specifically referring to the fully kitted cave diver and the factors that determine whether he floats or sinks.

The diver who tends to sink is said to have negative buoyancy. The diver who floats is said to be positively buoyant, or simply buoyant. A tendency to neither sink nor float but to remain in a constant mid-water position is termed neutral buoyancy. Whether a diver will sink or float or be neutrally buoyant is not simply coincidence, but can be determined and controlled.

NEUTRAL BUOYANCY

Archimedes Principle states that if an object is immersed in a liquid it will experience an upthrust equal to the weight of the liquid it displaces. If the object is heavier than the displaced liquid it will sink, if lighter, it will float. Since the human body unclothed is largely composed of water, most unclothed people are within a kilo or so of being neutrally buoyant.

However, due to the low temperature of cave water and the need therefore to wear insulative clothing (wet- or drysuits) and a wide variety of diving equipment, the kitted up cave diver may vary considerably from the neutral norm! Positive buoyancy is counteracted by the addition of lead weights, negative buoyancy by the use of one of several types of inflation device (drysuit, buoyancy compensator).

The ideal state for a cave diver is to be neutrally buoyant or slightly negative, depending on the task being performed. For this reason, most divers weight themselves to be neutrally buoyant at the surface as a point of reference. This is likely to make them increasingly negatively buoyant with depth, and this is compensated for by the use of a buoyancy device.

Achieving neutral buoyancy is done by weighting yourself so that you sink when fully exhaled, and float with full lungs. If wearing a drysuit or buoyancy compensator, this should be virtually empty of air. This takes some practise, and should first be experimented with in open water in full kit. With practise, a high degree of fine buoyancy control can be made by simply using breath control. It should be remembered that there is a great difference in buoyancy between different makes and sizes of cylinder, and between full and empty cylinders, and this should be allowed for in adjusting initial neutral buoyancy.

Factors Affecting Buoyancy During a Dive

1) Depth: As the diver descends, the water pressure increases, resulting in compression in his diving suit and the air within his body cavities. Because pressure and depth have a direct relationship, a wetsuited diver will become more negatively buoyant the deeper he goes. A diver in an expanded neoprene drysuit will also experience this, and all drysuit divers will experience a

reduction in the airspace between their bodies and the suit. In the case of a drysuit clad diver, buoyancy can be restored by the use of a direct feed inflation facility to re-inflate the suit.

How much buoyancy the diver will lose due to wetsuit compression is very difficult to measure, and only experience can give a rough indication.. However, to illustrate the problem, a diver of large build wearing a thick (6mm or more) wetsuit can lose up to 10kg of buoyancy at a depth of 30m.

2) Air consumption: The weight of an empty cylinder is the weight of the cylinder itself, the air inside having a negligible weight. A full cylinder, however, may contain 200 or 250 times more air, and this can add 3 or 4kg to the weight of a large cylinder. Several kilos of weight can therefore be lost during the course of a dive simply by breathing the air carried. The diver may end up positively buoyant at the end of a dive if this has not been anticipated, which may make for serious problems if decompression is indicated. The placement of additional weights at planned decompression stops can help to overcome this.

3) Saltwater diving: Saltwater is slightly denser than fresh water, so making a diver more buoyant. A general rule is to use 2 or 3 kg more weight in saltwater, but again buoyancy should be adjusted in shallow open water, and not on a serious dive.

4) Removal of weight during a dive: The use of stage tanks on long dives, or of lead weights as line belays, or of reels of positively or negatively buoyant line can affect the diver's buoyancy during the course of a dive. Stage tanks or positively buoyant items can be separately weighed if required to ensure neutral buoyancy on return, and negative reels and line weights should not be accounted for as part of the initial adjustment for neutral buoyancy. These can be compensated for by additional air in the drysuit or buoyancy compensator (BC) on the inward swim until such time as they are removed. The use of lumps of rock to help a diver sink is not recommended. Once the rock is abandoned at depth, the diver still faces the problem of uncontrollable ascent.

BUOYANCY DEVICES

It is apparent that on all but the shallowest and shortest dives you will encounter a continuous variation in buoyancy. There is equipment available that will compensate for changes in buoyancy. Drysuits have been mentioned already, and the term buoyancy compensator (BC) is here taken to refer to the adjustable buoyancy life jacket (ABLJ), stabiliser jacket and wing-type buoyancy compensator. In cave diving, buoyancy compensators are primarily regarded as just that, not as "life jackets".

Adjustable Buoyancy Life Jacket.

Owing to its cheapness and availability, the ABLJ was an early choice for the cave diver. The ABLJ is worn in a similar fashion to a standard surface lifejacket, and is designed on the "horse collar" principle. Earlier models were made from plastic or rubber with a single-skin construction, and tended to be stiff, bulky and heavy. More modern ones are often double skin, the outer layer of Cordura-type material providing a resistance to abrasion and physical damage, over the inner air bladder. They are lighter, and can be packed into a small space. Single skin bags have a tendency to develop leaks at the seams which can be difficult if not impossible to repair, and the rough handling they get down caves makes the double bag construction favourite. Inner bladders can be repaired or replaced without replacing the full bag.

The disadvantage of the ABLJ is its tendency to ride up around the diver's neck, keeping him in a head up position (and in extreme cases of misadjustment, virtually strangling him) though this can be reduced by taping the back of the yoke to reduce the buoyancy volume behind the neck. The chest bag also interferes with drysuit inflation buttons (if worn), though these can be moved to the arms. Most ABLJs come with a small emergency inflation air cylinder beneath the lower chest, which can be obstructive on entering or leaving the water. Most cave divers remove these and rely on both oral and direct feed inflation.

Stabiliser (Stab) Jacket

These have become popular amongst divers as an all-in dive pack. Though there are many varieties, the common features are that cylinder, buoyancy device and frequently weights are worn as one integral unit. The stab jacket otherwise performs the same function as the ABLJ though buoyancy is distributed more evenly. When used in conjunction with a waist cylinder harness, the stab jacket can bear some of the weight of waist-mounted tanks on the shoulders, and the open chest also allows drysuit inflation hoses to be reached. A crutch strap can be added when worn with side-mounted tanks to prevent riding up of the jacket.

Wings

In North America, a wing-type buoyancy compensator (figure 22) is often used, mounted behind the diver between his back and the cylinder pack. These adjust buoyancy only, do not keep him head up in the water if unconscious, but do provide him with a greater degree of streamlining and offer less encumbrance up front. They are perhaps best used with back-mounted cylinders, as to use them with side-mounts would require the construction of a special shoulder harness.

Drysuit

Besides the advantage of warmth, the drysuit offers similar facilities to the BC. It can be inflated by direct feed from the cylinder, or vented by means of a dump valve when it is necessary to become less positive. Drysuit diving is covered in greater detail elsewhere in

Fig. 22: Wing buoyancy compensator - best with back-mounted cylinders.

Movement & technique

this volume, but is should be noted that on long or deep dives, where there is a chance of a tear in the drysuit causing a catastrophic loss of buoyancy, a second form of buoyancy control is essential. This can be either an ABLJ or stab jacket (bearing in mind the position of inflation and deflation valves on the drysuit) or an inbuilt second bladder within the drysuit itself, valved separately to the main suit.

PRINCIPLES OF OPERATION

Inflation

There are three ways in which BCs can be inflated: orally, by direct feed, or by direct cylinder inflation. All BCs have the facility to be inflated orally through a mouthpiece on a large bore hose which is valved to inflate or deflate the bladder, depending on which button is depressed. Most modern BCs are fitted with a direct feed hose, which is attached to a low pressure outlet on the first stage of the demand valve. Inflation is by depressing a valve on the BC mouthpiece unit. The hose is connected to the BC by a low-pressure coupling. Direct feed has two advantages and is regarded as essential for cave diving. The need for oral inflation underwater is removed, making the system simpler and safer to use, and, in extreme cases, the BC can be used as a demand valve in the case of second stage failure. There are BC mouthpieces currently available which are specialised demand valves that double as BC inflation devices. Breathing directly from the bag itself is not to be recommended, due to problems with CO_2 build-up.

Direct cylinder inflation is not recommended for cave diving. Most ABLJs and many stab jackets are fitted with a small cylinder containing about 80l of air when full that can be recharged from the main cylinders. By operating a tap, the jacket can be filled instantly. This system was designed to allow open-water divers to achieve rapid buoyant ascent in emergency, not a practise to be recommended in cave diving. The extra bulk of the small cylinder generally outweighs any use it might have, and it can be removed and the inflation attachment on the jacket fitted with a blanking-off plug, if no non-return valve is fitted. Some BCs have a small carbon dioxide cartridge fitted in place of this air cylinder. This is a one-use only cartridge, and the possibility of it going off by accident far outweighs any possible advantage in cave diving. It should be removed and stored in a safe place.

Deflation

There are two methods of releasing air from BCs. One is by operation of the main dump valve, usually shoulder or collar mounted, and this is done by simply pulling on a cord attached to it. On some BCs the cord handle is not conveniently placed when wearing side-mounts, and in such instances it can be cut and shortened to be directly attached at the shoulder, where it can be more easily reached. The second way is via the inflation mouthpiece: raise the corrugated hose above the jacket, release air by depressing a purge button. This often allows a finer control of release than operation of the dump valve.

Many modern BCs and drysuits are fitted with automatic valves, which can be set to release air when pressure within the buoyancy device reaches a certain level.

DIVING WITH A BUOYANCY DEVICE

Though all BCs are basically simple in design, they can cause complications in what is already a stressful environment. Experience in open-water diving shows that buoyancy control is one of the major problems for novice divers.

As with all other techniques requiring any degree of skill, regular practise and training with the equipment will breed the competence and familiarity required for safe cave diving.

Preliminary training should take place in clear open water, or in a swimming pool, and the diver should take pains to familiarise himself with all the controls of the device, be it BC or drysuit. During training, the diver should practise obtaining neutral buoyancy with a variety of weighting and weight distribution, using only a depth gauge for reference in mid-water.

Drysuits can be deflated by releasing air through neck or wrist seals in addition to the dump valve. This should be practised, though it is usually difficult to do so in a cave where arm-mounted equipment, gloves or hood are worn, and seals can be damaged.

A problem encountered with drysuits is that of buoyancy inversion, where the air in the suit migrates to the diver's legs, turning him upside down. The diver should practise getting out of this position in open water or pool, fully-kitted. (See section on Drysuits) The possibility of inversion can be lessened by wearing a close-fitting suit, or by using ankle-straps to restrict air flow to the feet and ankles.

With BCs, the diver should practise inflating the jacket both floating and underwater by oral, direct feed and, for experience, by air cylinder (but beware the danger of a rapid ascent causing pulmonary embolism!). Deflation and fine buoyancy control by use of dump valve and mouthpiece should be carefully practised, with the aim of achieving neutral buoyancy in mid-water. A good diver should be able to control his buoyancy over two or three vertical metres simply by breath control once neutral, without recourse to inflation or deflation. These techniques should be practised in a variety of positions (eg vertically, upside down, prone). Weighting and weight distribution for buoyancy are crucial (see section on Harnesses & weightbelts).

DIVING WITHOUT A BUOYANCY DEVICE

It is not always practicable to dive with a buoyancy device. In such cases, correct weighting is essential, especially where depth may vary during the course of a dive. Dives below 20m should never be undertaken without some method of buoyancy control.

It may be advantageous to be slightly negative if progress can be made by pulling along a rocky bottom. This can conserve both air and energy, and it is possible to rest or work on the bottom without having to struggle to maintain position due to positive buoyancy. It is not advantageous to be negatively buoyant when swimming in mid-water, or when movement on or near the bottom would stir up sediment deposits, obscuring visibility.

It is rarely an advantage to be positively buoyant, for the tendency will be to float to the roof. It is difficult to make progress along an irregular roof, and floating line is essential if this is to be done, to avoid the possibility of losing sinking line. For short initial penetrations of large clear sumps, perhaps on a base fed line, there may be some advantages in being slightly buoyant.

Summary
When diving with a drysuit or BC, the first criterion is to be correctly weighted for the dive planned. After this, most problems can be solved by anticipation. The diver should anticipate ascending from depth and adjust buoyancy to suit as it becomes necessary. Similarly, he should be able to control descent by accurate inflation of the BC/suit before becoming too negative. When the desired depth is reached he should be able to remain in mid-water as second nature, and provide fine adjustment by use of careful breath control.

VISIBILITY IN UNDERWATER CAVES

UNFORTUNATELY, good visibility in British sumps is a luxury rather than a standard feature. Where good visibility exists, however, it is important to maintain it as much as possible for a number of reasons. These are:
1) To increase the safety of the dive.
2) To allow as full a visual examination of the passage as possible.
3) To make for easier route-finding.
4) To maintain visual communication between divers.
5) To preserve the cave environment.

Various factors affect the visibility in underwater caves. Percolation water usually produces clear "blue" sumps, whilst streamwater from major sinks is generally more contaminated with particulate matter. Conversely, percolation sumps tend to produce the worst visibility when disturbed, whereas stream sumps may be little affected by diving operations if care is taken not to disturb sediments unduly. Occasionally, flowing streamwater may overlie more static water (or vice versa), creating a layered effect similar to cloud inversion, where either the upper or lower layer is considerably clearer than the other. This may be due to temperature or density differences, and the phenomenon has not been fully studied.

Material in solution can seriously affect visibility, and this gives rise to the comparatively common brown-stained peaty water in many upland areas. This water can still be surprisingly clear, especially if hand-held light units are used to distance light from the eyes and create perspective.

Suspended material, due to either active surface run-off or human disturbance of cave or surface sediments, offers the greatest problems. Weather conditions obviously affect this, and care must be taken not to exacerbate the problem by careless use of technique or incautious movements. Even static sumps can be affected by adverse weather, with the addition of contaminated percolation water or overspill from active streamways. Heavy particles will settle fairly quickly, but fine, light particles may remain for hours, or even days, in suspension in the water. Any limitation in visibility on a cave dive increases the risk, and any reduction of visibility during a dive simply reduces the odds further. Again, lights held further from the eyes (eg hand-held) are more effective in reducing backscatter.

The rate of water flow may well affect visibility. High flow obviously is itself enough to disturb in situ sediments, but it may also clear induced particulate matter (stirred by a diver) more rapidly. It is thus often worth waiting some time before returning through a disturbed high-flow sump to allow conditions to improve. Low flow or static sumps work in the reverse way, and considerably more care must be taken in them to avoid disturbing sediments on the dive inward.

Variations in density or temperature between two water layers will also affect visibility if the layers are disturbed, due to the refractive differences of the intermingling densities. This gives a peculiar out-of-focus effect that can be discomfiting and disorientating to the diver. This commonly occurs in coastal caves in limestone areas abroad (such as the Bahamian Blue Holes) where fresh and salt waters meet, or in marine resurgences.

Lighting

The position and type of lights carried by the diver can affect visibility in a variety of ways. In clear water, it matters little where they are worn, as backscatter will be minimal, and the brighter the light, the more will be seen. When particulate matter is present, the closer the light source is to the eyes, the greater the degree of backscatter. In very low visibility, the common practice of wearing the lights on the helmet works against the diver, and having a bright light source available for hand-holding (perhaps a torch clipped to the harness) can considerably improve matters.

Some torches now come with variable beam angles. These are particularly suitable for low visibility conditions, where a concentrated narrow-angle beam can provide greater penetration than a diffuse wide-angle one.

For extreme situations, where visibility is absolutely zero, instruments can be read by using a small sealed perspex tube filled with air or clean water. Light is shone through the side of this while the diver looks down the length of the tube.

Diver Control

The diver's presence is one of the major factors in reducing visibility in an underwater cave. Some problems are virtually unavoidable, such as the disturbance of fine sediments from the roof by exhaled air bubbles. Extremely constricted sections offer the diver little opportunity for avoidance of sediment, and simply taking care is all that can be done to minimise the disturbance in passing. Careless motions increase the problem, and suggest that the diver is probably not competent to be there in the first place.

Many sites do respond well to careful treatment and technique, and cave divers should familiarise themselves with the skills of siltation avoidance and with the equipment for buoyancy control before diving in such caves.

When kitting up and entering the sump, try to minimise disturbance to the sump pool. Sherpas and onlookers should stay clear of the water at all times. If waiting in the water while fully-kitted, then the diver should minimise contact with floor or walls, ideally by inflating a buoyancy compensator and remaining in mid-water. Progress underwater should be slow and careful in silt-laden sumps, and care should be taken to stay out of contact with walls, roof and floor, as a simple touch may produce a cloud of fine silt. Body movement should be minimal and precise - excessive movements create eddies which also disturb silt.

Finning should be careful and delicate, a slight shuffle-kick with bent knees is better than deep powerful strokes which can disturb sediments up

Fig. 23: Ready to follow the line - but low visibility promises to present its usual problems in a British sump.

to 4m away from the diver (figure 24). There are a variety of finning techniques which have been developed in the USA to avoid raising silt. Many of these are perhaps a bit obsessive, but the simple ones work, and are all based on the minimal movement theory. In the smaller passages, finning by just using the ankles can be quite effective. If floor or walls are relatively clear, then carefully pulling on solid projections can avoid the need for finning over silt banks. Lines should be laid taut in mid-water, to avoid them being covered by silt banks in flood. Touching a buried line can wreck visibility far ahead of the diver!

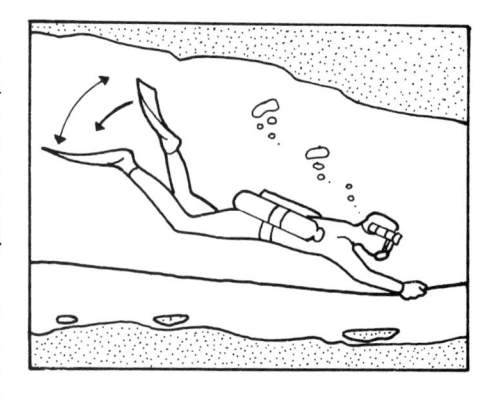

Fig. 24: The shuffle kick attitude - minimises sediment disturbance.

Where passage size allows, the use of buoyancy compensators is recommended. The ability to maintain position in mid-water is one of the best ways of avoiding sediment disturbance, and is too little used in British cave diving. Such control of buoyancy also improves air consumption and increases comfort and control so the benefits to the diver are considerable. Ideally, the diver should be weighted to progress slightly head down with feet raised and knees bent, to concentrate the fin thrust upwards and behind rather than down. Some buoyancy aids concentrate air around the neck, which pulls the diver's head up and tends to place him in a feet-down posture, with obvious results to the sediment below his fins. Such compensators should either be avoided or have their necks taped to reduce buoyancy in that region.

A diver at rest in the water causes more problems than he probably realises. Even if holding neutral buoyancy in mid-water, it is normal to maintain orientation with the fins, and there is a tendency for the feet to droop towards the floor. Care must be taken to avoid this habit. Holding onto a silt-free wall projection and keeping horizontal is probably a better way, and making oneself slightly buoyant may help.

If moving downstream, then turn to face upstream when engaged in any static activity like belaying or cutting a line reel free. If you continue to face downstream, any sediment disturbed by your movements will ruin your visibility far more than the disturbance you made by your earlier movement down the passage. Continue to exercise good buoyancy control throughout the task to further reduce the amount of disturbance. When setting off again, a gentle push suffices better than a powerful kick with the fins. If there is nothing to push against, try increasing your buoyancy to lift you clear of the floor before moving off.

Finally, remember that any disturbance of sediments is a disturbance to the ecology of the cave. Phreatic zones are often well-populated by cave fauna, and many of these creatures depend on organic substances in the sediment to survive. Exploration may not justify the serious disruption of phreatic cave ecology; in the great scheme of things, they may have more right to be there than you.

LINE LAYING & FOLLOWING

LINE laying is potentially the most dangerous cave diving activity, requiring maximum awareness and a methodical approach. The reasons are obvious, as this activity usually takes place in an unexplored sump with the extra clutter of a reel. There are two types of line laying, base-fed, and from a diver-controlled reel.

BASE FED

This method involves the diver being attached to base, with the line usually worn round a wrist. It is a useful method for initial, short penetrations, to see if a sump is going to "go". It has advantages in that the diver should not be able to lose the line, is less encumbered than with a reel, and can take advantage of better visibility. However it does have disadvantages in that the line cannot be weighted out of low beddings, and may well snag out of reach. Also, depending on the nature of the passage, the diver cannot always be felt by base, even if within 30m. Basically, the more corners you go round, the greater the drag on the line, so that after about three corners forward movement is no longer possible.

Most important is that the diver is only as safe as his attendants and, unless well-practised, the use of signals (tugs on the line) can be easily misinterpreted, and the line pulled into dangerous places. The complex system of signals used by the Royal Navy have little place in cave diving and the use of one signal is preferable as a sign for distress, with base instructed to feel the diver all the time, paying out and taking in line in response to the diver's movements. The BS-AC has almost given up using rope signals and no longer includes them in its basic diving training, but some people use six or more tugs to indicate distress, and three tugs to indicate "next thing" in accordance to a prearranged plan (eg "I'm through the sump, and you can now follow"). If a system of signals has been agreed upon, the signal should always be returned by the person receiving it to show that it has been understood.

A standby diver has a role to play when this method is used. As emergencies can be easily detected, they can quickly be acted on. The diver should not have lost close contact with the line, and the distance from base is short.

USING A REEL

This subject will be dealt with almost as a dive would be planned and carried out. There are details which are just as applicable to base-fed techniques, and are included here as this method of line-laying is the most commonly used. In addition to normal pre-dive planning, use the following procedures:

Movement & technique

Line Preparation

1) Relate the length of line put on the reel to the expected nature of the sump, and likely dive duration dictated by your third margin of air supply. If you have already laid some line in the sump and found it easy going, do not assume that the next unexplored section is going to be the same. Poor visibility, very large, very small or complex passage, and water depth can all hinder navigation, and hence reduce the amount of line that can be laid on one dive. In ideal conditions, a maximum of about 150m of line can be laid out safely whilst still absorbing passage detail, but with the introduction of one or more of the above factors this should be drastically reduced.

Note that the reel should not be filled to the edges - not only may this result in spillage but an initially well-stacked reel will not take all the line if it is reeled in again underwater.

2) In preparing the line on the reel, a simple method of tying knots underwater has been developed. This method only applies to man-made fibres which are sufficiently flexible to make non-slip knots. Assume that your first dive will not reach airspace or any natural underwater belay. Tie one end of the line to the centre of the reel with bowline and half-hitches. Then, leaving about a metre (depending on the diameter of your reel) so that the reel is easy to cut off, make a loop using a figure-of-eight knot. To attach a lead belay to the end of the line after it has been laid, proceed as follows (figure 25). A short loop attached to a weight can be easily passed through the loop at the end of the line. Then the weight can be passed through its own loop and pulled tight to secure it to the loop on the line. To ensure that the line is not lost while attaching the weight, put the loop over one forearm, or clip on with a karabiner, and do not remove it until the weight has been attached and the reel cut off.

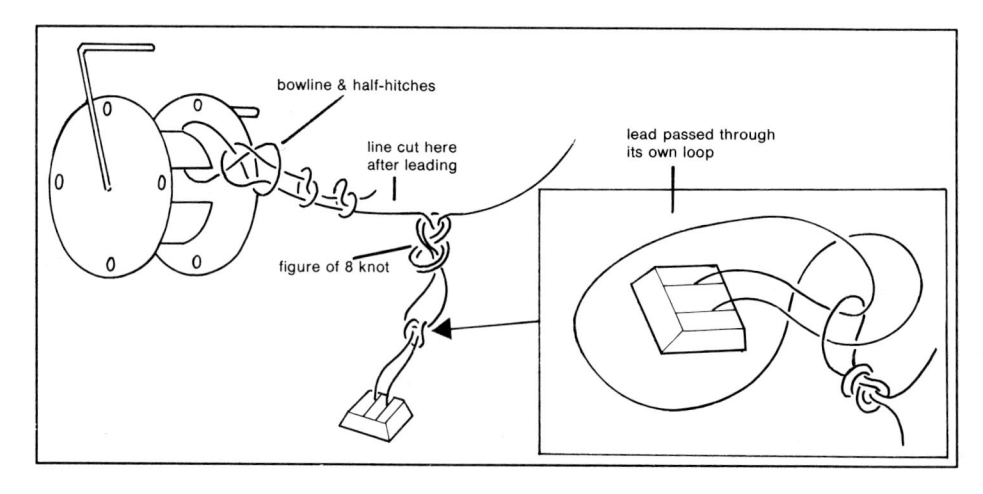

Fig. 25: Attaching a weight to a figure of 8 loop in the line.

On subsequent dives, when a new reel is taken in, make the same loop at the centre of the drum and, in addition, (see figure 26) a loop at the end, after all the line has been wound on. This loop should be large enough to pass the whole reel through easily. Leave a metre of loose end beyond this loop to attach securely to the reel to prevent spillage. This leaves the loop accessible, but the rest of the reel secure. It is best to keep the loop out of the way by attaching it to one rim of the reel with plastic waterproof tape or looping it through a hole drilled for that purpose. Then on reaching the limit of your previous dive, the loop on your new reel can be ripped free from the plastic tape and attached to the loop at the end of the old line, in the manner described above when attaching the weight. If the passage at this point is observed to have no complications (low beddings, junctions, etc) the weight can be removed and the new line laid out. The process can be repeated again and again without a knot being tied underwater.

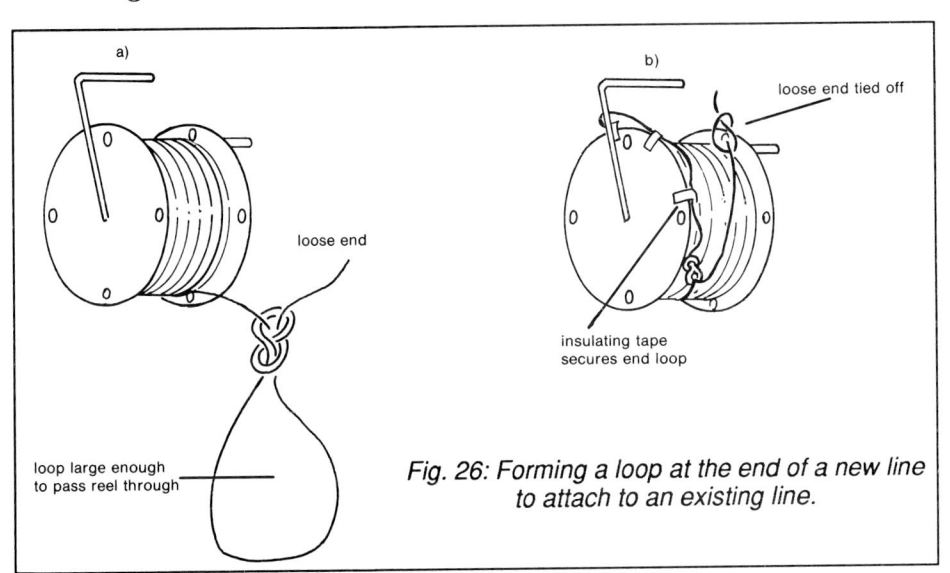

Fig. 26: Forming a loop at the end of a new line to attach to an existing line.

TAGGING

Before any line is wound on a reel, it should be measured and tagged at regular intervals (figure 27). If a light-coloured plastic tape is being used, distances can be marked on the tape with an indelible pen, which makes initial survey and navigation much easier, especially in poor visibility, where there may be little else to relate to. Plastic insulating tape is the easiest material to use for tags, and is simply attached by pushing one end between the strands (in hawser-laid line) and then sticking the tape ends together. This avoids slippage or loss. For plaited lines, where strands cannot be parted, the line must be bound tightly with tape for about 5cm and the tag attached at the end of that, to avoid slippage. A strongly contrasting tape/line colour combination is obviously important.

Where line loss and subsequent disorientation is a possibility, then dual tagging, with two colours, is advised. Yellow and black tags avoid problems with colour blindness, and the yellow tag is attached on the entrance (way out) side, and the black on the cave (way in) side. In such circumstances, the diver regaining a lost line knows in which direction out lies as soon as he reaches the tags. Alternatively, duct-tape arrows (figure 28) can be used to indicate the way out at regular intervals. These are made from triangular sections of duct tape folded across the line to form a simple arrow. More permanent arrows can be made from triangular shapes of perspex or PVC, drilled and slit and slotted on the line.

The intervals between tags depend on whether a potentially accurate survey is wanted, and whether the cave is complex or straightforward. For example, if the Keld Head (Yorkshire) exploration team had used tags every 5m (the CDG norm) they would still have been surveying months later, and tags would have been more confusing than helpful in navigation. They used tags every 30m, which provided more realistic references, and with experience it was possible to estimate subdivisions between tags with reasonable accuracy. Alternatively, major subdivisions can be marked in different colour tape, tagging the main line at 5 or 10m intervals, and using a different colour tag every 50m.

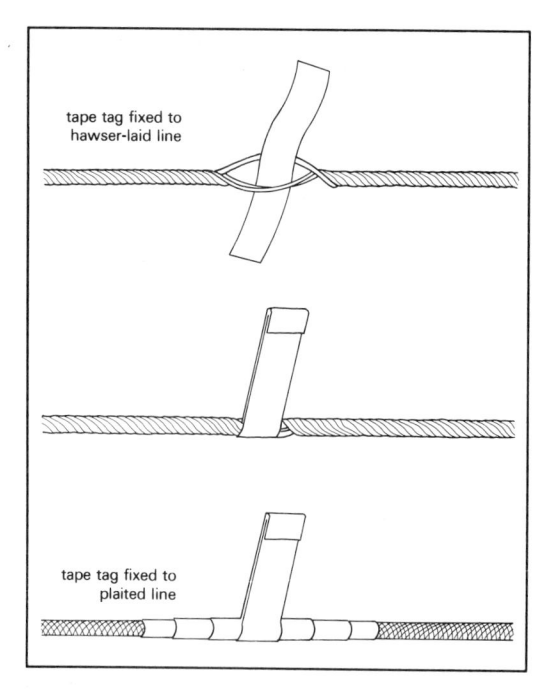

Fig. 27: Various methods of line tagging.

Where two or more lines diverge from one surface point, or at a major underwater junction, permanent tags should then be installed, with a written description of the destination and route taken by that line. White perspex squares, 5cm or more in width and length and at least 3mm thick, are attached to the line by drilling a hole in one corner and running a short loop through. Larger PVC/perspex arrows (see above) can also be used. Lettering should be etched in, or written in permanent ink with a clear varnish seal over it. Permanent tags should be inspected at regular intervals, and replaced when necessary. At junctions where tags are used, the way out line should also be very clearly labelled.

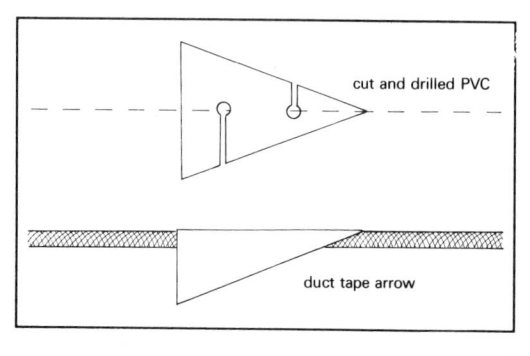

Fig. 28: Way out arrows using plastic and duct tape.

For just a temporary marking of junctions during a dive,

clothes-pegs can be placed on the entrance side of the junction. When more than one team is in the cave, different coloured pegs should be used. This has the additional benefit of indicating that a team is still in the system when the other team returns to the junction. Never rely on in-situ pegs, always take your own on each dive.

CHOICE OF LINE

This is extremely important, and there are a number of properties which a line must provide according to the diving conditions expected. These are as follows:

1) Strength
2) Resistance to abrasion
3) Diameter
4) Buoyancy
5) Colour
6) Texture
7) Knotability
8) Construction

1) *Strength:* Most synthetic lines are more than strong enough for cave diving, given that it is normally difficult to shock-load the line. Even line of only 2mm diameter (nylon or courlene) will hold the weight of a fully-kitted diver in the open air. If you are not sure of the strength of your line, see if it supports your own weight and give it a jerk. If it doesn't break, and has the other required properties, such a line would be suitable for horizontal diving. The static strength of lines for descending shafts should be double your own weight, because you may have to climb the line if you lose buoyancy control.

2) *Resistance to abrasion:* This quality is perhaps more important because even the gradual movements of a diver or of water can have a sawing effect where the line runs over sharp projections. For this reason it is unwise to use line of less than 3mm diameter (nylon or courlene) in British caves. In turbulent sumps, lines of even 5mm can be broken after only one flood, and for extreme conditions one has to look beyond the commonly used synthetic fibres. Glowline, a synthetic cord protected by a plastic sheath, or stainless steel wire (even in a single-wire form of 18swg) have proved to be extremely durable in virtually all conditions. For average British conditions, 4mm diameter courlene or nylon line is perfectly safe to lay, if well-belayed, but if the line is to be in place for some time it will need re-checking on a regular basis.

3) *Diameter:* Time and experience have suggested that 4mm diameter line is the best compromise for British conditions. It is strong, can stand up to short-term abrasion, a reasonably-sized reel can hold up to 150m of it, and it can be easily felt by a cold, gloved hand. On deep shafts or in major, high-flow or well-travelled sumps, 5 to 6mm line is more reassuring, as it is sufficiently tough and thick to pull on if necessary. The greater the diameter of the line, the easier it is to feel, and in poor visibility its more rigid quality means there is less risk of looping, spilling, or ensnaring. The limiting factors on the maximum diameter of line are its weight, the length that can be fitted on a manageable reel, and the effort needed to cut it in an emergency.

4) *Buoyancy:* For British conditions, a slightly buoyant line is preferable, such line being less prone to silting up, while encouraging the diver to keep in mid-water (thus reducing siltation). However, a buoyant line should be used

in conjunction with good, regular belaying, to avoid tangles round roof pendants, or to avoid it floating into less accessible parts of the sump cross-section. The 4mm courlene regularly used by the CDG is buoyant, yet 150m of it is not sufficiently buoyant to make a full reel too positive. A fully-laden reel should be just negatively buoyant, so that it doesn't float off if dropped or placed on the floor. A reel not in use should be clipped to wrist or harness. Positive buoyancy can be a big problem with thick synthetic lines (eg polypropylene), part of the problem being that it is difficult to get rid of tiny air bubbles held within the weave, particularly in shallow sumps. Nylon, steel and Glowline are all negative.

5) *Colour:* Courlene and Glowline usually come in fluorescent orange, and Glowline is the easiest to see. Nylon usually is white, though it stains after a while and becomes somewhat more camouflaged. Other materials hold their colour longer, and blue polypropylene is often used. Most synthetic lines can be obtained in a variety of colours and the use of different coloured lines can considerably aid navigation. In long single passages with no other landmarks, different coloured lines can give a rough indication of distance from base.

Fig. 29: Attaching a line of a different colour to an existing line to create a distinctive junction.

84 **Movement & technique**

Similarly, where there are one or more junctions or side passages, the use of a single colour line down the main passage and different colours of line on side passages can make such junctions considerably safer and individually distinctive.

Whatever colours are used, they should be bright enough to be distinctly seen in the often brown and tannic waters of the average sump in the event of losing hand contact with the line. Distance or direction tags should always be in a contrasting colour to the line.

6) *Texture:* How rigid or supple your line is will affect its handling on and off the reel. Basically, courlene, polypropylene, steel and Glowline are rigid, and nylon is not. Rigid lines do not gather up and loop so much in front of a moving diver's hand, and so tangles are easy to avoid. Nylon, especially when slackly laid, is almost impossible to feel with a cold, gloved hand because it is so soft. With rigid lines, always lay the line out on the ground before the dive to remove any twists, and to counteract the line's plastic memory. Then wind it in neatly so that the line does not have a tendency to spiral into coils when laid in a sump.

7) *Knotability:* This also relates to whether the line is rigid or supple. Rigid lines are easier to tie knots in underwater, because they can be felt more easily and do not flop about. But because they have more plastic memory, they more easily untie, and may even untie themselves. Glowline is particularly dangerous in this respect. Courlene and polypropylene need some care, and knots which present the maximum integral friction must be used (eg double fisherman's rather than single fisherman's, and figure-of eight rather than overhand). Plenty of loose end line must be left after the knot (this should be taped down with a few turns of insulating tape in case it creates a problem in murky water). It is best to avoid using Glowline in all but the shorter sumps, where one continuous length can be laid, and knots tied and left above water, where they can be inspected before diving. Stainless steel presents its own problems, and has not been much used in Britain. If its use is intended, practise and tests in various jointing methods and tools to be used is highly recommended, and wire cutters must be carried in addition to the diving knife.

8) *Construction:* This table looks at some of the materials and constructions of some of the lines in common use in British cave diving.

Material	**Construction**	**Comments**
Nylon	plaited, no core	continuous strand
Courlene	plaited, with core	continuous strand or hawser-laid
Polypropylene	hawser-laid	broken strand, furs up after a time
Glowline	plastic sheath over multiple strand	sheath can break, exposing threads
Stainless steel	single strand	beware kinking; steel needs wire cutters

Hawser-laid line is preferable, because the strands can be parted to make tagging easier. Whichever line is used, the knife or clippers carried must be able to cut it easily.

LINE REEL CONSTRUCTION

Few cave divers will ever have seen a perfect line reel. Many will have given much thought to designing one, but also, along with every other cave diver, will at some time have used an appalling one. Often the reel is the last thing to be considered, and Friday nights spent scouring building sites for plywood or electrical cable reels, then struggling to bend a handle/axle from a piece of reinforcing bar, is a technique known to most of us. Beachcombing is not the best way of making a reel. Some time should be spent on making one that does not fall apart. On the other hand, there is no need to get involved in complicated machining, moulding handles, fixing bearings and so on. The simplicity of construction and operation is most important, so that there is little in the fabric to go wrong.

The properties of a line reel should be as follows:

1) The spool should be of reasonable size and proportion. If the diameter or width of the spool exceeds 30cm, then it will present a considerable drag in the water. If the width of the reel is greater than the diameter, it can become unwieldy to hold and operate, though the wider the spool the easier it is to locate the line on the reel when rewinding. A reel with a width slightly less than the diameter is easier to handle, but with a width of less than 10cm, rewinding may be difficult. An ideal width might be between 15-20cm, and diameter 20-25cm.

2) The diameter of the spool core should not be too small (5cm minimum), or the last few metres of line will be difficult to unwind, and the reel operation may be too jerky, and the extra effort involved may pull the line into dangerous places behind the diver. This is especially true with thicker lines.

3) There should be a hole drilled in the side-plate or core to attach the line to before winding on.

4) Four equally-spaced holes should be drilled in each side-plate on the outside edge to attach the end of the line to after being wound on. The line can also be looped through the nearest hole to the re-wind knob and then over it. This prevents line spilling off the reel in the event of the diver having perform other tasks in mid-dive. These holes should be about 10mm in diameter so that a frayed end can be easily passed through them with a cold, gloved hand.

5) A rewind knob should be attached to the right-hand plate (left plate if left-handed) about 2cm from the edge. This can be fixed, or allowed to rotate, and should be large enough to be easily felt, without catching slack line. About 3cm long by 1cm diameter is fine. It should be attached with a round-headed, low-profile bolt so that the head of the bolt does not catch on line being wound on or off.

6) The position and size of the handle are crucial. The handle should be as near to the centre of gravity of the reel as possible, to minimise leverage on the wrist. The handle should be of similar size to a motorcycle grip, and should have sufficient clearance from the spool to avoid the latter catching on the hand. A loop of line or clip attached to the handle allows it to be attached to wrist or harness.

7) The axle should run freely and be firmly attached and washered (ie a threaded bar with lock-nuts, or a drilled bar with split pins). Washers and/or nylon bushes ensure free movement of the spool.

8) The reel should be light in weight, but sufficiently robust to withstand

Fig. 30: Diver ready for the passing of a virgin sump in Peak Cavern, with the line reel fully loaded.

porterage. Plywood side plates with a steel core are commonly used, but regular painting is needed to prevent the ply splitting. Plastic reels are fragile and don't stand up well to porterage. Aluminium discs make excellent sideplates, though it should be remembered that aluminium quickly work-hardens when regularly bent, so 2mm thickness or more should be used. Steel axles have a long life, but quickly wear through and enlarge holes drilled through aluminium endplates. Nylon bushes can be used to prevent this. Alternatively, the sideplates can be screwed directly on to the spool core, and an axle hole drilled through this to spread the load.

Figure 31 shows a lightweight aluminium reel and figure 32 a basic plywood reel. The former can be constructed with just a vice, hacksaw and drill. The latter, in addition, needs turning and welding. The aluminium reel has the advantages of light weight, and a more comfortably-positioned handle, with a better centre of gravity. The two designs are not suggested as definitive designs but are included as simple reels with no complicated additions. Many variations are possible, such as line feeder, one-way ratchets, torch holders, or even totally enclosed reels to prevent spillage. Unless such additions are well-constructed, however, they might well create one problem while solving another. Total enclosure can prevent spillage, for example, but several such designs have been very prone to jamming. Also, sophisticated reels need sophisticated line management skills - not all divers have these.

AVOIDING ENTANGLEMENT

Cave diving equipment should have been tried and tested in open water, and it is assumed that cylinder harnesses function well. As few items as possible should form snares for line entanglement. Anything that hangs free from the body can be ensnared by loose line.

When line is being laid, however well belayed it may be, there will always be a potential for slack line between the previous belay and the reel. When pausing to perform a task, or to belay the line, any slack should be wound onto the reel, and the line kept as taut as possible behind the diver. Major potential for entanglement comes from contents gauges (which should be fastened to arms, or wrapped around the neck of the cylinder and taped down within view), arm gauges, knife sheath or fin straps. As much ancillary equipment as possible should be worn on the arms, where tangles can be sorted out within vision.

Fin straps should be taped down with duct tape or insulating tape so that it is impossible for lines to get snagged in them. Bolts for securing cylinders in harnesses should be mounted at the front of the harness, so that they are within reach of the diver's hands. Hand-held torches should be held in the hand opposite to the reel, and should be clipped to the wrist in such a manner that they can be let go of without becoming detached or entangled, and without twisting to dazzle the diver. Hand-held bulb units for waist-mounted battery packs can be slung round the neck out of the way when not in use.

BELAYING

Good belaying is essential for safe exploration, and is most important in low, meandering beddings where the line may pull into places too narrow to

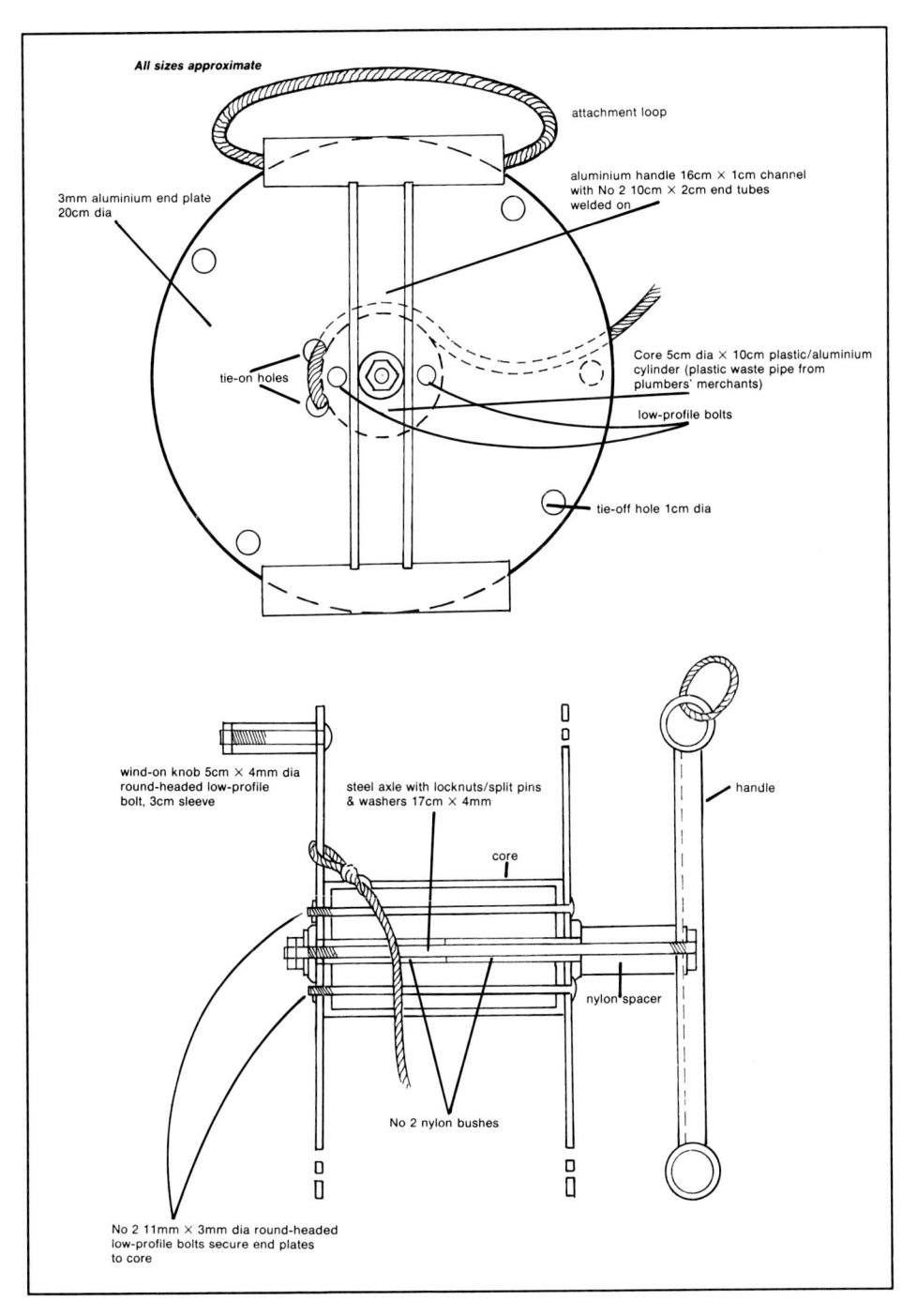

Fig. 31: Lightweight aluminium line reel.

Movement & technique 89

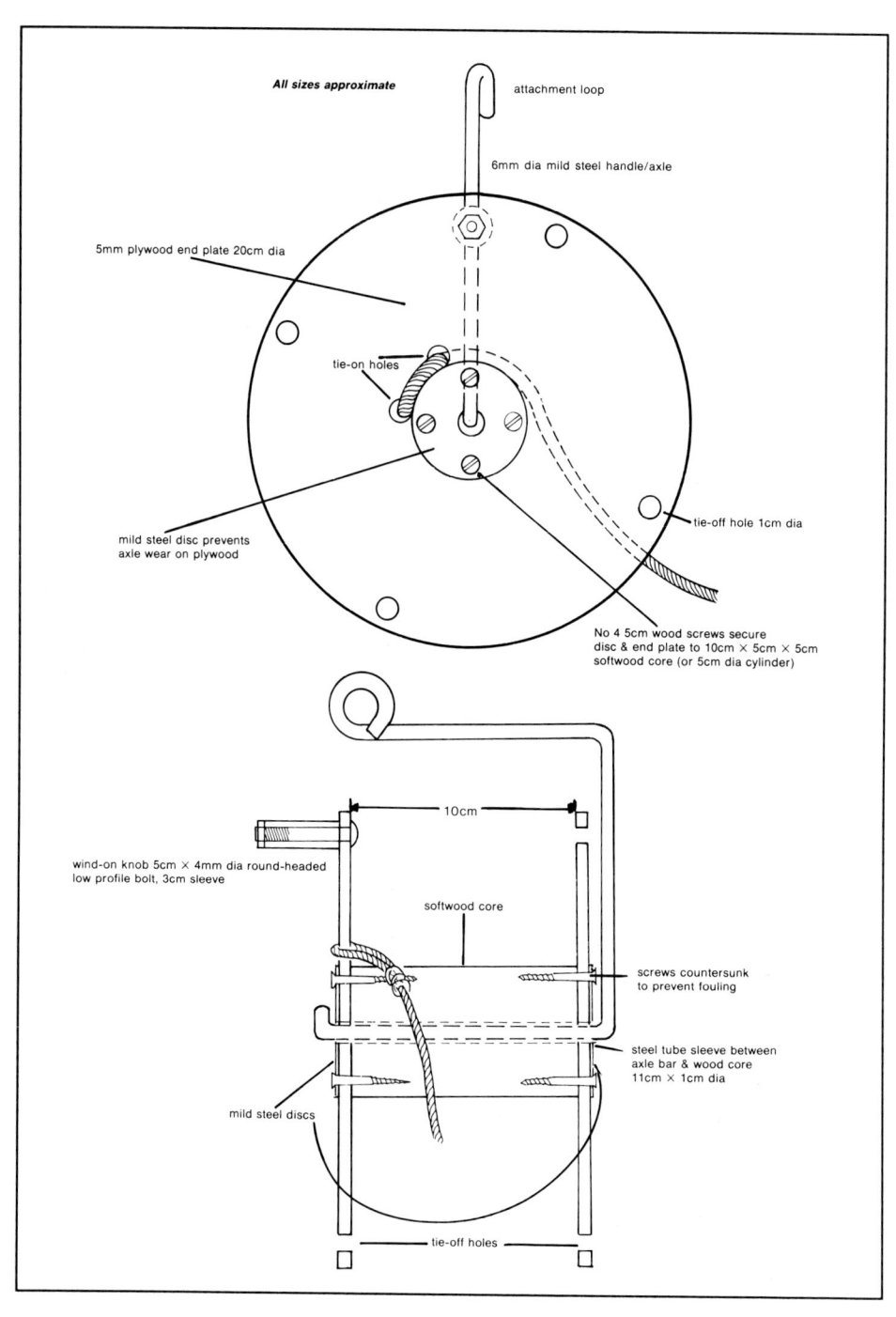

Fig.32: Basic plywood line reel.

Movement & technique

negotiate on the return (figure 33). The person laying the line has a real responsibility for the well-being of divers coming after him, and must lay the line in the safest manner possible in the circumstances.

In addition to providing navigational aids, the walls, floor and roof of the cave also provide natural belays. Whether or not they later prove to be unnecessary, it is sensible to secure the line to any suitable rocks, flakes or eyeholes the passage offers. If potentially mobile belays are being used, care is needed in paying out the line. Using one hand to hold the reel, gently feed the line out with the other arm, keeping it outstretched to avoid equipment tangles, and just taut enough to feel the belay. Dubious stone belays should be replaced at the first opportunity with lead or other permanent weighted belays. With eyeholes, it is easiest to form a loop in the line, which is passed through the eyehole. The reel is taken round the other side, and passed through the emerging loop, which is then pulled tight. No knots are required.

There are various types of artificial belay commonly used when no natural belay is available (figure 34).

1) *Lead weights*: These are the most commonly used form of weighting. They are reliable, expensive, and naturally very heavy. The latter point is the most important, especially if you do not have any means of variable buoyancy control. A wetsuited diver can find himself ascending rapidly after weighting the line with weights removed from his person. Three or four 1kg weights individually attached to waist-mounted karabiners (avoid loops dangling!) is the usual upper limit carried.

2) *Fish-net & nylon bags with draw string*: These are grand for passages containing small pebbles or stones, which can be placed inside the net and the drawstring tightened. This is then looped to the line. No buoyancy problems are encountered (a bag can even be taken for rocks to compensate for dropped-off lead weights). Experimentation in open water is needed first, but no doubt cave divers will eventually develop a small selection of bag sizes to suit different passage conditions.

3) *Buoys*: These are not generally used, but are effective in kicking-water airbells with no natural belays. If the bell is off the main line route, a jump-line, preferably of a different colour or thickness, must be laid. The main line should be tagged on the out side of the junction, as it is quite easy to lose one's bearings on descending back to the main line. Placing your own tag on the way in, and removing it on the way out, places the onus on the diver, and allows no confusion with previously placed tags. Coloured clothespegs, duct-tape arrows or small clips are ideal for this purpose. For buoys, one gallon juice/milk containers with handles on are eminently suitable. The handles give a belay attachment, and the bottles are swum in filled with water and emptied in the bell, or inflated by use of the second demand valve.

4) *Snoopy loops*: These have become a common item in the exploratory diver's kit. They are extremely easy to make and use, have no effect on buoyancy, and are highly adaptable.

They are made by carefully cutting a car inner tube into loops approximately 2cm wide. A clean cut is important, as the slightest nick or hole may start a tear when stretched over a rock. A length of courlene line about 30cm long is passed through the rubber loop, and then tied to form a second loop by a double-fisherman's knot. When belaying with a snoopy loop, the courlene line is passed around the main line and back through itself to attach it firmly,

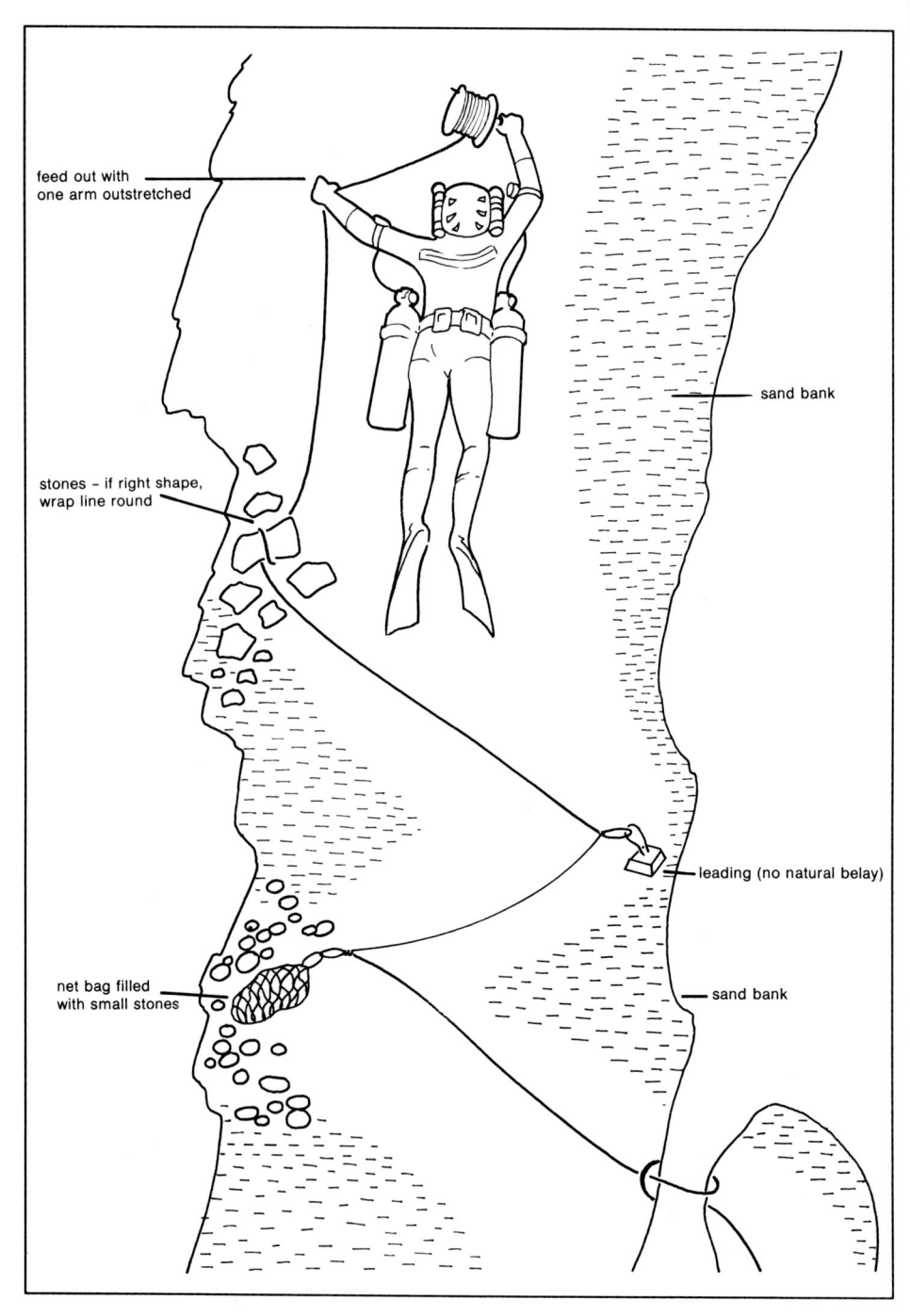

Fig. 33: Line belaying through a sump.

92 Movement & technique

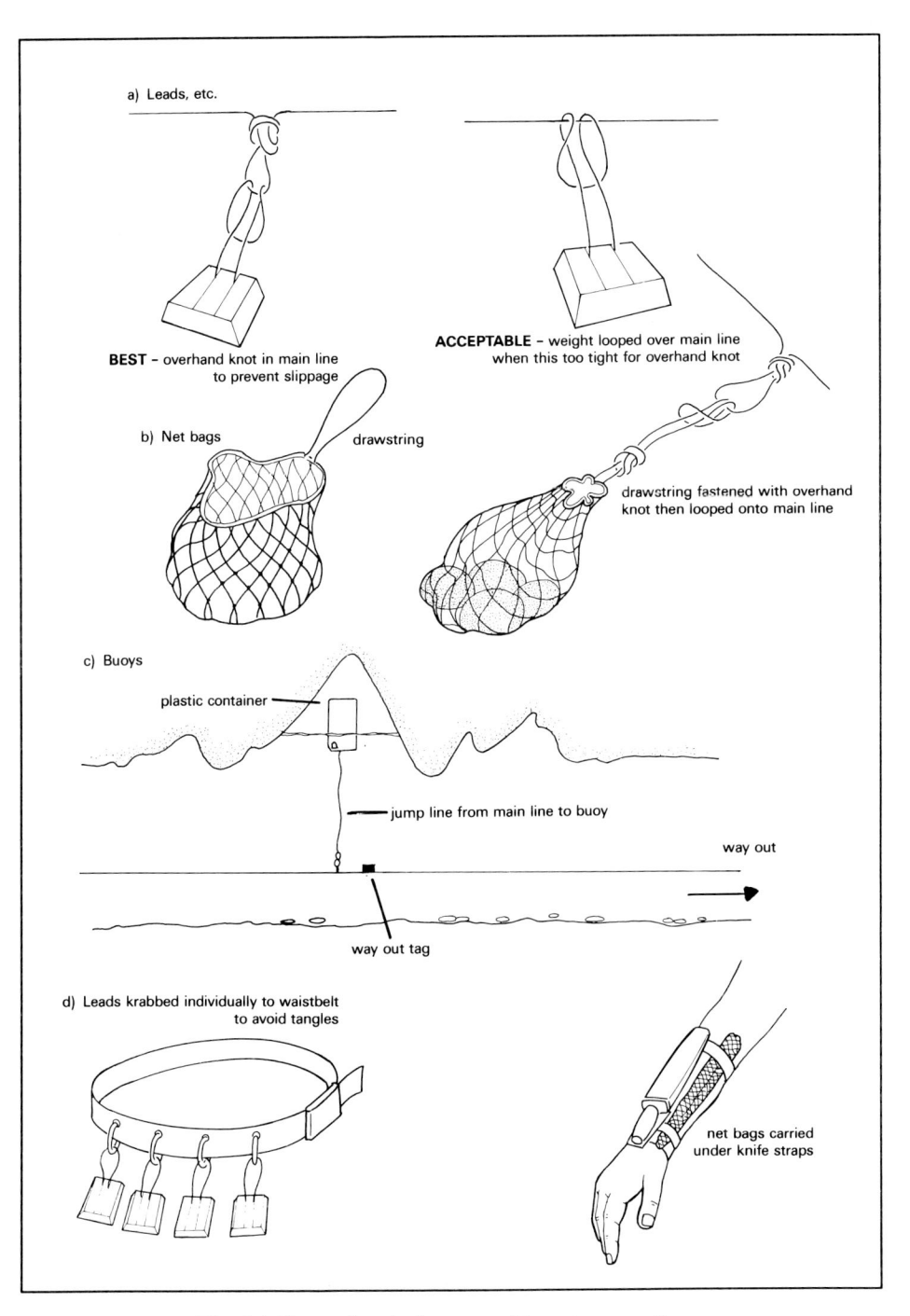

Fig. 34: Some line belays - and how to carry them.

and the inner tube is then stretched round a suitable rock or projection to complete the belay.

While they can be slipped under a strap on arm or thigh, this can result in all the loops sliding out when one is pulled. Clipping them to a single karabiner usually results in an awkward tangle, and so a holder for snoopy loops should be made. A piece of plastic wastepipe cut to the required length, and notched at either end, allows each inner tube to be stretched between the notches. As the second loop is fitted on the holder, the first courlene tail is secured beneath it. The same pattern is followed with all ensuing loops, so that when the holder is full only the toptail is free, allowing it to be easily removed with one hand, releasing the next tail in the process.

This system is a delight to use, especially in rocky passages, and the feeling of security it creates during exploration dives is on a par with the bombproof chock runner behind a lead climber. However, they are more suitable for exploration, and should be replaced when possible by more solid and permanent belays if the sump is to be passed regularly. They are very prone to dislodgement in floods, and badly placed ones, like badly placed chocks, can be pulled off by random tugs on the line.

FOLLOWING LINES & AWARENESS OF SURROUNDINGS

Before entering a sump, the diver must check over all the equipment worn and carried, and be sure that it is safe. This done, time should be taken to mentally prepare for the dive, and to make sure that the mind is in an aware and receptive state. There is often an impulse to get on with the dive, encouraged by the coldness of the water, onlookers and general apprehension. This should be suppressed until your breathing rate is down, and you are mentally and physically settled. This is especially important before long or deep dives.

Once underway, move as slowly and effortlessly as possible. Hold the line on the side which gives you most passage room, with your arm outstretched to keep the line as far as possible from potential equipment snares.

Whatever the visibility, sight is the most useful sense, so this is the time to glean all possible information about the character of the passage to aid a safe return. Move your head from side to side and observe as many landmarks as possible. Recording on the slate your general direction can give helpful information in case of line loss. This should be done regularly between each tag, particularly when laying line, or when the going is difficult.

Following the floor is most useful, as roofs and walls tend to be complicated by solution pockets and cross rifts. The floor is full of useful navigation aids. Deposits of silt display ripple marks, and together with bits of flood debris and the movement of particulate matter in the water can indicate the direction of flow. Good neutral buoyancy, and good control of the same, is needed to avoid getting too closely involved with the sediments, however. In static water, or where there is no other indication of direction, scallop markings are a useful clue (the sharp edge points downstream). Proper use of direction tags in such sumps is better practice! Pebble deposits can indicate a change of flow direction, or a rise or fall in passage depth.

In very bad visibility, it may be better to follow one wall, feeling for low beddings and weighting the line wherever possible. Here your sense of touch and balance will begin to take over from sight. If possible, hold the line with both hands and your sense of balance will pick out any change in direction or dip. It is very important to look ahead at all times, before any murky water stirred by your passage catches up with you and ruins visibility completely. Disorientation can be immediate in poor visibility. For example, an ear-clearing stop on the way in between Wookey 20 and 22 on Mendip led two divers to drift around in poor visibility and mistakenly end up back in 20.

More serious disorientation can occur where the line has been badly laid, as coils of loose line can drift into beddings, between boulders and around divers. Always deal with loose line before it builds up, by belaying it whenever possible and making sure that sufficient belays are used to allow the line to run as tautly as possible without pulling into awkward sections.

Make sure that the line behind you is sufficiently belayed for your return journey. In poor or decreased visibility there is a tendency to hug the line, and if it has drifted into a low section this may even result in a temptation to force one's way along it. Unless this is a well-known, documented squeeze, such a practice is best avoided, and a good memory of the route in allows a competent diver to avoid such errors. The best approach to such low sections is to belay a way round them properly in the first place.

Should you find yourself in the unenviable situation of being caught in a low bedding, use an outstretched arm like the proverbial blind man's white stick to locate the highest route, trying first one side and then the other. It is possible to over-react when your helmet jams against the roof, giving the first sign of a lowering section. Do not immediately lurch off to one side, but first sink to the floor, turn your head sideways, and gently ease forwards to see if things improve. It may just have been a roof projection!

Line junctions can be very confusing in a cave new to the diver. Unless familiar with the situation, always mark the way out with a suitable tag (clothespeg, plastic-coated copper wire twisted round line, duct-tape arrow, etc) so that it can be seen and felt on the way out. Take a bearing, and note the colours of lines. Airbells, especially the kicking-water variety, can be equally confusing where the ways in and out look similar. The airspace can give rise to undue complacency. All the diver has to do is turn round a few times while performing some task, and the way out can be lost. This emphasises the need to be aware of bearings.

As cave divers, we are taught to regard losing the line as unthinkable and unlikely. It happens. Clipping onto the line by means of a karabiner would seem to be the obvious solution, but this would create as many problems as it would solve, a bit like, say, being handcuffed to the steering wheel of a car. Valuable time is lost snagging, passing belays and obstructions, and in changing position relative to the line. More important is the need to see the passage shape in front before bad visibility catches up with you. Lines are rarely laid perfectly - a hand is a much more adaptable "natural karabiner", well-suited to keeping in contact with the line in virtually all conditions. It allows the added sensation of touch to the basic task of line contact.

The problem with hands is that they are ordered by heads. Under pressure, these are not as vigilant as they might be. Potentially dangerous situations occur when more than one thing is happening at once, and the order of priorities essential for survival in a sump may be momentarily forgotten. For example, while following a tight line round a low bedding corner

Fig. 35: A diver follows a well-laid line above silt banks down the centre of a passage.

using an outstretched arm to remain in line contact, the diver's mask becomes dislodged and floods. The rush of cold water round the face and up the nose can create a strong impulse to let go the line and refix the mask. Nice being able to see again, but not if there is no line in sight! Far better to move somewhere roomy enough to use both hands to clear the mask and yet remain in contact with the line by looping it over a forearm.

Looping the line over the forearm is commonly used for simple manoeuvres like clearing ears, but krabbing on with a short cow's tail sling may be advisable for awkward activities, like removing or replacing a stage tank, or attaching a new reel, especially in poor visibility.

Entanglement

Maintaining too close a contact with the line is also best avoided where the risk of becoming ensnared is high. Hold the line at arm's length when you cross it or change hands. Do your travelling at a leisurely pace; this allows most snags to be felt before they become knots, or before they drag the line behind you into a horrible place and disturb belays.

To get out of a tangle, move slowly and methodically. Locate the line behind you, and run your hand along it to find the offending tangle (usually at bottle taps or finstraps). If, in extremes, your attempts to untie the mess are unsuccessful, you may have to consider cutting the line. Get firm hold of the way out side first. You may have to cut the way in side first if the line is laid tight. If there is enough slack, make a loop on the way out side, tie an overhand knot, and get an arm through it or clip into it. Only when firmly linked to your exit, start cutting the line. It may need cutting on both sides of the tangle. If you have plenty of air and line, you may feel like repairing the break, or at least belaying the way out, or even both cut ends, if possible. If enough slack exists, it may be possible to simply rejoin the lines. Pass the cut end through the overhand loop already made, and knot it substantially, ideally with a bowline and several hitches. If in real doubt, wait for another day.

There is a certain onus on a diver who cuts a line to repair it. If this is not possible, every effort must be made to publicise the fact the line has been cut, so that the break will not endanger other divers. If the way out lies downstream, it is worth trying to belay the line as near to the cut end as possible so that the line does not float downstream and cause a serious and dangerous obstruction.

PAIR OR TEAM DIVING

Following lines with a partner or partners should create a feeling of confidence that comes with the duplication of equipment and minds. Equally, it can increase psychological and practical problems. This is especially true at depth, where misunderstandings or problem-solving between divers can increase narcosis problems. Countless divers must have had their masks dislodged by the fins of a diver they are following too closely; or, conversely, been freed from tangles by a diver following behind. Knowing that he is being followed can put pressure on the leading diver to hurry through potentially dangerous obstacles better passed in the individual's own good time. There may be a tendency to overlook equipment problems so as not to spoil the dive. Buddy diving in caves is a double-edged sword.

In most British caves, it is virtually impossible to buddy dive in the open water sense. It is thus most important that all those diving in pairs or teams to be totally independent of the other diver or divers, and treat any possible buddy assistance as a bonus. Do not assume, for example, that when passing a junction the diver in front knows the way out. This lemming instinct is too prevalent in ordinary caving, with often only one man in a party knowing the way out. It should not happen underwater! Do not allow yourself to be shown round a new dive route without taking it all in. Read up about it first, ask questions beforehand, and do not hesitate to mark points (eg junctions) yourself where you are uncertain - you may have to return alone.

Diving with others is most effective when individual aims and roles are pre-planned, and best when the divers have developed a considerable rapport based on years of diving and caving together. They must be familiar with the use of signals and slates, and should agree beforehand on any marks and techniques to be used at junctions or difficult sections. Otherwise, especially on original exploration dives, it is probably safer to dive alone, properly equipped. An experienced diver will always have his self-support capabilities lessened if he has to nursemaid a less experienced diver, and this can make

Movement & technique

original exploration of a cave unduly dangerous. Buddy diving is perhaps best done in larger, clearer passages, along a relatively well-known route.

LOSING CONTACT WITH THE LINE

At some point in a cave diver's career, he will probably lose contact with the guideline. While most divers regain it within seconds, without the use of specialised search techniques, such misfortune has ended in fatalities. There are ways of searching for, and finding, the line that every cave diver should be practised in and familiar with. Most divers now carry a small search reel that can be used specifically for line retrieval.

Search Reels

The essential characteristics of a search reel are that it should be sufficiently compact so as to be hardly noticeable as an extra item, and that it should be quick and easy to use in typical British conditions of restricted passage dimensions and poor visibility. As with other ancillary equipment, it is best mounted on the forearm (on the opposite side to the slate). The size of the reel is determined by the size of the forearm and also by the length of the line which would be needed to traverse the entire cross-section of the passage being explored.

In most sumps, 15m of line is sufficient to cross the width of the passage, and it is extremely unlikely that a lost line will have drifted that far from the diver if he has remained stationary in the interim period. The reel described here (figure 36) is suggested as a robust and reliable item of equipment. It will hold 15m of 2-3mm diameter courlene line and both the plumber's plastic solder spool/fishing line spool and the 15mm copper tube are easily obtained. The only maintenance required is to periodically check the condition of the line and its attachment to the reel. The reel is fixed by a loop to a wrist-mounted karabiner or brass thumbclip and stowed under an inner-tube loop on the upper forearm. There is no wind-on facility, so this must be done by hand. After all the line has been wound in, placing an inner tube loop over the drum of the reel will keep the line secure. When in use, it is pulled from the inner tube and swivelled round into a handgrip while still attached to the clip. A suitable weight is then looped on to the end of the search line before reeling out commences.

Too much, or too thin a line, on a search reel can create problems of entanglement that outweigh its usefulness.

Use of the Search Reel

It is always useful to have a short length of spare line even when following existing routes, for such purposes as repairing a break, or to conduct short searches off a main line for side passages. However, the principal use of a search reel is to recover a lost line.

The use of a search reel should be practised in open water and not in a cave. Remember, while its use can increase your chance of a line recovery, it should never be regarded as an infallible technique.

It is in the interests of every cave diver to analyse and anticipate situations where the line could get lost. If you do lose the line, your awareness of surroundings, and calmness, together with search reel and weight, will make an early recovery of the line very likely. Use the following procedure.

1) Write down main line bearings of the sump on the inward journey (or from earlier compass surveys).

2) Always be aware of your position relative to the line.

3) Having lost the line, do not disturb silt further by sudden movements.

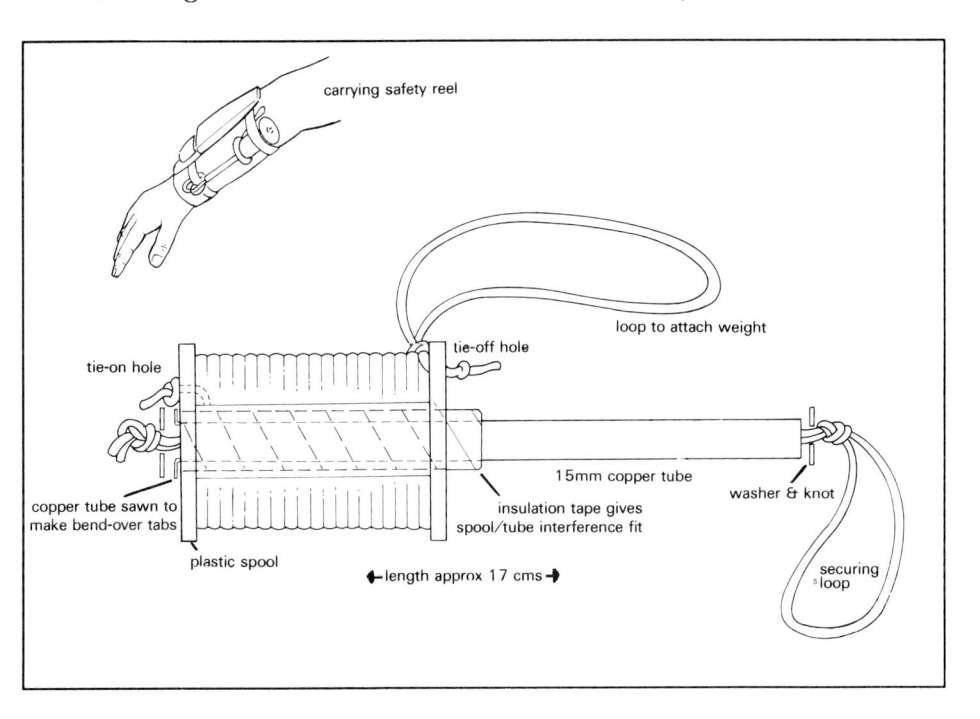

Fig. 36: A typical search reel - and how it may be carried.

4) Slowly scan the side of the tunnel on which the line ran relative to you, before the line was lost. Move no more than one metre in that direction.

5) If you are being followed by another diver, splay your arms and legs and wait for a few minutes (if air reserves allow) so that he is likely to bump in to you. Watch for his lights and, in poor visibility, hold your breath for a few seconds to listen for his exhaust bubbles. This has proved a successful method in the past.

6) If the line is still elusive, and you are alone, you will need to resort to your search reel. A random search is the best that is possible with just a compass and a knowledge of the main line bearing of the sump. Travelling at right angles to the main line bearing (figure 37), it is possible to do a search of the cross-section of the tunnel along the floor, over the roof and down the walls, with arms outstretched to try and trap the line in poor visibility. Passages are rarely more than 4-6m wide, whereas they can be very long, and it is quite possible to run parallel to the line in bad visibility and still not find it, even though you may feel you are zigzagging.

Coming out into clearer visibility on an outward swim may mean you have simply got ahead of your silt-cloud, and can find the line, but equally it may mean you are off route, and may be heading up a side passage, or even be beyond the limit of exploration.

This kind of random search, if extended beyond a few metres, leaves a lot to be desired. Knowing that the line is unlikely to have moved more than a metre or two away, attach your search reel to a small lead weight and then, facing the side of the passage where the line was last seen, record the bearing on your slate. Reel out carefully, at floor level, in that direction, trailing your free hand along the floor to catch the line (important if you have no visual contact with the floor). In most British sumps, a side wall or bedding will have been reached within 15m. If no wall has been seen, you will probably have been travelling at other than right-angles to the passage. Reel in to your lead weight. Then either add or subtract 90° from your first bearing and reel out

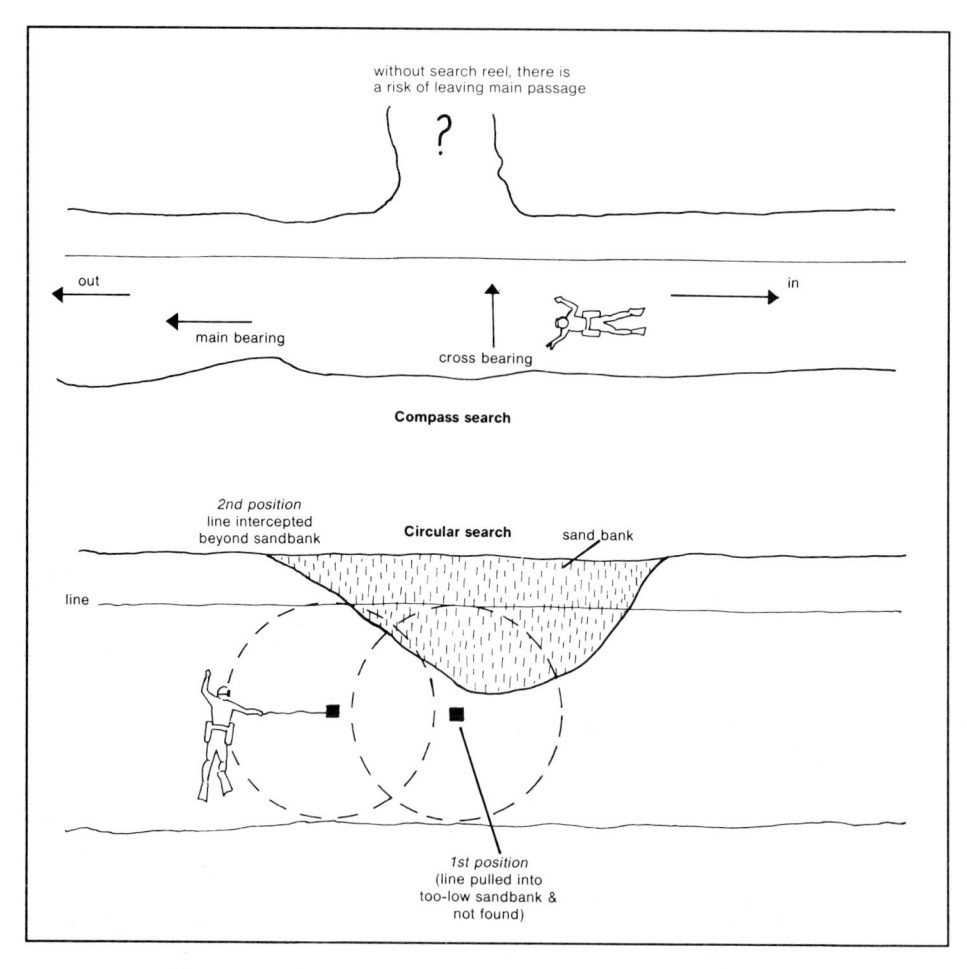

Fig. 37: Relocating the line using (top) a compass bearing at right angles to the line, and (below) a search reel.

100 **Movement & technique**

again, having recorded the new bearing. Once the wall is found, turn round, and add or subtract 180° to get the back bearing. Follow the roof over to the opposite wall. Turn again, and follow the floor on the other bearing back to your weight. Reeling in the line should ensnare the lost line, if it has not already been recovered.

If this fails, move out down the tunnel on the main line bearing to the limit of your search reel, wind in the weight, and start another search from your new position, as the line may have pulled into a bedding adjacent to your first weight position.

If the line is known to be negatively buoyant, a circular search at floor level around the weight may be more appropriate. Always try and use your search reel in conjunction with compass and slate to complete a 3D survey of the passage.

Obviously, having made your original mistake of losing the line, you have to weigh up the options, which are limited by your air supplies, and will have to decide when to attempt to follow a bearing out, knowing that poor visibility indicates your inward journey. The floor is most likely to show signs of flow direction, as indicated earlier in this chapter.

Of course, if there is absolutely no visibility, only a vague search by touch could be attempted, even with the search reel, following the roof, walls and floor in an attempt to ensnare the main line. Thus prevention rather than cure is all-important. If a difficult swim is indicated - carrying gear, or where line loss is possible by necessary tasks en route - clipping onto the line may be the answer.

Whatever the conditions underwater, line laying and control is one of the most important skills that can be learnt by a cave diver, whether he anticipates exploration diving or not. Laying line carries with it responsibility for others who may follow, and divers following existing line have an equal responsibility to maintain its integrity for those coming after them. It is the only item of cave diving equipment not carried into the cave by each diver using it, and it must thus be cared for by all.

Fig. 38: Laying new line, but fish lead the way in Zodiac Caverns.

AIR MARGINS

THE concept of third margins, using one-third of the air supply for the inward dive, and one-third for the return, whilst retaining the final third to deal with emergencies, was first applied to single cylinder dives. The use of only one breathing set in cave diving is now frowned upon, except as a back-up in very short or free-diveable sumps. The concept of the third-margin has been expanded, however, and its application developed to cover dual and multiple cylinder systems.

With two separate breathing sets, use of the third margin will effectively give a 100% safety margin, in that if one set fails, then the other set should get the diver out from any point on the dive, providing both sets were of equal capacity. In practice, the 100% margin is slightly less, because there is always the potential for further failure, and air consumption may well rise as a result of the stress associated with the emergency. If one system fails during a dive, the dive must therefore be abandoned at that point and an immediate return made to base.

The standard way of achieving third margins with two tanks is to use one third of the air in one cylinder, change to the second cylinder, and turn for base when one third of the air has been breathed from that in turn. Continue to breathe from that cylinder until it is two-thirds empty, then change again to the first cylinder. If no incidents occur to delay you, you should reach base with one full third left in each cylinder.

This can be modified by changing tanks every ten minutes or so, so that the diver can regularly assure himself that both systems are in full working order and can take action immediately if one fails. The system can simply be extrapolated for use with three or more cylinders on long dives; simply change to each new cylinder in turn as the previous one reaches its third. It may be worth colour-coding demand valves on multiple tank dives to aid underwater identification, and using matching colours on the relevant pressure gauges (coloured insulation tape is ideal for this).

Often divers will use cylinders of different sizes. While using cylinders of too great a variation in capacity is not recommended, the following rule should always be applied: where 2/3rds of the larger cylinder is greater than the total contents of the smaller, use the biggest first.

Various factors can complicate the simple system of thirds. It is worth noting that a neutrally buoyant, wetsuited diver wearing twin 5.5l cylinders following a known line at about 5m depth will cover about 150m in 10 minutes, using 1 cu ft of air/minute. A nervous, inexperienced, very cold diver could drain a cylinder doing the same dive. Similarly, if a bulky burden is carried, such as a scaling pole, stretcher or tackle-bag, the same dive might take several times as long, using proportionally more air.

Strong currents, whether river, tidal or flood, will have a dramatic effect on the thirds rule. Divers who have followed a resurgence, even in slow flowing conditions, have turned round on using their inward thirds to reach the surface with more than thirds in reserve. Conversely, turning round on thirds in a strong downstream flow could prove fatal on the return. Downstream sumps should be taken in small steps until a clear picture of air requirements is built up in all flow conditions, and the thirds rule can be adjusted proportionally to suit the circumstances.

The actual equipment worn can affect the rate of air consumed per unit of distance swum. A change from wetsuit to drysuit, or the addition of a buoyancy compensator, can all slow progress by increasing drag, though they provide other positive advantages by making the diver warmer or neutrally buoyant, thus compensating for air loss by reducing effort or improving physical conditions.

On very long dives, it has been found that weight around the waist can give rise to extreme backache when a drysuit is worn. With legs and chest inflated, the resultant arched posture slows the diver and increases air consumption. The facility of adjusting buoyancy or distributing weight more evenly (see sections on drysuit diving and buoyancy) can virtually eliminate this problem.

If using several breathing sets, the failure of more than one may present additional problems which using thirds may not adequately cover. A small delay at depth can result in greatly increased air consumption, both directly and as a result of the extra air required for associated additional decompression. When using diver propulsion vehicles (DPVs), the distance that may have to be swum in the event of a DPV failure should be planned for (see section on DPVs in this manual). THese factors should be taken into consideration when calculating the safety margins for air consumption.

When laying line, a well-prepared compact reel together with accessible associated equipment, and a practised technique, will reduce consumption of air considerably.

Individual sumps will each present particular problems of sustained awkwardness with constrictions, poor visibility, depth, length, cold, and water flow which require individually matched air reserves. In new territory, the diver should be prepared to take small steps at a time to glean the necessary information for safe progress and controlled air consumption.

Long Distance Diving

As soon as it becomes necessary to carry more than two cylinders, whether for long or deep dives, the 100% air margin at your furthest point is no longer possible. The thirds rule is still applied, but the details of application will vary according to the type of dive.

In long sumps broken by appropriately-spaced, usable airspaces, additional stage bottles (see section on *Stage diving*) can be left in an airspace having used the inward third. Leaving stage cylinders en route allows the diver to move more efficiently and with less drag (and thus use less air) in his exploration. In such a situation, no one cylinder will get the diver out from the furthest point reached, but the additional security of stage sets en route compensate for this. Airspace staging also allows good valves on used cylinders to be exchanged for faulty ones on fuller ones in safety. While such a practice is possible underwater, it does the valves little good, and may mean the pressure gauge has to be changed. It is a useful emergency procedure to be aware of in desperation, and can be practised with an old valve (minus pressure gauge!) in a swimming pool.

If there are no suitable airspaces, all the cylinders can be worn throughout the dive, providing maximum safety bailout but also increasing air consumption due to the drag and additional swimming effort involved. It may also affect the ability of the diver to pass constricted sections of passage, affect buoyancy adjustments, and dramatically increase the potential for entanglement. Clipping part-used tanks to the line underwater is the preferred method, and air margins are dealt with in the same way as with cylinders left in airspaces. At the sharp end of the dive, the diver has the fullest mobility possible to make exploration easiest and safest. It is critical that the diver does not stray beyond the limits imposed by the thirds rule, and each cylinder must be capable of reaching the previously staged tank/s in case of failure on any point of a dive, especially when cylinders of varying capacities are used.

Finally, divers must remember that just as more air is used swimming against a strong current, so there is an optimum speed at which to fin with differing amounts of equipment. Do not attempt to propel yourself along in a drysuit with three cylinders at the same rate as you would in a wetsuit with two. Like a ship trying to gain maximum speed, more fuel will be used. It is noticeable how the comparative relaxation of survey diving can result in less air being used, even though more time is spent swimming through the same distance of passage.

Alterations to equipment to make thirds margins more effective all have the same intention of being able to get all the air out of all the cylinders carried in emergency. The simplest technique is the use of self-sealing mid-hose snap-connectors on all low-pressure hoses. For example, if one valve has a massive second stage leak, we would normally turn off the cylinder, and turn it on only on actual demand. By breaking the connection to the second stage, the air loss is stopped by the release of the upstream valve in the connector. The now-redundant cylinder can be linked quickly by hose and snap connector to either the other valve when the other tank is breathed dry, or could already be linked by a previously fitted connector and hose on the spare low-pressure outlets on the two first stages. The remaining air can then be used by the other demand valve.

The American system of dual valve manifolds, where a dual manifold on a twin back-mounted set allows both demand valves access to all the air in either tank is a different approach to the problem. Apart from the fact that few British sumps offer suitable conditions for back-mounted cylinders, the possible failure of O-ring seatings, or the potential damage to taps by regular banging against the roof, mean that if one first stage or seating fails then a lot of air from both tanks can be lost before that tap can be turned off. In constricted passage, where the diver may not be easily able to reach the tap to isolate it, this can prove fatal. Inverting the tanks can help, and using DIN-fitting valves is considerably safer, but the fact remains that air from both tanks can be lost through a single component failure. The use of a low-pressure snap connector between the cylinders allows for dual access when required, without the continuous potential for uncontrolled release.

The Y-valve is another answer to the possibility of first or second stage failure on a single cylinder, allowing two separate demand valves to be mounted on a single cylinder, and for the isolation of either valve in emergency. This adds to clutter if two cylinders are used, though cave divers have linked the spare take-offs on each cylinder together by using two linked first stages to allow dual access if required. If one valve fails, the cylinder can be drawn on by the other just by turning the linked taps on.

STAGE DIVING

STAGE diving is the general term used to describe the technique of using cylinders which are carried for a part of the dive only. The simplest method is to wear two permanently side-mounted cylinders as usual, and to carry an extra cylinder which can be easily removed. The detachable cylinder is breathed whilst carried and then deposited at a suitable point, normally when 1/3 of its contents have been used. The diver continues breathing from his side-mounted cylinders and retrieves the stage cylinder on his return through the sump.

It is also possible to have support divers carry stage cylinders for a lead diver, leaving them at key points in the sump, or in suitable airspaces. The lead diver can then proceed through the staging points, exchanging partially-depleted cylinders for full ones. Exit is made using the stage cylinders in reverse order.

In general, stage diving enables a diver to increase the maximum penetration into a sump with available capacity cylinders, to reduce the amount of equipment carried beyond a staging point, and in addition it improves buoyancy, manoeuvrability and streamline profile when using large quantities of air.

SAFETY CONSIDERATIONS

Using more than two cylinders decreases the vulnerability of the diver to individual system failure. However, it is still necessary to maintain air reserves at all times, to ensure that the diver can withstand the failure of any item of equipment at any point in the dive. The following points may be worth considering:

1) Breath no more than 1/3 of any tank on the way in (possibly less, eg when swimming with a current behind the diver). If reserves are concentrated into one cylinder and that fails, insufficient air could remain for a safe exit.

2) Don't use stage cylinders which are larger than the total side-mounted capacity. This again concentrates the air reserves into an individual cylinder and, in the event of stage cylinder failure or loss on exit, insufficient air could remain.

3) Have independent decompression air and tables available. Stage dives by their very nature are long dives, and it is easy to exceed no-stop time. If an emergency requires the use of the reserve air then the bottom time is increased and the problem magnified. Stage cylinders should not be regarded as being available for decompression.

CARRYING STAGE CYLINDERS

There are many methods of carrying stage cylinders, and a little ingenuity is required in order to get the best from any system. Listed here are the main options:

1) *Hand Held*: This method is the simplest and easiest to set up, and can be used well. The cylinder can be picked up, set down and manipulated

Fig. 39: An electrolytic drink before a long dive on a Blue Holes expedition.

through awkward sections with little difficulty. A longitudinal strap to put your arm through makes it possible to free both hands without letting go of the cylinder. Access to the cylinder tap is good. The use of a nearly neutrally-buoyant cylinder can also make life easier. However, if the stage cylinder is breathed through an awkward section of passage, it is possible for the second stage of the demand valve to be pulled out of the mouth.

2) *Front Mounted*: This technique requires a little more preparation, but once underwater it is probably the best. Two karabiners are attached to the stage cylinder, one at either end. The cylinder is then krabbed to the waist harness and to a shoulder strap, and so held diagonally across the chest. During the dive the diver's hands will remain free and easy access to the cylinder tap is assured. The cylinder is removed and replaced easily underwater, as long as the attachment points are large enough (see **figure 40**).

3) *Back Mounted*: This is only suitable in large clear passage. The safest technique is to invert the cylinder to protect the tap and improve access to it. A long hose should be used between first and second stages on the demand valve. It may prove difficult to remove and replace the cylinder in low or silty conditions, or if much gear is worn on the arms.

4) *Side Mounted*:
Wearing stage cylinders on separate belts is a workable technique, especially if the cylinder is not too large. However, it is easy for confusion to arise as to which demand valve belongs to which cylinder, unless a clear colour coding system is adhered to. It is difficult to balance large cylinders in this way, and it may affect the diver's trim and buoyancy.

Whichever system is chosen, it is worth considering colour-coding demand valves to contents gauges to avoid the confusion which may arise with more than two cylinders. Coloured insulation tape is fine for this. The technique adopted will normally be the one that the diver feels most comfortable with, and which best suits the situation.

AT A STAGE POINT

Being separated from a significant portion of your air supply is a reasonably serious proposition, so it is worth minimising the risks involved. The main objectives are firstly to be able to find the stage cylinder, and then to find it in working order. The following rules can help achieve both aims:

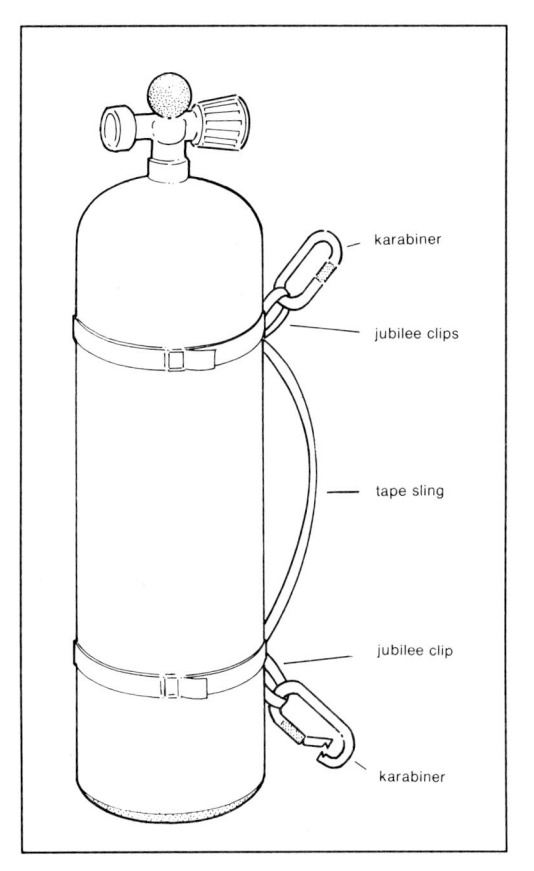

Fig. 40: A cylinder rigged for front mounting.

1) Securely attach the cylinder to the line in a manner which is easy to reverse. For instance, use a karabiner through a lark's foot sling knot. If the cylinder is buoyant, or there is a strong current, it is wise to leave it at a good line belay point.

2) Remember where you left it! If there is a lot of silt and/or poor visibility, it might be worth leaving a buoyant light, such as a Cyalume, on the cylinder so that you can find it in bad visibility.

3) Turn the cylinder off when you leave it, but leave the valve pressurised. In this way you ensure that the cylinder retains its contents whilst protecting the first stage of the valve from the ingress of silt and water. This also reduces the risk of blowing O-rings whilst repressurising.

4) Protect the second stage of the demand valve from silt, especially if the cylinder is to be left for some time. This can be done as simply as by putting it in a plastic bag and sealing with an elastic band.

5) If working in a silty area in a strong current, face upstream when

Movement & technique 107

recovering the cylinder; your body and fins are not disturbing the silt in your immediate sphere of vision, and the operation becomes easier. It may be convenient to inflate your buoyancy device and work on the roof to minimise the reduction of visibility.

Stage diving forms an integral part of long-distance diving, and has an obvious relationship with air margins. After reading this section it is worth referring to the sections on *Air margins* and *long-distance cave diving*.

Fig 41: Constricted sumps present a new category of challenge, and risk, for the cave diver. (Top) Pushing forward as the roof closes down; (bottom) a helper kits a diver in close confines as he prepares to dive an even more constricted sump.

Movement & technique

TIGHT SUMPS

DIVING in a tight or constricted sump has its own particular set of problems in addition to those of normal cave diving. These are further accentuated if the sump also happens to be long and deep.

A constricted sump can be defined as one in which progress is impeded by the small size or shape of the underwater route. As divers vary in size, some may find a particular sump more constricted than others do. Generally, a sump that has a vertical or horizontal dimension of 50cms or less is a constricted sump.

Some sumps may be constricted only in parts, whilst others may be constricted for almost all their length, presenting a more severe undertaking. The location of the constrictions within a sump must also be taken into consideration, such as whether they are situated far into the sump, or whether their depth presents further obstacles to the diver, both practically and psychologically.

Equipment

The equipment used is the same as that used for all cave diving, except in the case of an initial exploratory dive, when only a single cylinder, valve, knife and mask might be used. Line might be base fed, and the torch carried in the hand.

A wetsuit is preferable as drysuits are generally more bulky and may impede progress. The additional risk of catching an inflation valve in a constriction, inflating the suit and trapping the diver against the roof, should be borne in mind. The addition of a direct feed also provides more potential for snagging.

Long fins should be avoided, though small fins are probably better than boots if only that they preclude the temptation to pull on the line. Buoyancy is less of a problem in constricted sumps as the diver is usually in body contact with most of the passage, and a buoyancy compensator should not be taken unless the sump is deep. In shallow constricted sumps, even a weightbelt may be superfluous. If one is worn, perhaps to keep a diver away from an unstable roof in other parts of the dive, then care should be taken not to stack weights, or to allow cylinders to ride up on weights.

A low-volume mask that sits close to the face will stand less chance of getting dislodged as the diver is moving. A short strong knife that sits on the forearm is best. A depth gauge is useful as few constricted sumps give any indication of depth. The gauge face, as with that of the watch and pressure gauge/s, can be covered with clear plastic or inner tube to prevent them from becoming excessively scratched should they come into frequent contact with passage walls, roof or floor. A slate and compass is essential for surveying and maintaining orientation in any sump. A helmet may be an impediment, but some protective head covering, perhaps an additional wetsuit hood, is useful. Hand-held torches, perhaps mounted in holders on forearms, should be as bright as possible.

Search reels are essential even in constricted sumps. If the line is lost in a low bedding area, a search reel will greatly facilitate recovery, or reversal of route through wider sections during the search. To assume that the line will not be far away in a constricted sump is not good practice.

The way in which equipment is worn is important. All equipment should be as close-fitting and as streamlined as possible. Demand valve hoses should lie against the body where they are less liable to snag; they should be able to be reached with ease if they do snag. Any lamp cables should be run under the arm and along the body, rather than up the back where they are out of reach.

The size of cylinder must be equated with the spaciousness of the sump. For very constricted sumps, the smallest size that still allows for a comfortable air margin should be used. Cylinders are better on separate belts as this assists their removal should it be necessary. A Hryndyj or Troll belt makes this manoeuvre virtually impossible. Accessories such as knife, search reel, compass, slate, depth gauge, snoopy loops and the like must all be worn on the arms. Worn anywhere else they might be out of reach when needed, and may just as well be left in your car. Pressure gauges also go on arms, with care being taken when positioning the hoses. Here they can be easily read without having to fumble for them. It is inadvisable to let them dangle, or to wind them round the cylinder valve where they might snag or entangle, or where they might be impossible to reach.

Techniques

The greatest asset to a diver in constricted sumps is familiarisation. The more familiar a diver is with a particular sump, the easier will be his progress through it. Get to know a sump first; time spent on a few familiarisation dives is a good investment on longer explorations.

In initial exploration, a base fed line is useful. It should be tied to the diver's wrist or arm and the attendant should be fully conversant with both the technique and any signals that may be used. A complex sump usually means that for longer dives a diver must lay a line himself.

Good quality line-laying is of critical importance. A constricted sump can sometimes only be negotiated through a particular part of the passage, and the route may zig-zag. There is therefore not the same margin for error as in a spacious sump. If the line drifts about, negotiating the return can be difficult or impossible. The diver should lay the line to one side of the passage and not underneath him, as the latter encourages entanglement. Laying the line down one side of the passage creates a certain uniformity, and makes it easier to follow. Use plenty of belays to keep the line in place, and do not hesitate to use lead weights or other artificial belays if no natural ones are available. In the worst cases, leaving a marker on the line (eg a coloured duct-tape arrow or knotted snoopy loop) as an aide memoir can remind the diver to move right, left, up or down at this point.

Good quality line-laying cannot be overstressed, as it enables constricted sumps to be negotiated safely and efficiently (see the section on line-laying). Line reels with a simple straight handle have been found to be the easiest to use in constricted sumps, especially if visibility is low.

Passage modification is a useful technique. This can be as simple as moving a few boulders, or as extreme as the use of explosives (where permitted) to enlarge sections of extremely constricted cave. Either way, it makes a passage easier to negotiate and should be considered where relevant.

Time spent on such activities should not be seen as unproductive.

If difficult obstacles are encountered during a dive, avoid trying to pass them all in one go. It is better to go half-way through and then return to pass all the obstacles on the second or third attempt than to try in one go and get irretrievably stuck, or to get through and face additional unforeseen problems with an already high stress load and reduced air supply.

When passing a constriction, it is good practice to hold the spare demand valve in one hand as this prevents it being dragged through sediments, and also means that a change-over can be rapidly effected without the valve being trapped under the diver's body. Do not attempt to plough head first through sediment-filled restrictions with only one demand valve. Purge buttons can be jammed open by sediment, and a second valve is essential for this practice. Careful excavation rather than ploughing is a much safer technique. Some sumps were never designed to be passed in the first place.

If difficulties are experienced due to poor visibility, and yet the sump has a good water flow, try alleviating the situation a little by lying still in the water and giving the sump a chance to clear. This is especially relevant when facing upstream if you are all that is disturbing the visibility.

If your air cylinders are coming into frequent contact with the walls or roof or the sump, do check occasionally to see they are not being slowly turned off by such contact. The removal of equipment, especially cylinders, should be done with great care and usually only in an emergency. In a large sump with good visibility, the process is reasonably straightforward. In constricted sumps with poor visibility, it is very much more difficult. Taking them off may be simple, but replacement can present real problems, resulting in all sorts of tangles and taking a very long time. If removal and replacement is anticipated, it should be well-practised beforehand.

It is seldom practical to carry a cylinder for any great distance into a constricted sump, as it impedes progress. As a result, extreme measures, such as the penetration of a sump feet first while dragging the cylinders behind, can only be done over short distances. The image of cave divers removing all their equipment, passing a constriction, refitting it and swimming on is a rather fanciful one. It is seldom done, and then only by experienced divers in situations that occur after some planning and forethought.

Diving constricted sumps is generally done on a solo basis as there is little that can be achieved by having more than one diver in the sump at the same time. The only exception to this is where a stage tank is carried in, or to carry out a separate task. Even so, it is unwise to have two divers in a constricted sump at the same time, especially if there is only one known exit. The additional stress loading may be too great for safe diving. A stand-by diver may be of some use in short exploratory penetrations into constricted sumps, but his actions must be planned carefully beforehand.

As a general rule, the diving of any constricted sump should be done in a methodical and unhurried manner, with a well-practised and well thought-out approach.

FREE-DIVING

FREE-DIVING is the technique of passing a sump without the aid of breathing apparatus. Free-diving is usually undertaken as part of a standard caving trip, when a short flooded section of passage has to be passed, or during exploration of a new system for brief reconnaissance purposes. Whatever the reason for free-diving, good technique and awareness of passage dimensions and cave conditions are important.

Free-diving is an activity in which there is virtually no margin for error, and the right mental attitude is important. Often on arrival at the sump, one of the party may suddenly exhibit reluctance to continue. Such wishes should be respected; the pressure from his peers may endanger the life of the reluctant caver, and careful consideration should be given to any pressures put on the individual to dive.

The degree of difficulty of a free-diveable sump depends on its length, shape and depth. This can alter considerably between high and low water conditions, and by the position of any guideline through the sump. All this must be assessed in the light of the experience of the whole party before deciding whether to undertake the trip.

Equipment

1) *Clothing*: A full wetsuit is virtually essential - a cold diver is more likely to make a mistake or panic. Wetsuits are less likely to snag than are loose-fitting garments, and offer less resistance to motion underwater. They also keep the diver warmer for any return swim. Except for the very shortest of dives, or the warmest of water, a wetsuit hood and facemask should be worn. These are easily transported through a cave (eg down the front of the wetsuit). Without a hood, headaches produced by cold water can be incapacitating. Cold water on the face can trigger a breathing reflex, and this can be dangerous in a high-stress situation. The mask gives additional insulation to the face, and allows the free-diver a degree of visibility underwater. This not only gives a psychological advantage, but may ease route-finding and allow the line condition to be checked. Helmets must be worn. These should be tight-fitting, with a secure chin strap, and allow for adjustment so they can be worn with a wetsuit hood.

2) *Lighting*: Electric caving or diving lights are essential for free-diving. Acetylene lamps should not be used; not only are they impossible to keep alight underwater, but relighting them in confined airspaces will cause toxic fumes. With electric lights, any cables must be routed across the chest, and offer minimum potential for ensnarement. Cap lamps should be a firm fit in their helmet holders. Diving torches should be helmet mounted, hand-held torches being dangerous.

All non-waterproof lights should be dried and cleaned after the dive, especially if it was made in brackish or saltwater.

3) *Weights*: Wetsuits give positive buoyancy, and it may be advisable in certain cases to wear weights. For the longer freedives, the diver should be neutrally buoyant. This degree of buoyancy adjustment should not be worked out at the sump, but before the trip, in open water or a swimming pool.

(Consult the sections on buoyancy control, and weighting for diving.)

Wearing too much weight can be as dangerous as wearing too little. Losing the line in a large sump through being over-or underweight can prove fatal, and the extra effort required to pull the diver through can cause breathlessness. Weights should be on a separate belt from the light, with a quick-release buckle for emergency dumping.

4) *Fins*: Fins are rarely required in a short sump, especially where a good hauling line has been fixed through the sump. Boots allow a greater feel for walls, roof and floor. In longer sumps, or in lake approaches or exits, fins may add a degree of security and give extra propulsion.

Warning

The free-diver must not be attached to the guideline by a lanyard, however short. There are recorded cases of such lanyards snagging on obstructions, and causing near-fatal incidents.

Planning

Before the dive, find out as much as possible about the sump. Look for surveys and descriptions. Talk to people who have dived the sump about any special conditions to look out for. How long and deep is it? How wide and how high? Any special hazards - silting, bends, flakes in the roof? Is the line in good condition? Which side of the passage does it run, and where is belayed on each side? Are weights needed and how much? All this knowledge will help with preparation and should reduce apprehension.

Diving

Ensure that everyone involved has the correct equipment. Before diving, inspect the condition of the line before and where it enters the water. Check the soundness of the belay by pulling on the line. Take up the slack: there should not be too much - ideally about 1m (if more, it could be dangerous). Give a few tugs to test the security of the belay at the other side. A line designed for pulling on should be at least 10mm in diameter to ensure strength and adequate grip. Only the very shortest sumps (maximum length 1m should be attempted without a line. Pulling the line taut should give an indication of the direction of the dive, and may help indicate which side of the line the diver should be on.

Pre-arrange line signals for communicating through the sump. For example, three tugs when through can indicate "I am through, it is safe for the next person to come". The signal should be repeated by the next diver before following. Tugs should be clear, and clearly separate, to ensure no confusion arises with ordinary rope movements during a dive.

Make sure there are no accessories worn that might get entangled or ensnared during the dive. Do not wear SRT gear - racks have been known to trap divers in the shortest of sumps! Tackle-bags should be hauled through separately on a haul rope taken for that purpose. Do not wear them or hand-carry them. Safe free-diving requires both hands should be free to maintain contact with the line.

It may be an advantage, especially in longer sumps, to acclimatise briefly to the water temperature. Dip body and head underwater so that immersion below a rock roof does not come as too much of a shock. Balance can be affected, breathing can be triggered, and apprehension heightened. Get used to the water first, breathe normally, and concentrate before diving.

Try to avoid hyperventilation (rapid deep breathing). In extreme cases, it can induce blackout. Probably, if hyperventilation is required, so is full diving equipment. A few good deep breaths is the most that should be required.

Position in the water is largely a case of individual preference, but most free divers swim on their sides, which side possibly depending on where the line runs. If the diver is positively buoyant, short sumps can be passed along the roof, swimming face up whilst pulling on the line. In large sumps, where there is room to turn round, head-first entry is usual and recommended. In constricted or unknown sumps where there are any doubts about being able to get through, feet-first is strongly recommended.

Base-fed Lines

Feet-first entry is also recommended for diving on a base-fed line where the sump is short and unlined, or previously unexplored. With base-fed line, secure it both to the diver's wrist and to the base controller. The line should be strong enough to enable the diver to be pulled out if required, and should never be allowed to become slack during a dive. Again, rope-pull signals should be agreed by the team before the dive.

Free-diving should always be done in a cool and unhurried manner. A stressed diver who travels hastily is more likely to suffer entanglement and get stuck than one who lets his body feel the passage and respond to events before they become obstructions.

General Hazards

A number of hazards and risks can crop up in free-diving. It is important to be able to anticipate these, and to be familiar with the more common ones:

1) *Sediments*: Some sumps are prone to shingle or silt accumulation (eg Swildon's One on Mendip). This may make the dive harder, or occasionally impossible.

2) *Visibility*: This can vary enormously, but will probably be reduced considerably after the first diver has passed, and on the return trip. (see section on *Visibility*).

3) *Foul air*: Foul air can build up in small airbells to the extent that it has asphyxiated divers before they realised what was happening (as in Langstroth Cave, Yorkshire). If small airbells are used, stay in them as briefly as possible, and do not take a large party. Do not use carbide lamps.

4) *Debris*: In some sumps, debris can accumulate after flooding. In the case of Rowten Pot, Yorkshire, for instance. there is often a liberal spread of broken glass on the floor of the 8m sump, presumably caused by people throwing bottles down the main Rowten shaft. Other caves may contain trees or branches.

5) *Water levels*: Airbells are not always easy to find (or even may not exist) during high water levels. The presence of a jump line into them cannot always be relied on, even if previously present. Where no jump line is present, it is quite possible to miss even large bells if the diver is swimming face down (eg in Notts Pot Extension 10m sump). The belays of free-diving lines may be immersed in the highest water levels, and sumps can be considerably longer. Unless you know the line to be good, do not free-dive in high water conditions.

6) *Sump identification*: Mistaken identity is a real problem - ensure you are at the correct sump!

7) *The line*: The line may have been moved, or if hooked on an object underwater, may take a different, dangerous route in the sump. Be prepared to turn round if such an obstacle is encountered. It is good practise to pull with the back hand and run the front hand along the line to feel for frayed points or breaks. Rough hand-over-hand pulling is not recommended.

8) *Currents*: It is easy to disregard a current if it is running in the diver's favour, but it may cause serious problems on the return. It will obviously be stronger after rainfall, and in constricted sumps.

Conclusion

Training for free-diving can include underwater swimming in swimming baths, or even at a cold water open site. training in full free-diving attire in cold open water will both accustom the diver to cold water and identify buoyancy problems. The diver should attempt easy sumps first and build up to more difficult ones. If a sump is accessible from both sides, it might be beneficial to explore both sides first. Consider the use of a small air tank (if trained in SCUBA use) so that prior examination of a difficult sump can be made.

Whenever possible, free-diving should be done with someone reliable who has dived the sump before. It is their responsibility to instruct others at the sump pool, and to dive first to check that all is well.

Remember - don't dive on the spur of the moment. Plan the dive, train for it, and above all, be prepared to say no.

LONG-DISTANCE SUMP DIVING

IN the last decade, the vast improvements made in the equipment available to the cave diver have had a pronounced effect in breaking down both the practical and psychological barriers encountered in the exploration of long sumps. In the 60s and early 70s, penetrations of over 300m into a single sump were remarkable achievements. Nowadays they are fairly commonplace.

It was in the north of England, with the notable explorations in the long sumps of Boreham Cave, upstream Rowten and Keld Head, that a new attitude towards cave diving emerged. This school of thought felt that the diving of a sump was not just a means to find new dry cave passage, but that the exploration of the underwater passage itself was equally important. There were fewer and fewer constraints to the length of a sump that could be dived (except depth), and several sites offered the potential for long underwater journeys unhindered by having to travel through dry cave passage.

The passage of a lengthy sump requires essentially the same equipment as that of a normal cave dive, with the primary exception that a greater amount of air must be carried as the duration of the dive is considerably longer. In this section therefore, only certain modifications to standard cave diving equipment and techniques applicable to long sumps are dealt with. Deep diving in caves has a section of its own in this manual.

NATURE OF THE UNDERWATER CAVE

1) *Movement*: If the diver is going to be in the water for a long time, he should plan his movements to conserve both energy and air. A slow, methodical swim through the cave to the previous limit of exploration allows him to mentally prepare himself for the task ahead, to become familiar with his equipment again, and to accustom himself to his surroundings. Notice should be taken of the prevailing environmental factors (visibility, current, etc), and the diver should be planning how to make best use of these during the inward swim. In strong flows, it may be advantageous to keep near one wall, or to pull gently along roof or floor, to reduce finning effort.

2) *Presence of usable airspace*: The diver should be aware of all usable airspaces en route, and should take note of the precise location of any found during the course of exploration. Although they may not be entered during a normal dive (if, for example, they lie off the main route, their location being marked by jump-lines rising to marker buoys) their existence is advantageous for the following reasons.

a) they can be used as a refuge in an emergency;
b) they enable the diver to sort out small problems more easily than he could do underwater;
c) they provide points in which two divers can communicate easily;
d) knowledge of them is a psychological advantage in a long cave dive;
e) they may provide safer staging points on a long multi-cylinder dive.

3) *Constrictions*: One of the main enemies of the long distance diver is a section of constricted underwater cave. Such obstacles immediately place a limit on the amount of air and equipment the diver can carry beyond the constriction, they may prevent the use of backpacks in the sump, or they may not be passable with large side-mounted tanks. If near the start of an underwater passage which is likely to be extensive, it is worth considering the careful enlargement of the passage, possibly using explosives, before major dives take place.

4) *Large passages*: Where a passage is large, and visibility is clear, then it may be worth considering the use of diver propulsion vehicles (dealt with in more detail elsewhere), useful in reducing diver effort and therefore air consumption. Enough air should always be held in reserve for an outward swim should the vehicle malfunction deep inside the cave.

EQUIPMENT

Clothing

For long dives in British cave waters, it is undoubtedly better to wear a drysuit. If a wetsuit is to be worn, it must be of very high quality and in very good repair. A wet- dry suit may be suitable, but one of the major hazards of long cold water immersions is hypothermia. It can creep up on a diver without him realising it, will severely affect his decision-making ability, and will reduce his physical ability to cope with his surroundings. Where a drysuit is worn, the underclothing must be of a high thermal standard. Remember that deeper diving can reduce the insulative properties of closed-cell neoprene (in both wet and dry suits) by compressing it, and take this into account.

If a drysuit is worn, be aware that on long dives you may need to urinate. When underwater, the body gets tends to produce more urine (as a way of getting rid of a blood surplus caused by buoyant suspension of the body) and you may find yourself caught out. Commercial divers usually wear the largest nappies they can find, but there are some drysuits with catheter attachments should you desire to experiment with these. The thermal value of a membrane-type drysuit is considerably reduced when fluid is sloshing round inside it.

Whatever you wear, you must be as comfortable as possible. Make sure your fins fit well, and that there are no undue restrictions on blood or air circulation. You are going to be inside your outer shell for some time, and you ought to be as comfortable as you can to reduce physical and mental stress.

Air Supply

If the underwater cave is long and spacious, there is no real limit to the amount of air which may be carried. In some parts of the world, cave divers have designed systems that allow up to six cylinders to be attached to the diver. However, the greater the number and size of the cylinders carried, the greater the drag the diver experiences in the water. This increases both air consumption and fatigue. This problem can be solved by staging the cylinders at given distances into the underwater passage (see section on *Stage diving*). The stage cylinder is used according to the thirds rule, and when one-third of the air is consumed, the cylinder is attached to the line by a karabiner or other method, and the next cylinder is used. The first cylinder is retrieved on the outward swim, when another third is used to exit the cave, always reserving the final third for emergencies. Staging is used:
  (a) to reduce the number of cylinders worn (and therefore the drag);
  (b) to enable a diver to continue beyond a constriction which he would otherwise be unable to pass.
The method of carriage is largely a matter of personal preference, and is dealt with elsewhere.

Weights

A major problem encountered during long duration dives is caused by the concentration of weight applied to the small of the back. This results from wearing two or more cylinders combined with several kilos of lead, as well as battery packs and perhaps a line reel. Air contained in any drysuit worn then tends to collect in the chest and legs, making these areas more buoyant and leaving the diver with an acutely arched back.

This situation can be remedied by redistributing the weight to chest and or legs by one of several methods:

1) *Chest plate*: (figure 42). This is worn over the undersuit, but under a drysuit, where the harness straps are unable to snag. It is most easily made by melting lead to a depth of about 2cm in a frying pan about 30cm in diameter.

2) *Ankle weights*: These can be worn below the drysuit, but can also double as ankle retainers if worn outside, to reduce air migration into the feet of a drysuit. They should be light, less that 0.5 kilo each, otherwise they will cause undue strain on the legs during finning. They can be made either by slotting a small belt weight onto a strap, or by filling hollow climbing tape with lead shot and attaching Fastex clips to the ends.

3) *Shoulder weights*: Standard belt weights can be mounted on shoulder straps of either a backpack or one of the proprietary cave diving harnesses. These are worn outside the suit, and have the advantage that the diver does not have to undress to adjust his weight.

Additionally, individual cylinders can be weighted to distribute the load further, this being a distinct advantage with cylinders which become positive when empty. On long dives where several cylinders may be worn, a diver's trim can be severely affected by having buoyant cylinders on one side, and this should be anticipated before the dive.

Lighting

It is sufficient to mention here that the duration of the cells used in helmet-mounted lighting units may be inadequate for dives of long duration. In this case, it is often satisfactory to use twin caving cells, preferably with halogen bulbs, to reach the previous limit of exploration on the inward dive. The lighting is then supplemented with helmet-mounted torches, or a large primary light, to enable the diver to see more clearly when exploring new ground. Rechargeable caving cells are obviously economically preferable in this respect, but for extremely long dives, prime alkaline cells should be used for the helmet-mounted torches. Note that ordinary caving lamps do not work well in salt-water, and that one of the fully-waterproof caving cells, for example the Speleotechnics unit, should preferably be used when long immersion in water is anticipated.

Finally, it should be remembered that long distance cave diving is very tiring, both physically and mentally. The diver should make sure he is both sufficiently fit and sufficiently experienced to undertake the planned cave dive, and that his equipment is more than adequate for the task to be attempted.

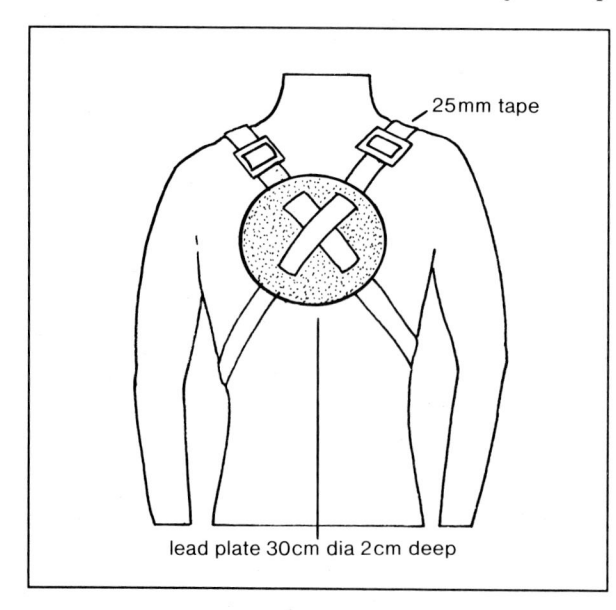

Fig. 42: Fitting a chest weight.

Chapter 4: Safety & Rescue

DIVING ACCIDENTS

SEVERAL attempts have been made to analyse the reasons why accidents have occurred to cave divers. Apart from the well-documented hazards of conventional cave exploration before and after the sump, cave divers have problems of a different nature once underwater. Some of the risks of ordinary caving are absent (there is little chance of injury due to a fall, for example). On the other hand, a lot of new dangers must be taken into account.

A brief analysis of all British cave rescues where divers assisted was made in the first British Sump Rescue Symposium. Interestingly, the main involvement in those incidents (more than all other such rescues put together) was to help ordinary cavers or would-be divers who had become trapped beyond sumps. However, this type of incident is not representative of the main hazards of real cave diving.

It must be remembered that although incidents may be categorised according to their main cause, they often arise as a result of a number of seemingly trivial problems occurring together. The main factor in cave diving accidents has consistently proved to be an inability to follow the line back to base. Equipment failures are a relatively minor cause, usually allied to diver error, where a diver was unfamiliar with the equipment, or misusing it in a place or fashion in which it was unsafe. Such incidents cannot really be regarded as equipment failure, simply as bad workmanship. Several deaths from unknown causes have been recorded, which is most unsatisfactory. Every effort must be made by divers unfortunate enough to be involved in a body recovery to ascertain exactly what went wrong. Only by doing this can cave diving safety continue to improve.

Inexperience is often a factor. Unfortunately, the only real way to gain experience is by going cave diving. Extra precautions by inexperienced divers, such as greater air reserves, overkill on lighting, etc, are strongly advised. So is getting the best gear you can afford; do not learn on second-hand gear that may be unsafe in the cave environment. Remember, however, that the most expensive equipment may not actually perform the best in a given situation. Take time to learn what you need, rather on what looks attractive at the time.

It could be argued that there is no such thing as a training cave dive. In the past, many of our best divers were largely self-taught. Unfortunately, so were many of those who made mistakes and paid for it with their lives. Fortunately, there is now every opportunity for those who are genuinely keen to train properly within the Cave Diving Group.

No record exists of any British cave diver having suffered from decompression sickness actually within a cave. However, with the increase in frequency and duration of deep cave diving, this will inevitably feature in future cave rescue statistics. The problem requires very special treatment, and it is to be hoped that both the divers and cave rescue teams concerned will have made adequate preparations.

Ordinary caving accidents occurring to divers who are exploring dry passages beyond sumps are rare in cave rescue statistics. This is misleading, however, as there are known to have been several fairly serious injuries in such circumstances, where the parties concerned have managed to effect self-rescue. It is vital to adhere to the standard safe practices recommended for dry caving beyond sumps, referred to elsewhere in this manual. In cave rescue terms, any accident location beyond a sump is considered as being very remote.

CAVE RESCUE PROCEDURE

If an accident occurs beyond a sump in a cave, then the actions outlined in the sections *Accident & rescue procedures* and *Solo caving & self-rescue* should be taken.

The nearest cave rescue team should be notified as quickly as possible, by dialling 999 and asking for CAVE RESCUE - not police, fire or ambulance!

Make very certain that the operator is aware that it is a diving emergency, so that the rescue team will be able to call out its rescue diver list immediately. Otherwise there will be an additional (and perhaps fatal) wait while divers are contacted after the rescue team arrives on the scene. Do not attempt to return to the casualty unless absolutely essential until members of the rescue diving team are present: they will need to be briefed on the situation.

CAVE DIVING RESCUE ORGANISATION IN BRITAIN

The CDG has no constitutional role in cave rescues, and if divers volunteer their services to cave rescue teams they do so as individuals. There are 13 separate cave rescue teams in the UK, all of which are represented on the British Cave Rescue Council.

Unfortunately, most active members of CDG prefer to spend their free time involved in cave diving projects, and many are reluctant to train in conventional cave rescue techniques. Another problem is therefore that all divers who are on the call-out lists of their local cave rescue teams are not necessarily competent in basic rescue techniques, even though they may be very skilful divers. A third problems is that cave diving conditions in Britain are often very difficult, with frequently bad visibility, many underwater restrictions, and an increasing number of long and deep dives being made in remote locations. All of our main caving areas have long sumps with extensive dry passages beyond in which conventional caving accidents are a real possibility, and the Group is concerned that there are several of these from which we could probably not rescue a victim alive.

Two meetings, in 1986 and 1988, brought cave divers and cave rescuers together for the first time at national level, to work jointly on the serious problem of how to rescue injured persons through long and difficult sumps. The first meeting served mainly to highlight the main aspects of this serious problem. The second one concentrated on practical aspects of such work, and examined the progress made in tackling the problems previously identified. Undoubtedly, however, the most useful way to make progress is for small

*Fig. 43: Surfacing from a long free-dive
- a sump-passing technique which demands scrupulous control.*

groups of cave divers to approach their local rescue teams and work with them to prepare for major incidents in their own area. There are many problems still to overcome, and the CDG would not consider itself as expert in cave diving rescue techniques.

All rescue work in Britain is the responsibility of the police. Once alerted, they are able to call on a wide variety of resources and specialist teams. In the event of a cave rescue, the police immediately contact a local cave rescue controller who then takes charge of the operation. Where cave divers are involved, an agreement exists that the divers concerned have the final say in what can or cannot be achieved by them.

Victims are never charged for the services of a cave rescue team, but many do make donations of money after being rescued. This, along with help from the police (eg loan of radios, vehicles, etc) and local fund-raising events (a more social aspect of cave rescue team membership) means that cave rescue teams can be self-funding.

Until recently, it was felt that the best way to get an injured victim through a sump (once his injuries had been treated) was to strap him on a stretcher and use a full-face mask and associated SCUBA whilst towing him out. Most cave divers would now agree that it is much better to use splints and local anaesthetics on the affected limb and, if possible, allow the victim to dive out himself, using his own equipment with which he is familiar. He can be supplied with larger cylinders and better lights, etc, and should be attended by other divers, who will give the advantage of better visibility by following him closely through the sump. It is unlikely that the Group will use conventional cave rescue stretchers, but will, depending on the circumstances of the rescue, adopt one or another of the several specialised stretchers or splint combinations now available to suit particular injuries.

In the event of serious facial injuries, or if the victim is a non-diver and unwilling to use demand valves, it may be necessary to resort to a full-face mask. Such equipment might be appropriate if there is a possibility that the victim may lose consciousness on the dive out. Theoretically, such a casualty should never be immersed in water, but certain situations may require action urgently enough to justify the risks involved.

There can be no hard and fast rules about the right way or the wrong way to perform a cave diving rescue. Individual circumstances will demand different specialised methods in each case, and those cave divers who are unfortunate enough to be called to the scene and expected to perform miracles will have to decide which action is most appropriate. They must be prepared to make important decisions on the basis of their own experience and judgement of the particular problems inherent in the situation, and to call for additional help and experience if necessary. They should contemplate the consequences of a poor decision made as a result of not having spent enough time and thought in preparing for such a rescue in their own home area. Underwater cave rescues are at the extremes of cave rescue techniques, and if not handled well may easily kill the victim. All cave divers have a responsibility to become involved in sump rescue techniques as a fundamental part of their training.

CAVING BEYOND SUMPS

ANY caving trip requires care if accidents are to be avoided. The main difference between a caving trip to a sump and one beyond a sump is that in the latter the difficulty of rescue is greatly increased. The subject of through-sump rescue is now beginning to receive attention and the results of a symposium on the subject have been published (*Cave Science*, Volume 14, No 1, 1987). It was, and is, the opinion of most divers and rescue organisation personnel that the rescue of an injured person through a sump would be extremely difficult and in some cases impossible. The following quotation should be engraved on the mind of every cave diver:

"The problems of rescuing an injured person through... a section of flooded cave have yet to be solved. Current techniques of sump rescue will probably prove woefully inadequate in coping with such an eventuality..." (Rob Palmer, Rescue through Long and Deep Sumps, *Cave Science* 14/1. 1987)

It is with this thought in mind that this chapter has been written. The suggested plans and precautions outlined here are designed to reduce the chances of a serious accident happening. They consider the time before a dive, when planning should take place, the necessary equipment gathered and contingency plans laid, and the time spent beyond a sump after it has been passed. The diving of sumps beyond the first is also considered but very little will be said of underwater caving as this is treated in the rest of the manual. Since accidents can happen, even to those taking the greatest of care, a brief account of what to do should something go wrong is also given.

PLANNING & EQUIPMENT

The safety and success of a caving trip depend very much on the type and condition of equipment used. It must be suitable for the job it is asked to do and must be in the best of condition. The information provided below is of a general nature and you may need additional equipment for a particular sort of exploration. Equally important is the planning carried out before the trip is undertaken and it is not advisable to undertake a serious trip (and this includes any trip beyond sumps) without some careful planning.

Planning

You should take note of all the following when planning a trip: weather conditions, strength of party, length of time underground, and whether your objectives are realistic. Be sure to tell someone where you are going, what time you expect to return (allowing some extra time for cock-ups and inefficiency) and what to do if you do not return. Remember to inform that person when you do get out. If you are caving during the summer months (particularly July and August) bear in mind that many of the divers in the local rescue team may well be away on expeditions.

Equipment
It is essential to wear the proper equipment for beyond-sump exploration. Study the sections on equipment in this volume, and bear them well in mind when planning your trip.

Clothing
Usually, the only suitable clothing both for diving and dry caving is a wetsuit. Alternatively, there may be situations where the use of a diving drysuit (for sumps), exchanged for a normal caving oversuit (for dry passages), is more suitable.

Footwear
It is essential that rugged footwear is used in dry passages; it is both unpleasant and unsafe to cave in wet-suit socks! The best way of carrying footwear is to wear it, so it is advisable to buy a pair of fins which will fit over your boots or wellingtons. This is now common practice. Whatever method is chosen, boots or wellingtons should be used and not pumps or training shoes as these are not sufficiently supportive.

Lights
Two or more lights should always be carried. The best combination is an accumulator of some sort (eg lead-acid, NiCad or FX2 with the cells protected against the ingress of water) that will provide ten or more hours of primary light, and at least two diving torches. Small light torches can be left on the helmet in dry passages without discomfort, whereas larger torches tend to be rather heavy when used out of water. Ensure that all batteries are fully charged if not new. Some of the less bright torches such as the Aquaflash have very long durations when used with 4Ah rechargeable NiCad cells, so that a waist-mounted caving lamp becomes unnecessary.

Helmets
The only really reliable helmets for dry caving are climbing or purpose-designed caving helmets. However, these have certain disadvantages for diving so canoeing or skateboarding helmets have tended to be used. It is often not feasible to carry a helmet through a sump so the diver foregoes the security of a proper caving helmet. This means the dangers associated with falling and from loose boulders must be minimised (see below). In caves where pitches or loose boulders are encountered before or after the dive it is advisable to wear an appropriate caving helmet which can then be exchanged for a specialist diving helmet.

Food
Food should always be carried. For most trips a number of chocolate bars will suffice but for longer or more strenuous trips self-heating cans or the use of lightweight stoves to provide warm and substantial meals should be considered.

Safety Items
A caver is not fully equipped without some safety and emergency items. The most important is a survival bag; this can be kept in the top of the helmet.

Once the bag has been used, replace it. Other items required are spare lights (divers will should have these anyway) and a first-aid kit. Details are given in the appendix of three personal first-aid and emergency kits. The Aquaflash kit is the most suitable for diving since it is waterproof, but the others can easily be packed into waterproof containers and can be more comprehensive.

Other Items

A whistle, for signalling on pitches and attracting the attention of a rescue team should rescue be needed, will prove useful, as will a pear-shaped steel Italian Hitch karabiner. This versatile device is excellent for safe lifelining.

Tackle

Any caving tackle required for the exploration of the cave (eg electron ladders, ropes and scaling poles) must be in good condition. If tackle is to be left in the cave for an extended period it is best to use ropes rather than ladders as ropes do not rust and weaken. Despite the opinions of many caving club tackle masters, the use of throw-away tackle for leaving beyond sumps is very unwise. When it is anticipated that tackle will remain beyond sumps for more than a few weeks, metal components will need to be protected from corrosion

Fig. 44: Beyond the sump - back to basic caving techniques.

Safety & rescue

(eg by greasing karabiners, dipping ladders in lanolin or diesel, etc). In certain cases, permanently fixed iron ladders have been used beyond sumps.

Dekitting & Storing of Diving Gear

Once the sump has been passed, the diving gear (which is heavy and cumbersome) must be removed and placed in a safe place. The first priority is to safeguard the air supply by turning it off but the valves should remain pressurised to stop the ingress of mud and to reduce the risk of blowing an O-ring when preparing for the return dive.

The next job is to find a suitable place for stowing the gear. Whenever possible this should be above flood level so that nothing is washed away and you can get back to the equipment if the water should rise. The kit dump should also be free of loose rocks which could fall on the delicate equipment. ("he dekitted and started climbing. About ten feet up, a large portion of the wall fell off onto his gear." Jingle Pot, *CDG NL* 40:20, 1976). A level floor helps to stop the bottles rolling around. If there is any chance of the gear getting washed away, or of it falling, a bolt or similar device should be installed and everything fastened to it. Dekitting should preferably be carried out slowly and methodically with gear being removed in the reverse order in to which it was donned. Once all the gear has been removed and placed in its storage place the weight belt (if worn separately) should be placed on top of everything else. Be particularly careful with the mask as it is easily broken. The example set by two cavers in Wookey Hole is not to be encouraged: "Panting furiously... they stripped off their gear and let if fall willy nilly to the floor..."! (*CDG NL* 39:23, 1976).

MOVING THROUGH THE CAVE & DEALING WITH OBSTACLES

Apart from flooding, fractures sustained by falling and by boulder falls are the most common cause of rescue. The way that you move through the cave, and the care you take (or don't!) will determine whether or not you will get injured and require a rescue team to get you out.

A constant watch for danger and slow, methodical progress will reduce the chances of an accident. In a new passage it is all too easy to go Hell for leather (understandably so) but caution should always be observed.

Free Climbs

If there is the slightest possibility of someone falling off a free climb, it should be equipped with at least a good handline. This should be belayed well back from the edge, especially where the top of the climb is a convex slope. If an upward free-climb is necessary be sure to protect it properly and be very cautious with the handholds, which may be loose, and with any boulders encountered. Remember that not everyone has a high standard of climbing ability so, if in doubt, always install that handline.

Pitches

Pitches require great care anywhere. Make sure that the tackle is sound and properly belayed. If ladders are used to descend pitches a lifeline, preferably operated with an Italian Hitch or similar device, must always be used.

Scaling Avens

Be much more careful than usual; do not do anything risky. Seriously consider the consequences of a fall, and be over-generous on climbing protection.

Boulder Chokes

Boulder chokes are the most dangerous of all caving obstacles. Always think of the return journey and the difficulty of rescue. If you are in any doubt, stay out.

Diving Another Sump

Many caves contain more than one sump. After the first has been passed and any dry passages have been explored the time will come when a dive in the second one will be proposed. Logistical problems will usually dictate that the first dive in the new sump will be carried out by one diver with the support of others who have passed the first but do not intend to enter any subsequent sumps.

There are two primary considerations for such operations: the total amount of air required and the number of bottles that contain it. The second of these requires considerable thought.

On a two-man trip through a short sump where both divers are using single sets it may be tempting to use both sets to put a diver in the second sump thereby cutting down on the amount of gear carried. This is, however, an unwise strategy because if the exploring diver does not return, his companion is stranded. This method has, however, been used! No matter which way the air supply is organised (and this will depend on numerous factors) the divers who are not entering the second sump should retain sufficient air in a sufficient number of bottles to ensure a safe exit from the cave. It is not good practise, anyway, to pass a sump without a reserve air supply.

Digging and Blasting

Digging: Care and forethought are always required when you are digging, especially for example, if boulders or unconsolidated deposits are involved. As with all other activities beyond sumps keep the difficulty of rescue in mind and be prepared to give up if the going gets too dangerous.

Blasting: The use of explosive charges is always very dangerous, for obvious reasons. Explosives should only be considered as a last resort, and only by those who are trained in their use. When used beyond a sump there are additional hazards to those normally encountered. Always check the draught before banging. Will the fumes be blown to your dekitting site - or will the passage be filled with fumes? If between two sumps is there sufficient passage for you to hide from the shock wave?

Anyone who is considering using explosives in a cave should read the two articles by Williams and Williams (see bibliography) where the potential dangers are graphically described, and the section on blasting in *British Caving and Practice*.

EXTRA PLANNING & PRECAUTIONS FOR PASSAGES BEYOND LONG SUMPS

For anyone who is injured or otherwise incapacitated in a cave, the greatest enemy is time. It takes time for a message to be sent out of the cave, time for the rescue to be organised, time for the rescuers to get themselves and their equipment to the casualty and the longest time of all to transport the casualty out of the cave.

For someone who has suffered an accident in an extensive series of passages beyond a long or deep sump this time factor can be very great. During the period of waiting the casualty will get cold, may be losing blood and be in shock. To survive it is essential that heat is conserved, that food is available for energy and that first-aid supplies are at hand to control bleeding, immobilise fractures, etc. This section describes some of the actions and equipment that can increase the chances of survival.

In caves such as Notts Pot, Daren Cilau, and others where numerous exploratory trips are being carried out, it makes very good sense to place a permanent rescue dump in a dry passage. If it is not considered necessary to install a large and permanent rescue dump divers should certainly carry one of the smaller emergency kits (see this section's Appendix I).

Some means of communication should also be considered since this will greatly reduce the time required for messages to be passed. It will, however, require a base party. The best possible device is the Molefone but this is not generally available. Telephones should not be too difficult to arrange and are well worth considering, especially as the necessary cable could be laid in place of (or in parallel with) the diving line and the phones themselves left in position for the duration of the exploration. (Bob Mackin deals in detail with through-sump communication in *Cave Science*, Vol 14 No 1.)

IF SOMETHING GOES WRONG

Accidents do happen, and planning for such an eventuality is an integral and essential part of any trip organisation. Caving safety and survival is a complex subject and it cannot be covered in depth here. Several of the articles included in the bibliography discuss the subject well and should be consulted by any serious caver. Elsewhere in this manual there are details of various emergency procedures which can be followed and it is important that these are read in conjunction with this chapter. A thorough knowledge of first-aid is necessary in dealing with injured persons and anyone who regularly participates in front-end caving should be trained in it. The bibliography contains a list of useful books and articles which should be consulted and there are addresses of first-aid organisations.

Survival of all the party in the event of anything going wrong requires an appropriate set of responses. First is the *immediate response*, where any further danger is assessed and if possible eliminated. Second is the *survival response*, which will only be required in the event of an enforced stay in the cave.

Immediate Response

Priorities for action in the case of an accident or other incident. (NB: 4 may follow 1 if there are sufficient people in the party.)
1) *STOP AND ASSESS THE SITUATION*
2) Possibility of further danger: position of safety.
3) Airway, breathing, circulation and other first-aid.
4) Message out of cave.

Whatever it is that has gone wrong (whether a flood trapping you beyond the sump, an injury to one of your party, or some other incident) you should put into action the *immediate response*. First, *stop and assess the situation* (1). This should be done as rapidly as possible but not be so hurriedly as to overlook important points. Take note of what has happened, how it happened, and of any further consequences. This information could be highly important especially if someone is injured, trapped by boulders, or the cave is flooding. Once you are in possession of this information you should act quickly (but unhurriedly and without panic) to remove or avert further danger, either to the whole party or to the injured individual (2). The specific response here will depend on what it is that has gone wrong. With a single injured or trapped individual you should do what you can to remove him to a safe place but take the greatest possible care to avoid further injury, *especially if a spinal injury is suspected*. Only move the victim if it is necessary, eg to get out of water or away from further rockfall. In case of a flood threatening the whole party (and assuming all to be fit and uninjured) it will be necessary to find a refuge above flood level where you can wait for the water to fall.

Any injuries will require first-aid (3), noting the priorities for the preservation of life:
Airway - ensure a clear airway, especially in an unconscious person
Breathing - give exhaled air resuscitation (EAR) if the person is not breathing
Circulation - if the heart is not beating begin external cardiac compression (ECC), and apply direct pressure to any open wound to control bleeding.

No further details of first-aid will be given here; see the relevant chapter in this manual, read the articles given in the bibliography and attend a first-aid course.

If the problem has been solved, or the injury is minor, you should attempt to leave the cave immediately, taking the greatest care of the casualty and providing support at all times. If it is not at all possible for the casualty to leave the cave and a rescue party is needed you should now send a message out of the cave, sending two people if they can be spared (4). Ensure that all details are given to the rescue controllers, write the details down on site before the messenger departs. If the party is large enough for two more people to be spared, a second message can be sent after the situation has been assessed. This is preferable if it can be done because of the time it will save.

Survival Response

If an enforced stay in the cave is necessary either because of flooding or because the casualty is too ill be be moved the survival response should be initiated:

1) Lights   4) Location
2) Protection 5) Water
3) Food

There are five priorities for survival and they should be tackled in order. Priority number one is to safeguard your supply of light; without it you are completely helpless (1). You should be carrying at least two lights each but it makes sense to use as little as possible. Use candles and the dip-beam of the electric. If you are sitting out a flood, turn off all lights unless you are watching an injured person. In this case, keep at least one light on so that you can monitor any changes in condition.

The second most important response is to protect the party from heat loss; hypothermia is very likely to set in during a prolonged wait and is an insidious and dangerous condition (2). The polythene (or other survival) bag and candles should enable you to keep warm for quite some time. Use any ropes, tackle bags etc, to protect you from the ground and wear your diving hood and gloves if you can get at them.

Eat small amounts of food at regular intervals because generating body heat requires energy (3), but be careful to make the supply of food last. If you are sitting in an obscure side-passage write a message (4) on a piece of plastic paper (or your diving-slate) and leave it where the rescue team will see it. To prevent thirst, and to aid the body in its metabolism of the food you have eaten, you should take small sips of water now and again (5) rather than a lot of cold water at one go - this would cool the body core rapidly, not advisable when trying to avoid hypothermia.

Finally, it cannot be stressed too strongly that this is merely an introduction to caving survival; please read the articles given in the bibliography and heed the advice.

CONCLUSION

British caving has now reached the stage where diving is one of the most common ways of exploring new passages and this is reflected in the great increase in the number of man-dives a year over the last ten years. Recently, British divers have been pushing sumps in France, Spain and elsewhere, and their efforts have been rewarded with some extensive finds. We have now reached the stage where many beyond-sump passages are being extensively and intensively explored with the use of digging, blasting, aven-climbing and further diving. In terms of intensity of activity, cave diving has now reached the stage that ordinary caving reached in the early 1960s.

Between 1960 and the late '80s the caving population has grown enormously and so has the number of people requiring a rescue team to extricate them. If this trend is continued by those who cave and push beyond sumps we are likely to see a great increase in the number of serious, extended rescues and quite probably in the number of fatalities. The only way in which the accident rate in ordinary caving can be reduced, and the likely increase in accidents beyond sumps forestalled, is by encouraging a safer approach to caving in general.

This chapter has attempted to outline some ways of reducing the chances of an accident, and of surviving if one does occur; at the end of the day, however, it is up to you. *PLAN* the trip; *EQUIP* yourself adequately; *MOVE* through the cave slowly and methodically with a constant eye for danger; *RIG* any verticals with ropes or ladders with lifelines and *BE PREPARED IN ADVANCE* for something going wrong.

CHAPTER APPENDIX I:
CONTENTS OF EMERGENCY KITS

A) Major Emergency Dump
First-aid kit
    1l saline plus giving set
    Temgesic (powerful pain killer)
    Codeine (less powerful pain killer)
    Amoxyl (penicillin-based antibiotic for use with open wounds)
    Indigestion tablets
    3 Suture sets
    Assorted bandages (including several triangular)
    Assorted waterproof plasters
    Cotton wool swabs
    Hypodermic needle (for cleaning dirt out of wounds)
    Inflatable splints (upper and lower limb)
    Splint bandages
    Airway
    Eye anaesthetic
    Subnormal (rectal) thermometer
    Disposable gloves
    Neoprene mitten (for splinted fingers)
    Warm packs (for use in cases of hypothermia)
    1 pair scissors
    1 pair forceps
    Waterproof notebook and pencil.
    (All contained in two rocket tubes)

Survival kit
    2 large heavy-duty survival bags
    Karrimat or similar
    Large nylon sheet plus poles and string (for use as shelter)
    Fibre-pile sleeping bag
    4 balaclavas (30% heat lost through head!)
    4 pairs gloves
    Gas stove plus cartridges
    2 boxes waterproofed matches plus striker
    Pan
    Carbide lamp(s) plus carbide and prickers
    Food - 6 self-heating cans, assorted tinned food, chocolate and
      high- energy sweets
    Candles

Repair kit
    2 adjustable spanners
    Assorted O-rings
    Blanking-off caps
    Small tube silicone grease
    Spare face mask
    Plus full contents list on plastic paper

B) Basic Personal Kit
First-aid
- 2 Melolin 5 x 5cm wound dressings
- 2 Melolin 10 x 10cm wound dressings
- 20 Assorted waterproof plasters
- 1 Triangular bandage
- 1 Crepe bandage
- 1 Medium plain lint dressing
- 1 Nylon stretch bandage
- 2 Packets Steristrips (wound closures)
- 2 Mediprep disposable swabs (cleaning wounds)
- 1 Subnormal (rectal) thermometer
- 1 pair scissors
- 2 Safety pins
- 2 warm packs (for use in cases of hypothermia)
- 20 Paracetamol tablets
- Nasal decongestant spray

Lights
- 1 6ins candle
- 2 6ins (12-hour) Cyalume light sticks
- Spare batteries
- 1 carton waterproof matches plus striker
- 1 spare bulb

Other items
- 4 pieces A6 plastic paper
- 1 pencil, sharpened both ends
- 1 pack glucose tablets
- 1 pack food tablets
- Plus contents list on plastic paper

Weight 900g (2lbs). Cost around £20. Packed in medium (200 x 110mm) BDH drum. This kit was designed for ordinary caving. It may need slight modification for use beyond sumps (eg by including some valve spares and spanners) and will need packing in a watertight, pressure-proof container.

C) Small Personal Kit
First aid
- 2 Melolin 5 x 5cm wound dressings
- 10 waterproof plasters
- 1 large plain lint dressing
- 1 nylon bandage
- 2 packets Steristrips (wound closures)
- 2 Mediprep disposable swabs (cleaning wounds)
- 1 roll zinc oxide plaster
- Nasal decongestant spray

Light
- 1 4ins candle
- 2 4ins Cyalume light sticks
- 1 carton waterproofed matches plus striker
- A spare bulb

Other items
>4 pieces A6 plastic paper
>1 pencil (sharpened both ends)
>Plus contents list on plastic paper

Weight 225g (0.5lb). Cost around £10. Packed into small (145 x 80mm) BDH drum. This kit was designed for ordinary caving. It may need modification for use beyond sumps.

D) Diver's Personal Emergency & Spares Kit
First-aid
>Temgesic (powerful pain killer)
>Codeine (less powerful pain killer)
>Amoxyl (penicillin-based antibiotic)
>Suture set
>Hypodermic needle (for cleaning wounds)
>Eye anaesthetic
>1 pair scissors
>1 pair forceps
>1ins gauze bandages
>Nasal decongestant spray

Repair kit
>Screwdriver
>2 small adjustable spanners
>Allen keys
>Blanking-off cap
>O-rings
>Tube silicone grease
>Packed into watertight torch with batteries & reflector removed.

CHAPTER APPENDIX II:

ADDRESSES OF FIRST-AID ORGANISATIONS

The following organisations run first-aid courses for the general public in Britain. They have local branches throughout the country and the address of your nearest branch can be obtained from the head offices at the addresses given.

St John Ambulance Association,
1 Grosvenor Crescent,
LONDON SW1X 7EF.
Tel: 01-235-5231.

British Red Cross Society,
9 Grosvenor Crescent,
LONDON SW1X 7EJ.
Tel: 01-235-5454.

St Andrew's Ambulance Association,
Milton Street,
GLASGOW.
Tel: 041-332-4031.

SOLO CAVING & SELF-RESCUE

SOLO CAVING

IN the past, some of the more notable explorations beyond sumps have been made by CDG members who, for various reasons, chose to cave on their own. Although this is perhaps inevitable during initial solo explorations when a sump is first passed, it is less inevitable on successive trips.

It has been argued that if a diver is competent to operate safely enough alone underwater, it must also be safe for him cave alone beyond the sump. This is simply not true. Although there are many British sumps in which a solo diver is undoubtedly safer than if accompanied, safety in numbers definitely applies in dry passages at the far side. The lone diver in the caving environment, with its very different hazards, is truly out on a limb. For reasons of safety, solo caving beyond sumps cannot be recommended, except in certain special circumstances. Those contemplating such solo explorations should think seriously about the potential dangers involved, and be more than adequately prepared for all eventualities.

SELF-RESCUE

It is assumed that all cave divers are totally independent whilst underwater - the complete opposite of normal open-water diving philosophy. Self-rescue in an underwater emergency is fundamental to standard cave diving practice. This section deals mainly with the problems of divers who are injured or stranded in dry passages beyond sumps.

One possible cause of stranding is an inadequate supply of air for the return journey, due to cylinder leakage or equipment failure. It may be possible to deal with this by exchanging cylinders between members of a party, should more than one diver be present. Otherwise, air can be decanted into depleted cylinders by connecting a high-pressure hose between two suitable first stages. This is not possible unless a small tool kit is carried containing suitable spanners, allen keys or screwdriver, and fittings are compatible or an adapter is available. Equipment failure, for whatever reason, may strand a diver beyond a sump. In a group, the relevant item can be borrowed from another diver after use if sufficient air supplies allow a third diver to ferry it back in through the sump. With longer dives, this becomes impractical, so it is worth considering taking certain vulnerable but important items as group spares, such as an extra facemask. Solo divers should take these as standard.

A solo diver, faced with a broken valve and no suitable airspace in which to exchange demand valves from one tank to another on the return swim, is undoubtedly better staying where he is and waiting for outside assistance. In an extreme situation, it is possible to exchange demand valves underwater from one tank to the other, but for obvious reasons this is not a recommended practice. It can be done with relative ease if three tanks are carried and there are two operable valves, but if only two tanks and one valve are available, then the tank valves must be close and accessible, and the full tank must not have the broken valve attached. Carrying the tanks strapped together and held in front of the diver is probably better than wearing them on the sides if such an underwater change-over is envisaged, but things will have to be pretty desperate to consider such a move. Changing regulators underwater does the regulator itself no long-term harm if serviced afterwards, but is likely to damage the pressure gauge. The regulator will work quite normally once any initial water has been purged from the system.

Apart from equipment problems, conventional caving accidents are a possibility beyond sumps. A diver may, for example, fall and sustain injuries and require assistance on the outward journey. Even though these injuries may be serious, the victim often has a greater chance of surviving in many situations if a self-rescue is attempted by the party. A cave rescue team will take quite some time to respond fully to a diving incident, and the condition of the casualty may deteriorate considerably during the wait, through cold, stress and physical decline. If a particular area of remote cave is to be frequently visited by the same group of divers, one of the first things they should take through and leave is an emergency medical kit. Self-rescue may then be considerably safer and a more viable option.

Self-rescue must be considered by the divers present at the time of the incident, and will obviously depend on several factors, such as the condition of the casualty and the distance and complexity of the journey to the cave entrance. If possible, one member of the team should immediately leave to alert the rescue team. It is essential to have support on site as quickly as possible, even if evacuation of the casualty has already begun.

Many cave rescue divers do not live in to main caving areas, and there is likely to be a long delay before they arrive at the scene. Whatever the victim's injuries are, they will be compounded by hypothermia, which will rapidly render him unable to help himself to any real degree as he will be unable to generate sufficient body heat without movement. If self-rescue is an option (precluded only by serious spinal or head injury or an unconscious victim) it must start quickly. Splinted limbs will be supported by the water, and makeshift splints can be made from all kinds of diving equipment - knives, fins, the other leg, or the body. Caver's belay belts make good straps, or emergency tourniquets. A diver is best evacuated using his own equipment, preferably having been equipped with the fullest cylinders available from among the party. (It is useful if members of a party have familiarised themselves with other divers' equipment before the dive.)

The decision as to whether the victim should be self-propelled or towed will depend on many variables, but if the first is the choice, thought should be given to the position of the casualty within the group. Visibility is one consideration - the better the visibility for the casualty, the easier it will be for him. If the sump is large enough, he should be accompanied by another diver swimming alongside to assist him. It may be that he will need help exiting from the water at the far side of one or more of the sumps, and in a constricted sump a central position within the group might be best in some circumstances.

If he is to be towed, then his equipment should be as streamlined as possible, to reduce the potential for snagging. The minimum for a safe exit should be worn. Where side-by-side manoeuvring is impossible, it may be worth considering linking him by a long sling beneath the shoulders, or to the wrists, to another diver in front, if his condition might deteriorate enough underwater for him to need towing.

The success of an attempted self-rescue will depend very much on the use of intelligence, experience and commonsense, and on having prepared for such an eventuality (buddy checks on equipment, carrying emergency packs, first-aid training, etc). If the normal practices of the diving team include good line laying, use of appropriate gear, plentiful reserves of air and lights, then the survival chances of a casualty will be greatly improved.

Cave rescue teams are no panacea - there are many frequently visited parts of caves beyond sumps from which non-self-rescue would be virtually impossible, or would probably result in the death of the victim. The best advice is to always assume that you will have to get yourself out of any predicament in which you are unfortunate enough to be stranded. If you are not prepared for this, then you should probably not be there at all.

Fig. 45: A hand-held light illuminates the entrance - and the way on beckons to the probing cave diver.

FIRST AID BEYOND LONG SUMPS

AS the length of explorable passage beyond extensive sumps increases the chances of a significant accident occurring must also increase. This observation has been confirmed already by a major accident in a Yorkshire cave and a less serious accident in Wookey Hole. Solo explorers have no safety margins at all and must, obviously, be totally self-reliant. The following lines are for those working in teams.

First aid beyond sumps should be aimed at achieving these goals:

1) Treatment of injury sufficient to allow the diver to leave the cave safely.

or

2) Treatment of injury sufficient to allow the dive to pass the sump prior to receiving further help.

or

3) Treatment of any injury resulting in a stabilisation of the victim's condition, hence allowing time for further help to be brought to the victim.

Let us consider these goals in relation to injuries likely to be sustained. Major injuries are likely to be caused by falls or crushing by boulders.

Head Injury Causing Loss of Consciousness

This has got to be top of the list. Loss of consciousness may be temporary or prolonged. In all cases follow these rules:

a) Check the victim is breathing.

b) Check the victim's pulse.

c) Place the victim in the recovery position and keep him there until he regains consciousness.

If the victim vomits make sure his airway is clear, and return him to the recovery position. Make observations on:

a) Length of time unconscious.

b) Depth of unconsciousness (ie deep coma; responding to pain; rousable but drowsy or alert).

c) Pupils of the eye - do they contract when light is shone in them?

A victim who remains in a deep coma for any length of time and whose pupils start to expand is likely to have a severe and life threatening injury to which prompt hospitalisation is the only answer.

Lesser degrees of head injury may allow the victim to recover consciousness. However, the victim may be confused, have forgotten the accident, and also have a very defective short-term memory. Evacuation through a sump should be delayed for as long as possible to allow the victim's behaviour to be observed. A deep sump (over, say, 9m could prove further detrimental to brain function - with, in particular, fits - due to increased partial pressure of oxygen. Rarely, some sufferers from head injury may look well for a while before internal bleeding causes a further deterioration.

Severe Bleeding

This may be external, from a deep cut, or internal, from a rupture or tearing of abdominal organs such as the spleen or liver, or as a result of fracture of the thighbone.

Rapid and severe bleeding results in the signs of shock. These are:
a) Rapid and increasingly weak pulse.
b) Rapid and deep breathing.
c) Loss of colour in the victim.
d) Possible confusion and agitation in the victim.
e) Cold extremities.
f) The victim may complain of thirst.

These are the results of the body's attempt to make the best of the remaining blood in circulation.

With external bleeding, immediately apply pressure to the site where the blood is emerging. Arterial blood loss (blood coming out in spurts) can be rapid, so move quickly. Bleeding from veins occurs as a steady ooze, and if this from a leg it can be halted rapidly by raising the leg.

With most bleeds, firm pressure for a time may allow the cut ends of the blood vessels to seal over and the victim to be moved. However, physical activity may start the bleeding again so be cautious.

Tourniquets, applied to a limb above the site of bleeding, are dangerous if left on too long because tissues will die if deprived of a blood supply. However, in an emergency, to get a diver through a sump, they could be useful. The affected limb would be useless but an injured diver could pull himself along a line one-handed if desperate. Further blood loss underwater would be avoided.

Remember to allow a shocked victim to stabilise before moving him. Even after significant blood loss the victim may improve as fluid is moved around the body to replace that loss. Giving the victim plenty to drink, *if* there is no evidence of internal bleeding, will help.

Drowning

This is the only likely emergency in which cardio pulmonary resuscitation (CPR) would be used with a fair chance of success. CPR means using artificial respiration and heart massage to get the heart and breathing going again.

I do not here want to go into the details of mouth to mouth respiration or heart massage; any trained diver should have learnt them before getting near the water. The only comment I would make is that efforts should be prolonged before one should think about giving up.

Some people have wondered if the use of a demand valve second stage and its purge button could be used to force air into the lungs. The ideas seems good and might be something to consider in certain situations. Remember that gas blown in like this may over-inflate the lung and that if it goes into the stomach it could encourage vomiting.

Broken Bones

Broken bones are painful and prevent useful movement of the limb beyond which they occur. In the case of the pelvis or femur significant blood loss can occur. To get a casualty out of a cave, splint the affected limb with whatever materials are to hand. For example, belts, etc, can be used to strap legs together or to provide slings for arms. Immobilising broken bones will reduce pain and increase the victim's morale.

Broken ribs may cause pain in deep breathing and if several are broken may severely affect the breathing by moving the "wrong way" with breathing. They can also puncture the lung causing it to collapse (pneumotherax). Severe chest injuries would be a nightmare for the diver and would pose problems for would-be rescuers.

Spinal Injuries

The word spinal refers to the spinal cord, not the backbone - that can be hurt without damage to the spinal cord. Suspect such injuries after an awkward fall if the victim has:
- a) Pain in a band around the body.
- b) Pins and needles below a certain level.
- c) Numbness below a certain level.
- d) Inability to move legs (or, in neck injuries, arms as well).
- e) Inability to pass urine.

Check by asking the victim about sensation and movement. Back pain in itself is not indicative of severe injury.

Decompression Sickness

This may occur even if tables have been adhered to. Consider the possibility if the victim becomes unwell shortly after surfacing. Symptoms may include skin irritation or rash, odd patches of pins and needles or symptoms similar to those seen with a spinal cord injury. The victim may become irritable or irrational. Management will depend on the severity of symptoms but oxygen if available is helpful. I will assume that in most serious deep dives communication with the outside is present and therefore expert advice can be sought. Underground, make sure the victim is kept warm and given plenty to drink.

Recent medical research indicates that people with even tiny holes between the left and right atria (chambers) of the heart are predisposed to decompression sickness, and that a large number of diving bends victims have such holes. You may have one and not realise it. Should decompression symptoms appear even after a cave dive conducted well within diving tables, treat them as indicating a potential bend.

FIRST AID DUMPS

On the far side of some sumps sophisticated first aid kits have been set up, and this procedure could be extended to all caves containing significant lengths of passage beyond long sumps. Certainly the materials can be left in sealed containers for long periods without deterioration, rather like food dumps. Doctors will always disagree on the precise contents of a first aid kit. Here is one suggestion for a kit which could be used by somebody with a little bit of training.

Gauze pads for compression of bleeds.
Elastocrepe bandages for holding dressings in place.
Triangular bandages for arm slings.

Strong painkiller, eg Temgesic (now a controlled drug in the UK).
Mild painkiller, eg Paracetamol or Ibuprofen.
Local anaesthetic, eg 1% lignocaine which can be injected round deep cuts to allow stitching.
Stitching material, eg silk with a built-in needle to allow deep wounds to be closed.
Antibiotics for deep or very dirty wounds if rescue is going to be prolonged.
Dentanurse kit for tooth injury.
Bags of warming gel.
Oropharyngeal airway for unconscious patients.
Lightweight splinting material which can now store indefinitely.
Sets for giving intravenous fluids.
Intravenous fluids, eg saline, plasma expanders (increase blood volume in shock).

SUMP RESCUE APPARATUS

Sump rescue apparatus should be considered when there is:
1) A deeply unconscious victim.
2) Strong evidence of spinal injury.
3) Multiple injuries where victim is unable to move independently or to be towed.

Fig. 46: A volunteer is prepared carefully for a cave rescue practice through Wookey Hole's sumps.

THERAPEUTIC RECOMPRESSION

THERAPEUTIC recompression is undertaken to treat the untoward effects of rapid or inadequate decompression. These are pulmonary barotrauma with arterial gas embolism (AGE), decompression sickness (DCS) and miscellaneous forms of barotrauma resulting from gas expansion in body cavities such as the gut or abdomen.

The only satisfactory way of treating dysbarism (a catch-all term for the above symptoms) is by recompressing the victim until relief of the symptoms is obtained, and then slowly decompressing him. Medical treatment by drugs, intravenous fluids or pure oxygen at atmospheric pressure is generally unsatisfactory. Recompression facilities are few and far between, and it therefore important to know their location and the best method of summoning assistance. In the last few years, various doctors involved in treating diving injuries have been trying to rationalise the system and is hoped that in the not-too-distant future anybody in Britain will be able to get advice and referral for treatment by making a 999 emergency call.

Firstly, it it worth stating that the likelihood of some forms of dysbarism occurring after a standard British cave dive is remote. Pulmonary barotrauma is virtually always associated with rapid and uncontrolled ascent, a luxury which cave divers rarely achieve in emergencies! Likewise, it is becoming clear that, in general terms, DCS seems to be linked to the speed of ascent. Most dives in this country follow an inclined profile, resulting in relatively slow ascents. However, we cannot afford to be complacent.

REQUIREMENTS FOR RECOMPRESSION

Equipment

A hyperbaric (pressure) chamber is obviously the first essential. Chambers vary in size from the coffin-sized portable one-man chamber to the huge saturation complexes capable of supporting several individuals under pressure for weeks at a time. A practical and effective chamber for therapeutic recompression should accommodate two individuals comfortably and have a lock-out and -in airlock to enable support personnel to change and supplies to be passed through. It needs to be in an environment where the temperature can be reasonably well-controlled. It should be capable of being pressurised to a depth equivalent of 50m. (Note that bends cases which involve mixed gas diving can only be treated at those chambers set up for heliox treatment, and for depths greater that 50m.) There should be an ample supply of breathing gas (usually compressed air), which usually means having a bottle bank and powerful compressor available on site. Pure oxygen should be available. Gas concentration monitoring is not specifically necessary, but it should be possible to flush the chamber regularly, and of course to remove excess carbon dioxide.

Personnel

Often not much thought is given to the number of personnel who may be required to man a treatment schedule. Obviously a trained chamber operator is needed, but an attendant trained in first-aid is just as important. He also needs to be "clean" (ie he must not have dived over the last day or so), thus avoiding complicated decompression schedules and bent attendants. Other personnel may be required to operate compressors, obtain supplies, etc. A doctor on site is not essential, but one needs to be on or near the end of a telephone, and may be required to attend if the patient has severe symptoms.

Decompression Schedules

The ideal decompression schedule should effectively treat the patient in the fastest time with the least risk of hazard to the chamber attendants. Various organisations, both civilian and military, have their own decompression tables, and to make matters seemingly even more complex, some are amenable to alteration during treatment.

Originally, treatment schedules involved recompressing the patient using ordinary compressed air either to relatively shallow depths or to greater depths, usually with a 50m maximum. Some of the deeper air tables had the embarrassing effect of producing decompression sickness in the chamber attendant! When it was realised that pure oxygen would increase the dissipation of inert gas (eg nitrogen) from the tissues by producing a more favourable gradient, oxygen tables were introduced. These had the advantage of being both shorter in duration and highly effective. Pure oxygen can be used in reasonable safety at pressures equivalent to a depth of 18m in chambers - in water the limit is around 9m. Probably one of the most commonly used schedules is the US Navy Table 6, which lasts about five hours with pure oxygen being breathed at increasingly longer intervals during the decompression. Shallow oxygen tables with pressurisation to no more that 12m, and exposure to pure oxygen for two or three hours at a time, have been used for mild cases. However, pure oxygen breathed for any length of time actually damages the lungs, so this kind of treatment needs careful monitoring of the patient.

One emergency system for treating bends has been used successfully in Australasia, where casualties may be hundreds of miles from a treatment chamber. This may be of interest to experienced CDG divers who are out on a limb with a bent diver. It involves the use of pure oxygen for in-water recompression at a depth of no more than 9m.

This technique obviously has dangers. It is for this reason that the equipment has been standardised. A full-face mask is used, supplied by an umbilical hose no more than 12m long, connected to a supply of pure oxygen. The site selected for treatment should be shallow, so that the victim is on the cave floor and not hanging on a shotline. The problems envisaged for use in a cave environment is that if a cave is used as the treatment site then observation of the victim is going to be difficult and hypothermia could be a very real hazard.

Treatment is given for a period of less that three hours. In severe cases, the victim is taken to a depth of 9m for up to 60 minutes, and then brought up to the surface at the rate of 1m every 12 minutes. Edmonds, Lowther and Pennefather (*Diving and Subaquatic Medicine*, 1984) suggest the technique should be considered as being in the realms of very sophisticated first-aid. They report some quite remarkable cases of severe neurological sickness being successfully treated by this technique.

Finally, it behoves any cave diving expedition contemplating deep diving to consider taking along a supply of pure oxygen. This can be used as a first-aid treatment for a victim of decompression sickness in the absence of a chamber or re-immersion facilities, or where there may be a long delay in evacuating the victim to a chamber. It is best supplied using a full-face mask, or ordinary demand valve that has been cleaned for oxygen use. Pure oxygen will help to speed up the dissipation of inert gas from the tissues and at the same time helps to keep the levels of oxygen in areas affected by the bubbles as high as possible, which may reduce damage.

The forgoing is not intended as a do-it-yourself guide, merely as an indication of the modes of treatment available. For any diver contemplating doing deep or prolonged dives far away from chambers, further research on the subject is essential.

DRUG TREATMENT FOR DECOMPRESSION SICKNESS

Although this chapter covers therapeutic recompression, for the sake of completeness drug therapy should be mentioned. There is no current effective treatment in the way of drugs for DCS. Advocates of aspirin who suggest taking a daily tablet for several weeks before a deep dive do so on the basis of research rather than positive evidence (aspirin reduces the stickiness of platelets involved in blood clotting around bubbles in the circulation). In the case of a bent patient in shock, where fluid has moved from the blood stream into the tissues causing a reduction in the circulation, what are known as plasma expanders (Haemacell) may help to maintain circulation. Other drugs have no proven value.

EXPERIENCING TREATMENT

The following is an account of what might happen to a diver with acute DCS who presents himself promptly to a chamber for treatment. It should be noted that just turning up at the nearest chamber without warning is not really a good idea - it may already be in use.

On arrival, the diver is asked to give a history of the dive with relation to depth, duration, decompression stops and previous dives (your dive computer would be a helpful item to take, if you have been using one). He will be asked about his symptoms and their relation to the time of surfacing. He is then likely to be quickly examined if there is a doctor or trained paramedic present, before being placed in the chamber with an attendant. The lock doors seal with a clunk, and the chamber is pressurised. There is a loud roaring as air enters the chamber and ears have to be cleared rapidly. The atmosphere becomes warm and humid as the pressure rises. The temperature and humidity settle after a while, and during the decompression drop considerably. The occupants will be glad of the warm clothing with which they have been provided. Then follows the tedious business of decompression.

After an interval at the greatest depth (18m on standard US Navy oxygen tables) the pressure is gradually reduced with the casualty breathing pure oxygen for increasing lengths of time, and with decreasing intervals between breaks as he is brought nearer surface pressure. The oxygen is supplied through a BIBS apparatus (built-in breathing system) which means theoretically that only the victim gets the oxygen. In practise, oxygen will often leak out through the mask the victim uses, so that the chamber will require periodic flushing to restore the gas levels. Breathing through a BIBS mask is extremely tiresome - you are not really allowed to talk!

Eventually the chamber reaches atmospheric pressure, the lock opens, and the grateful victim clambers out into fresh air again, hopefully cured, and wiser.

Do not ignore symptoms of decompression sickness, however mild they appear - especially if your dive was doubtful in relation to depth and/or duration. It is coming to be recognised that even minor symptoms can conceal "silent" damage to the central nervous system. Minor symptoms can precede more serious symptoms by some hours.

If you have been diving, and have symptoms resembling those of decompression sickness, you have it until proved otherwise, regardless of what your tables, decompression meter or dive computer may have indicated for the dive. Seek treatment early!

OBTAINING TREATMENT

Currently (1990) the number of the nearest recompression chamber in Britain should be obtained by ringing HMS Vernon at 0705-822351 extension 24875/24866 during working hours, and asking for the Superintendent of Diving, or extension 22008 after working hours and asking for the Duty Officer. In extreme emergencies, if there is no reply, ring 0705-818888.

For those in the south-west, the Diving Diseases Research Centre at Fort Bovisand have an emergency number which in the daytime is 0752-408093, and out-of-hours is 0752-261910. This number will usually get a doctor specialising in diving medicine.

In Scotland, there is the new National Hyperbaric Centre in Aberdeen. A diver suspecting he has a bend can provide the doctor attending him with the following number, which is a hot-line to a consultant in diving medicine. It is 0224-681818. It is not intended for divers who suspect they have DCS to use themselves.

These two recompression centres are also capable of dealing with bend cases involving mixed gas diving. It may be worth priming the nearest one to you before the dive takes place.

Eventually, it is hoped that DCS can be dealt with through a central notifying authority using the 999 emergency call arrangement in the same way that one does for cave rescue.

Chapter 5: The Effects of Pressure

DEEP DIVING PROBLEMS

THE advances made in cave diving, from passing short, shallow sumps to pushing deep, long ones, increase the problems facing the diver.

Psychological Problems
    The mental pressure of cave diving is present from the start of a dive (see section *The Effects of Stress*). Dark, cold water, poor visibility, manoeuvring in confined spaces, route finding, distance from airspace - all these contribute to the normal apprehension felt during a dive. Due to narcosis and added stress, these problems are amplified by increasing depth, and the threshold of the onset of panic comes closer. These problems can be lessened by correct training, adequate experience, the use of appropriate and reliable equipment, thorough dive planning, and by building up to deep dives with adequate practice.

Physiological Problems
    With increasing depth, the effort a diver has to put into the dive increases, and a high degree of physical and mental fitness is required. Adequate nourishment, fluid intake and rest before a deep dive are additional necessities, especially if the trip to the dive site is arduous and long.
    Another major problem associated with depth is nitrogen absorption into the body. Nitrogen has a narcotic effect similar to alcohol, although the effects disappear more rapidly. This effect of nitrogen is not noticed by most divers until a depth of about 30m, then the degree of narcosis increases steadily beyond that point. Nitrogen narcosis can cause a diver to become confused and less able to deal with any task. Poor diving conditions and apprehension can increase the effects of narcosis, and can also make it start at shallower depths. The deeper the dive the greater the effect. The effects decrease on ascent, and the diver may not even be aware of having suffered narcosis. The effects can be made much worse by the prior consumption of alcohol, by tiredness, stress and hard work at depth. The effects of nitrogen narcosis can be reduced by progressively working up to greater depths. The diver should make a point of not making any important decisions or complex calculations at depth.
    Always plan deep dives carefully beforehand, especially where decompression is concerned. Usually, a depth of 40m is considered to be a safe depth limit for diving on compressed air. Diving to depths in excess of this normally

requires the nitrogen content of the air to be reduced or replaced, or requires a considerable degree of experience and tolerance to narcosis. Dives have been made in underwater caves to depths well in excess of 60m on air, but these have been done by extremely experienced and very fit divers, who have made intricate pre-dive plans and followed elaborate safety procedures. In countries where deep underwater caves are common, deep diving is one of the prime causes of fatalities.

Nitrogen, while not being required by the body, is always in solution in all body tissues, and at constant atmospheric pressure is in equilibrium. When under increased pressure, the body absorbs more nitrogen into the bloodstream and, as well as causing narcosis, it is absorbed into body tissues to maintain equilibrium with ambient pressure (Henry's Law). The rate of absorption is dictated by the external pressure and by the density of blood vessels in each tissue; the greater the density, the faster the absorption. On reducing the pressure, the balance must still be maintained, but if the pressure reduces too quickly then nitrogen will come out of solution as free gas bubbles in the tissues and blood vessels before being released through the lungs. This can create a variety of symptoms - itches, pain (usually in the vicinity of a joint), blockages of blood vessels (which can reduce the flow of oxygen around the body and lead to severe pain, paralysis, breathing difficulties and unconsciousness or death), or even embolism. This is known as decompression sickness, or the bends, and the avoidance and treatment of it is covered elsewhere in this manual.

Physical Problems

Buoyancy supplied by the suit worn by the diver is lost with increasing depth, due to any gas spaces contained within it being compressed. The rate of this buoyancy loss becomes less with greater depth (Boyle's Law). A diver who is weighted for neutral buoyancy in a shallow sump will thus be overweight in a deep one. This may cause the diver to create poor visibility by bottom contact, and to breathe more heavily (and thus become exhausted more quickly, be more prone to narcosis, cause more rapid depletion of his air supply, and make himself more susceptible to carbon dioxide poisoning). An ascent of an underwater shaft in this condition would be very tiring. If the diver is weighted to be neutrally buoyant at the deepest part of the dive, he would be positively buoyant in shallow water, which would make decompression dangerous and difficult, and cause him to float to the roof in shallow passages. To overcome the buoyancy problem, a buoyancy compensator must be used, or a variable-volume drysuit. A diver planning to use such in an underwater cave must have prior experience with it in open water. In very deep sumps, the loss of buoyancy may be severe, and it is possible that some of the lead might have to be staged near the entrance to the sump to avoid undue exertion at depth. If surfacing is likely at the far side, enough lead must be taken through to counteract too great a degree of positive buoyancy there.

Compression of a diving suit will also reduce its insulative properties, and so a thicker wetsuit will be required, or, if using a drysuit, extra or more efficient undergarments worn, to minimise the loss of body heat. The diver should not be cold before the dive (or too hot) and should be adequately nourished to maintain the extra energy required to maintain the correct body temperature.

Air becomes denser with increasing depth, and thus the effort required for breathing increases. Demand valves should therefore be in top working condition, and be capable of delivering an air flow on demand at depth that will be adequate for heavy work requirements. Note that many demand valves are not capable of supplying adequate air flow below 40m. The workload of a deep dive should be kept to a minimum to avoid extra air demand and associated physiological problems.

Because of increases in air density, air supplies will be consumed more rapidly at depth, and third rules may not be applicable. Allowance *must* be made for the air supply necessary to maintain the recommended ascent rate specified by the decompression tables in use (typically 10 or 15 metres/minute), which may be much slower than the descent rate. The ascent air requirements may be considerably different from the descent air requirements. Problem-solving and emergencies at depth will also consume air at a drastically faster rate than at shallower points during the dive. To maintain acceptable safety standards, it may be necessary to leave a greater percentage of the available air supply as reserve.

The effects of the constituent gases of air become more apparent at greater depth. Oxygen, though it is essential in sustaining life, becomes toxic at pressures approaching 2 bars in most individuals. With pure oxygen, such as in a rebreathing system or in decompression tanks, this can occur by a depth of 10m. With ordinary air, containing 20% oxygen, a depth of 90m is attained before a partial pressure of 2 bars is reached (Dalton's Law).

Oxygen poisoning takes two forms: acute (sudden, short-term) and chronic (slow onset, long-term). Both conditions are possible if oxygen-enriched mixtures are used, and theoretically can occur at 90m depth if air is being breathed (though a diver is more likely to have succumbed to nitrogen narcosis before that depth). The symptoms of acute oxygen poisoning are lip and facial twitching, nausea, irregular breathing, convulsions similar to an epileptic fit, and unconsciousness - and thus, if underwater, death. Chronic oxygen poisoning occurs if pure oxygen is breathed at or near atmospheric pressure for a long time, and causes irritation of the lung tissues, congestion and discomfort as in pneumonia. It is not usually encountered in diving, but may be where long oxygen-supported decompressions take place.

Oxygen poisoning is treated by restoring normal air breathing at atmospheric pressure (which would be difficult on a cave dive where a long swim to an air surface was necessary). Partial recovery will be made by returning to air breathing at ambient pressure. Oxygen poisoning is best avoided by not using oxygen-enriched mixtures, or by careful planning of decompression procedures (see section on *Oxygen decompression*).

Other trace gases found in air can also cause problems at depth. Carbon dioxide, which as a waste product of the body's metabolism triggers the respiratory cycle, can accumulate in dead spaces within airways or demand valves. At a content of 5% atmospheric pressure it will cause breathlessness, and at 10% will lead to much greater problems. Yet again, this condition is brought about much sooner with an increase in depth, and leads to greater breathing rates, confusion, headaches and eventually unconsciousness and death. Modern demand valves are designed to minimise dead spaces, and a steady progress underwater, breathing normally, will keep the body's production of carbon dioxide at a reasonable rate. Shallow skip breathing in an effort to conserve air, or panting without fully exhausting the lung's contents between breaths, can also lead to carbon dioxide build-up in the diver's airways. If an increased breathing rate develops, then the diver should stop activity until breathing returns to normal, then take a few deep breaths, exhaling fully, to clear the build-up, or abort the dive. Note that carbon dioxide build-up can occur in restricted air bells in caves, and has been responsible for deaths in the past. Anyone using a full-face mask may also encounter this problem, depending on the design of the mask.

Carbon monoxide (CO) can be introduced into the breathing supply by a badly-sited or badly-maintained compressor. As this gas is more readily carried by the blood than oxygen, it can cause hypoxia (oxygen deficiency). A purity standard of 5 ppm is recommended for diving air. Even smoking immediately prior to a dive can leave residual carbon monoxide in the lungs and cause a mild form of poisoning.

Symptoms of carbon monoxide poisoning are dizziness, headache, mental confusion, staggering and exhaustion, followed by flushed cheeks and lips, coma and death. treatment in mild cases is to restore breathing of pure air and rest, whilst in serious cases oxygen under medical supervision will be required.

On a more physical note, it is possible to burst an ear-drum when returning through a deep section if the diver's sinuses are unable to be cleared. Repeated clearing of middle ear and sinuses can, on a saw-tooth dive profile, become a real problem. Here, the diver must decide whether to wait until the ears can be cleared, or whether other factors (cave conditions, hypothermia, etc) warrant risking a burst ear-drum with its attendant severe physical problems during the swim out.

Response and Behaviour

At depth, the potential for all the above effects adds up to increase the demands on the diver and - in the underwater cave environment, hampered by cold, darkness, low visibility and enclosure - the judgement of the diver can be severely clouded, as can his ability to assess dangers and respond to them correctly. A cave diver on his own in a sump is very vulnerable, and only correct training and acclimatisation to working at depth will give him the necessary experience and skills to minimise these dangers.

The problems associated with deep cave diving have grave consequences for the ill-prepared diver. The cave diver who is properly trained, has built-up his dives at increasing depths and is aware of all the problems likely to be encountered, can plan the dive accordingly and so reduce the dangers involved.

The diver should be very fit, and be properly rested and nourished before the dive. All equipment should be in top condition, the air in the cylinders should conform to British Standard 4001 (or, where other gas mixtures are used, should be properly analysed), potential dive profiles and bottom times (together with associated decompression calculations) should be worked out as far as is possible in advance, and the plan should not be altered to push the cave outside these plans however inviting it looks. Always plan the parameters of your dive in advance, and *dive the plan*.

DIVING AT ALTITUDE

DIVING at altitude is complicated by virtue of a drop in ambient atmospheric pressure. This affects the reading of non-compensated depth gauges, introduces changes in the decompression procedures necessary to compensate for altitude, and increases the potential for narcosis at shallow depths. Unfortunately, many of the world's major cave systems lie at high altitudes, and exploration of sumps within these caves necessitates the use of different decompression procedures from those relevant at sea level.

The lower oxygen level at altitude affects the body's ability to perform efficiently, and time must be taken to acclimatise before diving takes place. Even diving at comparatively low altitudes (500m or less) affects nitrogen absorption rates and thus decompression times. Making such a dive after a rapid ascent from sea level counts effectively as a repeat dive, because the body has not had a chance to fully decompress from the ascent to the dive site, and tissues still have a nitrogen load carried from lower altitude. A wait of at least 12 hours is recommended to allow the body to readjust to the new altitude.

There is an accepted formula for determining the equivalent depth at sea level for a dive at altitude, and this can be used as a basis for planning decompression dives at altitude:

$$\text{Equivalent depth} = \frac{\text{Dive depth at altitude} \times \text{sea level pressure}}{\text{Atmospheric pressure at altitude}}$$

For example, a 15m dive at 1524m would give:

$$\frac{15 \times 14.7\text{psi}}{12.2\text{psi}} = 18 \text{ metres equivalent depth.}$$

This requires use of an accurate barometer on site to measure atmospheric pressure, and a knowledge of current pressure at sea level. A rule of thumb measurement of the addition of 5% of the dive depth for every 300 metres of elevation is commonly used.

An inexpensive capillary depth gauge can be used to measure the approximate equivalent depth at altitude, as such gauges measure the ratio of water pressure to the actual surface pressure. At 5500m, atmospheric pressure is about half of that at sea level, and such a gauge would read 40m at an actual depth of 20m, and decompression stops would be made according to the capillary depth.

Ascent rates become slower with altitude, corresponding approximately to a subtraction of 0.6m/minute for each 300m of altitude. For example, the standard US Navy ascent rate of 18 metres/minute would alter at an altitude of 2000m to:

(2000/300) x 0.6 = 4 metres/minute slower ascent, thus the new ascent rate would be 14 metres/minute.

It should be remembered that exertion underwater during a dive at high altitude will not only increase the likelihood of decompression sickness and

The effects of pressure 149

narcosis, but can also cause problems on surfacing due to the rapid decrease in available oxygen in the air.

Many of the new decompression computers are self-compensating for altitude, but some are not. Ensure that any computer used to measure decompression stops is programmed to perform within the altitude range in which you are diving.

Do not mix altitudes in repetitive diving. Altitude decompression profiles are theoretical enough without adding to the problem.

Altitude diving is really a specialised branch, and as such should not be undertaken lightly. If at all possible stick to dives that do not involve decompression.

FLYING AFTER DIVING

Whilst it is theoretically possible to extrapolate decompression schedules to allow for the lower pressures experienced during flying, it is generally inadvisable. Aeroplanes do not always fly at predicted altitudes, and even cabin pressure can fluctuate in pressurised cabins.

In most cases, no-decompression diving at sea level entails a minimum surface interval of two hours before flying in any commercial aircraft with a cabin pressure equivalent to an altitude of 2000m. Longer is advisable, 12 hours is recommended, and 24 hours should be allowed if decompression dives have been made.

In the case of a decompression incident where flight to a chamber is essential, the pilot should be aware that he has to maintain as low an altitude as possible, ideally below 70m.

AIR DECOMPRESSION

DECOMPRESSION occurs when there is a decrease in ambient pressure. This may involve either a drop in pressure from sea level atmospheric to altitude sub-atmospheric or a reduction from increased pressure (due to depth or artificial pressurisation) to atmospheric pressure at sea level. For divers, the crucial effect that this has is on gases dissolved in body tissues.

On compression, nitrogen, oxygen and carbon dioxide, the main constituents of air, are dissolved into the bloodstream and body tissues. On decompression, they are released. Oxygen and carbon dioxide are easily dissolved and released, but nitrogen takes more time both to dissolve and to re-emerge safely from solution. As far as air decompression goes, nitrogen is therefore the limiting gas.

When pressure is released from a bottle of lemonade, bubbles form immediately. If the bottle is shaken, a large quantity of bubbles form, causing the fluid to froth and spurt from the bottle. The fluid is suffering rapid decompression, with inevitable consequences. It is these consequences we have to avoid by adopting safe decompression procedures to control the rate of bubble formation within safe levels.

On decompression, nitrogen bubbles form in body tissues and the bloodstream. Tiny bubbles may pass through the capillaries of the circulatory system, large bubbles will not. The effects of such blockages can include damage to nerve tissues, interference with and damage to blood supply to various parts of the body (including brain and organs) inflammation and haemorrhage in affected areas, and embolism.

Nitrogen absorption and elimination is affected by three factors:

1) *Pressure gradient*: The greater the nitrogen pressure difference between lungs, blood and tissue, the greater the uptake or elimination. As a tissue approaches saturation (ie the pressure differential, or gradient, decreases) the rate of uptake or elimination also decreases.

2) *Tissue type*: Fat absorbs large quantities of nitrogen, and takes longer to desaturate than non-fatty tissues. Nitrogen absorption rates vary depending upon the particular body tissue, and fat people are more susceptible to the effects of decompression than are healthy people, (though conversely, thin people can have problems with absorption into other tissues, and with thermal considerations). When no more nitrogen can be absorbed into the body, or into a particular tissue type, it is said to be saturated. The time taken to reach this state of equilibrium is called saturation time. If a rapid ascent is made, the saturation ratio for a given time/depth can be reached and exceeded, resulting in super-saturation and the inevitable messy consequences, when large bubbles form in the blood and body tissues. An ordered method of ascent is therefore required to avoid such adverse effects on the body.

3) *Blood flow*: The rate of blood flow varies greatly between different body organs, thus the rate of absorption or removal of nitrogen varies. Exertion at depth, or even great exertion before the dive, increases the rate of blood flow to tissues, and can greatly increase the amount of nitrogen absorbed into different tissue types. Decompression tables are based on a particular absorption rate per individual tissue type, and variance from this can increase the potential for decompression sickness. For this reason it is better to avoid undue exertion at depth, or immediately prior to and after a deep dive.

DECOMPRESSION TABLES

Professor Haldane, experimenting in the early part of this century, produced a set of tables based on the premise that a diver would stop at intervals during his ascent to allow the nitrogen in his body to be gradually released without forming large bubbles. The first stops are comparatively short, but as the pressure within the body (ie the pressure gradient) decreases, nitrogen comes out of solution at an increasingly slower rate and thus the stop times progressively increase as the surface is neared. The longest stop is that at the shallowest depth.

Haldane's tables were very safe, and were used for many years. Modern tables, however, have been developed which reduce decompression time whilst keeping decompression incidents to an acceptable minimum for their particular requirements. Examples of these are the Buhlmann tables (Swiss) and those produced by the Royal Navy and US Navy, all commonly used in British cave diving circles. The tables vary according to the mathematical models used, water temperatures encountered, the number of recorded dives used in the modelling, and the percentage of bends considered acceptable. Military tables may consider a higher percentage of bends cases acceptable in a military situation, sports tables may be more conservative. Military tables may also use younger and physically fitter divers as their model group. Most active cave divers are comparatively physically fit, but those less healthy should treat military tables with care, and ideally use a more conservative table.

Tables produced by these different diving authorities may give different times for stops given the standard variables of depth and duration. It would be an unwise cave diver who opted for the most lenient tables, thinking to save on air and time. Cave diving is a high-risk activity, and decisions should be made that are based on more than simply a superficial knowledge of the subject. In considering no stop times (the maximum time that can be spent at a given depth without having to decompress), the Swiss and US Navy tables allow 200 minutes at -12m, and RN allow 137 minutes. At -35m, the Swiss, US Navy and RN tables all allow 15 minutes. None of these tables is considered to be "right"; all are based on experimental calculations. It all depends on the decision of the individual as to what conditions he is working under, and what risk factor he is willing to accept. There is no heroic status in having a spinal bend.

Virtually all tables agree that dives involving a total decompression time of over 30 minutes (all stops added together) expose the diver to a risk factor in excess of 0.1% of getting a bend. In the Royal Navy tables, this is formalised as the limiting line, and thus decompression for British naval divers involving more than this time necessitates the on-site availability of recompression facilities in case of mishap.

APPLICATION TO THE CAVING ENVIRONMENT

The *CDG Training Manual* of 1975 stated that "the cave diver in the British Isles runs very little risk from decompression sickness, because he does not carry enough air". This is manifestly not true today. Decompression cave diving frequently occurs both on mainland Britain and abroad on expeditions. Deeper sumps are being explored and long duration dives are taking place, often with the two factors combining, as in the Three Counties system (Witches Cave and Gavel Pot), and in Wookey Hole and Gough's Cave. The problems facing cave divers as opposed to open water divers in relation to decompression are serious, but not insurmountable.

Recompression

In the event of mishap, therapeutic recompression facilities are never available at dive base. Indeed, these may be geographically distant, and there may be other sumps and cave passage between the diver and daylight. A recompression chamber could only be made available at the cave entrance on a very heavily-financed expedition, and is out of the question for the normal diver.

Emergency recompression in the event of minor bends can take place in the water, but this requires the continuous availability of breathing gas (air or oxygen) and increases the potential for hypothermia, and is not generally advisable or successful.

Other members of the support team must be made aware of the procedure for dealing with and evacuating a diver with decompression sickness, and must be aware of the phone number of the nearest recompression facility, and of the methods for transporting the casualty there.

The use of oxygen during the shallowest stops, at 6 and 3m considerably increases the safety levels of the dive, as long as the full air times are carried out, and decompression is not shortened in any way. The diver *must* be familiar with the use of oxygen, the equipment must be suitable, and the oxygen must be of breathing quality. The availability of oxygen in the cave following a decompression dive is medically advantageous, and a bent diver should breathe it during evacuation to the nearest chamber. The procedures for the use of oxygen are dealt with elsewhere.

Dive Profiles

Most of the published tables rely on a rectangular dive profile, that is, a steady descent to a given depth, a fixed duration at that depth, and a steady ascent to the surface, during which stops may be required. Caves rarely conform to this. One only has to consider Wookey Hole with its five major sumps beyond Chamber 9, or Hurtle Pot, where there are no airspaces, but where the main route drops to -28m, rises to -8m, then it drops gradually to -35m before a shaft rises to -26m. Such multiple variances of depth can themselves trigger decompression sickness, and can seriously affect the rate of nitrogen absorption/removal beyond the parameters of decompression tables.

Tables are available which allow multiple decompression dives to take place within a 24 hour period. The Buhlmann, the US Navy tables (and those based on them) and the new generation of BS-AC tables allow repetitive dives to take place. These work on the principle that credit is given for short-term decompression during surface intervals by converting it to residual nitrogen time, which is added to the time of the following repetitive dives.

This works well where distinctly separate sumps have a rectangular profile (eg Wookey Hole) followed by an evenly graded return to the surface. The repetitive principle has been extended to the RNPL model to allow up to four repetitive dives in one day. As stated above, Wookey has five major sumps beyond Chamber 9. Using the new RNPL model, only the first two of these could be passed and returned through on the same day. Either the diver must camp, or he must use other tables and accept a possibly greater risk.

There is a danger with all repetitive tables of extrapolating them beyond the limitations of both their mathematical and testing models. In all repetitive dives, the model works on the assumption that the deepest dive is made first, and that successive dives are shallower. If this is not the case, problems may occur with the differential absorption rates of nitrogen into body tissues which are still de-saturating from previous dives. This can effectively create dangerous bubble concentrations in such partially-saturated tissues. Making the deepest dive last in a series is a good way to get bent. This is a problem cave divers will have to face when deciding how to explore irregular profile dive sites, and such exploration may involve setting up camps beyond sumps until the tables indicate that the body has desaturated from the previous deep dive.

Another actual example is that of Keld Head. here, a dive to Dead Man's Handshake and beyond would involve an inward swim of over 1km, and a descent to -20m. Dive duration would be about two hours. If all the cave were at -20m, decompression stops would be required. However, depth is gained gradually throughout the length of the dive, and, more importantly, is lost gradually on return. The return therefore contributes significantly to the decompression requirements, as decompression is taking place gradually through the return swim. However, the ascent rate was far slower than that indicated by any tables, and even such a simple profile does not necessarily mean a simple decompression schedule.

On variable profile dives, many cave divers are now using decompression computers, which calculate decompression stops based on actual profiles, and which give credit for time spent above maximum depth during a dive. These instruments, described elsewhere in this volume, must be used in conjunction with tables, and with due regard to the physical boundaries of applied decompression research. Their improper use can get a diver bent very quickly.

Most cave diving is strenuous, involving the transport of heavy loads to dive sites or between sumps, adding the danger of high blood flow rates and increased nitrogen delivery to the body tissues. Ways to solve this problem are relatively straightforward. Keep exertion to a minimum, and rest for enough time to allow physical stabilisation before entering any sump. Call in other divers to help if necessary.

EQUIPMENT

Cave divers undertaking, or anticipating the possibility of, a dive involving decompression must add the following items to their standard cave diving equipment.

1) A reliable watch or bottom timer. Decompression dives should never be undertaken without some way of accurately measuring time and depth. The use of a depth gauge with a maximum depth indicator is also recommended, but this does not remove the need to monitor depth frequently.

2) Sets of waterproof decompression tables. Three sets of identical tables (*never* mix types of tables) must be taken into the cave. One is kept on the diver for the duration of the dive. One set should be placed at the deepest anticipated stop, attached to the line or shotline. One set should be left with the support party at the dive site. This support party should remain at the site until the diver returns, in case of premature abortion of the dive following an incident underwater. No decompression dive should be made without such a support team.

3) One or more reserve cylinders of air should be placed in the water, attached to the line or to a shotline at the deepest stop anticipated. This should ideally be twice the amount required to last for the planned decompression period. The air carried by the diver *must not* be regarded as being available for decompression, as an emergency may arise underwater which entails its use - this includes the reserve third. Oxygen taken must be staged no deeper than 6m and must not be used below this for decompression.

4) The use of a thick marked shotline is encouraged. This should be attached to the guideline at its deepest point, or should form the guideline

itself down the line of descent (the exploration reel can be attached to a figure of eight knot at the base of the shotline. The shotline must hang vertically, and should be weighted. Stop depths should be clearly marked in whatever intervals are indicated by the tables and gauges in use (metres or feet). This forms a reliable back-up to depth gauges, which may be difficult to read in low visibility. There should be a mark on the shotline which is calibrated to water surface by the surface team, to allow for changing water conditions, especially in tidally-influenced caves.

If securely attached at the surface, a non-stretching shotline can be modified to cope with long decompressions by the prior tying of loops in the line at each stop. The diver can clip himself to the shotline, make himself slightly negatively buoyant, and be held securely at stop-depth by the shotline. This enables him to relax more efficiently, and to move arms and legs to maintain circulation without having to constantly worry about monitoring depth. Even in this situation though, a regular check should be made to ensure that the specific stop-depth is being maintained.

Cave divers must chose tables which fit both themselves and the environment (and which match those used by any decompression computer being taken), develop dive plans and stick to them, consider the availability of recompression facilities and be aware exactly where they are. Decompression tables must be available in the water at the first anticipated stop, with the surface support team, and with the diver, whether dive computers are used or not. The use of oxygen should be considered for stops at 3 and 6m, and reserve air for decompression should always be carried or staged at the deepest anticipated stop. A watch or bottom timer *must* be worn throughout the dive.

FACTORS PREDISPOSING DECOMPRESSION SICKNESS

History of recent injury
Using DCS tables to their limits
Alcohol ingestion prior to dive
Diving on gas mixtures other than air
Deepest point not early in dive
Use of less conservative tables
Poor maintenance of stop depths
Short term repetitive diving
Previous DCS history
Moderate/heavy exercise after a dive
Diving in very cold water
Provocative medication
Flying/driving at altitude after deep dives

Hypoxia
Deeper dives
Increasing age
Dehydration
Obesity
Cold during decompression
Hangover
Saw-tooth profiles
Sex (women more susceptible)
Improper ascent rate
Hypercapnia
Diver fatigued before dive
Prolonged stay at low altitude prior to high altitude dives

BS-AC 1988 DECOMPRESSION TABLES AND BUHLMANN TABLES

Towards the end of 1988, BS-AC published its replacement for the old RNPL/BS-AC decompression tables, which had been in use for many years. The emphasis in the seven new BS-AC tables is away from the old idea that decompression was a thing to be avoided, and which led to penalties (stops) if you strayed beyond the no-stop time, towards an approach which stresses that decompression must take place towards the end of any dive in every case, whether this be during a slow, controlled ascent, or during specified stops. Accordingly, the 1988 tables are far more finely-graded than the old, which went up in blocks of five minutes, with the result that very small (eg one or two minute) stops may be all that is needed if you stray beyond no-stop time for five or ten minutes at medium depth.

Another emphasis is on slow ascent, with or without stops. The ascent rate must be no faster than 15m/minute up to 6m depth, and then one minute from there to the surface (ie ascent rate of 6m/minute). Stops are all at -6m, or -9m and -6m. There are no deeper stops, and no stop at -3m. The maximum depth catered for is -51m. The tables allow for repeat dives to be undertaken by coding the diver after each dive, and referring him to a new table according to the surface interval after each dive. They are applicable from sea level to 250m above it.

As far as cave diving is concerned, what have these new tables to offer? Being intended for sports diving only, these new tables cannot cater for very long, deep dives. The maximum time that can be spent at, for example, -42m is 32 minutes, requiring stops of three minutes at -9m and 18 minutes at -6 metres. This is nine minutes less than the old RNPL/BS-AC tables. There is also some suspicion that they have been designed to allow greater bottom times for less decompression, in response to pressure from sport divers.

The following example makes this even clearer. On a dive from Jingle Pot into upstream Hurtle Pot, a depth of 35m is reached for 25 minutes. On the old RNPL/BS-AC tables, this requires 20 minutes decompression (five minutes at -10m, 15 minutes at -5m). On the new tables, only three minutes at -6 metres is required! (A computer would probably give even less, due to the gradual ascent from the Low Arch to Frog Hall).

These tables seem to offer reduced stop times under most circumstances, and repetitive diving. They do not cater for deep, long dives, or dives requiring more than 21 minutes decompression. They are available in a waterproof condensed version of the three main tables, which comes with the full set on purchase.

It is worth noting that the reduced stop times might also reduce safety in some cases, especially where the predisposing factors in the table above are taken into account. The BS-AC tables have not been fully tested, but are probably as safe as any. Treat any table carefully, and with due respect to conditions.

The Buhlmann tables are given as an appendix to this manual. After careful consideration, the Cave Diving Group have decided to recommend use of these tables, due to the fact that they have a tested safety standard, and are those used by the decompression computers most commonly worn by cave divers in the UK (eg Aladin, Aladin Pro, Monitor). Again it must be remembered that any table is only as good as the mind applying it, and that full consideration *must* be given to environmental, psychological and physiological conditions before their application to the underwater cave environment. Waterproof copies of the basic Buhlmann tables can be obtained from the Sub-Aqua Association.

Fig. 47: An expedition diver decompresses on a shotline.

OXYGEN DECOMPRESSION

STANDARD air decompression tables are based on the diver breathing air during both the dive and decompression. During decompression, the nitrogen in the air (79%) limits the rate at which the nitrogen in the body tissues is released. The nitrogen release rate can be increased by decompressing on pure oxygen, thus shortening the time required to lower the levels of nitrogen in body tissues.

This can be used to the diver's advantage by either increasing his margin of safety or by reducing his decompression time. However, breathing oxygen at high partial pressures can have dangerous side effects.

This section refers specifically to in-water decompression and so the advice given does not refer to any compression chamber techniques which might be considered. Pressures in this section are absolute: they include atmospheric pressure.

Oxygen Poisoning

Breathing oxygen at partial pressures approaching and beyond 2 bar can bring on a condition known as acute oxygen poisoning. This is a condition which affects the central nervous system, and can vary from simple blackout to uncontrolled convulsions. If oxygen is breathed at partial pressures as low as 0.6 bar for prolonged periods, chronic oxygen poisoning can occur causing serious lung damage. However, chronic oxygen poisoning is not usually a problem to cave divers due to the time required for damage to occur. All forms of oxygen poisoning can be fatal to the lone cave diver.

For most people it is safe to breath pure oxygen at depths shallower than 9m. However, as oxygen poisoning is both pressure and time dependent, it is wise to alternate air and oxygen use at depths approaching 9m. It is unwise to breath oxygen below 9m.

Exertion can also increase susceptibility to oxygen poisoning due to the increased level of carbon dioxide in the body (high levels of carbon dioxide in the body can also increase susceptibility to decompression sickness). Caution is therefore advised if decompressing on oxygen after a hardworking dive.

Oxygen Decompression to Increase Safety Margins

An air decompression schedule derived from standard tables can be made safer by breathing oxygen for part of decompression. To reduce the risk of oxygen poisoning and decompression sickness the following guidelines should be followed:

1) Follow the air decompression schedule fully. (In this situation the benefits of breathing oxygen are not quantifiable.)

2) Do not breath oxygen at depths below -6m.

3) Alternate the use of air and oxygen over suitable periods (eg five minutes) on stops at or near -6m. At depths of -5m and shallower oxygen can be breathed for about 2½ hours with little risk.

4) Rest from exercise before ascending to the first stop of the decompression schedule.

This method of using oxygen to decompress is especially recommended where the risk of decompression sickness is high, such as after an exceptional exposure or a hard working dive.

Oxygen to Reduce Decompression Time

This can only be undertaken if a set of oxygen decompression tables are available. Even then, it should be remembered that the only available tables have been developed for use in chambers, where the diver is warm and rested. The risk in using these tables in an underwater environment is greatly increased. Until oxygen decompression tables based on more detailed and reliable data are developed, use them only with extreme caution if at all.

Extended Decompression on Oxygen

When a diver is following a long oxygen decompression schedule, it might be sensible to guard against the consequences of oxygen poisoning as well as the possibility of it occurring.

1) Wear a full-face mask - in the event of oxygen poisoning the diver will not lose his gas supply.

2) Have surface controlled air and oxygen supplies to the diver; in the event of oxygen poisoning, oxygen can be turned off and air delivered instead.

3) Have a stand-by diver available to keep the decompressing diver at the correct depth and to provide diver-to-surface communication.

4) If possible, do not bring to the surface a convulsing diver when the symptoms have receded after switching to air unless the risk to the diver's life outweighs the consequences of decompression sickness.

The equipment required is specialised and dictated by the dive site conditions. However, relatively basic equipment can be used to construct a suitable decompression rig: two demand valve first stages connected via an in-line, non-return Y valve to a length of low-pressure hose and the second stage. The first stages are connected to air and oxygen cylinders respectively and the second stage fits into the full face mask.

The wellbeing of the diver suffering oxygen poisoning then depends on the speed of reaction of the surface team and the presence of a support diver in the water. Even so, nothing is guaranteed.

Care of Oxygen

Pressurised oxygen in contact with even minute amounts of oil or dirt forms a spontaneously explosive mixture. Oxygen should therefore be kept in special tanks which are cleaned and inspected regularly. They should also be clearly marked and painted green in accordance with commercial standards. Only silicon grease should be used on tanks, demand valves and any decanting equipment used with oxygen.

When obtaining oxygen, ensure it is a breathable grade of gas (medical or diving grade, rather than welding quality).

Like all aspects of cave diving, oxygen decompression has to be carefully considered and planned before it is used. When used within its limits, it does provide a valuable extra safeguard against decompression sickness to a group of divers who are all too often a long way from recompression facilities.

DIVE COMPUTERS

THE use of no-decompression and decompression computers by cave divers is becoming commonplace. No recommendations are made by the CDG as to the advisability of such use, other than that the operator must be thoroughly familiar with the safe operation of the unit being used, and of its specific limitations (eg depth, duration, altitude).

Why are such computers considered useful? Decompression tables lack flexibility; they cannot be used for dive profiles other than those for which they were compiled nor do they allow adequately for previous diving history, as needed for a succession of dives (repeat dives).

Tables assume that a dive consists of a descent at uniform speed, say 30m a minute, followed by a period at a constant depth and then a return to the surface, usually at a slower rate, say 10m a minute. Whereas definitions of dive time and bottom time, etc, may vary from table to table, this so-called rectangular profile is a feature of all tables. It is not representative of many actual dives since depth may vary considerably with time throughout the dive.

Similarly, the penalty to be taken into consideration for a second dive can, in a table, only be given for set time intervals, eg two, four, or six hours. Also, some portion of the first dive is assumed for tissue saturation purposes at the start of the second dive, whereas in fact the release of nitrogen is an exponential process. The calculation of nitrogen levels is complicated by the fact (not allowed for in the tables) that the rate of release varies greatly from tissue to tissue so that while some tissues may be desaturated during the actual ascent, others will remain saturated for several hours. Therefore, while a second dive may be safe according to some tables, the gradual build-up of nitrogen in the slow tissues may seriously affect further dives even if they are on the following day.

These considerations are of particular concern in many cave diving situations, as profiles are often far from rectangular and dives through a series of sumps invoke the repeat dive principle with its associated problems. Any exploration involving a return trip through a deep sump encounters the same problem.

To take these factors fully into account (variation in depth with time, varying rates of absorption or release of nitrogen by different body tissues during and after a dive, residual nitrogen in body tissues when starting subsequent dives) requires a multitude of calculations and predictions at regular and frequent intervals, commencing before the start of the first dive. It is beyond the scope of any table. This almost continuous calculation and recalculation is possible, however, with modern technology in the form of a microprocessor linked to a pressure sensor and programmed with a suitable model of nitrogen saturation and desaturation for different body tissues.

The device is worn by the diver and after the dive it is left switched on if further diving is contemplated. After being switched on, the device first of all measures atmospheric pressure, enabling it to take account automatically of altitude and weather. When the diver enters the water it automatically starts timing, usually once a depth of 1.5m is reached. Depth, elapsed time, remaining no-stop time, and when to return to the surface (including stops if any are necessary), are displayed. If a no-stop time is exceeded, stops are displayed in the order to be observed; the deepest stop is at 27m then in 3m increments to 12m, 9m, 6m, 3m. After the dive, dive time and maximum depth reached are displayed sometimes with total desaturation time and dive particulars are recorded for a second or subsequent dive.

Fig. 48: Various decompression aids on a set of water-sealed US Navy tables - (clockwise from left) SOS decompression meter; MK1 Decobrain; depth gauge; Aladin dive computer.

The computer calculates the nitrogen uptake and release for a variety of different body tissues, depending on make, and updates all displays every few seconds. It is able, therefore, to take into account wide variations in depth throughout the dive, and is thus able to reduce considerably the decompression times given by any table which is based on a rectangular profile. For a truly rectangular dive profile, the no-stop time and the stops will be the same as those given by the table on which the machine is based. For example, the Decobrain gives 18 minutes no-stop time for a 30m dive; the old RN/BS-AC table gives 20 minutes, the small difference being to the rather more conservative Swiss tables on which the Decobrain is based.

The following example of the considerable saving in decompression time for a dive of irregular profile should make the value of these machines abundantly clear.

The dive profile is shown in the diagram (figure 49). The maximum depth is 33m and the dive time to the far end is 30 minutes. On the old BS-AC tables no-stop time expires at point C on the way in and by the time point D is reached

The effects of pressure 161

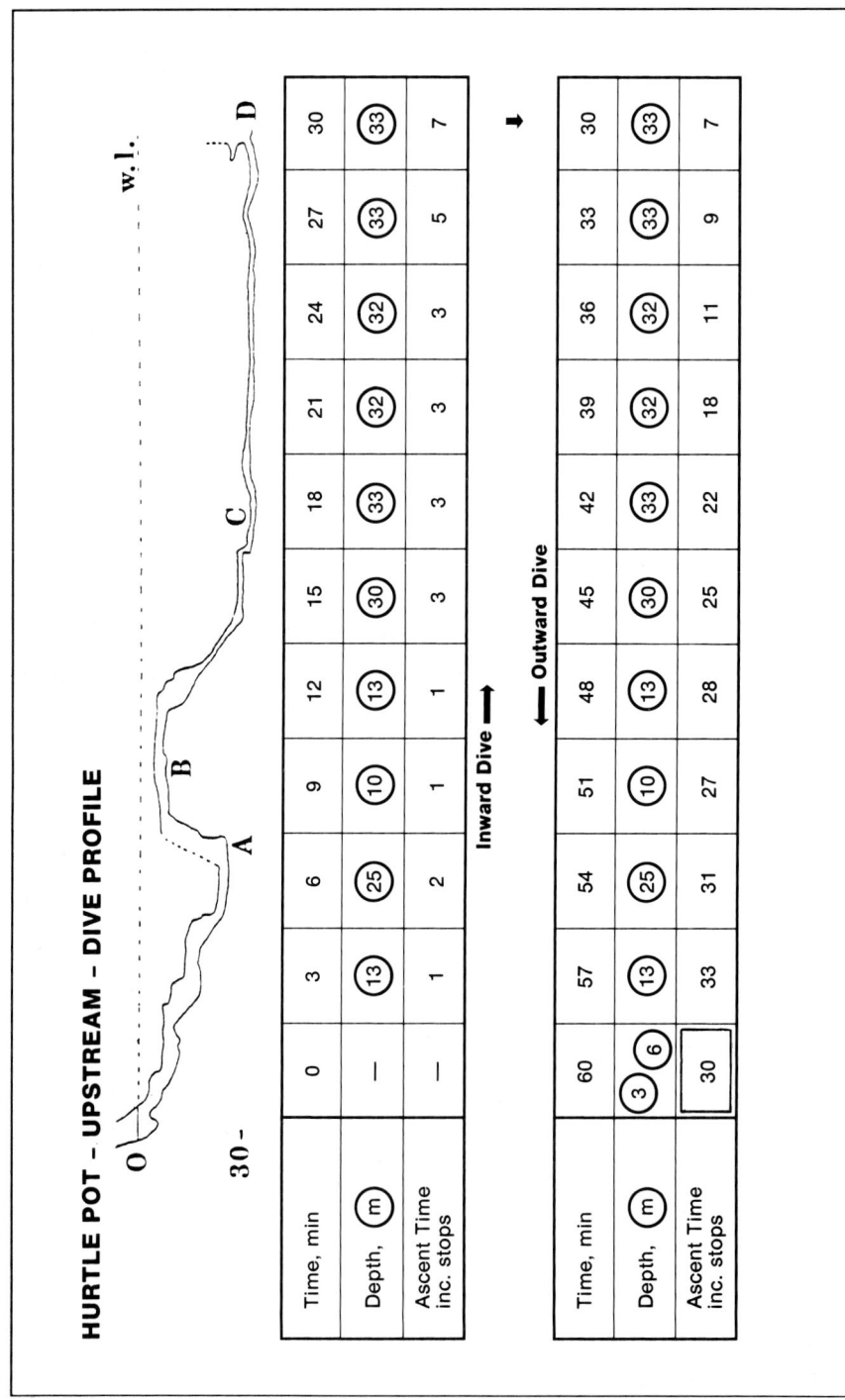

HURTLE POT – UPSTREAM – DIVE PROFILE

Time, min	0	3	6	9	12	15	18	21	24	27	30
Depth, (m)	—	⑬	㉕	⑩	⑬	㉚	㉝	㉜	㉜	㉝	㉝
Ascent Time inc. stops	—	1	2	1	1	3	3	3	3	5	7

Inward Dive ⟶

Time, min	60	57	54	51	48	45	42	39	36	33	30
Depth, (m)	③ ⑥	⑬	㉕	⑩	⑬	㉚	㉝	㉜	㉜	㉝	㉝
Ascent Time inc. stops	30	33	31	27	28	25	22	18	11	9	7

⟵ Outward Dive

Fig. 49: Hurtle Pot profile.

a total decompression time of 20 minutes would be necessary if the diver should return immediately to surface, were he able. On his return journey the diver ascends to 8m depth at B, during which time some decompression takes place but cannot be taken into account as the diver then descends to 28m at A. It is from A that the ascent must be deemed to begin when, with a decompression debt of 55 minutes, the dive is completely off the old BS-AC tables. RNPL tables give total decompression stops for this dive as 115 minutes, USN tables give 90 minutes (hence USN tables have been used by the few divers who have visited the far end of Upstream Hurtle). Even for this assumed rectangular profile, ie 55 minutes at 33m, a Decobrain gives only 60 minutes decompression time, presumably because of its analogue reading of depth, whereas, in the incremental tables for 33 the next stop, 34 must be used on BS-AC or 35 on RNPL. Using a Decobrain in a simulated dive of the actual profile, the figures in the next diagram were obtained:

Points to note

1) Stops first become necessary (no-stop time expires) after 24 minutes.

2) At the far end, D, a 3 minute ascent for decompression together with a 4 minute stop at 3m would be necessary if surface were attainable.

3) Total decompression time builds up quite rapidly on return through The Deep, but reduces slightly at B, ie the decompression achieved during the 10m deep section is small but valuable.

4) On descent to 25m the decompression total hardly increases beyond that required at C, and even reduces from 33 to 30 minutes during the gradual ascent to the first stop at 6m.

5) The final decompression after 60 minutes is 3 minutes at 6m and 27 minutes at 3m - a total of 30 minutes, much less than given by any tables.

(It must be stressed that this saving is mainly due to the dive profile and not to the machine itself. On a rectangular dive of 55 minutes to 33m the machine would register considerably more necessary decompression - twice as much in fact. It is the variations in depth, particularly the section at 10m, which reduce the decompression time since decompression occurring en route is now taken into account.)

6) The total desaturation time after this dive was 20 hours. A no-stop second dive immediately permissible was 17 minutes at 30m.

In conclusion, for dives with irregular profiles, and repeat dives, which includes dives through a series of sumps and return journeys, a computer is indispensable if decompression stops must be kept to a safe minimum. In simple one-off rectangular dives, tables give equally valid results.

It should be noted that there are specific decompression problems associated with multiple dive or irregular dive profiles. Degassing of some body tissues can be seriously affected by multiple decompression on an irregular profile dive, and several instances of decompression sickness have occurred as a result. Irregular profiles on long/deep dives should be treated with the utmost caution, and the use of oxygen at decompression stops above 9m is recommended.

USE IN CAVES

No-decompression computers are only of use if a dive is specifically to be made within the no-decompression limits of a specific type of decompression tables. Under *no* circumstances should a no-decompression computer calibrated for one set of tables (eg Buhlmann) be used with a different set of tables for additional calculated decompression (eg BSAC/RN). It is recommended that the deepest point of a no-decompression dive be made early in the dive profile when using these meters.

Different computers take different decompression tables as their source. It is strongly recommended that the diver be thoroughly familiar with the decompression tables used by his computer and that these tables be carried during all computer-aided dives. A copy of these tables should always be available in the water at a stop deeper than the first anticipated decompression stop in case of meter failure before or during a decompression period. Alternatively, if different tables are used, the whole dive must be recalculated using these tables in the water.

At no time should decompression computers be the only source of decompression information in the water. There should always be a spare set of waterproof tables available in the water in case of failure of the computer unit.

The diver should be aware that with many computers there is no way of recalling a dive profile after the event. A record of maximum depth and elapsed dive time should always be kept in case of post-dive complication. In case of a cave rescue incident involving chamber treatment, any computer used must accompany the diver to the recompression chamber.

The diver should also be aware that many computers do not give the total decompression time to be undertaken after a particular dive, only that to be spent at the current stop. When using such a computer, the diver must ensure that sufficient air supplies are available in the water to allow for a decompression duration longer than anticipated. On particularly long or deep dives, each diver in the water should have available a set of waterproof tables that will allow the approximate time duration of a particular decompression profile to be calculated in the water.

It is recommended that decompression computers be kept separate from heavy diving equipment to minimise the possibility of damage, and that they be regularly calibrated within a chamber designed for that purpose.

When moving though passages between sumps, or during any surface interval between dives, make sure that the sensors on decompression computers are dried off and that the computer is stored in a dry container or place. Moisture from wet clothing, hands or equipment can "re-start" the computer, or a high degree of humidity can prevent it from clearing from the dive in the first place. In such instances, it would not accurately measure the surface interval between dives.

During any series of dives, *on no account* should one computer be used by more than one individual unless it can be completely reset from its calculations of dives for the previous user. Decompression computers, when in use, are generally specific to one diver.

A summary of problems that must be anticipated in cave diving use of decompression meters are:
1) Difficulty of reading display in low visibility
2) Fragile - need protection from knocks
3) Diver-specific (one diver = one meter)
4) Lack of full decompression information (ie total stop times)

SPECIFICATIONS

The BS-AC specification for dive computers is as follows:
1) The device shall measure water-pressure to at least 7 bar with an accuracy of ±0.025 bar.
2) The device shall measure atmospheric pressure.
3) The device shall measure time accurately.
4) The device shall work within the temperature range -10 C to +50 C without loss of accuracy.
5) The device shall be capable of storing and displaying its information for a minimum of 24 hours.
6) Adequate warning shall be given of low-power state.
7) Replacement of power source shall not affect stored information.
8) The device shall be portable enough to be easily carried by a diver.
9) When used for a dive of rectangular profile the device shall give the same information as would be obtained from an acceptable decompression table.

In addition the following displays are deemed necessary:
a) Time to no-stop situation.
b) Depth and time of next decompression stop.
c) Time to surface.
d) Warning of excessive rate of ascent.
e) "Look ahead" for next dive.

The following displays are also desirable:
a) Elapsed time of dive.
b) Current depth of dive.
c) Maximum depth of dive.
d) "Log-book" entry facility after dive.

CURRENT DIVE COMPUTERS

Several different makes of dive computers are currently being marketed in the UK. Brief details are given below of these, plus one now only obtainable secondhand. Any intending purchaser or user is advised to acquaint himself thoroughly with the available functions and the information displayed by the particular type of computer before using it underwater.

Decobrain (Divetronic)
The Decobrain is based on a CMOS 8-bit microprocessor with a 10kbyte ROM for the assembler programme and database. The peripherals are a piezo-resistor pressure sensor and four four-digit LCD displays. Five rechargeable NiCad cells give 80-100 hours running time and recharge in 5-6 hours. The Decobrain calculates the diver's nitrogen saturation and desaturation for 16 different tissues having half-times ranging from 4-635 minutes, in accordance with the ZHL-12 system published by Prof A. A. Buhlmann. The differential equation is solved at two-second intervals for each of the tissues. Using these calculations the decompression stages, decompression times, no-decompression times and desaturation times are all determined and displayed, along with elapsed time and time-to-surface current depth and

maximum depth. On ascending, warning lights indicate if the ascent rate is too fast and also when the diver is at a decompression stop. It is, however, no longer commercially available in the UK. Secondhand models should be treated with great care and calibrated before first use.

Edge (Orca)

The Edge is based on 12 tissue types with half-times from 5-480 minutes. A maximum full function depth of 49m limits its use for deep cave diving. It reads the atmospheric pressure before the dive and automatically compensates for altitude. It displays similar information to Decobrain, except the time to surface. The visual display is graphic rather than numeric, with even tissue saturation being displayed graphically. Ascent rate is 6-18m/minute. The decompression status and stops are displayed automatically. Battery replacement is required after approximately 50 hours.

Aladin & Aladin Pro (Dive Dynamics)

Of the various makes on the market at the time of writing, the most suitable for cave diving use are the Aladin and Monitor (see below) meters made by Uwatec of Switzerland. The Aladin comes in two versions, the original Aladin and the Aladin Pro. These meters give maximum depth (to -100m), current depth, elapsed dive time (to 999 minutes), remaining no-stop time, current decompression stops (if required) (to a maximum of -24m), visual decompression-required warning, current elapsed time of any surface interval, and contains logbook data of the last five dives, (nine with the Pro model (Note: this would not necessarily be the full profile of a cave dive if more than five separate sumps are passed - eg Wookey 9-24 requires at least eight separate underwater dives in and out.) Ascent rate is 10m/minute. Only the Pro gives actual duration of any stops necessary, and total decompression time to the surface. With the Pro, there is a loud audible warning if ascent rate is exceeded, as well as display indication. If a rapid emergency ascent takes the diver completely out of the Pro's standard decompression data, the display freezes on the maximum depth and the last tissue group that still remains saturated. This information is extremely useful when arriving at the recompression chamber.

The Aladin is based on 6 tissue types, and the Buhlmann decompression tables. It reads atmospheric pressure and then selects one of four altitude groups within its memory; the lowest is from 0-750m, (ie all altitudes in this range are equivalent). They display stops and decompression warning automatically. Battery life is approximately five years, and the replacement battery must be fitted by an authorised dealer.

Suunto

SME-ML Nine tissue type model. (SME-USN version is based on the USN tables.). Ascent rate is 10m/minute. Depth rated to 57m, they display stops, remaining no-stop time, full stop time and decompression warning automatically. It will not allow more than 30 minutes of decompression, and then enters Error Mode. It is not recommended as a decompression computer for cave diving. It does have a good memory, however, and can even remember the previous ten hours of diving at three minute intervals. The altitude range is 0-300metres. Battery life is approximately 1,000 hours.

Monitor

The Aqua-Lung Monitor 2 is a fully-fledged decompression computer with the same internal chip as the Aladin Pro. Performance and readout information are as for the Aladin Pro above, save that the display is larger and easier to read. Memory function covers the last nine dives and total ascent time is given. It can be mounted on the wrist or as part of a console.

Mini-Brain

The Dacor Mini-Brain is depth rated to 70m with a 199 minute dive time, and has a ten year battery life.

Fig. 50: Taking the cue from a dive computer during a long decompression schedule.

The effects of pressure

Chapter 6: Mixed Gas Diving

NITROX

NITROX is a gas mixture of oxygen (O_2) and nitrogen (N_2) containing differing properties from those of standard air (21% oxygen, 79% nitrogen). A diving nitrox mixture generally contains a higher proportion of oxygen than air.

The use of nitrox as a diving gas is well-established in both military and commercial diving. The advantage of nitrox is that breathing a richer oxygen mixture reduces the decompression time, due to the fact that decompression is a function of the nitrogen content in the breathing gas and the diving depth. Replacing a part of the nitrogen content with oxygen would thus have the same effect as a reduction in depth. In nitrox diving, a commonly used term is equivalent air depth (EAD). This is the depth at which the nitrogen partial pressure when using air is equal to that of the actual diving depth on the nitrox mixture. The EAD can be established using the following equation:

$$EAD = \frac{(D+10)N}{79} - 10$$

(Where D = depth and N = percentage nitrogen in nitrox mixture.)

The result is the depth used to determine decompression from standard air diving tables.

Example: 30m dive using a 40% oxygen mixture:

$$EAD = \frac{(30+10)60}{79} - 10 = 20.4m$$

From a decompression standpoint, it could be suggested that the oxygen content should be as high as possible. However, this increases the risk of oxygen poisoning, and hence limits need to be established.

Oxygen Poisoning

The occurrence of oxygen poisoning is dependent upon the partial pressure of the oxygen breathed and the time for which it is breathed. The two major results are either chronic or acute oxygen poisoning. Chronic poisoning is usually the first to appear, and moderate levels of poisoning cause minor complaints which, if noticed in time, are fully reversible. The primary effects manifest themselves as a soreness in the chest and a shortage of breath. Acute poisoning affects the brain and central nervous system directly, symptoms are usually, but not always, preceded by advance warnings such as facial twitches shortly before the advanced symptoms appear (see section on *Oxygen decompression*). Acute symptoms are abnormal vision and hearing, dizziness and nausea, skin pricking (especially round the mouth), euphoria, breathing difficulties, convulsions and unconsciousness. It must be stressed that from the onset of early symptoms to the more serious ones occurring may be anything from a few hours to a few seconds! Assume the worst if in doubt.

With a maximum partial pressure of oxygen of 2 bar, acute poisoning should not occur. However, a maximum partial pressure of 1.6 bar of oxygen is more widely accepted to give a greater margin of safety, though pulmonary problems still occur even at the 1.6 bar oxygen levels. (The lower limit that no ill effects occur at is 0.5 bar.) To assess the oxygen dose (termed the unit of pulmonary toxicity dose, or UPTD), the following empirically-based equation has been developed:

$$UPTD = t(2P - 1)^{0.833}$$

where t = time, and P = partial pressure of oxygen.

The UPTD is calculated for each dive during a 24 hour period and the totals are added together. The accepted maximum UPTD is 1425, and is compiled from multiple dives plus the treatment for decompression sickness. At this dose level, a 10% reduction in vital capacity in 50% of divers is anticipated. It is only really safe to allow exposures up to this level under strictly-controlled circumstances (ie when undergoing treatment for decompression sickness in a chamber). The practical UPTD limit for in-water diving is 615.

Another added safety margin may be gained by the introduction of short periods of breathing ordinary air rather than nitrox. This is now common practice for divers undergoing pure oxygen decompression or treatment, on a 20 minutes oxygen, 5 minutes air basis. These air breaks may occur normally due to the nature of a cave dive (where airbells are reached) or can be introduced by changing to air underwater. They can be done without affecting decompression if the change-over occurs at a depth shallower than the EAD or during decompression stops.

Example: A dive to be carried out at a previously explored site. Sump 1 is 500m long and 16m deep, passed in 32 minutes to 100m of dry passage, which takes around 25 minutes to pass through. Sump 2 has been explored for 300m to -26m, the return journey taking 38 minutes. The dive plan has to cater for -30m for 60 minutes. (Norwegian tables will be used for this example).

Case 1: Using air
Sump 1, -16m/32 minutes. Table 18m/35 minutes, no stops, Repeat Group F.
Sump 2, -30m/60 minutes (repeat penalty 25 minutes). Table -30m/90 minutes.
95 minutes decompression. Repeat Group Z.
Sump 1 return. -16m/32 minutes. (repeat penalty 125 minutes). Table -18m/180 minutes. 60 minutes decompression.

Case 2: Using nitrox
For logistical reasons it would be intended to use one nitrox mixture only, and this would be a 40% oxygen/60% nitrogen mix, which at -30m would give a partial pressure of oxygen of 1.6 bar (figure 51).
Sump 1, -16m/32 minutes. EAD = 10m, Table -12m/35 minutes, no stops, Repeat Group D. UPTD = 1.07 x 32 = 34.
Sump 2, -30m/60 minutes. EAD = 20.9m. (repeat penalty = 20 minutes) Table -21m/85 mins. 25 mins decompression. Repeat Group M. UPTD = 116.

Mixed gas diving 169

Table 6/1a

TABLE OF EAD/p.p.O$_2$/UPTD per min.

% OXYGEN

D \ %	32	34	36	38	40	42	44	46	48	50
10	8/0.7/0.35	7/0.7/0.43	7/0.8/0.51	6/0.8/0.58	6/0.8/0.65	5/0.9/0.73	5/0.9/0.8	4/1.0/0.86	4/1.0/0.93	3/1.0/1.0
12	9/0.7/0.47	9/0.8/0.56	8/0.8/0.64	8/0.9/0.72	7/0.9/0.8	7/1.0/0.87	6/1.0/0.95	6/1.1/1.02	5/1.1/1.09	4/1.1/1.17
14	11/0.8/0.6	11/0.9/0.68	10/0.9/0.77	9/1.0/0.85	9/1.0/0.93	8/1.1/1.01	8/1.1/1.09	7/1.1/1.17	6/1.2/1.25	6/1.2/1.34
16	13/0.9/0.71	12/0.9/0.8	12/1.0/0.89	11/1.0/0.98	10/1.1/1.07	10/1.1/1.15	9/1.2/1.23	8/1.2/1.32	8/1.3/1.4	7/1.3/1.5
18	15/0.9/0.82	14/1.0/0.92	13/1.0/1.01	12/1.1/1.11	12/1.1/1.2	11/1.2/1.29	10/1.3/1.37	10/1.3/1.46	9/1.4/1.55	8/1.4/1.66
20	16/1.0/0.93	16/1.1/1.03	15/1.1/1.13	14/1.2/1.23	13/1.2/1.32	13/1.3/1.42	12/1.4/1.51	11/1.4/1.6	10/1.5/1.69	9/1.5/1.82
22	18/1.1/1.04	17/1.1/1.15	16/1.2/1.25	16/1.3/1.35	15/1.3/1.45	14/1.4/1.55	13/1.4/1.64	12/1.5/1.74	12/1.6/1.83	11/1.6/1.98
24	20/1.1/1.15	19/1.2/1.25	18/1.3/1.36	17/1.3/1.47	16/1.4/1.57	15/1.5/1.67	15/1.5/1.78	14/1.6/1.88	13/1.7/1.98	12/1.7/2.13
26	21/1.2/1.25	21/1.3/1.36	20/1.3/1.47	19/1.4/1.58	18/1.5/1.69	17/1.6/1.8	16/1.6/1.91	15/1.7/2.01	14/1.8/2.11	13/1.8/2.29
28	23/1.3/1.35	22/1.3/1.47	21/1.4/1.58	20/1.5/1.7	19/1.6/1.81	18/1.6/1.92	17/1.7/2.03	16/1.8/2.14	16/1.9/2.25	15/1.9/2.44
30	25/1.3/1.45	24/1.4/1.57	23/1.5/1.69	22/1.6/1.81	21/1.6/1.93	20/1.7/2.04	19/1.8/2.16	18/1.9/2.27	17/2.0/2.39	16/2.0/2.59
32	27/1.4/1.55	26/1.5/1.67	24/1.6/1.8	23/1.6/1.92	22/1.7/2.04	21/1.8/2.17	20/1.9/2.28	19/2.0/2.4		
34	28/1.4/1.65	27/1.5/1.78	26/1.6/1.91	25/1.7/2.03	24/1.8/2.16	23/1.9/2.28	22/2.0/2.41			
36	30/1.5/1.74	29/1.6/1.88	28/1.7/2.01	27/1.8/2.14	25/1.9/2.27	24/2.0/2.4				
38	32/1.6/1.84	31/1.7/1.98	29/1.8/2.11	28/1.9/2.25	27/2.0/2.39					
40	33/1.6/1.93	32/1.7/2.07	31/1.8/2.22	30/1.9/2.36	28/2.0/2.5					
42	35/1.7/2.02	34/1.8/2.17	33/1.9/2.32	31/2.0/2.46						
44	37/1.8/2.11	36/1.9/2.27	34/2.0/2.42							
46	39/1.8/2.21	37/1.9/2.36								
48	40/1.9/2.3	39/2.0/2.46								
50	42/2.0/2.39									

DEPTH (mm)

Fig. 51: Oxgen partial pressure table.

Sump 1 return, -16m/32 mins. EAD = 10.1m. (repeat penalty = 190 minutes)
Table -12m/225 mins, 15 minutes decompression. UPTD = 34.
Total UPTD of 184 is well within limits.

The use of nitrox for this example would be well worthwhile, since it reduces the required decompression by 115 minutes whilst being well within the UPTD limit. It should be noted that decompression time spent on high partial pressure of oxygen mixtures will also contribute to the UPTD, and should be accounted for if approaching the limit. The reduction in time spent decompressing would inevitably improve safety, as the diver would be less liable to hypothermia and hence decompression sickness. Another advantage would be the reduction in any narcosis effects at -30m.

When using this EAD method and standard air decompression tables, no reduction in stop times should be made. Any altitude corrections should be calculated within the EAD.

Apart from the inherent pre-dive planning required, the only other problem that may be encountered is actually getting a supply of the gas. Both diving and medical gas suppliers can provide pre-mixed gas to any composition, providing cylinders are colour coded and labelled with the chemical composition of the gas. The user would also be provided with an analysis certificate. This may, however, prove to be an expensive source, probably costing £5-10 per 12l cylinder at late 1980s prices.

The alternative is for the diver to mix the gas. This is achieved by decanting a known pressure of pure oxygen (medical or diving quality - industrial quality may contain impurities) into an empty cylinder and then subsequently filling to working pressure with air. Accurate gas mixing is reliant upon an accurate pressure gauge (standard contents gauges can vary by +/- 10% in accuracy) and it would be wise to have the resultant gas mix analysed prior to use. Gas mixed in this manner should be allowed to stand for 24 hours to allow the gases to intermix fully prior to analysis or use.

To determine the initial oxygen charge pressure for any mix, use the following equation:

$$\text{Oxygen (bar)} = \frac{P(79 - N)}{(79)}$$

Where P = cylinder working pressure (bar) and N = percentage nitrogen in final mix.

Example: Using a 12l cylinder, with a working pressure of 228 bar. A nitrox mix of 40% oxygen/60% nitrogen is required.

Oxygen pressure = 228 x [(79-60)/79] = 54.8 bar.

Therefore decant 55 bar of oxygen into the cylinder, and then fill to 228 bar with air. Allow it to cool and then top up with air to 228 bar again. Overcharging initially may dilute the gas mix.

Care must be taken when using pure oxygen for in-water decompression, even at the shallowest 3m stop when using a nitrox mix, to avoid excessive exposure to the gas.

HELIOX

The practical limits for air diving were established as long ago as 1915, when US Navy divers salvaged the submarine USSF-4 from a depth of 92m. Divers were able to work at this depth - just. Decompression penalties and the effects of nitrogen narcosis limited bottom time to ten minutes. A few years later, an inventor named Elihu Thompson estimated that by replacing nitrogen with helium, working depth would be increased by 50%.

In the ensuing half-century, experimental and military research pushed diving using helium and other inert gas mixtures (neon, hydrogen) to depths in excess of 300m. The practical limit for helium diving was between 230m and 260m due to a variety of symptoms and practical considerations discussed later. With the development of offshore oil fields in the 1970s, new techniques, equipment and decompression schedules were developed by private companies, shifting the emphasis from military use.

Saturation diving was introduced, whereby divers were pressurised at the start of their dive to their working depth, and then spent up to a month in a deck decompression chamber, travelling to work in a pressurised diving bell. Final decompression took place in the deck chamber, often taking a week or more to complete. Today, non-saturation mixed gas diving (or bell-bounce, as it is more commonly referred to) is virtually unknown in the North Sea.

ADVANTAGES & DISADVANTAGES

Helium is less narcotic than nitrogen when breathed at depth. If it was simply a matter of swapping 79% nitrogen with 79% helium for deep diving mixes, life would be very simple indeed. However, oxygen starts to become toxic at 2 bars (10m depth), and depth increases the oxygen toxicity of any breathing gas mixture with the result that breathing air at about 85m is as toxic as breathing pure oxygen at 10m depth.

To overcome this problem is simply a matter of reducing the oxygen content in a specific gas mixture. The diver must then be aware of two important factors:

firstly, an oxygen-weak mix may prove anoxic at shallow depths; secondly,

the stronger the percentage of inert gas, the greater the absorption of that gas into the bloodstream, and hence the longer the decompression.

Helium is not as readily taken up by body tissues as nitrogen, but once it has been absorbed, it is not so readily released. This can also lead to longer decompression times. However, nitrogen is four times more readily absorbed into the fatty tissues of the body than helium, and, due to the poor circulation of blood through these fatty tissues, takes four times as long to escape than helium. This explains why a nitrox decompression takes longer than a heliox one.

The small molecular size of helium enables it to escape from the most seemingly gas-proof joints, including sealed SCUBA cylinders, and this means that the actual oxygen content of any gas mixture must be checked prior to the start of any dive, or before the gas is put on-line to a diver.

The thermal conductivity of helium also creates problems. A body surrounded by helium loses heat far more rapidly than one surrounded by nitrogen, and body core heat is more rapidly lost through exhalation. As depth increases, so does the density of the gas. More molecules come into contact with the diver's body, and heat is conducted away even more rapidly (see figure 52). In commercial dives heated suits are worn when deeper than 50m, and the gas itself is heated when over 150m, or the body core temperature drops too rapidly. Where variable volume drysuits are used, these should only be inflated with air.

Finally, there is decompression sickness. Helium bends must only be treated with helium-oxygen mixtures and by suitably qualified personnel under the supervision of a specialist doctor.

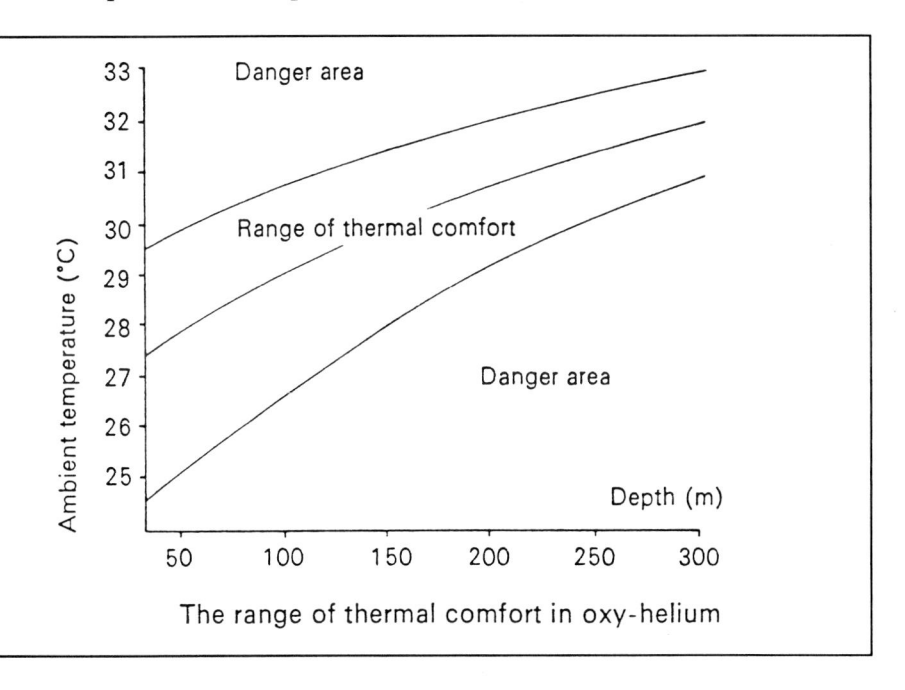

Fig. 52: Heliox use/temperature curve.

EQUIPMENT

Because the density of gas increases with depth, it is essential to ensure that the breathing apparatus can cope. Air becomes noticeably syrupy at 60m, with an accompanying increase in breathing effort. Heliox, with its smaller atomic size, is less dense and an easier gas to breathe at comparative depths, heliox at about 300m being equivalent to air at about 30m. By 500m, however, it also becomes too dense to use without mechanically-boosted assistance.

It is advantageous, therefore, to have a second stage with as high a flow as possible to allow easier breathing at depth, especially if hard work or hard finning is envisaged. Remember that most demand valve first stages work at a pressure of about 10 bars above ambient pressure. This means that the reserve air in a cylinder becomes progressively less available at depth. For example, at a depth equivalent to a pressure of 10 bars (-90m) there are 20 bars of gas unavailable to the diver in each cylinder. Though this becomes progressively more available on ascent, it should be calculated into margins available at the deepest point of the dive.

Any SCUBA equipment designed for heliox use must be specially serviced, and all potentially leaking joints or seatings cleaned, re-sealed (using oxygen-grade PTFE tape) or changed. This includes cylinder valves, which should be removed and serviced.

Drysuits used in heliox diving should have their direct feed air supply connected to a separate air cylinder, which must not be used for breathing at depth. The capacity of the cylinder will depend on the depth and duration of the dive to be undertaken, but the problems of ascending from depth without the availability of a direct feed supply are significant, and the amount carried should reflect this. Extra undergarments should be worn for heliox diving, and on no account should long dives be made on heliox without heated suits outside the depth/temperature boundary curve in figure 52.

Stage tanks to get to depth in the cave can be filled with air, which may be used to a descent depth of 60m, if the diver is nitrogen tolerant to that depth. These tanks must not be used on ascent - the heliox mixture must be breathed back to the oxygen decompression tanks or oxygen umbilical placed for decompression. The problems of reverse-gas diffusion, where denser nitrogen can hinder the expulsion of lighter helium from the tissues, exceed acceptable safety margins. Stage tanks to be used on a heliox dive should contain the same proportions of heliox as the diver's main mixture, unless due professional computation of time/depth/mix ratios has been made, and full back-up facilities are available on site.

To cut down on cost, and on the amount of gas that has to be carried by the diver, a semi-closed circuit or closed circuit rebreathing system may be considered for use. These have been used in cave diving both for nitrox and heliox mixtures, but are expensive. (See section on *Rebreathers*).

MIXED GAS DECOMPRESSION

Mixed gas diving is far more complex than air diving, but still allows a choice of operational procedures and equipment, and a potential for depth and duration far beyond that of air. Procedures for mixed gas decompression must be rigorously adhered to, as even in first-world countries support facilities for mixed gas decompression-related incidents are limited and rarely available.

Before making a mixed gas dive, the diver should ascertain where the nearest chamber capable of mixed gas therapy to cover his operating depth/duration is situated, and would do well to discuss the profile of the dive with them or with other expert medical sources first.

Due to the greater depths and times involved, the diver may be more liable to oxygen toxicity than in air decompression, and he and his colleagues must be constantly alert for the symptoms.

The US Navy Mixed Gas SCUBA decompression tables are only suitable for semi-closed or closed-circuit decompression where the percentage of

Fig. 53: A dry-suited diver prepares for a deep heliox dive wearing back-mounted dual-manifold cylinders and a separate air inflation cylinder to avoid heat loss.

Mixed gas diving 175

oxygen is varied to keep the partial pressure constant. They are therefore of no use with open-circuit sets. However, the surface supply tables allow for the use of all types of circuit and can be used in open water. These tables, also referred to as the partial pressure decompression tables, permit the use of heliox mixtures with a wide range of oxygen concentrations. The normal minimum oxygen content of a breathing gas is 16%, which will allow a diver on the surface to breathe without hypoxia developing. However, at this level any movement would probably render him unconscious. The maximum oxygen percentage is governed by depth and bottom time before oxygen toxicity sets in, and expert advice must be obtained before computing field mixtures. Partial pressure and exposure times must not exceed the limits.

On ascent from a heliox cave dive, the two shallowest stops should be made on pure oxygen. The use of open-circuit oxygen allows the inert gas to escape on a one-way basis, and theoretically accelerates decompression. Note that most commercial in-water tables require a deeper oxygen stop than 9m, possibly 15m. This is extremely hazardous, and should not be done unless in a hard hat or bell, with in-water medical support.

The use of a surface umbilical and full-face mask for long oxygen decompressions is highly recommended. This allows the gas mixture to be changed should symptoms of toxicity develop, and for the system to be fully-flushed with pure oxygen to remove all traces of helium. Note that rates of ascent for helium diving may be different from those for air.

This section has been included in the manual as an insight into the problems associated with mixed gas diving. It is not a training section.

Diving is dangerous. Cave diving is more dangerous than open water diving. Mixed gas cave diving is probably the most dangerous of all. Do not, under any circumstances, try any type of mixed gas diving without expert consultation.

TRIMIX

IT is well known that when nitrogen is breathed at a partial pressure of more than 4 bar it has a narcotic effect. Similarly, oxygen breathed at partial pressures of 2 bar or more can cause acute oxygen poisoning. If the breathing gas is air, these partial pressure limits of nitrogen and oxygen are reached at depths of 40m and 90m respectively. The depths at which these conditions occur can be increased by replacing some of the nitrogen and oxygen content of air with less narcotic and chemically-inert helium. The resulting three-gas mixture is called trimix.

Obtaining and using trimix is complicated and potentially dangerous. This section is not intended to give the cave diver enough information to carry out a trimix dive, but rather to give an appreciation of its use and the pitfalls to avoid.

All the pressures quoted are absolute pressures (ie they include atmospheric pressure) and all the percentages quoted are percentages by volume.

MIXING AND STORING TRIMIX

The proportions of each of the three gases in the trimix are determined by the depth at which it is to be used. At that depth the partial pressure of nitrogen should be about 4 bar, and that of oxygen should not exceed 2 bar. The oxygen content should also not be less than 0.15 bar on the surface (15% by volume) to enable a safe descent to be made. The remainder of the mixture is helium. For example, a mixture recently devised for use at 100m contained 38% nitrogen, 17% oxygen and 45% helium.

In practice, the trimix is a mixture of oxygen, helium and air because the nitrogen in air costs nothing. Vacuum is pulled on the cylinder, and oxygen put in first to minimise the pressure at which it is decanted. Even so, the equipment needs to be free of oil and dirt to avoid an oxygen explosion, and some suppliers will refuse to fill aluminium and aluminium-lined cylinders. The helium is then put in, and the final pressure reached by topping up with the correct proportion of air.

Having filled the cylinders, it is wise to check the proportions of the component gases with a suitably reliable technique, such as gas chromatography.

If the gas is then stored for a time before use, two further problems can arise. Firstly, helium can escape from nominally airtight cylinders because it is much less dense than air. So cylinder pressures should be noted before storage and checked again at the same temperature before use. If there has been a drop in pressure, it is likely that this cylinder contains an oxygen- and nitrogen-rich mixture, and would be dangerous at depth. Secondly, because helium is lighter than oxygen and nitrogen, the mixture can separate into layers if the cylinder is left still. Considerable agitation is then required to remix the gases and this must be done before the mixture is breathed.

DIVING ON TRIMIX

Although nitrogen narcosis can begin to occur at a depth of 40m when breathing air, trimix is not normally considered unless a dive entails going deeper than 50m. Beyond this depth, the advantages of trimix begin to outweigh the disadvantages.

The first obstacle is that of obtaining a suitable set of decompression tables. Very few are available, and some of those that are advise the use of pure oxygen below 9m (which is very dangerous and should not be considered for in-water decompression). However, the US Navy Exceptional Exposure tables can be used for helium diving if pure oxygen is breathed at the 3m and 6m stops. Trimix decompression schedules based on this advice have been successfully completed in both the USA and in Britain in caves. It must be remembered that this practice is experimental, and the risk of decompression sickness is high. Individuals should be experienced in decompression and therefore be aware of their own susceptibility to decompression sickness before embarking on this course of action and must be in perfect physical condition.

Helium has also an exceptional ability to transfer heat, so measures must be taken to avoid excessive cooling of the body. The first step is to ensure that the helium content of the mixture is at a minimum, replacing only that portion of the nitrogen and oxygen as is necessary for the particular dive profile. Secondly, a neoprene drysuit with a separate air supply for inflation (perhaps a pony bottle) should be worn, together with one or more layers of insulating underwear. The colder a diver gets, the more susceptible he is to decompression sickness, and to cutting short a decompression schedule because of problems with hypothermia.

To date, trimix has been successfully used in Wookey Hole and in Gavel Pot on Britain's two deepest cave dives. However, the mixture and decompression tables for both dives were obtained with the help of both the US Navy and the commercial diving industry. Both were tested in a chamber dive to the equivalent of 75m.

Though it is possible to produce a trimix mixture by drawing vacuum on a tank and filling it with the required percentage of helium, and then topping it up with the required percentage of compressed air from a compressor, care should be taken to ensure that the purity of the air is exceptionally high. Traces of carbon monoxide or other impurities that might be acceptable at shallow depths on short dives can be lethal on very deep ones. Such homemade mixes should be treated with great care, and analysis is every bit as important with these as with commercially-mixed supplies.

If trimix appears to be the best solution to a particular problem, then contact the relevant authorities and divers experienced in its use to gain advice.

REBREATHERS

WITH open circuit breathing apparatus, diving depth and time is severely restricted by the low efficiency of gas utilisation which results from the complete loss of each exhalation of breathing gas. The actual gas utilisation, based upon the consumption of available oxygen, is in the order of 5% at atmospheric pressure and decreases in percentage with depth. All types of rebreathing apparatus increase this gas utilisation efficiency in varying degrees by removing carbon dioxide from the expired gas and controlling the oxygen concentration within physiologically safe limits. This allows much of the exhaled gas to be reused.

The three main types of rebreather are discussed in the following sections. However, specific equipment varies, and this only offers guidance as to the principles of operation.

CLOSED-CIRCUIT OXYGEN

In its varying forms, this type of equipment has probably the highest gas utilisation efficiency of all breathing apparatus, since 100% of the gas carried is available for metabolic use. Figure 54 shows a single-bag oxygen system as typically used by the Cave Diving Group in the past.

The basic principle of operation is simple. Oxygen is fed at a fixed mass flow rate into the breathing circuit, this rate corresponding with the rate of metabolic consumption. The rate of metabolic consumption is proportional to the work rate, being typically 0.5l/minute at rest, and up to 3l/minute for heavy work. The flow control system shown is of the fixed flow type, which consists of an absolute pressure regulator (pressure output does not vary with depth) and a critical flow orifice (gas flowing through the orifice is at critical flow and as such will not vary with changing depth). The flow setting is usually around 1.5l/minute, corresponding with moderate work, though this can be increased or decreased by operation of a manual valve if required.

The breathing circuit consists of a breathing bag of usually 6-8l capacity, which is connected by a large-bore hose (to reduce breathing resistance) to the carbon dioxide (CO_2) scrubber. The scrubber is a watertight container holding a pelletised CO_2 absorbent material, such as Baralime, Sodalime or Sodasorb. These are all efficient CO_2 absorbents which produce the minimum of caustic fumes if inadvertently wetted. The capacity of scrubber units varies from 1kg to 3kg, thus limiting the set duration. Absorption capacity is usually taken at approximately 30 minutes to 1kg at a water temperature of 21°C. This can, however, be significantly reduced by lower water temperatures, with an 80% reduction at 4°C.

The outlet from the CO_2 scrubber is connected by another large-bore hose to the mouthpiece. With this type of apparatus, there is a considerable

A – gas supply
B – shut off valve
C – absolute pressure regulator
D – critical flow orifice
E – bypass valve
F – mouthpiece
G – CO_2 scrubber
H – breathing bag

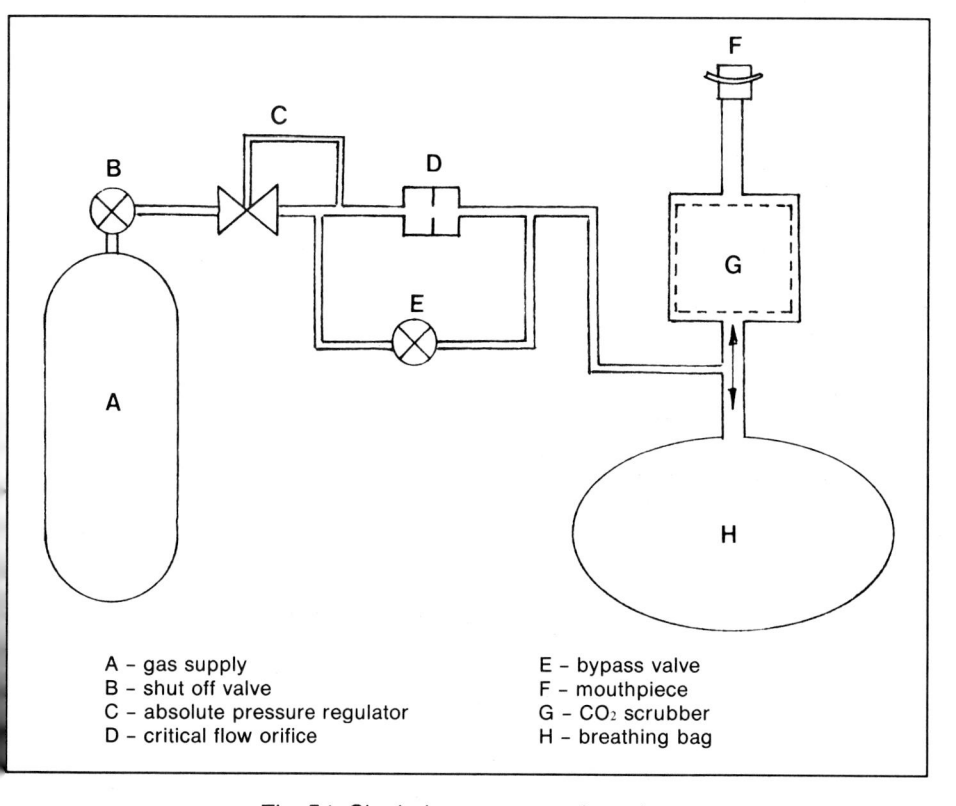

Fig. 54: Single-bag oxygen rebreather.

Mixed gas diving 179

dead volume within the single breathing hose and scrubber. Hoses should be as short as possible and shallow breathing should be avoided.

Figure 55 shows a more up-to-date oxygen rebreather, which uses the same principles as those discussed previously. The main difference in this set is that the breathing circuit is a loop, governed by non-return valves in the mouthpiece. This eliminates the dead volume in the breathing circuit and, since the gas has only to travel through the CO_2 scrubber once, it reduces the breathing resistance. The twin breathing bags, each of approximately 4l, help to balance the inhalation/exhalation resistance.

The other difference is that the type of oxygen flow control is a needle valve which can be adjusted during the dive to match the oxygen consumption. Flow is usually pre-set to around 1l/minute prior to the dive.

The main advantages of an oxygen rebreather are the long system duration (about 90 minutes for a 1.2l cylinder) providing the scrubber capacity is adequate, and the relative compactness and low weight of the unit. The disadvantages are the risk of oxygen toxicity (hypoxia) at depths greater than 10m, of anoxia due to nitrogen accumulating in the breathing bag if breathing is unduly shallow and the lungs are not flushed out (combined with nitrogen coming out of solution in the body tissues), of caustic poisoning due to water coming into contact with the CO_2 scrubber, and of the lack of system redundancy and the fragility of some of the components, such as hoses and bags.

SEMI-CLOSED-CIRCUIT MIXED GAS

The basic system is as shown in figure 55 except that the flow control is usually a replaceable critical flow orifice selected for the flow rate required, and that both breathing bags are fitted with exhaust valves.

The principle of operation is that a fixed mass flow of gas containing a higher percentage of oxygen than would be used on open-circuit is fed into the breathing circuit where it recirculates as in the oxygen rebreather. Since the gas fed into the system will contain a proportion of diluent (nitrogen, helium, neon), the pre-set flow rate is critical and must be maintained to constantly flush through the breathing circuit to prevent anoxia.

Having established that the rate of oxygen consumption is proportional to the work rate, it follows that the actual percentage of oxygen in the breathing mixture (given fixed gas composition and flow rate input) will vary with the work rate and will always be a lower percentage of oxygen than the gas feed. The actual percentage of oxygen in the breathing circuit is given by:

$$O_2 \text{ circuit \%age} = \frac{(O_2/100 \times \text{flow}) - O_2 \text{ consumption}}{100 \times \text{Flow} - O_2 \text{ consumption}}$$

Examples:
a) 40% oxygen/60% nitrogen mixture, with diver at rest and flow rate of 0.5l/minute. Flowrate setting is 12l/minute.

$$\text{Oxygen} = 100 \frac{[(0.4 \times 12) - 0.5)]}{[\quad 12 - 0.5 \quad]} = 37.4\% \ O_2 \ \& \text{ thus } 62.6\% \ N_2.$$

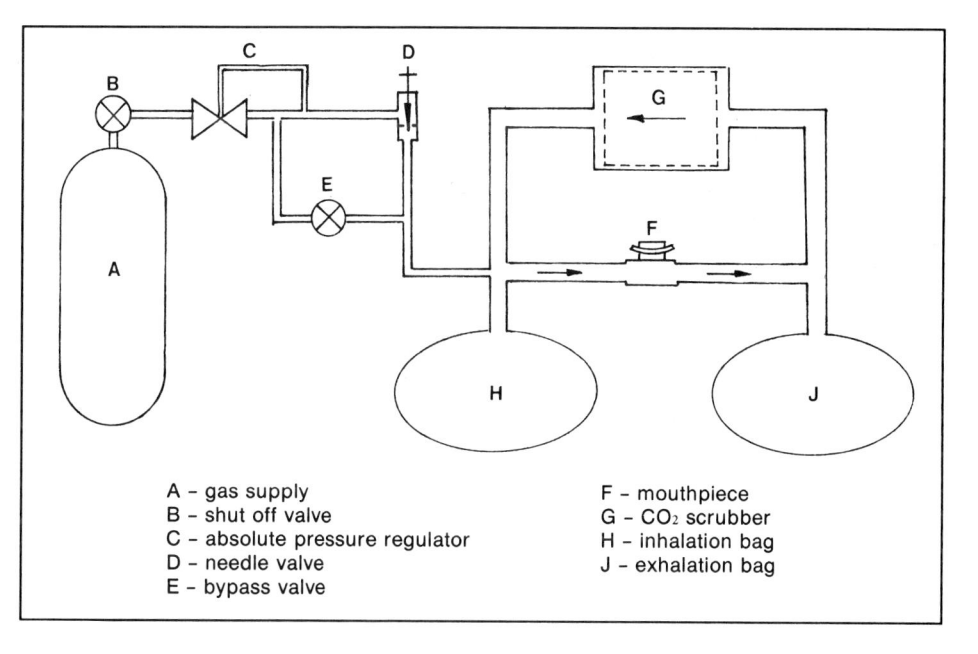

Fig. 55: A modern oxygen rebreather system.

A - gas supply
B - shut off valve
C - absolute pressure regulator
D - needle valve
E - bypass valve
F - mouthpiece
G - CO_2 scrubber
H - inhalation bag
J - exhalation bag

b) Mixture and setting as a), but diver undertaking heavy work (ie use at 3l/minute)

$$\text{Oxygen} = 100 \frac{[(0.4 \times 12) - 0.5]}{[12 - 3.0]} = 20\% \text{ O}_2 \text{ \& thus } 80\% \text{ N}_2.$$

As seen from the examples above, the oxygen and nitrogen percentages can vary significantly, and the flow rate settings and gas feed composition are critical. Tables of flowrate settings are published for particular apparatus, but are all based on the following guidelines:

a) Oxygen percentages should not fall below 16% under heavy work, to prevent anoxia at shallow depths.

b) The maximum depth for a mixture is determined by the oxygen in the delivery mix. This is normally based on a maximum partial pressure of oxygen of 1.6 bar absolute.

c) Decompression is normally determined for the maximum possible diluent gas content in the breathing circuit (ie when diver is undertaking heavy work).

d) Fresh CO_2 scrubber is used on each separate dive.

The main advantage of this system is the relatively long duration at greater depths than with closed-circuit oxygen (eg a dive to -25m would use a 40% O_2/60% N_2 mix with a flow rate setting of 12l/minute, thus an 8.5l cylinder would last for about 160 minutes compared with 20 minutes on open-circuit.). The disadvantages are that the maximum depth is restricted by the mix and flow setting, as well as those outlined for closed-circuit oxygen above.

CLOSED-CIRCUIT MIXED GAS

This type of system primarily evolved from the diver lock-out type of mini-submersible, where a self-contained system was required to give long durations at depth. The principle of operation is not unlike the semi-closed-circuit, but the flow of oxygen and diluent gas into the system is from separate cylinders with a microprocessor and oxygen sensors controlling the gas mixture within the breathing circuit to maintain it within the range of physiological tolerance (figure 56).

Early models of this type of system proved to be unreliable and complicated due to the necessary dual circuits, and a common complaint seemed to be that the diver spent all his time monitoring the equipment rather than working. Research waned when saturation techniques became more accepted, but in recent years there have been new developments in this system, generally for military purposes. These have much improved the reliability of the systems, and there are a number of systems in production. Availability is restricted, and the costs are generally prohibitive, but modified Rexnord Mk 16 rebreathers were used successfully by CDG members to reach depths of over 90m in Bahamian caves.

Theoretically, these units have a maximum operating depth of almost 500m and a duration of up to 8 hours if used at a fixed depth. Use on a mixed

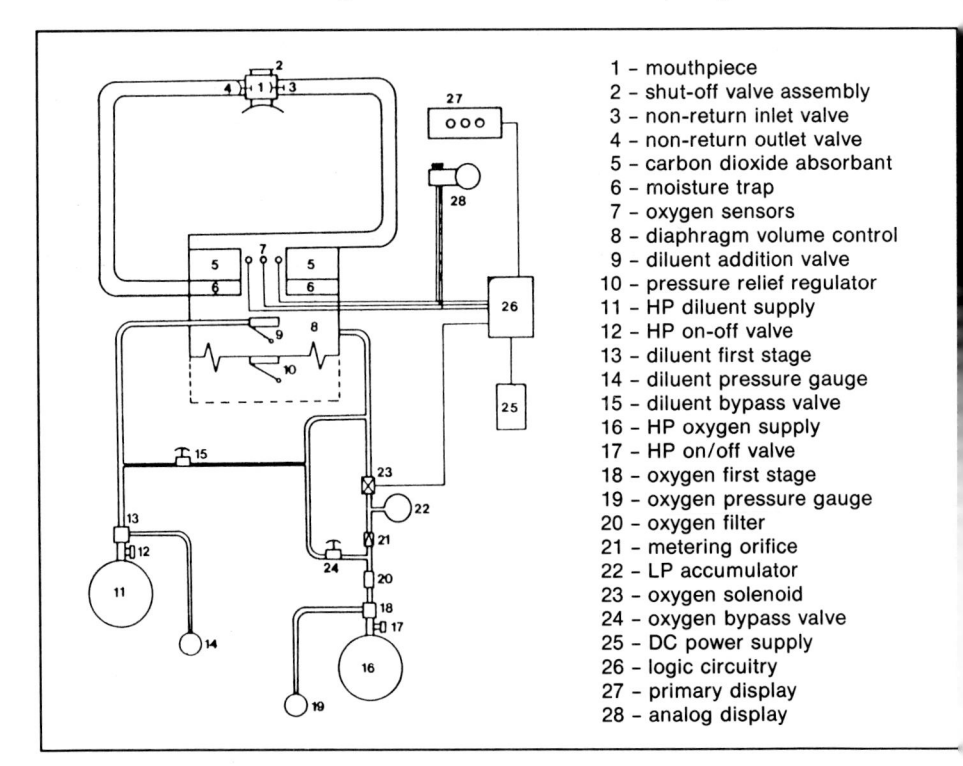

1 – mouthpiece
2 – shut-off valve assembly
3 – non-return inlet valve
4 – non-return outlet valve
5 – carbon dioxide absorbant
6 – moisture trap
7 – oxygen sensors
8 – diaphragm volume control
9 – diluent addition valve
10 – pressure relief regulator
11 – HP diluent supply
12 – HP on-off valve
13 – diluent first stage
14 – diluent pressure gauge
15 – diluent bypass valve
16 – HP oxygen supply
17 – HP on/off valve
18 – oxygen first stage
19 – oxygen pressure gauge
20 – oxygen filter
21 – metering orifice
22 – LP accumulator
23 – oxygen solenoid
24 – oxygen bypass valve
25 – DC power supply
26 – logic circuitry
27 – primary display
28 – analog display

Fig. 56: A closed-circuit mixed-gas rebreather system.

profile dive, where depth may vary throughout the dive, reduces the duration of the system due to excess pressure within the breathing bag being vented to allow for changes in external pressure.

New developments in closed-circuit mixed gas rebreathers will allow long-distance cave diving penetrations to be made in relative safety, and at far greater depths that open-circuit mixed gas would ever allow. A further advantage over open-circuit mixed gas is that the percentage of oxygen in the breathing mix is increased as depth lessens, giving an added safety factor during decompression. The disadvantage of most current units is a lack of redundancy and the relative fragility of exposed parts (such as the breathing hose), and the high initial price and ensuing operating costs.

The field availability of breathing-quality gases (oxygen and diluent) and of suitable recompression facilities for mixed gas diving are also limiting factors. Gas composition in the breathing mix, though generally accurately controlled by micro-processors and oxygen sensors within the unit, should be analysed before field use by a gas chromatograph or similar analytical apparatus to ensure maximum safety. Consideration should also be given in underground use to the availability of a bail-out system in the case of rebreather failure. This could be an open-circuit mixed gas system of one or more stage tanks per diver, and these must contain a gas mix relevant to the operating depth. If such a bail-out system is used, an additional facility for extended decompression must also be available in the water (eg surface umbilical rigged for heliox/nitrox/oxygen change-over).

For all rebreathing systems, it is imperative that the carbon dioxide absorbent in the scrubber system is changed after each dive, and that breathing hoses and breathing bag are regularly decontaminated to avoid bacterial infection. Water must never be allowed to enter the system through the mouthpiece - either it stays in the mouth while in the water, or a manual shut-off valve must be fixed so that it can be sealed while out of the mouth. Water entering the absorbent will react to form a caustic soda mixture that will burn lungs if inhaled. It is worth considering the use of an open-circuit back-up set to provide redundancy with any rebreather system.

*Fig. 57: Maytime, Agen Allwedd - a CDG discovery in 1972.
Finding a dry way there took another fifteen years.*

Mixed gas diving

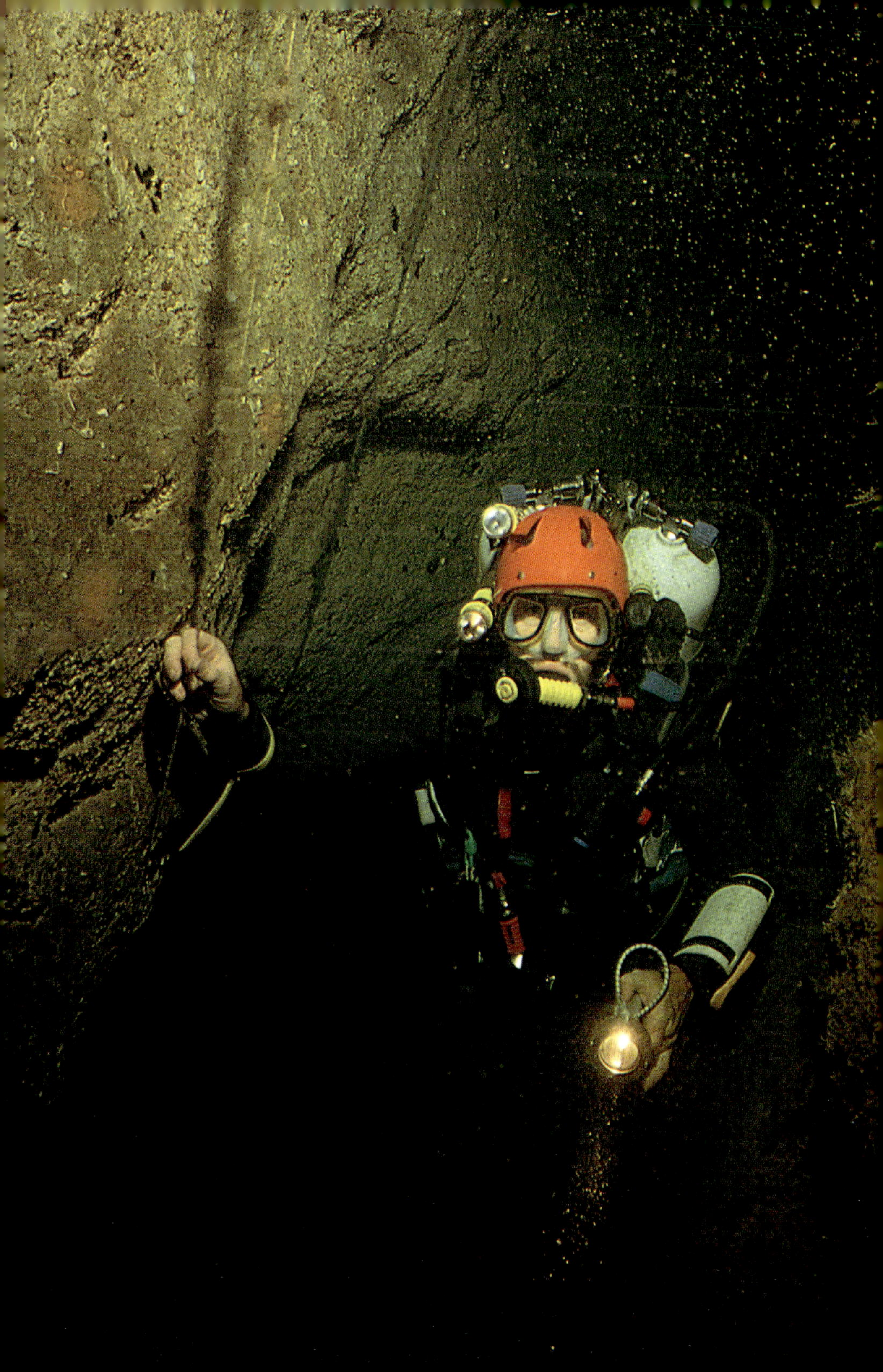

Preceding page: Surfacing from a dive with independently-valved back-mounted cylinders.

This page: Excellent visibility for this diver with side-mounts and triple helmet lights.

Opposite: (Top) Shuffle kicking through a clear North Florida cave. (Bottom) Setting out on an exceptionally deep cave dive, using multiple gas mixtures in various cylinder configurations.

Overleaf: (Top) With a tow-strap attached, a diver explores a sump with a Tekna scooter. (Below) Two divers decompress at the entrance to a submarine cave - facing into the outflowing current for stability.

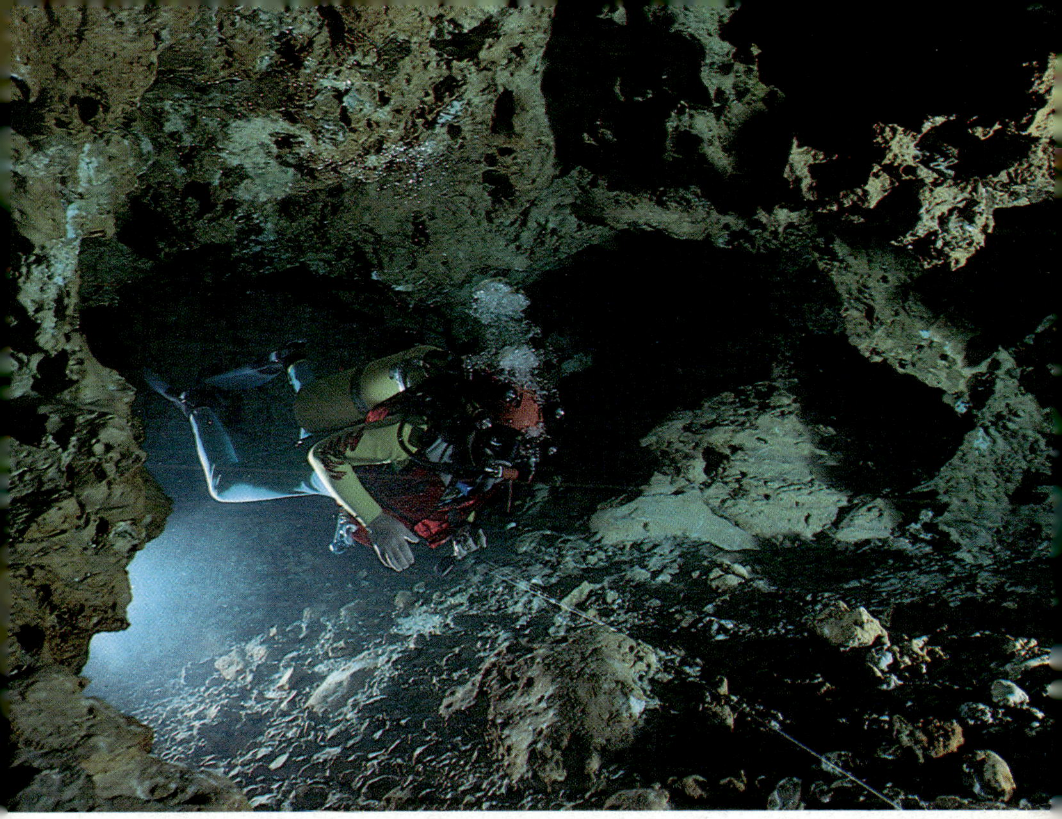

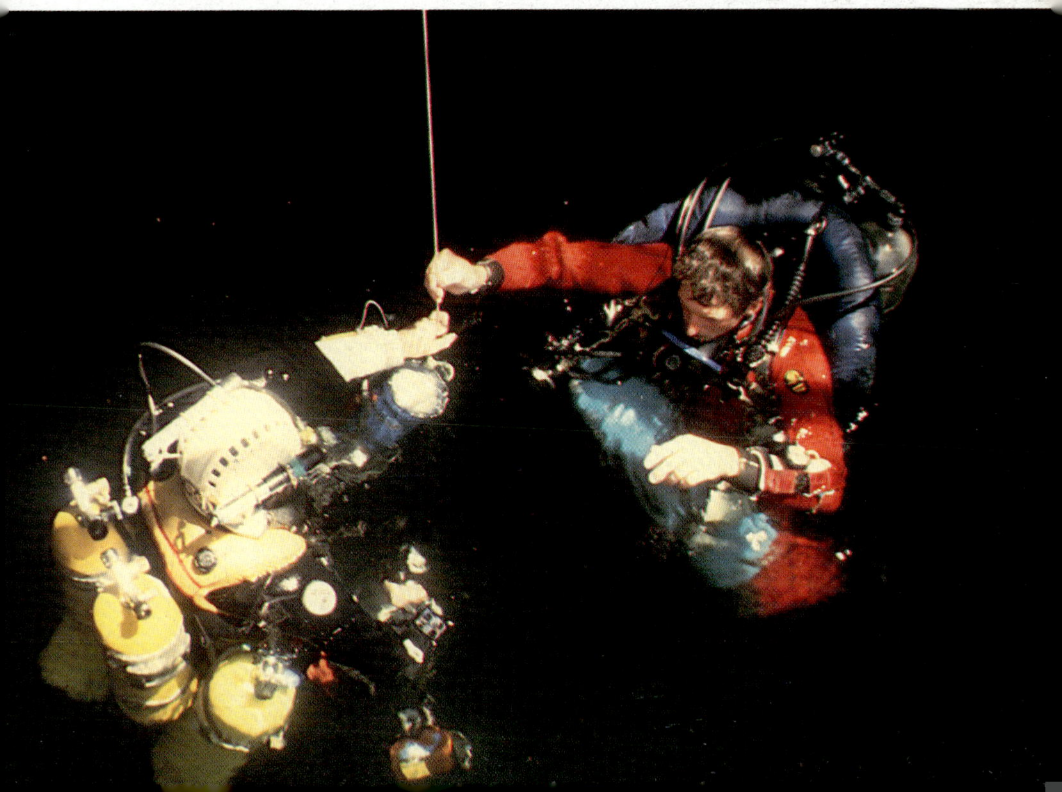

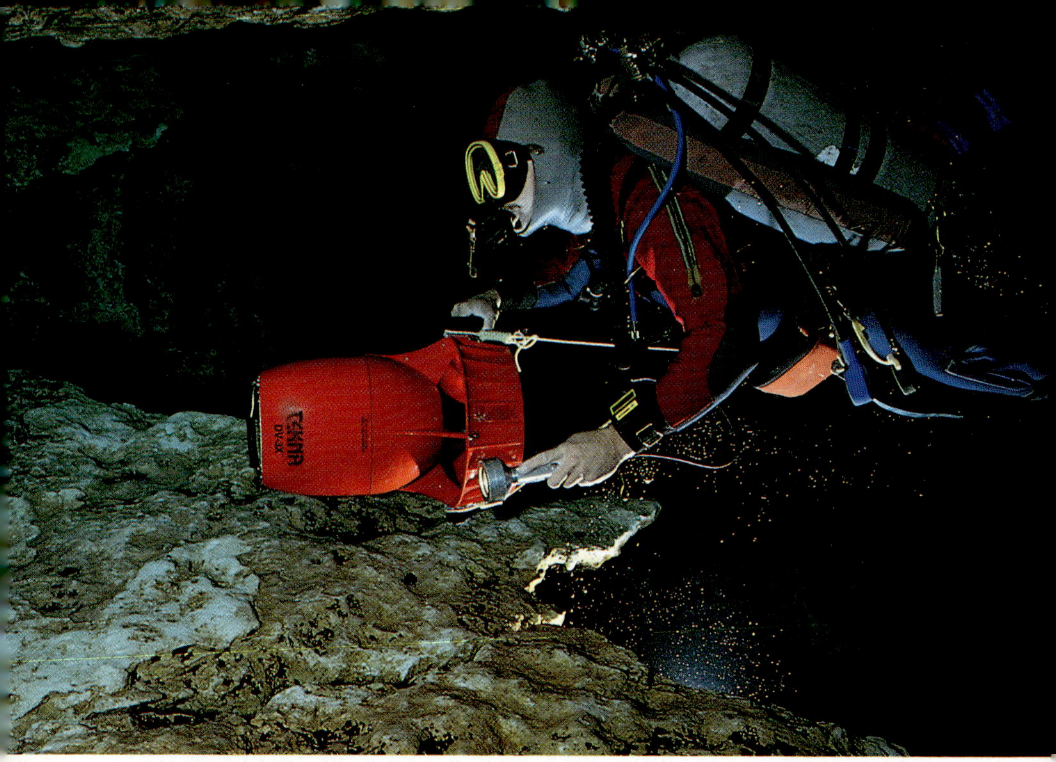
TEKNA
DV-3X

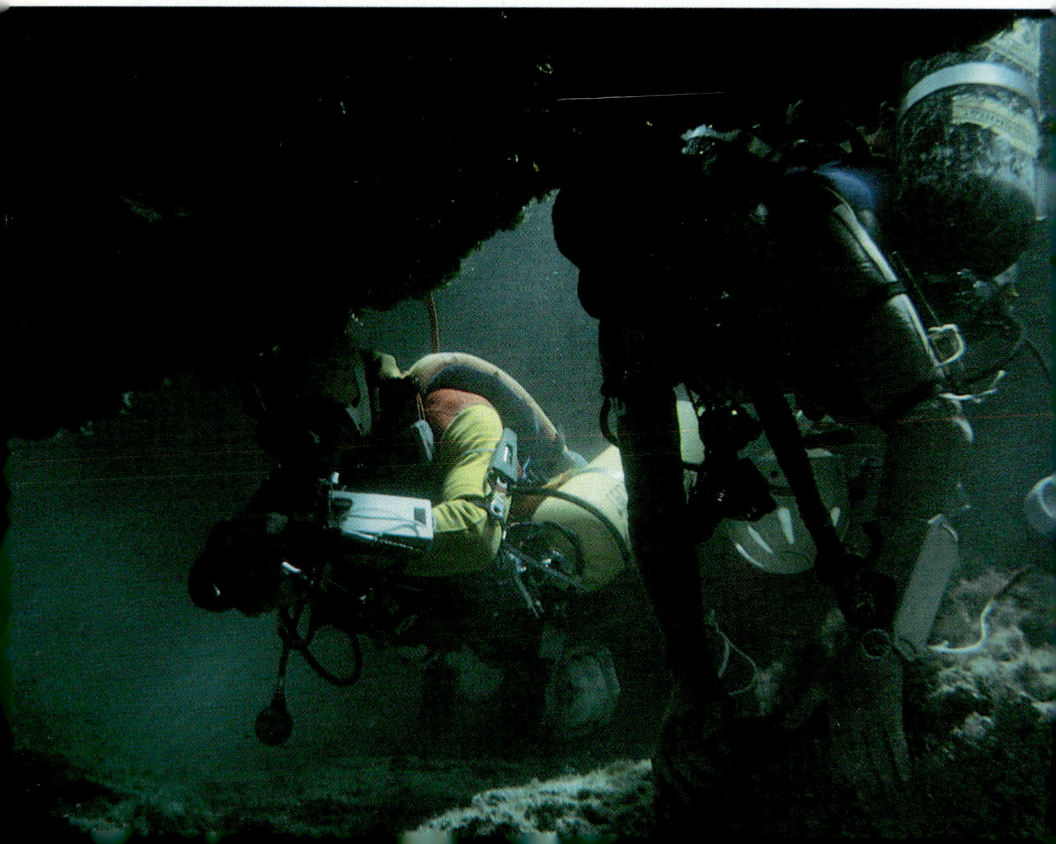

Chapter 7: Advanced Techniques

UNDERWATER CAVE PHOTOGRAPHY

CAVE diving photography is still in its infancy. This relates directly to the fact that cave diving is dangerous and that active practitioners of the sport are few in number. Not many experiment with photography in underwater caves.

CHOICE OF CAMERA

Divers have experimented with various forms of photographic equipment, such as cameras in elaborate housings and a variety of lighting equipment and film stock. Housings are bulky, and possess several limitations for cave use - it is, for example, extremely difficult to frame and focus through a single lens reflex (SLR) camera in a housing when in the confines of an underwater cave. Despite some limitations on depth and framing, small, self-contained amphibious cameras, such as the Nikonos or Sea & Sea range, are the easiest to handle in British cave diving conditions. "Splash-proof" cameras are virtually useless for cave diving.

The Nikonos cameras are guaranteed to withstand water pressure down to -50m, and the cameras weigh about 0.5kg. There are three bodies currently available - the Nikonos III, IV and V, with interchangeable lenses. Of these, the III (a manual camera) and the V (manual and automatic) are most suitable for underground use, the IV having a number of design faults. The III is now only available second-hand, but is extremely robust, and can cope with an occasional flooding if prompt action is taken to salvage it. The electronics of the V are less forgiving.

The interchangeable lenses - available in 15mm, 20mm, 28mm 35mm and 80mm sizes - are of similar construction, with two knobs that adjust focus and aperture respectively. These are large enough to be set when wearing gloves. Lenses *cannot* be changed underwater, relying on an O-ring seal to prevent water ingress between camera and lens.

All current Nikonos cameras are viewfinder rather than SLR, and the integral viewfinder covers only the 35mm and 80mm lenses. These are also the only underwater lenses that can be used on land, all the wider lenses being optically corrected for underwater use. (A 28mm splashproof lens is available for surface use in all weather conditions.) Wide-angle viewfinders are available either from Nikon or other manufacturers which cover the full range of lenses. Additionally, other companies manufacture a variety of wide-angle and close-up lenses and attachments that allow the 28mm and 35mm lenses to adapt to both wide-angle (to 16mm) or macro (down to twice life-size). The quality of the optics varies considerably, and basically you get what you pay for.

The Sea & Sea cameras are marginally less versatile. The simpler units, up to the Motor Marine 1, are probably not robust enough for cave diving, nor will they really give satisfactory results. The newer Motor Marine 2, which looks a little like a yellow plastic Nikonos V, has far better optics and is more robust than its stablemates. It comes with an integral 35mm lens and internal close-up adapter, allowing a full range of focusing from infinity to 0.5m. It is fully automatic, with auto-wind, transport and rewind, auto ASA reading (100 and 400 ASA only - other ASA's need the shutter speed or aperture adjusting accordingly to over-ride the sensors), auto-exposure and TTL flash. Aperture settings cover F 3.5 - 22, and there are various LED warnings and information displayed within the viewfinder.

The camera is depth-restricted to -45m. 20mm and 16mm wide-angle lenses attach on the front, underwater if necessary, via a simple bayonet mount. This makes it technically more versatile than the Nikonos, allowing close-up and wide-angle photography with limited equipment and simple underwater adjustment. For most purposes, optical quality will be acceptable. Two dedicated TTL underwater flashguns are available, and it has a small built-in flash for surface use.

The type of lighting used depends to a certain extent on the camera; the Nikonos III can use either bulb or electronic, the V and Motor Marine 2 can only use electronic, though they have the added facility of through-the-lens metering with dedicated flash units. The use of bulb and electronic flashes are discussed later.

ENVIRONMENT

There are innumerable adverse environmental conditions encountered underwater in caves. The water may be cold (less than 10°C in Britain) and so potential time can be limited by temperature as well as available air for both photographer and subjects. Weather is another major handicap - everyone is aware that caves flood, and this reduces the time available for photography, not simply in terms of access, but because it also affects visibility. This is one of the major problems of sump photography; visibility is poor in British caves, perhaps averaging 3-5m at best. Further, because cave passages are often relatively small, movement quickly disturbs the natural sediments and greatly reduces the visibility.

Other factors include depth, currents, passage configuration and the general physical restriction of the environment, making modelling difficult and having a generally detrimental effect on the photographic equipment itself. The cave diving environment is thwart with hazards; the photographer must be able to cope with these as second nature before he can turn his full attention to photography.

EQUIPMENT

Cave diving photography is not a cheap pastime. Not only does the photographer require a full set of caving equipment, but also a full set of first-class diving gear as well as his cameras. All must be maintained to a high

*Fig. 58: Use tripods inventively to give camera stability.
This one is being held against the roof, reducing cave floor sediment disturbance.*

Advanced techniques 187

standard. Damage to apparatus is frequent, and a cool methodical approach must be adopted at all times. This extends doubly to the photographic equipment, which is even more delicate and must be fully protected from abrasion, bumps and knocks. To transport underwater photographic equipment to the dive site, it requires both careful handling and packaging, either in padded boxes (such as the waterproof Pelican or Underwater Kinetics cases) or in cushioned ammunition boxes or waterproof tubes. Underground assembly, especially where mud and O-rings are likely to come into contact, should be kept to the bare minimum.

For full passage shots, high-speed film is recommended, either 200 or 400 ASA. General close-ups are best on slower film if lighting allows, either 50/64 ASA or general 100 ASA. Macro photography is best on the slowest film lighting will allow, to maintain fine detail. 25 or 64 ASA Kodachrome are best.

Guide numbers on flashguns or for bulbs offer little guidance to the correct exposure. On average, three-and-a-half to four times more light is required than for a similar distance in ordinary cave photography. This is based on the theory that 50% of the light output is absorbed by the water on the way from flash to subject, and 50% of the remaining light from the subject back to the lens. A great deal depends on the clarity of the water.

Much of the initial work in British sumps was done using flash bulbs. PF6B bulbs were originally used, but it was found that the cheaper PF1M clear bulbs were equally suitable. In normal colour photography the use of clear bulbs results in a very slight reddish tinge, but due to the fast absorption of red by water, this effect is cancelled.

Due to the very great difficulties experienced in communicating underwater in caves, pre-dive planning is essential if good results are to be obtained. The model must be aware of exactly where to place himself and where to point the flash. He must also be as competent a diver as the photographer - inexperienced divers are generally poor at buoyancy control and look and act in an uncoordinated fashion. The model must be in good rapport with the photographer, and able to imagine the end result from the camera position. A series of planned poses, taken on the move to avoid sediment problems, are perhaps best. This necessitates a good knowledge of the cave system itself and of the local passage configuration.

Both photographer and model must be aware of the refractive index of water - due to this objects appear to be 1.25 times closer than they really are. However, as the camera lens is fooled as well, the photographer need only set the focus distance as he sees it. It is only when precise focusing is needed, as for close-ups, that the camera/subject distance needs to be accurately measured, and the distance scale set to 0.75 of the measured distance. For extreme close-ups, macro attachments for the Nikonos generally have an integral distance prod and framer.

The positioning of light is critical. In all but the clearest water, having the flash close to the camera generally results in excessive back-scatter of light as it reflects off particles in suspension in the water. This results in very cloudy and flat pictures. It is essential to get the flash or flashes at a reasonable distance from the lens to minimise or avoid such back scatter. For simple shots, with a single flash on a fixed lead, this can either be held at arm's length by the photographer or carried on the end of an extended lead by the subject for silhouette shots. By using underwater connectors two or more flashguns can be controlled by the photographer, and the addition of light-sensitive slave flashes allows even greater freedom of composition. The common cave technique of open shutter non-synchronous flashes by the subject needs an elaborate and awkward technique underwater, due to poor communication and the need for minimum movement of the subject and photographer while the shutter is open. It is possible, but requires considerable practise by both model and photographer.

A simple system can be used employing two underwater flash units linked to the photographer by cables. The addition of a third diver as a front

Fig. 59: Man-made light dramatically silhouettes a diver.

model adds to the picture. By adjusting the position of the diver with the flash, he can be brought into the photograph as required. Cables can be extended by joining sections together with underwater connectors, or can be sealed together using a proprietary potting compound or self-amalgamating tape. The disadvantage of cable connectors is they can intrude into the photograph.

Replacing the cables by light-sensitive slaves removes this problem, but means that the subject divers must ensure that the slave is both pointing towards the primary flash unit and is within operating distance. The sensitivity of slave units is considerably reduced by the light-absorbing qualities of water.

The choice of bulbs or electronic flash units is the personal decision of the photographer. Bulbs are comparatively cheaper in original outlay, have a high guide number and offer a wider angle of even light (150°) than do most electronic guns. Surface bulb flashguns can be easily modified for underwater use by potting the electrics, or sealing them in a waterproof housing remote from the flashhead. If bulbs are used, then dead bulbs should be retained by the divers and disposed of outside the cave. Small bandoleers can be easily made from elastic and webbing to contain bulbs and can be worn on arm or wrist.

Electronic flashes are easier to use underwater, but powerful units with a wide beam are expensive, costing several hundred pounds. Many come with an integral slave for use in close-ups, but unfortunately this is most often in the front of the flash where it is of least use in a cave, save for backlighting, and such slaves are rarely very sensitive over more than a metre or two. Some flashguns have an integral spotting light, and the use of such a facility is of great assistance to the photographer. Even with bulb flash, the use of a powerful spotting light (20 watts or more) illuminates the scene more effectively for the photographer, allowing for easier framing and better communication.

Electronics also offer the potential for dedicated flash photography, which can be a bonus when conditions are poor and single flash photography is preferred, or when undertaking macro-photographic work. Underwater cave photography is difficult enough without ignoring the potential inherent within the best available technology. For close-up work, for example of aquatic cave fauna, close-up adapters with pre-set focusing aids are best and a low-powered electronic flash is generally adequate. Again, the angle of flash is important, and it should generally be held at one side pointing in toward the subject, or even from slightly behind the subject if the effect is considered desirable.

VIDEO AND CINEMATOGRAPHY

This is a relatively recent development in underwater caving, but the introduction of compact, low-price Video-8 and Super-VHS cameras with compatible underwater housings allows cave divers to take moving pictures underwater with comparative ease. Video is generally preferable to film for amateur purposes; the results are similar when viewed on a television set and the whole process is considerably cheaper at the home movie stage. Several of the housings now available also allow synchronised sound to be recorded underwater.

Most of the conditions above apply equally to video or film, and lighting divers must be aware that the film lights they carry are illuminating whatever they are pointed at. Taking them too close to walls induces flare-out, and pointing them into black passage illuminates nothing. Pointing them into the lens may damage the video tube, and is not good practice, save for silhouettes. Backscatter is still a problem, and light units should be used within their operating range, and as creatively as possible. For large open passage shots, a 250 watt light is a recommended minimum; for close-ups, 100 watts may suffice. A camera with a CCD tube and an automatic aperture will hide many slips, and as wide a lens as possible (8mm to 12mm) will allow focusing from infinity to a metre or so without the need for refocusing underwater.

Filming should be done in short sequences, and the camera held as steadily as possible. A moving shot should ideally begin on a static scene and then begin its motion (whether panning or tracking) a few seconds into the shot. The fluid environment helps keep cameras steady, and tripods are rarely needed save for extreme close-ups, where camera shake would be more apparent.

The advent of simple diver-to-diver underwater communications may well improve the lot of the underwater cave photographer, but until then there is little more to recommend other than trial and error and a considerable amount of patience.

UNDERWATER CAVE SURVEYING

THERE are several reasons why cave divers should take the trouble to record survey data underwater. Perhaps the most important is that of increased safety because it promotes a greater awareness of the surroundings. Apart from adding interest to a cave dive, the information collected is often an invaluable aid to further exploration. In deep sumps, an accurate knowledge of the dive profile is needed for the planning of future operations. The increasingly worrying problem of sump rescue will be eased if good quality surveys of sumps are available. Finally, as has been shown in the past, well-produced underwater surveys are helpful for gaining sponsorship for major projects.

SUMP SURVEY METHOD

Experience has shown that, with a minimum of effort and a little knowledge of surveying theory, it is possible to produce reasonably accurate surveys of sumps. The basic method has been described by Lloyd (1,2) and is a compromise between speed and accuracy. Attempts at improving the

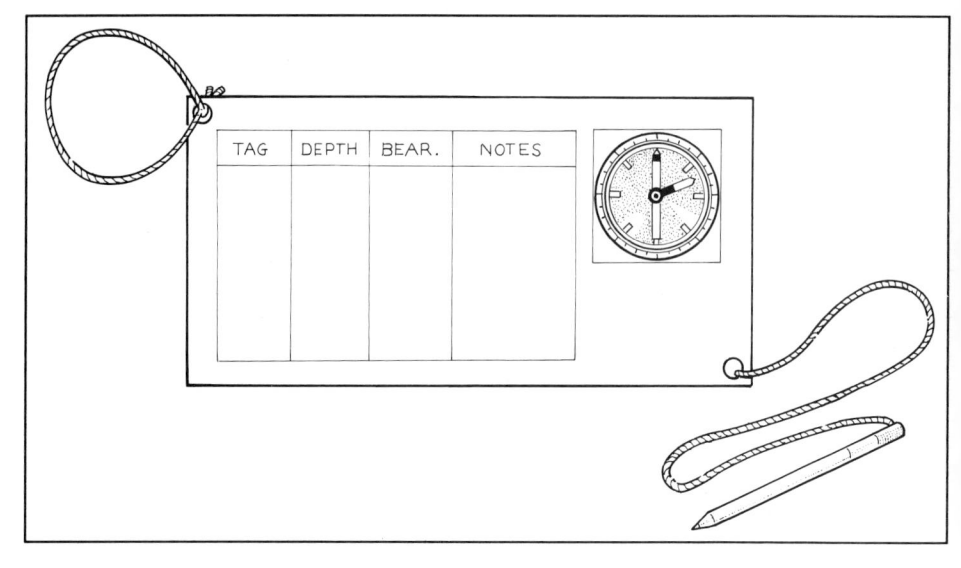

Fig. 60: A typical survey board.

accuracy tend to require a much more complicated and time-consuming technique, slowing the diver down so that a law of diminishing returns applies.

Before embarking on a survey, it is essential that the line be tagged at suitable intervals (usually every 5 or 10m) before it is laid in the sump. (Note that divers in the USA tag their lines at 10ft intervals, and that when diving abroad the British cave diver must tag or knot line in accordance with common local practice. Tags every 3m are a reasonable equivalent to 10ft, when belay wraps are allowed for.)

The tagged line is normally the guideline laid on the original exploration dive, and must thus not be laid slackly or its use for survey will become limited. The instruments used are normally carried by all divers for safety reasons, whether or not surveying is intended. They consist of an arm-mounted Formica (or similar) slate and pencil, a diver's compass and a good depth gauge (calibrated from time to time in open water against a vertical shot-line).

For more accurate surveying, a survey board can be constructed from a sheet of heavy-duty Formica, roughened perspex or similar material, upon which can be mounted a ruler, oil-filled compass, and sighting mark (figure 60). This can be held in front of the diver, and the line laid along the edge of the board, allowing for a more accurate sighting. There is more space available on the board for descriptive recording, and additional instruments can be mounted if required (depth gauge, thermometer, etc.) Pencils should be sharp (plastic replaceable-point pencils are ideal) and securely fastened (with a piece of rubber surgical tube or similar). There should be an attachment point for clipping the slate to the diver.

The first survey station chosen should be the final station of any previous survey done in the passage leading to the pool. If there is no previous survey data to tie into, a station should be chosen that is distinctive and close to water level. Whichever is the case, the start of the diving line must coincide with it. The compass is held against the line and the bearing recorded. The diver then enters the sump, following the line until it changes direction (at a belay or wall-corner), counting the tags to estimate the distance travelled. This information is written on the slate, together with the depth of the passage at the second station. The new bearing of the next section of passage is recorded at the second station, before repeating the procedure at the second deflection of the line (ie the third station). If the distance between two stations is greater than 20m, it is preferable to split the survey leg with another extra station to maintain accuracy, at whichever point is considered most appropriate.

Other passage details may be recorded at this stage, but it is often a good idea to do this on a consecutive dive in order to concentrate on getting the main line plotted properly. This is the most important part, and the surveyor should not load himself by taking on too much at once. Subsequent dives offer the chance to measure such information accurately, and reduce the temptation to invent detail and dimensions. More than once the exploration of important sites has been hindered because divers had not used a systematic approach to surveying sumps for other passages, or even the main route.

The furthest point reached during each surveying dive should be marked (eg by a piece of twisted wire) for continuation next dive. If possible, stations should be chosen at permanent features in the sump, such as recognisable boulders, or stalactites in airbells, so that if the line is torn out in floods before surveying is completed, it is possible to continue the survey. If a sump is re-lined, the old line can be measured before it is discarded.

Finally, although underwater surveying is a fascinating occupation, normal cave diving safety procedures must not be overlooked, just because the diver's mind is on something else.

ERRORS

To describe any survey as good or bad demonstrates a lack of knowledge of surveying theory. The important thing is to appreciate the limitations of the technique (3) which has been used. None of the existing British Cave Research Association (BCRA) grades of accuracy describe the above method well, but the results should be considered as being somewhere between grades 2 and 3. There is a need for divers to practise both the reading and making of underwater surveys to ensure that errors arise solely from the limitations of the instruments used rather than from poor technique.

The main source of error is directional. Both the lining up and the reading of the compass demands care. Most diving compasses are only calibrated to the nearest 5°, so that the bearing has to be estimated to the nearest degree. Although day to day calibrations are probably unnecessary (4,5,6) both the observer's ability to read the compass, and the instrument itself, should be periodically checked against a known true bearing. The difference between the recorded bearing and the true bearing is the correction factor which must be applied to all observations made. The diver should also be aware that errors may be caused by the proximity of steel equipment (knives, cylinders, etc) or the magnetic fields created by the bright diving lights that are gaining in popularity. Compasses can be diverted by the presence of iron-rich mineral veins in the surrounding rock (as in Gough's Cave).

Errors of distance should be fairly small. Experience has shown that when divers guess the distance of lines they have laid, they almost invariably over-estimate. When tagging a line, the distance from the start of a line (in metres) should be written on each tag to avoid confusion underwater. The total distance of the sump can therefore be read off directly, thus forming a useful check on estimations made while underwater. Shorter distance between tags can be made by rough, one metre hand-over-hand estimations along the line, a technique which becomes more reliable with practise. Station position error is minimised if the line has been previously frequently belayed along the sump.

Levelling errors are also small in a sump survey if an accurate depth gauge is used. Unlike a clinometer in a dry passage, errors are not transferred to all subsequent stations. The two ends of a sump will always be at the same level, no matter how long it is. However, water surface in airbells is occasionally below sump level (eg Ink Sump in Peak Cavern) or above it, (as in the Torricellian Chamber in Buxton Water Sump, Peak Cavern). Check your depth gauge when surfacing in enclosed airbells.

If possible, loop closure should be carried out, with the misclosure quoted as a percentage. If a loop has been formed by both ends of a sump being connected by dry passages which have been surveyed to a high grade, then it is probably preferable to distribute the error solely through the sump. If no natural loops occur, a closed loop can be created by resurveying the sump on the return. A misclosure of about 2-3% is typical.

PROCESSING DATA & DRAWING THE SURVEY

Pencil notes on a diving slate are in a very temporary form, and a few minutes of transport in a gritty diving bag can soon eliminate all trace of them! They should be transferred to a notebook immediately after the dive. However, access to the original survey notes is often invaluable at the drawing stage, so it is worth trying to preserve them. A permanent record can be made by simply photocopying the slate before it is cleaned for the next dive. Other relevant information is also better recorded immediately at the dive site, such as the date, calibration information, visibility, water levels, etc.

Before drawing the survey, all numerical data should be reduced to co-ordinates in the normal way (7). It is a simple matter to adapt a computer programme to accept depth information instead of clinometer readings. A line survey is then constructed either as a plan, or an elevation, or both, (depending on the eventual use of the survey) before passage details are added. Walls must not be drawn in as solid lines unless they have been definitely observed and their distance from the main line estimated. Any other useful information should be included, such as cross-joints, side passages, permanent stations, radio-location points, depths (on the plan view), faults, decompression points, flow markings, dip of limestone beds, floor deposits, direction of water flow, and so on, depending on the scale of the drawing. The position of the diving line is often worth showing if the route to be taken by divers is not obvious or straightforward.

Like any survey, it should also bear a title, scale, Grid North arrow and some indication of its likely accuracy. A detailed underwater survey is more clearly drawn without the cross-hatching which cavers normally use to depict sumps. Any symbols used must also be accompanied by a key. An example of a typical cave survey is shown in figure 61.

SURVEYING BEYOND SUMPS

Ideally this should be carried out to BCRA Grade 5. However, it often takes considerable organisation to get a team through a long sump, especially one in a remote location. The number of survey trips beyond the sump may be limited by long periods of poor weather. To be practical, there is obviously

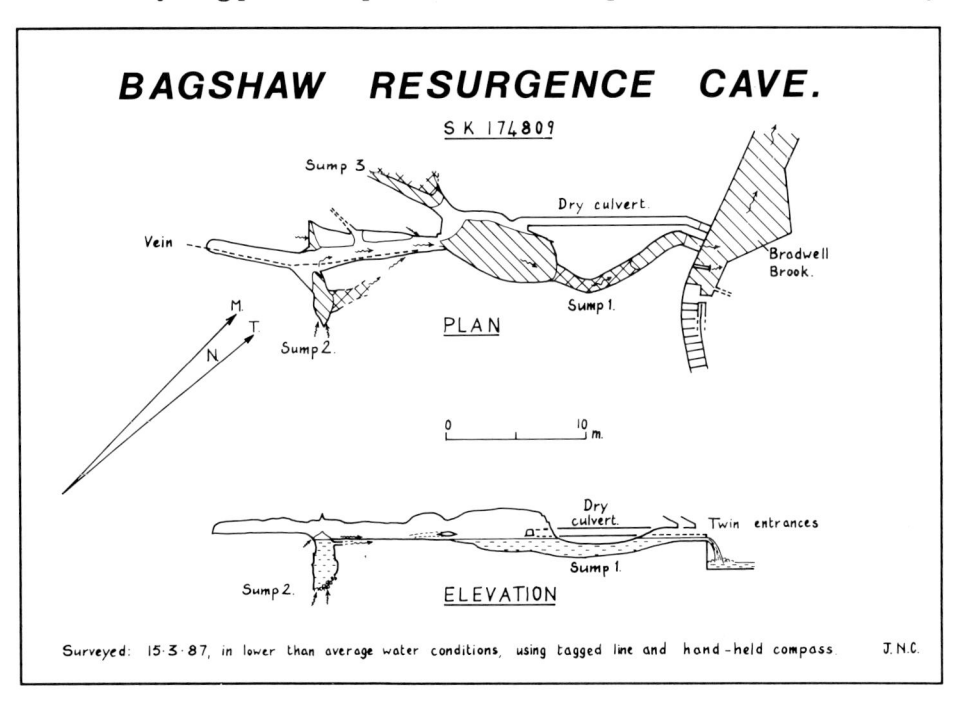

Fig. 61: An example of a cave diving survey.

a need for a faster, more efficient survey method. Again, there is a trade-off between accuracy and time, but it is better to have a reasonable survey of major extensions beyond sumps than to have a highly-accurate survey of only one small part.

A useful compromise is to perform a Grade 2 (pace and hand-held compass) survey, with key stations pin-pointed from the surface using a radio-location device such as the Molefone. The errors in the survey legs between each location can then be distributed, with the end result being quite acceptable. The above can be carried out by a solo diver. (1,500m of the downstream extensions in Notts Pot was surveyed in about five hours using this method).

If the use of a location device is not possible (due to lack of availability, excessive depth, proximity of mineral veins, or ferro-magnesian minerals in lava beds, etc) and a full Grade 5 survey is impractical, another useful technique to maintain some degree of accuracy involves using the diving line. A measured 10m length of line is cut from the reel and tied to a lead weight (which can be removed from the weightbelt). The diver lays this out along the passage floor, takes a back-bearing, then pulls the weight in before repeating the process. (8,9). Shorter legs can be measured by folding the cord in half, or into quarters. In level passages, this corresponds to BCRA Grade 3, as the compass can be lined up more reliably than when trying to sight along to the next (as yet undetermined) station. No other equipment is needed other than that which the exploring cave diver is already carrying, and the method is fairly rapid.

AVAILABILITY OF SURVEYS

Most British divers who make surveys submit them for publication in the CDG Newsletter, which is widely available. Another useful source of these is in the regional sump indexes, produced by the CDG on an occasional basis for each main British caving area. These surveys are not always well-detailed, because the scale is small. Accounts of more important discoveries made, along with larger scale surveys, are sometimes prepared for the journals of caving clubs of which the divers concerned are members. The most reliable source of information is undoubtedly by direct contact with the surveying diver/s, who will usually be able to supply larger drawings and, more importantly, the original survey data.

THE FUTURE

Continental and American divers (10,11) often make surveys of underwater caves which are considerably more accurate than those produced in Britain. Because their diving conditions are so much better than ours, they are able to work in pairs using normal tapes and sighting compasses. This approach is unlikely to be used in Britain, due to generally poor visibility.

Apart from variations on the normal technique (12) divers will probably rely more and more on electronic recording devices. Tape recorders in watertight housings have been used in the States, as have small housed key-recording units. Radio-location will become more common as an aid in position-fixing underwater as well as in dry passages.

Perhaps the most promising innovation being developed for underwater survey is a device which, though the diver must still count the tags, will record the station number (shown on a display) bearing, dip, depth, distance to roof, walls and floor, and temperature. These last two records might have applications as side passage detectors. To record the above data, the device is held at arm's length like a pistol before a button is pressed to store the information. This reduces parallax errors, and errors arising from the proximity of magnetic materials (cylinders, etc.). All data is stored on a micro-processor and the final processing can be done later on a home computer.

UNDERWATER DIGGING

NOTE that this section does not cover archaeological excavations. Specialist help should be sought if there is any possibility of the dig interfering with archaeological remains.

The objective of an underwater dig is exactly the same as for an above-water one - to gain access to passage where none was known before. There are both advantages and disadvantages in excavating underwater. Examples are:

Advantages: The diver can adjust buoyancy to make movement easier. Rocks weigh less underwater, so can be easier to move.

Disadvantages: Bad visibility can hinder communication and foul equipment. Air supplies and cold limit digging time.

Great care must be taken to ensure that mobile sediments (gravels, etc) do not trap the diver. Readjustment of passage obstructions may suddenly alter flow patterns. Digging should be treated with extreme caution, and it is advisable to have a kitted-up standby diver in support at the diving base.

SAFETY

Line: A stronger line than normal must be laid so that inadvertent pulls caused while digging do not break it. If working in a pool with an air surface, then the line may sometimes be omitted providing there is only one, easy way straight up to air. Alternatively, a base-fed line may be more appropriate.

Weights: If using additional weights to achieve negative buoyancy to make working at floor level easier, then these should be on a separate belt which is put on last. In the event of an emergency, it can then be ditched quickly to achieve normal or positive buoyancy,

Air margins: Allow at least twice the amount of air it took to reach the digging site to return to base. This may mean adjusting the standard thirds rule to allow a greater safety margin. Do not include digging time air in the inward total, or allow it to take you over thirds margins. Don't become so engrossed in the work that you forget to check your gauges regularly.

Boulders: A boulder underwater weighs less than in air. This reduction in weight is equal to the weight of water displaced by the boulder. Exhaled air mixes with water and forms a less dense medium. Any boulder entering this less dense medium suddenly becomes heavier. This can cause blocks to fall from the roof, but is especially dangerous in boulder chokes where all sorts of unexpected stresses can be generated as the air rises through the choke.

Pneumatic tools: Water is an incompressible fluid. Normally the eardrum does not come into contact with water carrying dangerously high-intensity sounds. If using any form of implement that can transmit loud noises into the water, then wear a hard hat or full-face mask with integral hood. These will ensure that only air comes into contact with the ears. Most compressed air drills, pneumatic jack-hammers, etc, come into this category of implement, and can seriously damage unprotected ears.

PLANNING

Because a dig is out of sight, it does not mean permission to dig should not be sought! Always check with the landowner or cave access authority that it is alright to dig in a particular location. The long-term effects of your work could mean a considerable amount of work or disturbance for someone else.

Because of limitations with regard to visibility, air supplies, cold, etc, the detailed planning of the dig is critical. All the options should be reviewed in advance so that, once the dig is reached, one option can be chosen and implemented immediately. Any communication signals between divers and/or their surface support must be simple and unambiguous.

Whenever possible, try and work with the water, rather than against it. This will keep visibility clearer at the work site, as fresh water coming downstream will clear away unwanted silt. It will mean, however, that your return swim will probably be in very reduced visibility.

TECHNIQUES

All the techniques used on an above-water dig can be used underwater. We will look only briefly here at such different techniques.

Explosives

In general, the amount of explosive required is greater underwater to offset the hydrostatic head. Larger shot-holes and closer spacing of these is recommended. For plaster charges where the head of water is sufficient (minimum 7.5m) no additional tamping is required.

Not all explosives are suitable for use underwater. The table gives some idea of the variables within those which are suitable.

PRODUCT	DESCRIPTION	HEAD OF WATER	DURATION OF IMMERSION
Special gelatine 80%	medium density medium strength gelatinous explosive paper cartridges	< 6m	a few days
Plaster gelatine	high density high strength paper/polythene-wrapped slabs	< 46m (deeper with special primer)	several weeks
Submarine blasting gelatine	high density, high strength gelatinous explosive paper/chipboard cartridges	< 450m (deeper with special primer)	several weeks

Cordtex, a plastic-coated detonating fuse, is suitable for use underwater provided the ends are sealed to prevent water getting in. If detonating fuse is used and initiated from above water, then any suitable detonator can be used.

For underwater initiation the use of a submarine electric detonator is advised. For initiation of submarine blasting gelatine the use of a Number 8 Star detonator is advised. The submarine electric detonator is tested to 135m depth. The diver must be well clear of the water when he detonates the charge.

Airbags

An airbag can be used for lifting heavy objects underwater. The basic idea is to attach one or more bags to the object to be lifted, and then to let air into the bag to give buoyancy. Problems underground are:

a) A large passage is required to use the technique efficiently.

b) If too much air is injected, then the bag will rise in an uncontrolled manner. This usually occurs either because the object was stuck in mud and only pulls free when too much air has been injected, or because the bag rises, allowing the air inside it to expand. The air will continue to expand and generate more buoyancy as the bag rises until air completely fills the bag, or the air surface or the roof is reached, and the excess spills out. The bag may then fall back down with increasing speed. For this reason, the use of several smaller bags is preferable to one large one. Each small bag should be completely filled until the required buoyancy is achieved. Then sudden lift will be counterbalanced by immediate spillage of air, and the bags can be re-adjusted accordingly. Err on the side of remaining slightly negative, as the diver can supply the final bit of lift required.

c) Once the airbag reaches the surface, it ceases to be an aid for further upward movement. Some form of additional lifting device, or brute force, is then required.

d) The mass of the load being lifted can still be dangerous, even if there is no apparent weight.

When making an airbag, aim for depth rather than diameter. Pear-shaped bags are quite common (figure 62). A small neck reduces the likelihood of air spilling out, but the neck must also contain the eyelets for attaching the lifting line, and must be of sufficient strength and diameter to bear the weight to be lifted by the bag.

Airbags are probably best used on resurgence digs, or digs vertically below a large water surface (figure 63).

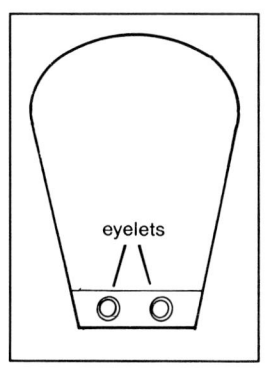

Fig. 62: An airbag showing standard pear-shape and eyelets.

Airlifts

Air entering the bottom section of an open-ended tube rises, and in doing so drags water up with it. This creates a suction at the bottom end, which can be used to lift silt and gravel up the tube. The airlift can be made sufficiently powerful to lift such debris and water over a metre above the water surface, and propel it sideways if required. Tube diameters of 10-15cm have been found suitable for use in conjunction with a compressor delivering 60-100 cu/ft/min at 100psi, (the sort seen at roadworks, not in dive shops). The use of plastic soil-pipe for the main tube is convenient, and different lengths can be created easily. A diagram of the airlift in use by the Welsh Section in their Pwll y Cwm dig is shown in figure 64.

The main problems are:
a) Twigs getting into the pipe being unable to leave at the top because of the bend, thus creating a blockage in the pipe.
b) The varying buoyancy of the lift whilst in operation (too much weight on the bottom causes it to slide down the debris cone, whilst too little causes the end to leave the bottom).
c) Maintaining a non-collapsible end-section sufficiently flexible for easy manoeuvring.

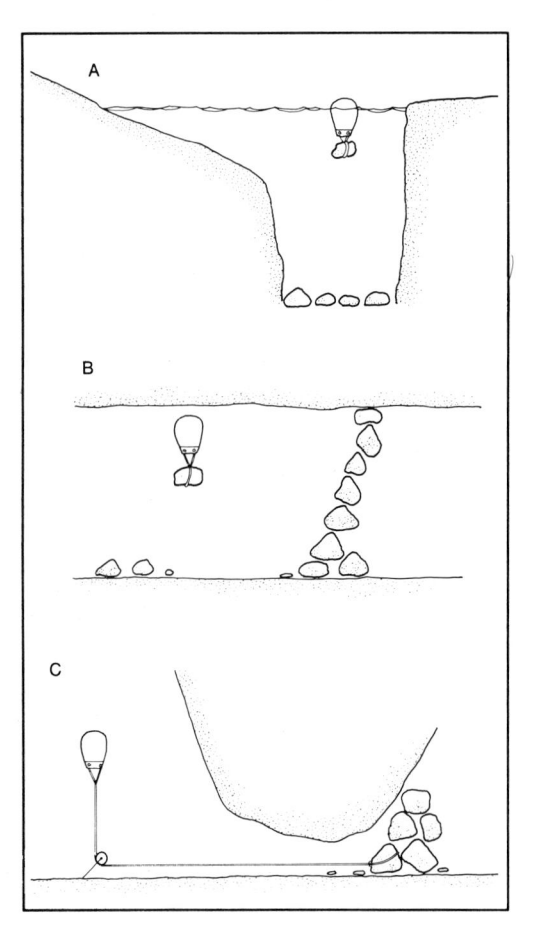

Fig. 63: Using the airbag - (from top) lifting a rock to the surface; moving a rock along a passage; pulling a rock sideways via a pulley.

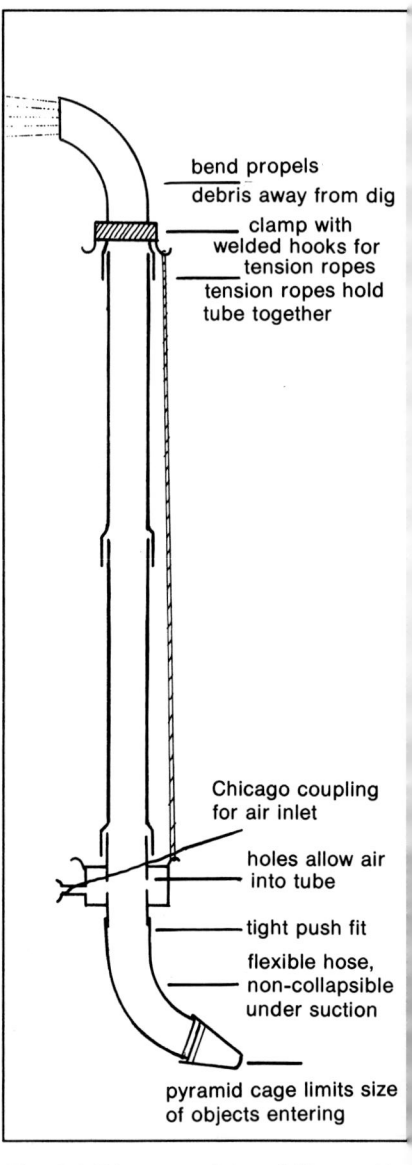

Fig. 64: Diagram of the airlift used by the Welsh section of the CDG in the Pwll y Cwm underwater dig.

DIVER PROPULSION VEHICLES

THERE are two basic types of diver propulsion vehicle (DPV): those you sit on top of and ride, (eg Aquazepp 714, Farallon IV) and those that pull you along (eg Tekna, Apollo, Farallon II/III and Aquazepp LS). Each has its own problems and advantages, and requires a different approach in technique. Whichever type is used, considerable practice in open, flowing water is required before the DPV is used in the cave environment.

Those which are sat upon must be fitted with a T-bar that allows the rider to slide his legs below the top of the bar, and sit comfortably and securely astride the DPV. The bars fitted to the standard DPV are generally not adequately strong or robust enough to withstand cave wear, or to cope with the weight of a fully-kitted cave diver. A robust home-made T-bar, fitted by stainless-steel jubilee clips, is probably more reliable. When in the legs astride position, the diver's fins hang over the rear of the unit, and can be used as rudders in the propeller wash for steering.

Weighting is crucial on sit-on DPVs, and side-mounts cannot be used unless the scooter is itself weighted accordingly. In some cases, where heavy loads are carried, it may be necessary to fix a buoyancy compensator to the DPV, run from a separate air tank fitted to the DPV as well.

When the pull-type of DPV is used, the cave diver *must* be attached securely to the DPV by a tow strap (see figure 65) to a D-ring on the diving harness. By pulling on either arm, you can change direction, and, with a properly adjusted tow strap, one-handed operation of some units (such as the Tekna) is possible. Smaller towing scooters are more suited to small passages, as they are more easily fine-controlled, and they allow a smaller end-on profile.

Either type of DPV should be fitted with a dead man's handle throttle switch. More than one good story exists of the "one that got away", and a lost scooter over a deep shaft, or a scooter towing an unconscious diver following a collision between head and roof under power, could prove serious. Major silt-outs can also be avoided. Scooters should be stopped and swum though low sections or constrictions or low-visibility sections.

Siltation can be a major problem with scooter wash. Avoid pointing the propeller at silt deposits whilst in operation - prop-wash is considerably worse than a careless fin-stroke. When starting a scooter within a cave, always adjust buoyancy so that both diver and scooter are in position in mid-water, with the prop-wash directed back down the passage.

There are many advantages offered by the use of DPVs. The obvious ones are that the diver can travel further for less air consumption, and spend shorter times negotiating deep sections of underwater caves (thus giving significant decompression advantages). This also involves a strict set of air management rules that over-ride the thirds rule. It's no good getting 1000m into a cave system on a DPV to find that, having hit thirds, your batteries have gone flat.

Fig. 65: Setting a series of staging tanks for mounting beneath an Aquazepp scooter.

202 **Advanced techniques**

There is no hard and fast rule with respect to air reserves versus distance swum; each cave has its own variables, such as depth, current flow, stress factor, etc. In a cave with no flow and easy swimming passage, inward use of 20% of the air supply might be acceptable, leaving 80% available for the outward journey and a potential emergency swim out. The diver must assess each situation and plan accordingly. In many cases, a buddy bottle is carried over and above the normal air supply, to be used only in emergency.

If you are using a DPV for deep diving, it is essential to have considerable experience of free-swimming at the maximum depth planned. Narcosis is a major problem in deep cave diving, and is greatly exacerbated if the diver is attempting to tow out a dead DPV. It is good policy to have a three-man scooter team for deep work, so that one diver can tow the broken scooter while the other two divers ride tandem on the third DPV. At least one spare tow strap should be carried per team, so that in the event of scooter failure the diver being towed does not have to grip on by hand. A diver being towed may have problems with out-of-air situations, and the use of a long hose between the first and the second stages on one regulator is recommended (2-3m hose).

Fig. 66: Aquazepp scooters rigged with stage cylinders for an extremely long dive. Note the modified on/off switch and seat.

Modifications can be made to DPVs to enable them to be used deeper than their initial specifications allow, but this is outside the scope of this manual.

DPVs have been used successfully to tow sleds of equipment through underwater caves (eg the Australian Nullarbor expeditions) and to tow more than one person for limited distances. Stage tanks can be mounted on the DPV, making due allowance for weight. These are generally slung below the rider. Divers must be aware that this can greatly limit the range and speed of DPVs and allowance must be made for this in the dive plan. The same is true about using the inbuilt light on some DPVs. This is often disconnected for this reason, but can be left connected as an emergency light source only.

It is recommended that DPVs are regularly checked for range by running them in open water until the batteries are showing signs of discharge. *Do not run NiCad batteries flat*, as this can damage them, and recharge immediately after such complete discharge.

Always use a helmet when riding DPVs, even in large caves, as hitting the roof at 50m a minute is enough to knock you unconscious. It is a good idea to have some means of mounting your primary light on your helmet, so that both hands are free for scooter operation.

One of the main reasons for scooter malfunction on a dive is a snapped propeller or drive shaft, due to an item of equipment being sucked into the propeller. All equipment must be securely strapped down.

Advanced techniques

The use of scooters necessitates a new list of gear checks before use:

a) Are all gauges securely fastened, and all equipment strapped down?
b) Is the battery freshly charged?
c) Are all scooter clips and plugs secure?
d) Are you clipped to the scooter?
e) Can you reach stage tank hoses easily?
f) Is your buoyancy correct?
g) Are you sure you can swim back?

SUBMARINE CAVE DIVING

WHEN considering the topic of cave diving under the sea, it is worth going back to first principles and considering the differences between freshwater and seawater sites. The main ones are:
1) *Salinity*: Seawater is a solution of many minerals, primarily salt. It is denser than freshwater.
2) *Tides*: The sea is subject to tidal variations in many parts of the world. These can range from 14m to less than a metre; in the UK, the range can be up to 6m.
3) *Weather*: The surface of the sea is subject to the effects of the weather, which can make conditions very unpleasant very rapidly.
4) *Marine life*: The sea nurtures myriads of organisms, some of which may be harmful.
5) *Boat handling*: Access to the diving site may involve crossing the sea in a boat, which demands the additional experience of boat-handling.
6) *Human competition*: Some diving sites may be in multi-use areas, eg in shipping lanes or harbours.

All of the above factors can make diving in submarine caves an interesting but frustrating experience. Let us take them in turn, and consider their effects in more detail.

Salinity

A salt sea means that all electrical equipment and non-stainless steel ferrous equipment is liable to corrode at an alarming rate. Lights need to be thoroughly sealed to prevent damage, even slight flooding can ruin expensive torches if they leak. After diving in seawater, rinse all equipment well to prevent corrosion and the accumulation of salt deposits which can prevent cylinder taps turning, demand valves opening properly, and so on. If electrical equipment is flooded, abort the dive immediately and flush it with freshwater or pure alcohol (not booze) and dry it thoroughly.

The density differences between salt, brackish and/or fresh water result in a halocline, a boundary layer which may appear as a sharp transition or as a fuzzy mixing zone. Passing through a halocline produces an alteration in visibility, which can be seen as a haze or a shimmering effect as the changing densities refract light differently. Haloclines occur where freshwater overlies saltwater, or freshwater resurges in seawater (eg Spring of Drakos, in Greece, or the Doolin Green Holes, in Eire). Such density changes can have an effect on buoyancy. Similar alterations in visibility can occur at thermoclines, where layers of seawater at different temperatures meet.

Tides

Find out the tidal range of your proposed diving site, and to what degree it is affected by local currents at each stage of the tide. An extreme example is the ocean Blue Holes of the Bahamas, where entrance is governed by tidally-related suck and blow currents at the entrance. Such currents are often out of phase with surface tidal changes, and may change two to three hours later. At other locations, there may be a negligible tide, as in the Mediterranean. Apart from the presence of tidal currents in the caves, entry and exit into the water may be affected. One looks foolish if a short 1m drop into the water on a falling tide is turned into a 4m high sheer wall on exit, as can happen on the Devon coast. Check that your point of entry will not be affected by the tidal range.

Tides also produce currents. Anybody who has seen a five-knot current knows how dangerous these can be. Check tidal streams and the time of slack water, near high or low tide, before tackling a site that can be swept by strong currents. Boat cover may be worthwhile. If currents are not a problem, check that your site is not out of the water on a low spring tide. Diving at low tide may give you a shorter dive (less air consumption, fewer decompression problems) and less problem with swell. Diving at high water may give better visibility, but swell surges into sea caves (particularly those which funnel in) may trap a diver, or ram him into passages from which he cannot escape. Diving in shallow caves with airspace may become unpleasant with pronounced surges, when a considerable shock wave may occur as air is compressed suddenly. This shock can be felt by the diver.

Weather

The effects of wind on the sea can be sudden and dramatic. Sometimes storms many miles from the diving site, particularly ocean-facing sites like the west coast of Ireland, can generate a huge swell which converts into pounding surf when it reaches the shoreline. Study the weather forecast each day, and inspect the site before diving. Entry and exit into the water may become epic if a surf is breaking. Remember that getting in is always easier than getting out, and that a fully-kitted diver can be dragged about helplessly in a strong undertow. Underwater, the surge from a big swell can reach depths of many metres, and affect not only the swim into the cave and the subsequent dive, but can also seriously affect any decompression stops.

The best weather for diving an exposed coastline is probably when the wind is coming from onshore, and the weather is settled.

Unsettled weather can have a bad effect on underwater visibility, which may take several days to clear fully. Additionally, where submarine caves are

Fig. 67: Aquatic dance through drowned formations in Gemini, Grand Bahama.

active resurgences, strong currents may be encountered running out of the caves, and visibility may be stained by organic run-off from the land end of the cave systems in bad weather. The calmer weather immediately after a heavy storm may, however, be a good time to go looking for active marine resurgences from the shoreline.

Marine Life

The sea harbours many living creatures, most of which are not only harmless but make diving a positive pleasure. Visibility may be affected by the smallest - plankton - to the extent that one can only see a metre or less through a soup-like haze of life. Jellyfish of some species can sting, and it is worth noting that they can be swept by wind and tides into sea caves in large numbers. In tropical waters, corals can cause nasty scrapes, and some small attached creatures can give nasty stings (eg fire coral, hydroids). It is always worth wearing some form of complete body cover, even a set of light overalls, when diving in close proximity to hard surfaces in the sea. Fish of any kind are unlikely to present a hazard if left alone, whatever their size, even if it is alarming to bump into a 2m conger eel in a small phreatic tube. Crustaceans such as the spider crab or crawfish seem to like caves, and the former has a habit of dropping from the roof when disturbed by exhaust bubbles. None of these will cause harm if not handled, and do remember that in most parts of the world it is illegal to take shellfish, lobsters, crabs and many fish from the water when using SCUBA gear. Check local regulations, and *do not break them.* The CDG will disown you if you do.

Boats

If you need to use a boat to reach the diving site, have somebody in charge of it who is competent to handle it. Be familiar with the use of boats for diving, and also make sure that the boat is up to the task. It is not advisable to dive and leave a boat unmanned, for fairly obvious reasons. It may float off or be stolen, you may surface with an emergency... Check the weather before setting off in a boat, and use the international diver down flag when in the water if other boats are likely to be present.

Seasickness afflicts some people even finning in a choppy sea. If prone to seasickness when travelling in a boat, keep your eyes on a static object, like the shore or the horizon. Sea sickness from finning on the surface usually disappears when the diver submerges - get below the surge zone quickly and settle for a while before moving off. Remedies for sea-sickness include drugs such as antihistamines. Some are totally unsuitable for divers, but others, such as Stugeron (cinnarizine), are claimed not to cause drowsiness. In the last few years, researchers have found ginger to be very helpful. The last word in non-interventionist treatment is an acupressure wrist band, which holds a stud that is said to press on the anti-seasickness acupressure point. Some have found this effective, and there is no harm in trying.

Harbours & Controlled Locations

Some diving sites may be in controlled locations such as harbours or shipping lanes, when your presence may endanger others as much as theirs endangers you. Check to see if there are any local regulations affecting diving at a particular site. Using the international diving symbol (figure 68) on the support vessel will warn other vessels to keep away - one hopes! If you are underwater and hear a boat engine, stay under until it has gone - don't come up for a look!

EQUIPMENT

Bearing the above factors in mind, we come to the specialised equipment required for sea diving. One important item is an adjustable buoyancy device which can act as a life jacket. It is rare for any submarine cave dive to start directly from the shore, and a buoyancy compensator which is also a life jacket provides better support than

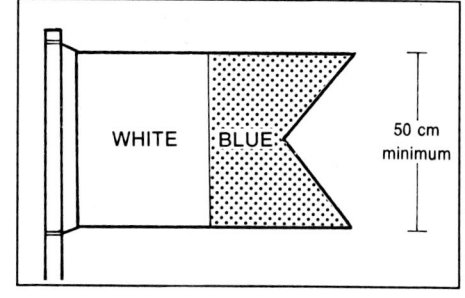

Fig. 68: International diver's flag.

Advanced techniques 207

one which is not during the surface swim to and from the site. Saltwater is denser and therefore more buoyant than fresh water, so weights will need to be increased accordingly. It may be that weightbelts will need to be jettisoned on the surface, either in an emergency or for getting back into the boat, and it may be worth altering normal cave diving practise and wearing the weightbelt on top of the cylinder harness.

A surface marker buoy may be useful at some sites (even an empty squash container on a cord) to help relocate them during the exploration period. Remove these when diving is completed at the end of an expedition so that sport divers are not tempted to follow. Such buoys can also aid in identifying locations from onshore, and enable precise bearings to be taken. For initial exploration, it may be sufficient to attach a small buoy to the end of the line reel, and run the line from the surface, belaying at the entrance before penetrating the cave.

LINE LAYING

Techniques in line laying will be largely as standard in freshwater cave diving. Some discussion has revolved around the permanence of any line laid in areas which may later be dived by sport divers (eg the Green Holes of Doolin, in Eire). In general, leaving line at an entrance is an open invitation for a non-cave diver to go beyond his safe limits, and it is best to belay the line beyond the limits of daylight, and make sure any line laid has direction tags which positively indicate which way the nearest entrance lies. (Lack of this practice almost certainly caused a fatality in Hodge Close Quarry, in Cumbria). Belaying line well inside the entrance has the further benefit of reducing storm damage. Any permanent lines should be thick, and capable of coping with storm surges and strong alternating currents. It should be well-laid, and well-belayed. Do not lay several lines down the same passage on successive explorations. If the original line is sound, use that. If it is damaged, then it must be removed and replaced. Broken lines can pose an entanglement threat not only to cave divers, but to marine life. Remember that a line reel may not last long in seawater if left in the cave.

SCIENTIFIC ASPECTS

Finally, to the raison d'etre of cave diving - original research, whether it be the exploration of new passage, the study and survey of its geomorphology, or, especially in sea caves, of the life it contains. Although it is unlikely that one is going to find unique blind cave fish or other exotic beasts in British sea caves, there is evidence that submarine caves may well harbour unusual species, or species which are normally found in quite different habitats. Certainly sea caves seem to harbour many organisms usually seen in much deeper waters. In Britain, the Marine Conservation Society is interested in such sites, and has an observation card system that any diver can use - contact them at 9 Gloucester Road, Ross-on-Wye, Herefordshire for further information. Cave divers may well be able to make a significant contribution to marine biology in this and other countries. The formation of submarine caves is also of interest, and links in with many other groundwater and geological research topics.

EXPEDITION CAVE DIVING

CAVE diving is increasingly used as an expeditionary tool, both to penetrate further in vadose cave systems that end prematurely in a sump (eg Gouffre Berger in France, Cueva del Agua in Spain), and in the exploration of phreatic systems that are expected to lie underwater for their entire extent (eg the Bahamian Blue Holes). For the purposes of this section, the two will be treated separately. As in the USA, diving at the end of vadose caves will be termed sump diving, and the exploration of entirely submerged systems will be termed cave diving. There are significant differences in technique and approach to each type.

SUMP DIVING

The first question to ask when planning a caving expedition to a system which may end in a sump is - do we want to pass the sump? The second is why?, the third, how?

Diving the terminal sump in a deep and difficult cave system demands a lot, not only of the diver, but also of the rest of the team. Psychologically, the focus of the expedition is suddenly on one or two individuals, and this itself can cause problems in a group in which the efforts and rewards of exploration had previously been shared. Whilst the exploration of the cave should come first, people's motives for being there differ, and it should be clearly decided before the expedition takes the field that the full team weight will be flung behind the diver in such a situation. This gives people time to adjust to the idea. If any team members feel strongly otherwise at an early stage, readjust plans accordingly, or include them out.

Having decided to plan for a diving contingency, commitment to that should be honest and complete. Given that it needs an expedition approach to get to the bottom of your cave anyway, any attempt at passing a "terminal" sump should be seriously undertaken, and not just a gesture made with a mask and the smallest of single tanks. This requires a commitment on the part of the diver, and the selection and commitment of a suitable support team.

A minimum plan for a lightweight attack on a sump at the end of a deep cave system might be to take one diver with equipment, two 4l tanks, and a reel with 100m of line on it to the site to allow a decent exploratory dive to be made. Then the expedition will at least be aware of:
   a)   how long and deep the sump might be;
   b)   what sort of approach might be needed to pass it;
   c)   whether or not it goes in the first place.

Equipment for such an attempt can be carried by two or three people in addition to those needed to tackle the cave. Difficult caves or long distance may demand more people if equipment is heavy (for larger or deeper sumps).

Once a sump has been passed, logistical problems mount. Putting two or three divers beyond a medium-length sump (100-250m long) and providing them with enough equipment to explore safely beyond, survey, and possibly camp, or pass further sumps, is a very serious commitment. Decide whether the expedition is going to be able to cope with that; such exploration is really the aim of an expedition in itself.

Sump divers undertaking exploration dives in an expedition situation must have considerable experience of exploration diving in difficult conditions in their home country, otherwise they are probably wasting their own and the expedition's time. It takes considerable effort to get a diver to the end of a long cave system, and it's not really the place for developing egos. Make it efficient and effective!

Finally, make sure that the support team is qualified for the trip. All the equipment must be taken out of the cave, ideally on the same trip. It is too easy to avoid going back for equipment later on, when people are tired, or when new challenges beckon. Diving gear is relatively delicate, and the team must be capable of getting it in and out without damaging it. Much of this seems obvious, but only if you already know it!

CAVE DIVING

Cave diving involves the exploration of a completely-flooded cave system for its own sake, without the expectation of reaching and exploring dry passages beyond, although the exploration of any such passages may be a secondary aim.

Cave types included in this category are marine caves (such as the Blue Holes), major springs (such as those in Florida) or cave resurgences (such as the Doux de Coly). The emphasis in such exploration will be on long-distance cave diving, often in excess of depths normally encountered in sump diving. Experience, equipment and attitude should reflect these conditions, and it is again a considerable advantage to have prior experience in long-distance cave diving in the home country, and of deep-diving in caves and open water. Experience in decompression diving and in buddy diving is an additional asset, as the large underwater caves encountered on such expeditions are often suitable for pair diving and there is no reason for this not to take place. Often it makes work more effective, and the dive safer.

In marine caves, other skills are essential. Sites may only be accessible by boat, and so experience in boat handling, coastal navigation and outboard motors and their maintenance is advisable. Be aware of the effects of tides, and their influence inside and outside the cave. (Read the section on *Submarine cave diving* in this manual.)

Other than the degree of diving commitment, the major differences between long-distance or deep-cave diving and ordinary cave diving are in equipment and experience. Equipment is discussed elsewhere, and experience does not come just from reading textbooks.

EQUIPMENT

This section is designed to complement the chapters elsewhere in this manual, and should be read in association with those. Personal diving equipment for a sump diving project will probably be similar to standard sump diving gear at home. Size and weight is often a problem on expeditions when a hard caving trip lies before a sump. Resist the temptation to skimp on safety, and take along a small spares and tool kit. Ensure that a spare regulator, mask, fins, etc. are taken with the expedition and are available at base camp. Minor repairs can be made on site, but it would be sad to have to abandon an expedition simply because a single major item of equipment is lost or irreparably damaged.

The choice of wet- or drysuit will depend on several factors, such as accessibility of site, water temperature and expected dive duration. Even in tropical waters, long decompressions can become hypothermic, and in colder European waters a drysuit is near-essential for long dives. In warm waters, or for relatively short dives, a wetsuit is probably best. Even for short dives in the warmest waters, a full, one-piece 3mm wetsuit provides better abrasion resistance than skin to coral and rock.

Compressors

Any expedition with a serious cave diving or sump diving programme would be well-advised to take their own compressor/s with them. The larger the expedition, the larger the compressor, or number of compressors, needed. For a sump diving project with two or three divers, a 150l/minute portable compressor would be adequate. For one involving four or more divers, perhaps with 10 - 12l tanks to fill, at least one 200l/minute compressor per six divers should be taken. Otherwise the machine will be working overtime, and may well fail after the first couple of weeks unless excellently maintained. Take a full spares kit, and take a course in maintaining your particular unit before you go.

Don't rely on "known" sources of air in a foreign country unless they are 100% reliable. Air is often the most difficult thing to get hold of abroad, especially away from main diving centres. You may well need a BS-AC or CMAS card to get tanks filled in dive shops.

Line Laying

Lines should be dictated by conditions - thick line in abrasive environments, thin in low current, clear water caves. Remember that you may not be the next person to use the line, and either remove after use or make sure it is absolutely safe to leave it. Always remove thin line from little-visited flowing water caves.

Be aware of the line-laying practices of any previous divers who have visited the site. Many countries use jump-reels to link over to set guidelines that split from the main passage, and rarely are lines directly joined together. Always carry a small spare reel, either for linking to other lines or as a search reel. Where a jump reel is necessary, always mark your way out, with a clothes-peg clip or some other reliable means.

Lighting

For sump diving in freshwater, the standard helmet-mounted torches used in British sump-diving are probably adequate. With fresh batteries and a water-resistant caving cell, they should allow plenty of light for beyond sump exploration at the end of a successful dive.

For large caves, or long and clear sumps, lighting should be more ambitious. Helmet torches should use a quartz-halogen bulb for a brighter

Fig. 69: Through the crystal waters of Cocklebiddy, under the Australian Nullarbor desert.

beam, though this will generally be at the expense of duration. The use of a larger 20-50 watt waist-mounted lighting unit, with the bulb unit held in the hand, allows better general vision in large caves. The boundaries of the cave can be more easily seen, and there is less chance of missing important leads. Brightness is a considerable psychological boost.

Prime (ie non-rechargeable) alkaline batteries undoubtedly last longer in torches, but the use of good-quality rechargeable batteries on expeditions has much to recommend it, if a reliable source of electricity is available. They can cut down considerably on equipment bulk and cost, but need careful charging to gain maximum benefit from their use. A few boxes of prime batteries should be taken for emergency use. Short-duration expeditions to remote areas may find prime batteries better, but the temptation to use them till exhausted should be avoided.

Rechargeable batteries are only as good as their charger, so take a good, variable output charger that allows you to charge NiCad batteries at their rated specifications. Don't just rely on a cheap, fits-any-battery-charger. You won't get the best, or a full charge, from your batteries.

Repairs

Experience has shown that several basic items are invaluable for keeping diving expeditions going. In addition to a basic tool kit, regulator, compressor and generator spares (diving equipment spares and tool kit are well outlined in *Scuba Equipment Maintenance* by Farley and Royer), pack two or three large rolls of good quality 5cm duct tape, stainless steel jubilee clips (various sizes and available by the roll), inner tubes, electrician's plastic pull-ties and a roll of 2cm nylon webbing. PVC hollow pipe is surprisingly useful for a number of things, and is readily available even in third world countries. Repairs to electrical cables (eg flashguns, lights) can use self-amalgamating tape.

MEDICINE

If diving is to be an integral part of your expedition, try and take a doctor already versed in diving medicine. If that isn't possible, get your medical officer to discuss the programme with one. There are several medical problems that affect diving and in foreign countries there may be things that bite and sting in the water. Be aware of their existence. In third world countries, beware of polluted water - there are lots of nasty little amoebas that can give you brain or liver damage if you are not careful where you dive. Be well-versed in life-saving techniques if marine diving is envisaged.

DECOMPRESSION

Be aware where the nearest operational decompression chambers (plural) are, and the procedures for getting there. You may need to operate through local police, coastguard, air/sea rescue or the military. Make sure that the chambers available can cope with the depths to which you are diving - many smaller ones cannot treat bends from very deep dives, or from mixed gas dives. Victims can find themselves several hundred miles away from the nearest operational chamber and suffer accordingly. Keep your dive limits within those which are medically supportable within a reasonable area. Make sure your insurance covers chamber treatment.

There are ways of keeping a decompression victim in reasonable comfort during long evacuations to therapy, but these should be done under competent medical supervision. Take a trained diving medic on any expedition involving serious decompression diving. Always have oxygen available in remote locations, both in the water for final decompression, and at base for emergencies.

SCIENCE

On a cave diving expedition, a tremendous amount of information can be gained for very little effort. It is worth discussing the possibility of, and techniques for, making basic biological collections of cave fauna in remote or unusual areas, or doing some basic geological or hydrological sampling as part of a survey programme. In most cases, the additional knowledge this adds to the overall picture of the cave environment is so great as to be worth the minute amount of extra effort involved. The diver doesn't have to be any sort of scientist to do this, and it certainly increases his awareness of the underwater cave environment in general.

Speak with someone familiar with collecting and preserving techniques, and find out who might be interested in analysing such specimens. Always check local regulations about scientific collection before you do it, though. In many countries, a permit must be obtained before such collection can be done. This is usually easy to obtain, and is simply to co-ordinate scientific research on a central basis. Always lodge results of your work with a reputable organisation in the host country.

Take great care if you find archaeological remains. Do not disturb them unless essential, and always record positions before any disturbance. Do not announce your find to the press, but contact the local or national museum discretely.

CONSERVATION

The phreatic zone of caves is often one of the most important areas of the cave as far as wildlife is concerned. Cave divers and sump divers can do an immense amount of damage to an underwater cave ecosystem by careless movement or thoughtless exploration. The use of a buoyancy compensating device is essential when the size of the cave permits. Caves in foreign countries are often different in content to British caves - tropical caves may contain more fauna, and sea-level or submarine caves may contain speleothems. Undue mixing of fresh and salt water in halocline caves can affect the fauna present.

Where speleothems have formed during low water conditions, such formations may have re-crystallised and will be extremely fragile. They can be broken by water movements created by a diver swimming near them, and certainly by being swum into. Try and avoid using such delicate features for belays!

POLITICS

Every country has its own rules, whether you agree with them or not. If you are diving underwater caves abroad, be aware of any regulations that may affect caving or diving. Diving politics are often more delicate than caving politics; in Greece or Spain, for example (two countries that regularly feature in the caving expedition scene) diving expeditions may have to fulfil additional requirements. If you break the rules, you will just be making it difficult for those coming after you, and you will justifiably lose support for future ventures of your own. Contact local cave diving organisations wherever possible. Play the ambassador and make social and sporting contacts. In many countries (eg France, USA) cave diving is treated in a much more professional manner than it often is in the UK, so be more professional in your own approach.

Getting air from dive shops abroad may need the production of a BS-AC or CMAS card. Check with the BS-AC in London on national diving regulations for the country you intend to visit.

ON RETURN

It should be unnecessary to say so, but thank your sponsors, especially any from the diving world. Cave diving expeditions have a good reputation to date, fostered by Cave Diving Group members over the last decade. Don't abuse the privilege of this foundation work; set a good example to the next generation of cave diving expeditioners who will follow you!

SCIENTIFIC CAVE DIVING

OUR pioneering divers took much more interest in their surroundings than did many generations following them. Many of the early dives were to recover archaeological remains from a Romano-British burial chamber, in support of archaeologists from Bristol University who were studying the early inhabitants of Mendip, in Somerset.

Developments in cave diving technique over the next few decades were largely aimed at the safe exploration of dry cave passages that lay beyond sumps. Cave divers in the UK would rarely have regarded themselves as scientists, though many were instrumental in mapping extensive caves systems that lay beneath the limestone hills of the major caving areas in the country. This itself added significantly to an understanding of the drainage network configurations in such karst environments, and helped reveal the hitherto unexpected complexity of such phreatic river systems.

More recently, and especially with a growing interest in the cave diving community in travelling further afield in search of new exploration territory, cave diving techniques have refined themselves to the point where long-distance cave penetrations can be made, even to considerable depths, with comparative safety, presuming a set series of rules are followed.

The development of safe cave diving techniques has enabled cave divers to take a more refined interest in their subterranean surroundings. Underwater caves provide one of the more faunally significant of cave habitats, much of the food budget of cave systems being brought in by drip water or flowing streams, and ending up within the phreas. Even in the early days of cave exploration in Wookey Hole, it was apparent that the divers shared the water with a diverse community of micro-fauna, several species of which proved to be troglobitic (genetically cave-adapted). The same has been found true of other major phreatic networks in Britain, notably the Leck Fell/Casterton Fell system and the Cheddar River Cave.

Cave diving scientists throughout the world have recently been very active in original research and exploration in many subaquatic caves. There is a whole field of study in the phreatic zone of British caves waiting for interested cave divers with scientific bent to come along.

BIOLOGY

Underwater caves can be loosely divided into three types: freshwater, anchialine and marine. Marine caves have for some time been regarded with interest by biologists as containing species which might otherwise be less commonly found in more accessible areas of the open reef or seafloor. Marine caves often contain reversing tidal currents, and act effectively as underground tidal creeks. These currents can carry the sustenance for life far into the cave passages, allowing studies of the zonation and community structure of reef organisms to be made in comparative ease in an environment very similar to both the interior of shallow coral reefs and to darker depths in the surrounding seas.

Anchialine caves are "bodies of haline waters, usually with a restricted exposure to open air, always with more or less extensive submarine connections to the sea, and showing noticeable marine as well as terrestrial influences" (Jan Stock). Though this is an extremely broad generalisation, these caves usually lie at or below the mixing zone between fresh and saline waters, and their isolation from both the freshwater cave environment and the marine environment (by both distance and degree of salinity) mean that in many cases a specialist fauna has evolved to fill the peculiar niches available in this isolated and stygian habitat.

An example of the importance of the anchialine habitat was the discovery in 1980, by American biologist Jill Yager, of an entirely new order of crustacea, Remipedia, in Grand Bahamas Lucayan caverns. During this decade, over a score of new species have emerged from anchialine caves in the northern Caribbean alone, with more still awaiting description. Many of these bear a close resemblance to similar animals from much deeper habitats on the open ocean floor, and there is evidence to suggest that the cavernous environment of anchialine caves may form part of a much more extensive crevicular habitat that links the inside of continents together via a trans-oceanic underworld of crack and fissure and cave. Similar organisms have been found in Mediterranean Afro-Atlantic and Pacific waters.

The fauna and flora of freshwater cave systems are often a good indicator of water quality, and here hydrology and biology may link together in their ability to monitor pollution. The possibility of cave divers being able to locate and monitor pollution within an underground aquifer by improving the accuracy of sample distribution in less accessible areas of underground cave systems is one which has implications for the third world as well as the first world.

GEOLOGY

Caves have long allowed geologists a direct opportunity to get inside the Earth and see its workings, down to the water table at least. Using cave diving techniques allows the geologist to penetrate further, and consequently see more.

Within northern Florida and the Bahamas, one of the largest and most stable limestone provinces in the world, the ability to reach clean vertical exposures to depths of over 100m allows in situ study of the landform development of the area, with its associated climatic ramifications, for the entire Pleistocene period. The presence of speleothems (dripstone formations) - which can only have formed during periods of low sea level due to glacio-eustatic exposures - within these caves and similar caves else where in the world enables the periods of such exposure to be dated with reasonable accuracy, using radio-isotope dating techniques. This provides additional information about the climatic record of the late Pleistocene, and about the effect of sea-level fluctuation on the formation of islands such as Bermuda, The Bahamas and Pacific atolls, or on coastal areas such as the Mediterranean or Yucatan peninsula of Mexico.

HYDROLOGY

Terrestrial underwater caves form potential conduits which can channel flow movements within their host rock. The mechanisms by which currents flow through vadose river caves are well understood, but those which initiate flow within phreatic conduits or island aquifers are perhaps more complex. Where caves have a conduit function, by carrying tidal waters beneath freshwater aquifers, as freshwater drainage routes, or as routes for deep upwelling of subterranean waters through reflux, they provide a method by which scientists can physically enter into the aquifer to examine such processes at work.

Many underwater island caves intersect the mixing zone, where fresh and saline waters blend in a chemically aggressive region of the aquifer. The diagenetic processes at work in this area are currently under study and may reveal much about the conjectural role this area plays in dolomite formation.

CONSERVATION & MANAGEMENT

There is a tendency when initiating conservation and management plans for terrestrial and marine ecosystems to forget that life does not stop at the surface. This is something that marine scientists have been aware of for many years, and which has long been a point of occasionally less than ribald controversy. The research work of scientific cave divers is revealing that the world beneath the sea, and beneath the water table onshore, is just as important and worthy of protection and management as the more visible world outside.

The recent development by the Bahamas National Trust of the Lucayan National Park on Grand Bahama, which includes what is currently the world's most extensive underwater cave system, is a brave and interesting exercise in complete environmental management of underwater cave systems.

The use of cave diving as a scientific tool is showing us that the good health of the water beneath our feet is perhaps as important as the health of the waters in the seas to the future good health of mankind.

Chapter 8: Researching & Recording

INFORMATION ABOUT SUMPS

WHEN researching site information, where dives are known to have taken place at a particular cave site by members of the CDG, the first resort should be the various *Sump Index* editions produced by the Group. Earlier indexes tended to use an historical approach, whilst more recent ones have been more site descriptive, with references to the relevant *CDG Newsletter* for precise details of previous dives. Indexes include surveys of major sumps and underwater caves. This obviously is good only to date of publication of the appropriate index, and should be supplemented by information from proceeding newsletters.

Newsletters are published every three months by the Group, and contain details of all exploration dives submitted to the Editor, as well as information about existing dive sites that is felt to be worth recording (condition of lines, changes in sediment patterns, dry exploration beyond, etc). These newsletters, together with the index editions, constitute the most easily accessible and thorough record of underwater caving in the UK. Annotated ten-year cumulative indices to newsletters help identify previous published accounts of dives at particular sites.

Other information, especially about early dives, may be gleaned from area guide books or caving club journals, where more detailed accounts of particular explorations are found. Caving magazines, such as *Descent* and *Caves and Caving*, occasionally contain accounts of exploration at major sites.

Information about foreign diving sites can be gained either by contacting foreign cave diving groups (see appendices at the end of this manual), or by subscribing to foreign cave diving magazines. The CDG Foreign Officer can help with preliminary contacts, and holds some foreign magazines in records. In some countries, groups or individuals are reluctant to publish exploration records, and personal contact may be the best approach.

For both British and foreign sites, approaching a CDG member known to have experience at that site or in that country can often give detailed information about sites and conditions.

RECORDING DIVES

Obviously, for information to be available for succeeding generations of cave divers, it is important that each original dive is recorded with the Group. Divers may also wish to send in notes on dives which may be otherwise

CAVE DIVING GROUP LOGSHEET (STANDARD DIVES)   LOG No: ......

Diver(s) name(s): ....

Date of dive: .... Area/Country: ....

Location: ....

NGR: .... Time: ....

Equipment: ....
....

(tank sizes in litres/water capacity)

Aim: ....

Dive record: (include map if relevant)

Duration of dive: .... hours/minutes.

Maximum depth recorded: .... metres.

Decompression required: Yes/No   Type of Tables used: ....

Stops: ....

Computer used: Yes/No   Type: ....

Drysuit used: Yes/No

Visibility (m): Inward: .... Return: ....

Current: ....

Names of surface support/sherpas: ....
....

Other information: ....
....

Signed: .... Date: ....

relevant to members of the Group, and to make a personal record of their own cave diving career.

Most cave divers keep some sort of personal logbook, and submit details to the Group *Newsletter* when they feel it relevant. Over the years, a form of submission has become common, with the following information being given for each dive: site; cave, area, county, country; Ordnance Survey 6-figure grid reference, or relevant national map co-ordinates; date; divers involved; aim of dive; record of results of dive.

Within the record of the dive, notes may be made as to the sump conditions encountered, original explorations made, condition of lines and belays, depth of sump, length of sump, equipment used (including size of cylinders) and its suitability, sediment patterns, flow conditions, visibility (outward and return) and any other information deemed interesting. The account should be detailed but concise - blow-by-blow accounts are rarely as exciting to the reader as to the writer. Mention of sherpas on long and arduous carries is polite, and will probably help getting them down for a return bout. All submissions should be on one side of the paper only, and typewritten whenever possible.

A survey is preferred where any original exploration is made, and this should be drawn *in black ink* as clearly as possible. This need not be detailed at first, and a rough sketch is better than nothing. When the occasion allows, a more precise survey should be undertaken and published in the *Newsletter*.

On the previous page is a sample record form that can be copied and clipped in a folder. Filling one of these in after each dive enables a record to be kept easily. The completed form can then be photocopied and sent in to the Editor for summary.

Where secrecy is preferred, perhaps because of access difficulties, conservation management or other reasons, the CDG Editor operates a Secrecy File. This is not available for publication within or outside the Group unless the diver concerned gives permission, but is useful to have on record for several reasons, a major one being an accident to the exploring diver when otherwise there would be no record of where he might be.

Where dives are made under circumstances that would be covered by the Health & Safety Executive regulations (for paid work including filming, journalism, scientific research, training, etc) more detailed information may be required from each dive. The diver is referred the HSE section of this manual for further information and a sample record sheet.

INTERNATIONAL CAVE DIVING BODIES

AT the time of writing there are two international bodies representing cave diving: the UIS Commission for Cave Diving and the CMAS International Speleological Commission. These approach cave diving from the two ends of the spectrum, the UIS Commission being part of the International Speleological Union and the CMAS Council being part of the world-wide sub-aqua organisation. Both have in the past provided only a very limited forum for contact between national cave diving groups, though there is recent improvement. Far more contacts between divers from different countries have been made outside these two organisations.

Cave diving standards and qualifications are formulated by national groups and are usually recognised formally only in the country of origin. In countries where diving is regulated, standards and qualifications often play an important role in determining who can dive and who cannot. Without internationally recognised standards, divers from another country could be excluded from diving, especially in show caves and government-controlled sites. At the moment (1989), CMAS and UIS are attempting to rationalise a set of internationally acceptable cave diving standards, which should be in force in some form by the early 1990s. UIS has an international code of safety recommendations, given at the end of this section.

An international body should, as a minimum, provide a more effective forum for exchange of techniques and ideas between national groups. Whether it could act as an effective administrator of a system of international cave diving standards depends entirely on the commitments of the national groups to such an idea. At present the interest is lukewarm, but increasing.

The UIS Commission have published irregular newsletters, and have recently brought out (1988/89) an international cave diving magazine of high quality, covering many aspects of cave diving such as training standards, international exploration reports, summaries of national cave diving status, reviews, and so on. Details of this are available from the CDG Foreign Officer, or from the editor of the magazine, Alessio Fabricatore, Via Fatebenefratelli 26, 34170 Gorizia, Italy. The annual subscription to the UIS magazine is currently US $10.

The Commission has a council, and several working groups covering the following aspects of cave diving: Equipment and Techniques; Training and Education; Safety, Rescue and Recovery; Accident and Dive Statistics; Cartography; Photography and Filming; Scientific Cave Diving; Medical Aspects of Cave Diving; Library and Bibliography. These groups seems to have a fairly flexible membership, and are open to any cave diver of any nationality who wishes to be involved with them.

The most practical arm of the UIS Cave Diving Commission is the international cave diving camp, run at two yearly intervals, usually in conjunction with the UIS International Congress of Speleology. This allows cave divers of all nationalities to come together and discuss techniques of cave

Fig. 70: Russian diver emerging from sump. Note - independently back-mounted cylinders, hand-held torches on wrist lanyards and modified exposure suit under layers of clothing.

living in open forum, and to dive together in practical sessions. It is open to anyone who wishes to attend, and details can be obtained from the CDG Secretary or Foreign Officer.

UIS SAFETY RECOMMENDATIONS FOR CAVE DIVING

1) No people outside cave diving should make safety rules, regulations or recommendations regarding cave diving.

2) Every cave diver should be able to exhibit the necessary degree of commonsense and judgement, and should be in good physical and mental health, to meet the hazards involved in cave diving.

3) Each cave diver should commence his or her training in the company of experienced cave divers. Cave diving certification courses or controlled training programmes should be preferred for this purpose.

4) Temporary or permanent guide line, or a combination of both, must be used when diving in a cave or in any similar closed environment, irrespective of visibility, cave environment, or other factors. Non-rotting, adequately strong line must be used.

5) Guide lines permanently installed in a sump must be provided with direction markers, showing direction out at least every ten metres.

6) Direction out should be marked at any crossing where two or more lines join.

7) Permanent lines should be properly placed and tensioned to minimise friction and the possibility of entanglement, while enabling easy following.

8) There must be a continuous line from any point of the dive to the surface.

9) Minimum equipment recommendations are that ALL vital parts of the life support system must be at least doubled, especially regulators, lights and decompression meters. Each cave diver should use at least the following equipment on any cave dive:

- Two regulators with independently-controlled tank valves.
- Submersible pressure gauge on each independent regulator.
- 3 or more independent lights, each of them having a burn duration exceeding that of the planned dive.
- Isothermic suit with thermal insulation properties appropriate to the water temperature and dive duration.
- Mask or diving helmet and a spare mask.
- Depth gauge.
- Watch. If there is no stay planned beyond a sump, a dive computer or bottom timer can be used.
- Protective helmet.
- Protective cover or cage on tank valves.
- Safety (back-up) reel.
- Fins where applicable.
- Buoyancy compensator or a drysuit suitable for buoyancy compensation, where applicable.

- If a dive computer is used, it must be doubled on complex dives, or backed up by the appropriate decompression tables, watch and depth gauge on more simple dives.

10) All the equipment must be arranged so that free-hanging pieces and sharp edges on equipment are avoided, and everything is streamlined to prevent entanglements or guide line damage.

11) Cave diving training should be organised in cave diving courses or controlled training programmes, complying with the UIS training standards.

12) Proper dive planning is an important part of any cave dive. It should involve information gathering, group planning, and individual planning. Specific of particular caves must be considered, as well as equipment requirements, training and experience levels of the cave divers involved.

13) Solo cave diving is considered a commonly acceptable practice, and should be preferred in caves where proper co-operation and mutual help of cave divers in team is not possible.

14) Cave divers should give due consideration to the cave environment, for safety and conservation reasons. Air in closed air spaces should be treated with caution.

15) A maximum of one-third of initial air supply should be used for penetration, two thirds must be reserved for the return journey, to allow for a reserve supply to meet any emergency that might arise on route. More conservative rules are recommended are recommended on difficult cave dives.

16) Any cave dive on which it is planned to exceed 40m in depth should be approached with due care, considering the increased risk, and the deep diving experience of the divers involved.

17) When cave diving, proper care must be given to guide line techniques (laying, following, etc.), taking into consideration that in more than 50% of cave diving accidents guide lines were involved.

18) Proper techniques of buoyancy control and propulsion should be followed to minimise silting of the cave and maximise diving efficiency.

CAVE DIVING AND THE HEALTH & SAFETY EXECUTIVE

DIVING OPERATIONS AT WORK REGULATIONS, 1981

WHEN cave divers are paid for the act of cave diving in the United Kingdom, or by a UK-based company for diving abroad where the money is paid in the UK, no matter for whatever reason, they become liable to HSE regulations for their activities. In theory this means full compliance with the requirements for medical tests, for supervision and for having support divers available at diving base, and with a number of other regulations governing such commercial diving operations. Divers are advised to make themselves familiar with the regulations.

For many purposes there is little likelihood of prosecution if the spirit of the regulations is followed. Major operations may require divers to be registered at least as Part IV Commercial Divers. The use of mixed gas or surface demand involves further regulations.

Exemptions for parts of the requirements exist for scientific, training, journalistic and archaeological diving, provided no person at work dives deeper than 50m, and that no routine decompression time exceeds 20 minutes. Each set of exemptions differs from the others, but these various exemptions would cover most cave diving in the UK. These exemptions do not completely remove divers from HSE regulations. Details of the listed exemptions are held by the CDG Secretary, and the exemption details for scientific diving (as being a likely type that some cave divers will encounter and which would technically cover exploration diving) are given as an appendix to this section. This exemption does not exclude the diver and contractor from filling the relevant diving log.

All commercial dives must be recorded in a personal log book; log books are available from most good diving shops, but the CDG Logsheets in this book will suffice if filled in fully.

More comprehensive details on HSE regulations and their current effect on paid cave diving can be obtained from the Secretary of the Cave Diving Group.

———————————————————————

HEALTH AND SAFETY EXECUTIVE

Diving Operations at Work Regulations 1981
Certificate of Exemption No. DOW/3/81 (General)

The Health and Safety Executive in exercise of the powers conferred on it by Regulation 14 of the Diving Operations at Work Regulations 1981 and being satisfied that the health and safety of persons who are likely to be affected by the exemption will not be prejudiced in consequence of it hereby exempt diving operations -

- a) which are primarily for the purpose of scientific research, and;
- b) in which no person at work dives at a greater depth than 50 metres or his routine decompression time exceeds 20 minutes, and
- c) where a full diving team comprising persons with duties under the regulations is not available.

from Regulations 4, 5, 6, 7(1)(a), 7(3)(b), 8, 9, 10, 12 and 13 of, and Schedules 1 to 6 to, the Diving Operations at Work Regulations SUBJECT TO the following conditions in relation to each diving operation:-

1. That every person diving at work and his employer, if any, ensures so far as is reasonably practicable that -
   a) the plant and equipment that he will use -
   i) includes a means of supplying a breathing mixture (including a reserve supply for immediate use in the event of an emergency or for therapeutic recompression or decompression) suitable in content and temperature and of adequate pressure, and at an adequate rate, to sustain prolonged vigorous physical exertion at the ambient pressure for the duration of the diving operation;
   ii) is properly designed, of adequate strength and of good construction from sound and suitable material;
   iii) is suitable for the conditions in which it is intended to be used;
   iv) where its safe use depends on the depth or pressure at which it is used, is marked with safe working pressure or the maximum depth at which it may be used;
   v) at whatever temperature it is to be used, is adequately protected against malfunctioning at that temperature;
   b) each gas cylinder he will use is legibly marked "breathing air".
2. That every person diving at work -
   a) is trained and competent to operate the plant and equipment he will use;
   b) ensures that the plant and equipment he will use is inspected by a competent person within the six hours immediately before he dives and ensures so far as is reasonably practical that it is maintained in a safe condition whilst it is being used.
3. That every person diving at work ensures so far as is reasonably practicable that -
   a) the diving operation is carried on in accordance with a code of safe diving practice;
   b) there is a person at the surface in immediate control of the operation;

c) there is another person available to render assistance in an emergency, that other person being either on the surface in immediate readiness to dive or in the water in a position to render assistance.

4. That every person diving at work enters the following particulars in the log book required by Regulation 7(3)(a) of the Regulations -
   a) the date;
   b) the name or other designation and the location of the work site;
   c) the maximum depth reached on each occasion;
   d) the time he left the surface, his bottom time and the time he reached the surface on each occasion;
   e) the type of breathing apparatus used by him;
   f) any work done by him on each occasion and the equipment (including tools) used by him in that work;
   g) any decompression schedules followed by him on each occasion;
   h) any decompression sickness or other illness, discomfort or injury suffered by him;
   i) any other factors relevant to his safety or health.

Signed: .... Date: ....
(a person authorised by the Health and Safety Executive to act in that behalf)

CAVE DIVING GROUP LOGSHEET (HSE work dives only)   LOG No: ......

Name and address of diver and/or contractor: ....

....

....

....

Date: ....

Site location(s): ....

Grid reference: ....

Name of diving supervisor: ....

Equipment used: SCUBA ....../Surface demand/other (state) ....

Breathing mixture used: Compressed air: .... Other(state) ....

Task (including tools): ....

....

Dive number:	1	2	3	4	5
Time of leaving surface:	......	......	....	....	....
Time of leaving bottom:	......	......	....	....	....
Bottom time (min.):	......	......	....	....	....
Time of surfacing:	......	......	....	....	....
Maximum depth (metres)	......	......	....	....	....
Stops at (m) depth: Time	......	......	....	....	....
Stops at (m) depth: Time	......	......	....	....	....

Decompression implemented? No/Yes

BSAC .... USN .... Other ....

Any decompression sickness? Yes/No

Any other illness/discomfort/injury? Yes/No

Any adverse health and safety factors? Yes/No

Action/comments if yes to above: ....

....

....

....

Signed: Diver .... Supervisor ....

[ALL THE INFORMATION ABOVE IS REQUIRED BY LAW AND MUST BE COMPLETED FOR EACH DIVE OR GROUP OF DIVES]

Additional Notes:
Name(s) of diving companion(s): ....

....

Equipment: Cylinder sizes (litres/water capacity) ....

Decompression computer details: ....

Water: Visibility (m): .... Temp. (°C): ....

Current (kt): .... Tide/swell: ....

List comments on the dive on reverse or separate sheet.

Chapter 9: Training & Tests

THE DEVELOPMENT OF THE CDG TRAINING PROGRAMME

BECAUSE cave diving is so extreme, the Cave Diving Group has always been acutely aware of a need for legitimacy and responsibility, whilst fostering and encouraging innovative techniques which other diving organisations would find impossible to support as an active policy.

This schizophrenia was shown when Professor J.B.S. Haldane wrote in the 1940s that if there was a Bolshevik revolutionary spirit to be found in the UK it was to be found in the ranks of the CDG. The CDG's response to this was to demote Haldane to non-diving status with the excuse that his oxygen tolerance was questionable.

In the beginning, there wasn't a problem. The caving pioneers of the 1930s were not only developing but inventing the concept of amateur self-contained diving. The strong links forged in this period with Haldane, Davies and Siebe Gorman were to relay the lessons hard won in those early days to military use in the Second World War, and also to lay the foundations for post-war amateur dive training programmes.

In 1946, the Wookey Hole divers founded the Cave Diving Group. The original test schedules can be read in the first edition of *British Caving*, formed out of the need to set standards of training, as all equipment in the 1940s and 1950s was based on military surpluses exclusively contracted to the Group. The CDG evolved on hierarchical lines during this period. The military post-war hangover can be seen in its literature. Each dive was briefed and de-briefed, and dives were actually termed operations. Aspirant divers were apprenticed on a who knew whom basis, and as the CDG had a monopoly on equipment, anyone contemplating a cave diving career had to be a member of CDG. By the early 1960s the Group was in rather a closed circuit, but there was to be great change.

The first change was the almost universal adoption of commercial open-circuit compressed air equipment, pioneered by Mike Boon and others. The CDG published Boon's *Cave Diving on Air*, and those first air tests were a cross between existing closed circuit schedules and revised parts from the BS-AC 3rd Class Diver standard.

The second and by far the greatest revolution came from social change. The post-war generation had come of age. Undisciplined insofar as National Service had been abandoned, the post-war bulge led to an increase in the caving population. This, together with more money and leisure time, and readily available diving equipment, meant that being a member of the CDG was no longer a prerequisite to becoming a cave diver. The point was underlined with the formation of the Independent Cave Diving Group. The CDG realised that if it would not change it might perish, and by 1965 the Group had opened its doors to all.

In the late 1960s, it was felt that the original air test was inadequate in that it did little to examine the candidates ability in actual cave diving. The CDG maxim was that the cave diver had to be a caver first and foremost, diving ability on its own was not enough. This led to O.C. Lloyd's update of the training schedule, with *A Cave Diver's Training Manual* being published in 1975. Even by the time it reached print, events had already dated its usefulness.

The boundaries of cave diving in Britain were being pushed in the 1970s not so much by the improvement of equipment, but by the superbly improved discipline of technique. Yeadon, Statham, Palmer, Farr and others were to legitimise underwater cave exploration as an end in itself, and take up a torch that had been left behind in the 1950s. Whilst the 1960s had agonised on the role of the cave diver, the 1970s and 1980s showed that diving for caving's and diving for diving's sake were equal goals. This change of attitude was marked by the publication of *Yeadon's Technical Review No.3*, on line management techniques, in 1981.

As a direct result of these changes, a sub-committee was formed to review training procedures within the CDG The tests had already been divided into two parts, the first being designed to display competence with the equipment in a safe water environment. The second, or open water section was to show competence with the equipment coupled with the more important elements of cave diving technique.

The sub-committee decided on two parameters in their review. The first was derived from the Group's historical schizophrenia: it being decided to align the first pool section with the CMAS Two-Star standard. Ever since the foundation of the CMAS in 1966, the CDG has sought recognition for two reasons. Firstly so that Group members could obtain air and other diving facilities abroad, and secondly to guarantee CDG's independent status in the light of any future legislation on amateur diving. By following the CMAS standards, it was hoped that at some future time they would recognise CDG's basic training qualification. The reality is that the CDG is not yet officially recognised as the authoritative training organisation for cave diving in the UK by CMAS, and as such continues its fully independent status of the last 20 years.

A far higher standard of cave diving technique was reflected by Yeadon's practice and philosophy in his *Technical Review*. The new training schedule and tests are outlined later in this manual.

So why have tests? In reading the evolution of our standards, an aspiran diver will realise that cave diving is a ruthless discipline, and that today it is harder than ever. The rewards to the individual go without saying. The penalties don't bear contemplating. To get it wrong and survive is getting away with it and this underlines why the trainee diver needs to learn and qualify as quickly as possible, if only to prove he's on the right track. Getting away with it isn't enough. By not qualifying, the trainee shows that he is a liability to his peers, and displays a dangerous lack of self-discipline. In the 1960s when most members were self-taught, it was a common attitude not to qualify, with

Fig. 71: Duke Street II, discovered by CDG divers in 1963 in Ireby Fell Cavern.

the argument that by the time the diver conformed he was over the hill anyway. Fortunately the Group's finest divers have consistently qualified early in their careers, which rather disproves that argument.

Another carrot is that members of the Group enjoy public liability insurance. A nasty fact of modern life is that sooner or later circumstances could arise whereby a member or members of the Group could be sued and found guilty of negligence by a third party, for example the dependents of a victim of a cave diving incident. This fact alone gives a member a deep moral obligation to strive to get qualified, as every qualified diver ensures that the CDG is recognised as a legitimate and responsible organisation.

NOTES FOR TRAINERS & EXAMINERS

Each of the Regional Sections of the CDG has a different requirement for training. Some Sections, with pools and a large membership, can follow a formal regime, whereas others need to be more flexible. Each Section should have appointed Trainers, selected from the ranks of their Qualified Divers. The trainer's mandate should not exceed Parts One and Two of the qualifying tests. Though the basics of diving and the theory of cave diving can readily be taught, full training in cave diving can only be gained by the acquisition of experience in the actual environment itself. The basic training programme is designed to ensure that the trainee cave diver has a good grounding in theory before trying to obtain experience in practice.

Trainers should be aware that training progress rates vary between individuals. Some take to cave diving easily, others may need ten times the teaching to become proficient in basic skills. There is no great need to assume that a caver/diver who takes considerably more time to feel comfortable in the applied use of cave diving skills is going to be an unsafe diver, perhaps simply a more cautious one.

MEMBERSHIP STATUS

Probationary Members

This can be something of a grey area. This category was designed so that the aspirant cave diver with no diving experience could begin elementary pool training before becoming a trainee. As a PM is not cave diving at this stage, he can be refused further training by his Regional Section, or he can discontinue his own membership without prejudice. Each Section has an obligation to train Probationary Divers, whether a pool is available or not. It is possible for already experienced divers, who have the required degree of caving skills, to bypass Probationary Trainee status if the Section is in agreement and the Part One test is taken. Probationary Members are awarded Trainee Diver status once the Part One pool test has been passed, and the Regional Section meeting has agreed to their promotion.

Trainee Divers

Once a member has trainee status, he may start, under the supervision of Qualified Divers, to acquire cave diving experience. The trainee should strive to become fully qualified. Once the required number of dives have been undertaken, and the open water tests completed, he can request a meeting of his Regional Section to award full Qualified Diver status. It is worth noting that access agreements at some of the country's major cave diving sites (eg Wookey Hole, Cheddar Caves) require the diver to hold Qualified Diver status before certain dives can be undertaken.

Qualified Divers

At the present time (1989), the Qualified Diver status is the highest qualification awarded by the Group. It is an award based upon the degree of experience needed to pass or explore simple sumps or underwater cave passages, and takes no account of additional training for deep diving, specialised diving or other high-experience skills, which are regarded as simply that. Many cave divers have little interest in acquiring such advanced skills, and it is recognised that the CDG has no facilities to promote such training. It encourages members to use commercial training facilities where possible for specialised techniques (such as mixed gas diving) but each Section can organise seminars on request to disseminate information on less specialised subjects, such as drysuit diving, cave diving rescue, decompression diving and the like. Here, members of the Group, and not simply the Regional Section, have an onus on them to share information by speaking at such seminars.

Trainers and Examiners

The sponsoring divers of the new member are currently regarded as being his trainers, though some sections have a more formal training programme in which any Qualified Diver available and willing can act as trainer. Examiners are appointed by the Regional Sections from among their most experienced Qualified Divers, and objectively examine the candidate on completion of his training. A candidate's trainers cannot act as Examiner.

Each Regional Section must appoint at least one Examiner (some like to work in pairs so as to be more objective in their judgement), and their task can be an unenviable one.

Verbal tests for all candidates should cover decompression theory and procedure, and the awareness of different tables, stage diving, basic diving physiology and mechanical understanding of equipment and technique. The Examiner should devise practical and written tests to prove the trainee's standard, and must be prepared to delay the qualification of the Trainee if there is any doubt of his ability to progress safely to the next stage of qualification - and to explain to the Trainee the reason why.

CAVE DIVING GROUP TRAINING SCHEDULE & QUALIFYING TESTS

TRAINING SCHEDULE

1) A trainee diver must be proposed and seconded by Qualified Divers of his Section.
2) His sponsors will thus be his Section, who will be responsible for his training.
3) a) The proposed trainee must be physically fit and must not be suffering from epilepsy. He will be required to sign a statement to this effect, and a medical examination will not be required.
   b) The trainee must be a caver of considerable experience, preferably extending over several years, and still beactive as a caver. The Group does not accept diving experience as a substitute for this.
   c) The trainee must have attained the age of 18 years.
   d) He must be elected by the diving members of his Regional Section (Probationary Trainees cannot vote at such election), after completing and presenting an application form together with his first year's subscription.
   e) The regional Section will decide whether to admit the candidate as a Trainee or Probationary Diver, depending on previous diving experience. The status and progress of a Probationary Diver will be reviewed after a period of one year.
4) The training may be divided into three parts:
   a) Basic training in air diving, including rescue and resuscitation. For this, prior training to CMAS 2 star standard or equivalent (eg BS-AC Sports Diver) can be accepted.
   b) Training oriented towards cave diving, including the use of side-mounted cylinders, line management and search techniques.
   c) Cave diving under supervision.
5) These parts may well overlap. Line management should be taught as soon as the candidate has become a diving member. Cave diving under supervision can be started at the Trainer's discretion as soon as the Part One training is completed, if the candidate is sufficiently proficient. A Probationary member will not be allowed to undertake any cave diving.
6) The trainee must keep a log of all his dives using breathing apparatus. This log will be inspected a) when he takes his Part Two tests and b) when the Regional Section considers qualifying him.

CONTENT OF TRAINING SCHEDULE

Basic Air Diving: (Part One)
The trainee should practise under supervision so that he is able to perform, at ease and with full competence, the following techniques.
1) Swim 200m using basic equipment (mask, fins and snorkel).
2) Swim 100m using snorkel and fins but no nose clip. At the discretion of the trainer this may be done in cold water, in which case a wetsuit and weights may be used.
3) Learn to assemble the apparatus which he intends to use underwater, and to understand its mechanism and simple maintenance. To log a total of at least 15 dives with the apparatus in open water, each dive being of at least 15 minutes duration.
4) To practise clearing both mask and mouthpiece underwater.
5) To practise mobility exercises and buoyancy control. This should include swimming upside down, somersaults, rolls, diving through hoops and breathing to control buoyancy.
6) Sharing breathing apparatus with another diver.
7) Practise kit dumping.
8) To study and practise methods of rescue and resuscitation, including towing, landing, the use of buoyant aids, EAR in and out of the water, ECC, and the symptoms of cardiac arrest, recovery and first-aid.

In addition, the trainee should study the CDG Manual in respect of all aspects not specifically covered in advanced training.

Training Orientated Towards Cave Diving: (Part Two)
1) Use of side-mounted cylinders.
2) Line laying and following
3) Exchange of equipment underwater (eg staging)
4) Search for known objects
5) Search for lost diving line
6) Survey methods
7) Applied decompression procedures
8) Use of buoyancy compensators and drysuits.

Additionally, the Trainee must study the whole of the Diving Manual, including aspects not specifically practised in advanced training (eg mixed gases, deep diving, transport of equipment).

Applied Cave Diving Training
This must be done in accordance with the CDG safety code. A total of 20 cave dives should be logged before Qualified Diver status can be awarded. These should show experience of a variety of diving sites, conditions and depths.

TESTS

Note: The Examiners should not be the candidate's trainers, except in Part One of the tests. They must be Qualified Divers.

PART ONE: ELEMENTARY POOL TEST

A test for basic air diving for Probationary and Trainee Divers, to be carried out in a swimming pool or an open water site with good visibility and calm water.

1) Assemble breathing apparatus, weight for swimming at surface and perform the following:
   a   Jump into at least 3m of water from a height of not less than 1m.
   b) Remove mask three times and replace. Breathe to clear mask each time.
   c) Remove mouthpiece three times and replace. Breathe to clear mouthpiece each time.
   d) Perform three forward and three backward somersaults.
2) Swim 50m using fins and breathing apparatus but no mask.
3) Descend fully equipped to a depth of 3m. Remove all equipment, surface and find shore. Dive and fit all equipment and then surface. (Note: if the candidate is wearing a wetsuit, he may put on another weightbelt before descending to don his equipment. He should remove the second belt after replacing his original belt, and hand it to the Examiner.
4) Share breathing apparatus with another diver for 50m, 25m receiving and 25m giving air.
5) Fully kitted, swim 50m to a point where a subject is lying "unconscious" at a depth of 3m. Dive and bring the subject to the surface. Give 4 cycles of EAR, then tow for 25m to the shore, giving EAR as necessary on the way. Land the subject (help with equipment permitted), and continue EAR for 6 cycles.
   Demonstrate an ability to recognise cardiac arrest and how to perform ECC (a dummy should be used for the latter). Assuming that breathing has recommended, put the subject in the recovery position and describe the treatment for shock. (Note: buoyancy aids on removal of victim's weightbelt may be used at the discretion of the Examiner).
6) Answer viva voce questions relating to the diving apparatus, (eg how it works and its upkeep), physiological problems and open water diving problems.

On passing the Part One test, a Probationary Member may be promoted to Trainee Diver by a meeting of his Regional Section.

PART TWO: ADVANCED TEST

The Part Two test must be carried out at a diving site with poor visibility and a muddy bottom, with a recommended depth of 3m. Full kit, as chosen by the candidate for cave diving, must be worn. Weight as for shallow swimming. The Examiner must not be the candidate's trainer.

1) Lay a tagged line for 50m and belay the end.
2) Lay a branch line from this to the surface, and fit a buoyant aid. Having previously marked the main line with a home tag, remove the buoyant aid, branch line and home tag.
3) On the way "home", the Examiner or helper will displace the candidate's mask and/or disrupt his air supply. The candidate must refix the mask and clear it, and/or reinstate his air supply.

4) Demonstrate the use of a compass and knowledge of cave diving survey.
5) Having "lost" the main line in bad visibility, demonstrate the use of a search reel to regain the main line.
6) Demonstrate to the Examiner's satisfaction the ability to clear tangled line.
7) Release the line from the belay and reel in back "home".
8) Demonstrate the use of buoyancy compensators, or, if drysuits are used, buoyancy control of such suits.
9) Answer viva voce questions relating to cave diving problems including: standard and specialised equipment and its maintenance, in-water techniques, use of decompression tables and specific decompression problems relating to cave diving, mixed gases and any additional technologies specified by examiner.

Note: Full kit in Part Two must include two independently valved breathing sets, and the candidate must demonstrate ability to change from one set to the other underwater.

On passing Part Two, a candidate may apply for Qualified Diver status at a meeting of his Regional Section, who will take all material matters into account before awarding it.

Fig. 72: Preparing for a training dive into the Aggy Risings, South Wales.

Chapter 10: Reference Section

CAVE DIVING GROUP CONSTITUTION

OBJECTS

1) The name shall be the Cave Diving Group. The objects of the Group shall be:
    a) to explore submerged caves and cave passages
    b) to lay down codes of diving practise for that purpose
    c) to review and publicise new diving techniques.

CENTRAL COMMITTEE

2) The Cave Diving Group shall consist of any number of regional sections and a central committee. The central committee shall consist of a President, a Chairperson, a Secretary, a Treasurer, a Foreign Officer, a Technical Officer and an Editor each elected at the Annual General Meeting, and in addition to these officers there shall be two committee members for each regional section, who will have one vote between them at committee meetings. The posts of any two of these offices may be combined.

3) The committee shall meet at least once a year between one AGM and the next, the meeting places being in each region by rotation, unless agreed by a simple majority of those entitled to at tend.
    The committee shall deal with the following matters:
    a) General administration and policy.
    b) To supervise and finance the publication of sump indexes, technical reviews, newsletters, updates to the Group's Manual and the five year index of dives.
    c) To maintain public relations with other bodies on a national and international level.
    d) To initiate new regional sections as and when they become necessary.
    e) Finance in respect of powers delegated by regional sections under Paragraph 23.
    f) To consider appeals against expulsion from membership.

REGIONAL SECTIONS

4) The functions of regional sections shall be as follows:
    a) Finance, except where delegated to central committee under Paragraph 23.

b) To encourage all members to use the Safety Code for divers and follow the Group's Rules.
  c) To supervise the cave diving and training of its members.
  d) To elect or expel members.
  e) To establish and maintain a regional equipment store.
  f) To consider all new forms of diving equipment and to make recommendations regarding their use on Group dives.
  g) To furnish the Editor with material for his publications. To prepare a regional sump index.
  h) To award or remove diving status or any category thereof.
  i) To present a report of their activities to the AGM.

5) The regional committee members shall be responsible to the central committee for ensuring the functions of the regional sections are implemented. They may delegate responsibility for any section.

6) The regional sections shall be named by reference to their geographical location, or by such other name as the members shall determine, providing the words Cave Diving Group appear in the title.

7) Each regional section shall elect at its annual meeting a Secretary and a Treasurer. The Treasurer shall receive all subscriptions from the region, present properly audited accounts to the section once a year for approval, and send a copy to the Secretary of the central committee. He or she shall be responsible for forwarding the annual subscription to the central committee. Where the regional section has no Treasurer, the regional Secretary must observe the rules relating to annual accounts.

8) Subject to the provisions of this constitution and the Rules the business of the regional sections may be carried out in whatever manner the members of that regional section shall determine.

MEMBERSHIP

9) There shall be three classes of membership, namely Honorary, Diving and Non-Diving membership.

10) Honorary members are to be proposed by regional sections for consideration by the central committee. The central committee will put its recommendations to the AGM where election shall be by simple majority vote. These positions shall be awarded to persons who have made a valuable contribution to cave diving or the Group. Honorary members are entitled to receive all the Group's publications and attend and vote at all General Meetings and attend but not vote at regional section meetings. They are covered by the Group's insurance, can borrow Group equipment and take part in Group dives and pay no subscription.

11) There shall be three classes of diving membership, namely Probationary Diver, Trainee Diver and Qualified Diver. The election of diving members and the award of qualifications is the function of regional sections in accordance with the Rules. All diving members are entitled to receive the Group's publications and attend and vote at all general meetings and regional section meetings of which they are a member, except probationary divers who cannot vote on the election of new diving members or matters of qualification. All diving members shall use the Group's Safety Code for divers and follow the Group's Rules.

Fig. 73: A diver greeted by the full-time residents of a submarine cave.

12) Non diving members are elected by the regional sections. They must be proposed and seconded by existing members of the Group and shall be entitled to receive the Group's publications. They are also entitled to attend and vote at all General Meetings and regional section meetings of which they are a member, except that they cannot vote on the election of new diving members. They are not covered by the Group's insurance and cannot borrow Group equipment or take part Group dives. Members ordinarily resident abroad will normally fall into this category.

13) The full subscription shall be determined by a majority of members attending and voting at the Annual General Meeting. It shall comprise an annual subscription (60%) and an additional subscription (40%) levied by the regional section. Non diving members shall not be charged an additional subscription. In the event of a failure to determine the rate of subscription for the following year the existing rate shall continue to apply. Possession of a current CDG Manual is a condition for the award of diving membership of the Cave Diving Group.

14) The full subscriptions are due on 1st January and shall be paid to the regional treasurer except as provided in Paragraph 15. If any member is more than a year overdue with their annual subscription their membership will be deemed to have lapsed. Their status as a member will however not be affected the their ability or failure to pay an additional subscription. No publications will be sent to members whose subscriptions have not been paid by the Annual General Meeting.

15) Where the regional section prefers not to have a treasurer (under Paragraph 7) the annual subscription must be paid directly to the central treasurer by the member, and falls due on 1st January.

16) Members expelled by their regional section shall have a right of appeal to the central committee whose decision shall be final. The appeal must be made in writing to the Secretary within three months of the member being notified of the expulsion by the regional section.

MEETINGS

17) There shall be an Annual General Meeting to be held in the month of May. The Secretary shall give six weeks notice of the meeting and twenty-one days notice of all proposals to be put to the meeting. Notice shall be circulated to all members.

18) The central committee or a regional section may call an extraordinary General Meeting by the giving of twenty-one days notice to all members and a similar notice of their proposals.

19) Proceedings at General meetings of the Group shall be by simple majority of those attending and voting. The decisions of a General Meeting are binding on the central committee.

20) There shall be a quorum of 5% of the membership at any General Meeting before the meeting is deemed validly constituted.

21) Amendments to the constitution take effect as soon as they are passed by a General Meeting.

OFFICIALS

22) The Secretary of the central committee shall call a committee meeting when necessary at his or her discretion, in accordance with Paragraph 3, giving notice of not less than one month to all committee members. After every committee meeting he or she shall circulate minutes to each committee member. He or she shall keep the minutes of all the meetings called (reference Paragraphs 17 & 18), keep the membership list, a copy of which must be submitted for publication in the January Newsletter, maintain contacts on a national level, and be responsible for general correspondence.

23) The function of the treasurer is to receive the annual subscription from the regional treasurers, or the annual subscription from the members of regional sections who have no treasurer, to keep up to date the Group's insurance policy, to pay the expenses of the Editor and Secretary and pay for Group publications and deal with all other matters relevant to the Group's finances. He or she shall present properly audited accounts to the Annual General Meeting.

24) The function of the Foreign Officer is to establish and maintain contacts with overseas groups including the exchange of newsletters. He or she shall also ensure Group representation at relevant overseas meetings where possible and maintain a library for overseas publications.

25) The Technical Officer is responsible for the update of the Group's Manual. He or she is also responsible for the review and publication of all items of technical interest and correspondence on all technical matters.

26) The Editor will keep a record (supplied by regional sections) of all dives carried out by the Group and will be responsible for the publication of a five year index of dives. He or she will also publish a newsletter quarterly and the deadline dates for copy will be March 1st, June 1st, September 1st and December 1st.

27) The President shall preside over all general Meetings and central committee meetings, but these meetings shall be chaired by the Chairperson.

GENERAL

28) Every person, whether a member or not, taking part in any activity or expedition organised by the Group, or in which any member or officer of the Group takes part, shall do so at his or her own risk, and he or she or his or her legal and person representatives or assigns or dependents shall have no claim or right of action against the Group or any member thereof in respect of damage or injuries to persons or property and whether fatal or otherwise notwithstanding any negligence of any member or officer of the Group or of the body of members of the Group.

29) On a cave diving trip, which is conducted by a member of the Group observing the Group's Safety Code, the equipment used is deemed as being on loan to the Group. This applies to the trip itself and to the journey to and from the diving site. It applies equally to open water training.

30) Recommendations for changes to the Group's Rules or safety Code shall be put forward to the central committee for consideration. All such changes must be adopted at a General Meeting.

USEFUL TELEPHONE NUMBERS

WEATHER FORECASTS

Yorkshire Dales: (West Yorkshire) 0532-8091; (Lakes area) 0966-25151.

Derbyshire: (Sheffield) 0742-8091.

Wales: (Glamorgan/Gwent) 0222-8091.

Mendip: (Somerset/Avon) 0272-8091.

EMERGENCY RECOMPRESSION ADVICE

HMS Vernon:
    Day: 0705-822351 ext: 24875/24866
    (Superintendent of Diving)
    Night: 0705-822351 ext: 22008
    (Duty Officer)
    Extreme emergency: 0705-818888 (if no reply above)

DDRC Ft Bovisand:
    Day: 0752-408093
    Night: 0752-261910

Aberdeen (NHC):
    Day/Night 0224-681818 (doctors only in emergency)

PHYSICAL LAWS RELATING TO DIVING

IN order to understand the principles of air and mixed gas diving, and to allow for the planning of a dive, it is useful to know and understand the physical laws governing gases under pressure. These are Boyle's Law, Charles' Law, Dalton's Law and Henry's Law. (It is also worth bearing one none-textbook law in mind: Murphy's.)

1) *Boyle's Law*: At a constant temperature, the pressure of a gas is inversely proportional to its volume. (Ie if you double the pressure, you halve the volume)

2) *Charles' Law*: The pressure of a gas at constant volume is directly proportional to the absolute temperature of the gas. (Ie the pressure in your tank depends to a certain degree on the temperature of its surroundings)

3) *Dalton's Law*: In a mixture of gases, each gas exerts the pressure that it would do if it occupied the volume alone. (Ie each constituent gas has its own partial pressure.)

4) *Henry's Law*: The amount of gas that will dissolve in a liquid is directly proportional to the partial pressure of the gas. (Ie if the partial pressure of a gas (eg nitrogen, helium) is doubled, then twice as much is absorbed into the body.)

There is one other law with a direct bearing on cave diving. There are many variations, but one basic law that covers all cave diving ventures. This is Murphy's Law, and it is just as important as those above. Remember it next time you cave dive.

5) *Murphy's Law*: If anything can go wrong, it will, usually at the most inconvenient moment.

Buhlmann Decompression Tables

The tables have been compiled with a safety factor of 2 m for the depth of the dive; therefore, for a dive to 32 m decompression is carried out in correspondence with the table for 30 m. For intermediate stays at the bottom, the next length of stay should be used; thus for a stay of 35 min at 30 m decompression is undertaken as for a stay of 40 mins.

With repeated dives time supplements for the bottom time must be considered; the values for repetitive dives are marked for every dive with a letter. The supplements are determined from Tables 1 and 2.

If diving is done daily, the total time of diving, whereby the intervals at the surface are included in the total, should not exceed 6 h in any 24 h.

Examples for Repeated Diving

1. *No Decompression Dives.* After a stay of 53 min at 18 m ascent to the surface may be effected in a bare 2 min without a stop for decompression. If the stay at 18 m has been only 20 min, the diver is in Repetitive Group C, which can be found in Table 2. He may dive again for 32 min to a depth of 18 m and then return to the surface without a stop for decompression.

2. *Dives with Decompression.* After a first dive with a stay of 50 min at 30 m, following decompression the diver is in Repetitive Group G. After an interval of 60 min at the surface Repetitive Group D is applicable with an addition of 18 min for a second dive to the same depth. After a stay of 32 min at 30 m, decompression must be accomplished in correspondence with a stay of 50 mins at the bottom. At the end of decompression, Repetitive Group G is again applicable; if the stay at 30 m is 50 min, decompression must be accomplished as for a stay at the bottom of 70 min.

Table 1. Table of intervals at the surface (Reprinted with permission)

Repetitive group at the end of the interval at the surface

	L	K	J	H	G	F	E	D	C	B	A	"O"
L	160	240	300	400	530	600	700	800	1000	1200		48
K		120	150	210	270	330	420	480	560	660		34
J			45	70	90	120	160	210	300	420		24
H				30	45	60	90	150	180	260		17
G					25	45	60	75	100	130		12
F						20	30	45	75	90		8
E							10	15	25	45		4
D								10	15	30		3
C									10	25		3
B										20		2
A												2

Repetitive group at the beginning of the interval at the surface

Duration of the intervals in minutes, for group "O", in hours. This table is valid for up to 3,500 m above sea level.

For stepwise descent and ascent, the depth and duration of the first dive ascertain the repetitive group with an addition of time calculated for the depth that is averaged over the entire duration of the dive. An example is given by 20 min at 18 m is in Group C, plus 15 min at 24 m, plus 15 min at 18 m, and plus 15 min at 35 m, yielding 65 min at an average depth of 22.8 m, for which the supplement in Group C is 20 min for 21 m. The decompression will be as for a stay of 90 min at a depth of 21 m.

Table 2. Time supplements for repetitive dives

Repe-titive group	Depth attained in the repetitive dives (m)																
	9	12	15	18	21	24	27	30	33	36	39	42	45	48	51	54	57	60
L	450	300	240	180	160	140	120	110	100	90	80	75	75	65	60	60	55	50
K	430	270	200	150	100	100	90	75	70	65	55	55	50	50	45	40	40	40
J	410	220	150	100	80	75	70	60	55	50	40	40	40	40	35	35	30	30
H	300	150	100	90	75	60	55	50	50	45	35	35	30	25	25	25	20	20
G	145	115	80	65	55	45	40	35	30	25	25	23	23	20	20	18	15	15
F	115	100	75	60	50	40	35	30	25	23	20	18	17	16	15	14	13	12
E	90	75	45	40	35	30	25	23	22	20	18	16	14	12	11	10	10	10
D	70	50	35	30	25	23	20	18	17	16	15	14	12	10	9	8	7	6
C	45	30	25	20	20	20	18	16	14	12	10	10	9	8	7	7	6	5
B	30	25	20	18	15	12	10	10	9	8	7	7	6	6	5	5	5	5
A	20	18	15	14	12	10	9	7	6	6	6	6	5	5	5	5	5	5

The time supplements are valid for up to 3,500 m above sea level.

Table 3. Air decompression table (0–700 m above sea level)

Depth m	Bottom time min	Time to first stop min : s	Decompression stops m min							Total ascent time min : s		Repeti-tive group
			24	21	18	15	12	9	6	3		
9	300										1	0	H
12	120										1	10	G
	150	0 50								9	9	50	G
	180	0 50								14	14	50	H
	210	0 50								18	18	50	H
	240	0 50								24	24	50	J
	270	0 50								29	29	50	K
	300	0 50								34	34	50	K
15	75										1	30	G
	90	1 10							6		7	10	G
	120	1 10							20		21	10	G
	140	1 10							25		26	10	H
	160	1 10							31		32	10	H
	180	1 10							38		39	10	H
	200	0 50						2	43		45	50	J
	220	0 50						5	46		51	50	K
	240	0 50						6	49		55	50	K

Table 3. *(continued)* Air decompression table (0-700m above sea level)

Depth m	Bottom time min	Time to first stop min : s	Decompression stops m min								Total ascent time min : s		Repetitive group
			24	21	18	15	12	9	6	3			
18	53										1	50	F
	60	1 30								4	5	30	F
	70	1 30								9	10	30	G
	80	1 30								16	17	30	G
	90	1 30								23	24	30	G
	100	1 30								28	29	30	G
	110	1 10							1	31	33	10	H
	120	1 10							3	33	37	10	H
	130	1 10							7	35	43	10	H
	140	1 10							10	38	49	10	H
	150	1 10							13	41	55	10	J
	160	1 10							15	44	60	10	J
	170	1 10							17	46	64	10	K
	180	1 10							19	48	68	10	K
	190	1 10							20	50	71	10	K
	200	1 10							21	52	74 · 10		K
21	35										2	10	E
	50	1 50								6	7	50	F
	60	1 50								13	14	50	G
	70	1 50								23	24	50	G
	80	1 30							3	28	32	50	G
	90	1 30							7	31	39	30	H
	100	1 30							10	33	44	30	H
	110	1 30							15	36	52	30	H
	120	1 30							20	39	60	30	J
	130	1 30							23	43	67	30	J
	140	1 30							26	46	73	30	K
	150	1 30							29	48	78	30	K
	160	1 10						2	29	51	83	10	L
	170	1 10						5	30	52	88	10	L
	180	1 10						7	33	73	114	10	L
24	25										2	30	E
	40	2 10								6	8	10	F
	50	2 10								15	17	10	G
	60	1 50							3	23	27	50	G
	70	1 50							8	29	38	50	G
	80	1 50							13	32	46	50	H
	90	1 50							18	33	52	50	H
	100	1 30						1	24	38	64	30	H
	110	1 30						4	26	43	74	30	J
	120	1 30						6	29	46	82	30	J
	130	1 30						10	29	49	89	30	K
	140	1 30						13	30	52	96	30	L
	150	1 30						16	33	61	111	30	L
	160	1 30						18	36	94	149	30	L

Table 3. *(continued)* Air decompression table (0–700m above sea level)

Depth m	Bottom time min	Time to first stop min : s	Decompression stops m min							Total ascent time min : s		Repetitive group
			24	21	18	15	12	9	6	3			
27	22										2	40	E
	30	2 20								4	6	20	F
	40	2 10							1	12	15	10	F
	50	2 10							4	22	28	10	G
	60	2 10							10	28	40	10	G
	70	1 50						1	16	32	50	50	H
	80	1 50						4	21	34	60	50	H
	90	1 50						8	25	39	73	50	H
	100| 1 50						11	28	44	84	50	J
	110| 1 50						15	29	49	94	50	K
	120| 1 50						19	30	52	102	50	L
	130| 1 30					1	23	33	55	113	30	L
	140| 1 30					3	24	38	94	160	30	L
30	20										3	0	D
	25	2 40								4	6	40	E
	30	2 20							2	6	10	20	F
	40	2 20							5	16	23	20	G
	50	2 10						1	10	26	39	10	G
	60	2 10						3	16	31	52	10	H
	70	2 10						7	21	34	64	10	H
	80	2 10						12	25	40	79	10	J
	90	1 50					1	15	29	45	91	50	J
	100| 1 50					4	19	29	50	103	50	K
	110| 1 50					6	23	32	51	113	50	L
	120| 1 50					9	24	37	79	150	50	L
33	17										3	20	D
	25	2 40							2	6	10	40	F
	30	2 40							4	10	16	40	F
	40	2 20						2	7	22	33	20	G
	50	2 20						4	14	30	50	20	G
	60	2 20						8	20	33	63	20	H
	70	2 10					2	13	25	39	81	10	J
	80	2 10					4	16	29	45	96	10	K
	90	2 10					8	20	29	51	110	10	K
	100	2 10					12	23	33	53	123	10	L
	110	2 10					14	26	38	95	175	10	L

Table 3. *(continued)* Air decompression table (0-700m above sea level)

Depth m	Bottom time min	Time to first stop min : s	Decompression stops m min							Total ascent time min : s		Repetitive group
			24	21	18	15	12	9	6	3		
36	15										3	40	D
	20	3 0							2	4	9	0	E
	25	3 0							4	7	14	0	F
	30	2 40						2	5	14	23	40	G
	40	2 40						4	10	26	42	40	G
	50	2 20					1	8	16	33	60	20	H
	60	2 20					4	12	23	37	78	20	H
	70	2 20					7	15	28	44	96	20	K
	80	2 20					12	19	29	50	112	20	K
	90	2 10				2	14	24	33	53	128	10	L
	100	2 10				5	16	26	39	102	190	10	L
39	12										3	50	D
	15	3 40								4	7	40	E
	20	3 20							3	6	12	20	F
	25	3 0						2	4	11	20	0	G
	30	3 0						3	6	17	29	0	G
	40	2 40					2	6	13	29	52	40	G
	50	2 40					4	10	20	33	69	40	H
	60	2 20				1	7	15	27	41	93	20	J
	70	2 20				3	11	19	29	49	113	20	K
	80	2 20				5	14	23	33	52	129	20	L
	90	2 20				9	16	26	39	95	187	20	L
42	10										4	10	D
	15	3 40							2	4	9	40	E
	20	3 20						1	4	7	15	20	F
	25	3 20						3	5	14	25	20	G
	30	3 0					2	3	8	22	38	0	G
	40	2 40				1	3	8	16	31	61	40	G
	50	2 40				2	6	13	24	37	84	40	H
	60	2 40				4	9	17	29	46	107	40	K
	70	2 40				7	13	22	31	51	126	40	K
	80	2 20			2	10	15	26	38	84	177	20	L
45	10	4 10								2	6	10	E
	15	3 50							3	5	11	50	E
	20	3 40						3	4	10	20	40	F
	25	3 20					2	3	6	17	31	20	G
	30	3 20					3	5	10	25	46	20	G
	40	3 0				2	5	9	18	34	71	0	H
	50	3 0				5	7	15	27	41	98	0	K
	60	2 40			2	6	12	20	29	50	121	40	K
	70	2 40			3	10	14	25	35	57	146	40	L
	80	2 40			6	12	19	26	42	130	237	40	L

Table 3. *(continued)* Air decompression table (0–700 m above sea level)

Depth m	Bottom time min	Time to first stop min : s	\multicolumn{8}{l}{Decompression stops m min}	Total ascent time min : s	Repetitive group
			24	21	18	15	12	9	6	3		
48	10	4 30								4	8 30	E
	15	3 50						1	4	5	13 50	F
	20	3 40					1	3	5	13	25 40	F
	25	3 40					3	4	8	21	39 40	G
	30	3 20				2	3	6	13	28	55 20	G
	35	3 20				3	4	8	17	32	67 20	H
	40	3 0			1	3	6	12	22	34	81 0	H
	50	3 0			2	6	9	16	29	45	110 0	K
	60	3 0			4	8	14	23	31	52	135 0	K
	70	2 40		1	7	11	17	26	40	100	204 40	L
51	10	4 30							1	4	9 30	E
	15	4 10						2	4	7	17 10	F
	20	3 50					2	4	5	15	29 50	G
	25	3 40				1	4	5	9	25	47 40	G
	30	3 40				3	4	7	15	30	62 40	G
	35	3 20			1	4	5	10	20	33	76 20	H
	40	3 20			2	5	7	13	25	38	93 20	J
	50	3 0		1	4	7	12	19	29	49	124 0	K
	60	3 0		2	6	10	15	25	36	60	157 0	L
	65	3 0		3	7	12	17	26	40	106	214 0	L
54	10	4 50							2	5	11 50	E
	15	4 30						3	4	8	19 30	F
	20	4 10					3	4	6	18	35 10	G
	25	3 50				3	3	6	12	27	54 50	G
	30	3 40			2	3	5	8	17	32	70 40	G
	35	3 40			3	4	6	12	23	35	86 40	J
	40	3 20		1	3	5	9	15	27	41	104 20	K
	50	3 20		2	5	8	14	22	29	52	135 20	K
	60	3 20		5	7	12	17	26	39	103	212 20	L
57	10	5 10						3	5		13 10	E
	15	4 30					1	4	4	11	24 30	F
	20	4 10				2	3	4	8	22	43 10	G
	25	3 50			1	3	4	6	15	29	61 50	G
	30	3 50			3	3	6	9	20	33	77 50	H
	35	3 40		2	3	4	8	14	25	39	98 40	K
	40	3 40		3	3	6	10	16	29	45	115 40	K
	50	3 20	1	4	6	9	15	24	34	52	148 20	K
	55	3 20	2	5	7	11	17	26	39	95	205 20	L

250 Reference section

Table 3. *(continued)* Air decompression table (0–700 m above sea level)

Depth m	Bottom time min	Time to first stop min : s	\multicolumn{8}{c}{Decompression stops m min}	Total ascent time min : s	Repetitive group
			24	21	18	15	12	9	6	3		
60	10	5 10						1	4	5	15 10	E
	15	4 50					2	4	5	13	28 50	F
	20	4 30					3	3	5	9	25	49 30	G
	25	4 10				2	4	4	8	16	31	69 10	H
	30	3 50			2	3	4	6	12	22	35	88 50	J
	35	3 50			3	3	6	8	16	27	42	108 50	K
	40	3 40		1	3	5	7	12	19	29	48	127 40	K
	45	3 40		2	4	5	9	14	23	32	52	144 40	L
	50	3 40		3	4	7	11	16	26	37	82	189 40	L
	55	3 40		4	5	8	14	19	26	42	133	254 40	L
63	10	5 20						2	4	6	17 20	F
	15	4 50					1	3	4	6	15	33 50	G
	20	4 30				1	3	4	6	11	27	56 30	G
	25	4 10			1	3	3	6	8	18	33	76 10	H
	30	4 10			3	3	5	7	14	24	38	98 10	J
	35	3 50		2	3	4	6	10	16	29	46	119 50	K
	40	3 50		3	3	5	8	13	22	29	51	137 50	L
	45	3 50		4	4	7	10	15	25	35	56	159 50	L
	50	3 50		5	5	8	13	18	26	41	114	233 50	L

Table 4. Air decompression table (701–1500 m above sea level)

Depth m	Bottom time min	Time to first stop min : s	\multicolumn{7}{c}{Decompression stops m min}	Total ascent time min : s	Repetitive group
			18	15	12	9	6	4	2		
9	180									1 0	G
12	90	1 0								1 10	G
	100	1 0							2	3 0	G
	110	1 0							6	7 0	G
	120	1 0							10	11 0	G
	130	1 0							13	14 0	G
	140	1 0							15	16 0	G
	150	1 0							17	18 0	H
15	63									1 30	F
	70	1 10							4	5 10	G
	80	1 10							9	10 10	G
	90	1 10							15	16 10	G
	100	1 10							20	21 10	G
	110	1 10							24	25 10	G
	120	1 10							27	28 10	H

Table 4. *(continued)* Air decompression table (701–1500 m above sea level)

Depth m	Bottom time min	Time to first stop min : s	Decompression stops m min							Total ascent time min : s	Repetitive group
			18	15	12	9	6	4	2		
18	43									1 50	F
	50								2	3 40	F
	60	1 40							9	10 40	G
	70	1 40							17	18 40	G
	80	1 40							24	25 40	G
	90	1 20						3	27	31 20	G
	100	1 20						5	30	36 20	H
	110	1 20						9	31	41 20	H
	120	1 20						13	33	47 20	H
21	30									2 10	E
	40	1 50							3	4 50	F
	50	1 50							11	12 50	G
	60	1 40						1	20	22 40	G
	70	1 40						5	25	31 40	G
	80	1 40						9	29	39 40	H
	90	1 40						14	30	45 40	H
	100	1 30					6	17	32	56 30	H
	110	1 30					6	19	36	62 30	H
24	25									2 20	E
	30	2 10							3	5 10	E
	35	2 10							5	7 10	F
	40	2 0						1	9	12 0	F
	50	2 0						3	18	23 0	G
	60	2 0						8	25	35 0	G
	70	1 50					2	12	29	44 50	H
	80	1 50					6	15	30	52 50	H
	90	1 50					10	18	34	63 50	H
	100	1 30				2	12	20	39	74 30	H
27	18									2 20	E
	25	2 30							3	5 30	E
	30	2 20						1	5	8 20	F
	35	2 20						2	10	14 20	F
	40	2 20						3	14	19 20	G
	50	2 10					2	7	24	35 10	G
	60	2 10					5	11	29	47 10	G
	70	1 50				1	9	15	30	56 50	H
	80	1 50				4	11	19	35	70 70	H
	90	1 50				8	14	20	40	83 50	J

Table 4. *(continued)* Air decompression table (701–1500 m above sea level)

Depth m	Bottom time min	Time to first stop min : s	\multicolumn{7}{c}{Decompression stops m min}	Total ascent time min : s	Repetitive group
			18	15	12	9	6	4	2		
30	16									3 0	E
	20	2 50							3	5 50	E
	25	2 40						1	5	8 40	F
	30	2 40						3	8	13 40	F
	35	2 20					1	4	14	21 20	G
	40	2 20					2	6	19	29 20	G
	45	2 20					4	7	24	37 20	G
	50	2 10				1	5	10	27	45 10	G
	60	2 10				3	9	14	30	58 10	H
	70	2 10				7	11	19	35	74 10	H
	80	2 10				12	14	20	41	89 10	J
33	14									3 20	E
	20	2 50						1	4	7 50	E
	25	2 40					1	3	6	12 40	F
	30	2 40					2	4	12	20 40	G
	35	2 20				1	3	5	18	29 20	G
	40	2 20				2	4	7	24	39 20	G
	45	2 20				3	5	11	27	48 20	G
	50	2 20				4	7	12	30	55 20	H
	60	2 20				8	11	18	32	71 20	H
	70	2 10			2	13	14	20	40	91 10	J
36	11									3 40	D
	15	3 20							4	7 20	E
	20	3 10						3	5	11 10	F
	25	3 0					2	3	10	18 0	G
	30	2 40				2	3	4	16	27 40	G
	35	2 40				3	4	6	23	38 40	G
	40	2 40				4	5	11	26	48 40	G
	45	2 20			1	5	8	12	30	58 20	H
	50	2 20			1	8	10	15	30	66 20	H
	60	2 20			4	12	12	20	38	88 20	J
39	10									3 50	D
	15	3 30						1	4	8 30	E
	20	3 20					2	3	6	14 20	F
	25	3 0				2	3	3	13	24 0	G
	30	3 0				3	4	6	20	36 0	G
	35	2 40			1	4	5	10	25	47 40	G
	40	2 40			2	6	6	12	30	58 40	H
	45	2 40			3	8	9	15	31	68 40	H
	50	2 40			5	9	11	18	34	79 40	H
	55	2 40			6	12	13	18	40	91 40	J

Reference section 253

Table 4. *(continued)* Air decompression table (701–1500m above sea level)

Depth m	Bottom time min	Time to first stop min : s	\multicolumn{5}{c}{Decompression stops m min}					Total ascent time min : s	Repetitive group
			18	15	12	9	6	4	2		
42	15	3 50					3	4		10 50	F
	20	3 20				1	3	3	8	18 20	G
	25	3 20				3	3	5	16	30 20	G
	30	3 0			2	4	4	8	24	45 0	G
	35	3 0			3	5	6	12	28	57 0	H
	40	2 40		1	3	8	9	14	30	67 40	H
	45	2 40		1	5	9	12	17	33	79 40	H
	50	2 40		2	6	13	14	20	38	95 40	H
45	10	4 20						3		7 20	D
	15	3 50					2	3	4	12 50	F
	20	3 40				3	3	4	12	25 40	F
	25	3 20			2	3	4	6	20	38 20	G
	30	3 20			3	5	5	10	27	53 20	G
	35	3 0		1	4	6	9	12	30	65 0	H
	40	3 0		2	5	9	11	16	31	77 0	H
	45	3 0		3	6	12	12	20	37	93 0	J
48	10	4 20					1	4		9 20	D
	15	3 50				1	2	3	6	15 50	F
	20	3 40			1	3	3	4	15	29 40	G
	25	3 40			3	4	4	8	23	45 40	G
	30	3 20		2	3	6	6	12	29	61 20	H
	35	3 20		3	4	8	10	15	31	74 20	H
	40	3 0	1	3	6	11	12	19	35	90 0	J
	45	3 0	2	4	8	14	15	20	41	107 0	J
51	10	4 40					2	4		10 40	E
	15	4 10				2	3	3	7	19 10	G
	20	3 50			2	4	4	5	17	35 50	G
	25	3 40		1	4	5	5	9	26	53 40	H
	30	3 40		3	4	7	8	13	30	68 40	H
	35	3 20	1	4	5	10	11	18	32	84 20	H
	40	3 20	2	5	7	13	14	19	39	102 20	J
54	10	4 50					1	3	4	12 50	E
	15	4 30				3	3	3	10	23 30	G
	20	4 10			3	4	4	6	21	42 10	G
	25	3 50		3	3	6	6	11	28	60 50	H
	30	3 40	2	3	5	8	10	15	31	77 40	H
	35	3 40	3	4	6	12	12	20	36	96 40	J

BIBLIOGRAPHY

THIS section is divided into two parts, a general bibliography and a chapter reference section. Not all chapters have a reference list to accompany them, but much material of common interest will be found within those which do. A look through both sections is recommended.

GENERAL BIBLIOGRAPHY

The Darkness Beckons Farr, M.J., Diadem Press, 2nd Ed. 1990.
The Great Caving Adventure Farr, M.J., Oxford Illustrated Press, 1986.
The Blue Holes of the Bahamas Palmer, R.J., Jonathan Cape, 1985.
Deep Into Blue Holes Palmer, R.J., Unwin Hyman, 1989.
The Wakulla Springs Project Stone, W.C., US Deep Caving Team, 1989.
UNESCO Code of Practice for Scientific Diving Flemming, N.C., & Max, M.D., UNESCO/CMAS, 1988.
NSS Cave Diving Manual Exley, S., and Young, I., Cave Diving Section, National Speleological Society (USA), 1982.
NSS/CDS Instructors Cave Diving Manual Prosser, J., NCC-CDS, 1985.
Basic Cave Diving Exley, S., CDS-NSS, 1986. (5th Ed.)
The Art of Safe Cave Diving Training Manual of the National Association for Cave Diving (USA), 1988.
Cave Diving in Australia Lewis, I., and Stace, P., CDAA 1980.
Techniques de Plongee Souterraine Thiry, J.P., SSW 1986
Pesteri Scufundate Lascu, C., & Sarbu, S., Editura Academiei Republicii Socialiste Romania, 1987.
BS-AC Sport Diving Manual British Sub-Aqua Club, Stanley Paul, London, 1987.
Professional Divers Handbook Sisman, D., Submex 1982.

CHAPTER REFERENCES

The effects of stress
a) Numerical section references:
1) *BSAC Manual*, 1987 Edition, p86. Stanley Paul, London.
2) Thomas, R., & McKenzie, B., *The Diver's Medical Companion*, p24, Diving Medical Centre, Australia, 1986.
3) Cordingley, J.N., "The First British Sump Rescue Symposium", *Cave Science* 14(1), p13, 1987.
4) As (2), page 127.
5) As (1), page 157.
6) *NSS Cave Diving Manual* (Eds Exley, S., & Young, I.) National Speleological Association, USA, 1981.
b) General chapter bibliography:
Bonington, C., *Quest for Adventure*, Pan Books, London, pp292-302, 1983.
BSAC Manual 1972, pp59-69, The Riverside Press, London.
Hasenmayer, J., "Angst Ist Nur Ein Wort" (Fear is Only a Word) in *Submarin*, pp25-35, 1977.

Fig. 74: The sump is passed, the diver becomes an ordinary caver again.

Knutson, S., "Getting the Edge" *NSS News* 14, (12), December 1988.
Murphey, M., "Psychological Considerations", *UIS Cave Diving Magazine* 1, pp14-17, Gorizia, 1987.
Smith, R., "Stress in Cave Diving", in *Safe Cave Diving*, Ed Tom Mount, NACD, Florida, pp168-188, 1973.
Wooding, M, "Cave Diving, Extending the Limits of Exploration", *BSA Bulletin*, New Series 1, p7-8, 1970.

The demand valve
Scuba Equipment Repair and Maintenance, Farley and Royer, Marcor Publishing, 1980.

Free-diving
ULSA Review 13, University of Leeds Speleological Association.

Safety & rescue
1) "Proceedings of the First British Sump Rescue Symposium", *Cave Science*, 14 (1) pp7-30, 1987.
2) "Sump Rescue Symposium", *CDG Newsletter* 88, pp7-14, 1988.
   The following books and articles contain much useful information on safety and survival [SS] and first-aid [FA] and some of them should be consulted by anyone who is considering caving beyond sumps.
Bryson, Dr P., *Underwater Diving Accident Manual*, obtainable DDRC, Fort Bovisand, Plymouth, Devon.
Incidents & seminars: *CDG N/L new series No. 62*, pp27-28; *CDG N/L new series No. 77*, pp26-27; *CDG N/L new series No. 81*, pp4-7; *CDG N/L new series No. 87*; *CDG N/L new series No. 88*, pp7-14; *Cave Science Vol 14 No. 1*, pp7-30.
Emergency Procedures for Everyone at Home, at Work or at Leisure, Authorised manual of the St John Ambulance Association, the St Andrew's Ambulance Association, and the British Red Cross Society, 1982.
Danilewicz, C.J., & Proudlove, G. S., editors. "Proceedings of the First British Sump Rescue Symposium", *Cave Science* 14 (1), pp7-30, 1987.
Frankland, J., "Medical Aspects of Cave Rescue",. *Trans of the BCRA*, 2(2), pp53-64 1975.
Frankland, J., "Hypothermia and Cavers", *Trans of the BCRA*, 8(4), pp225-228, 1981.
Frankland, J., "Hypothermia in Cavers", *Trans of the BCRA*, 11(3), pp154-159 1984.
Gardner, A. W., & Roylance, P. J., *New Advanced First-Aid* Wright, Bristol, 1984.
Gibson, D., "Caving Injuries: Management from Site to Surface", *Journal of the Northern Pennine Club*, 4(1), pp61-67, 1987.
Harper, N., "Temperature Regulation in Man: the Problem of Hypothermia", *Trans of the BCRA*, 2(2), pp47-52, 1975.
Houghton, T., "Underground First-Aid", *Proc of the Oxford University Cave Club*, 12, pp26-27, 1986.
Kirby, N. G., & Mather, S. J., *Baillieres Handbook of First-Aid*, 7th Edition, Bailliere Tindall, London, 1985.

Lyons, T., "Principles of First-Aid Treatment following a Major Cave Accident", *Trans of the BCRA*, 11(3), pp167-170, 1984.
Mackin, R., *Through-Sump and Diver Communications*, 1987. Danelewicz, C. J., & Proudlove, G. S., (Eds). "Proceedings of the First British Sump Rescue Symposium", *Cave Science* 14(1), pp7-30.
Parcel, G., *Basic Emergency Care of the Sick and Injured*, C. V. Mosby Company, St Louis, 1982.
Proudlove, G. S., "Caving Helmets", *Caves and Caving* 31, p34 and Descent 63, p32, 1986.
Proudlove, G. S., (not yet published) "Caving Safety and Survival: an Integrated Approach", *Caves and Caving*.
Ramsden, P., "Cave Flooding and Underground Survival". *Trans of the BCRA*, 11(3), pp160-166, 1984.
Steele, P., *Medical Care for Mountain Climbers*, Heinemann, London, 1976.
Walker, F., "Care after Caving Accidents", *Trans of the BCRA*, 8(4), pp233-235, 1981.
Wilkerson, J. A., *Medicine for Mountaineers*, The Mountaineers, Seattle, 1975.
Williams, R. M., & Williams, M. A. M., "Hazards of Using Explosives", *Trans of the Cave Research Group*, 6(2), pp69-78, 1975.
Williams, R. M., & Williams, M. A. M., "Hazards of Using Explosives in Caves", *Trans of the Cave Research Group*, 2(2), pp89-72, 1975.
Wilmshurst, Dr P. (Ed), *Diving Emergency Handbook*, (UK edn), Obtainable BSAC.

First-aid beyond long sumps

Emergency Procedures for Everyone at Home, at Work or at Leisure, Authorised manual of the St John Ambulance Association, the St Andrew's Ambulance Association, and the British Red Cross Society, 1982.
Frankland, J. C., "Medical Aspects of Cave Rescue", *Trans of the BCRA*, 2(2), pp53-63, 1975.
Gardener, A. W., & Roylance, P. J., *New Essential First Aid*, Pan, London & Sydney, 1979.
Glanvill, Dr P., *First Aid For Cavers*, obtainable Ambit (publishers of Descent magazine).
Harper, N., "Temperature Regulation in Man: The Problem of Hypothermia", *Trans of the BCRA*, 2(2), pp47-52, 1975.
James, J. M., Pavey, A. J., & Rogers, A. F., "Foul Air and the Resulting Hazards to Cavers", *Trans of the BCRA*, 2(2), pp79-88, 1975.
Lloyd, D. C., "Some Medical Aspects of Cave Diving", *Trans of the BCRA*, 2(2), pp65-78, 1975.
Mills, J. N., "Speleology and Circadian Rhythms", *Trans of the BCRA*, 2(2), pp95-97, 1975.
Mitchell, D., *Mountaineering First Aid. A Guide to Accident Response and First Aid Care*, Snohomish Publishing Co Inc, Snohomish, Washington, 1978.
Standing, P. A., "Medical Care on Caving Expeditions", *Trans of the BCRA*, 2(2), pp99-105, 1975.
Standing, P. A., "Miscellaneous Medical Problems", *Trans BCRA*, 2(2), p93, 1976.
Steele, P., *Medical Care for Mountain Climbers*, Heinemann, London, 1976.

Williams, R. M., & Williams, A. M., "Hazards of Using Explosives", *Trans of the BCRA*, 2(2), pp89-92.
British Sub-Aqua Club, *Sport Diving*, Stanley Paul, London, 1986.

Deep diving problems
1) Stone, Dr W. C., *The Wakulla Springs Project Report*, US Deep Caving Team, 1989.
2) Palmer R., *Deep Into Blue Holes*, Unwin Hyman, 1989.
3) Exley and Young, *NSS Cave Diving Manual*, NSS-CDS, 1982.

Dive computers
1) "BS-AC Specification for Dive Computers", *DIVER*, Nov 1985, 30 (11).
2) Divetronic *Decobrain User Manual*.
3) *Diver*, May 1985, 30 (5).
4) *Skin Diver*, Nov 1985.
5) *Diver*, May 1987, 32 (5).
6) *Diver*, July 1987, 32 (7).
7) *Sport Diver*, January/February 1989, 1 (1).

Mixed gas diving
1) *The Wakulla Project Report*, Stone, Dr W. C., US Deep Caving Team, 1989.

Underwater cave photography
1) Rowlands P., *The Underwater Photographer's Handbook*, Macdonald & Co. 1983.
2) Church, J. & K., *The Nikonos Book*, 1979.
3) Church, J. & K., *Beginning Underwater Photography*, 1977.

Underwater cave surveying
1) Lloyd, O.C., "An Underwater Cave Survey", *Trans Cave Research Group*, 12(3), pp197-199, 1970.
2) Lloyd, O.C., "Surveying Submerged Passages" in *Surveying Caves*, Ed. Bryan Ellis, BCRA, pp61-62, 1976.
3) Cordingley, J.N., "Sump Survey Accuracy", *CDG Newsletter*, 72, pp4-5, 1984.
4) Stanton, W., "Compass Corrections", *CDG Newsletter*, 70, p8, 1984.
5) Stanton, W., "More About Surveying", *CDG Newsletter*, 72, p4, 1984.
6) Abbott, J., "Correspondence" *CDG Newsletter*, 71, p2, 1984.
7) *Cave Science*, 14(2), various authors, 1987.
8) Cordingley, J.N., *CDG Newsletter*, 79, p12, 1986.
9) Cordingley, J.N., "Far Sump Extension, a Survey Description", Technical Speleological Group *Journal* 12, 1986.
10) Exley, S,. and Maegerlein, S., "Surveying" in *NSS Cave Diving Manual*, pp241-262, 1982.
11) Thiry, J.P., *Techniques de la Plongee Souterraine*, p63, 1985.
12) Cordingley, J.N., "Towards a better sump survey method", *CDG Newsletter*, 81, p3, 1986.

Submarine cave diving
1) Woods, E., (Ed), *Sea Life of Britain and Ireland*, Immel Publishing, 1988.

2) Erwin & Picton, *Guide to Inshore Marine Life*, Immel 1987.
3) British Sub-Aqua Club, *BS-AC Sport Divers Manual*, Stanley Paul, London 1988.
4) Palmer, R., *Blue Holes of the Bahamas*, Jonathan Cape, 1985

Expedition cave diving
1) Farley, M., and Royer, C., *Scuba Equipment: Care and Maintenance*, Marcor Publishing, 1980.
2) Palmer, R., *The Blue Holes of the Bahamas*, Jonathan Cape, 1985.
3) Palmer, R., *Underwater Expeditions*, Expedition Advisory Centre, Royal Geographical Society, 1986.
4) Palmer, R., *Deep Into Blue Holes*, Unwin Hyman, 1989.
5) Stone, W., *The Wakulla Project*, 1989.
6) Willis, D., *Caving Expeditions*, Expedition Advisory Centre, Royal Geographical Society, 1989 ed.
7) Winser, N. & S., *Expedition Planner's Handbook and Directory*, Expedition Advisory Centre, Royal Geographical Society, 1988/9.

Scientific cave diving
1) Palmer, R.J., *Cave Diving in Caving Expeditions*, (Ed: Willis R.) Expedition Advisory Centre, London. pp115-121, 1896.
2) *UNESCO Guide for Scientific Diving*, (Eds Max, M., & Flemming, N.C.) UNESCO/CMAS, 1988.
3) Cunliffe, S., "The Flora and Fauna of Sagittarius, an Anchialine Cave and Lake in Grand Bahama", *Cave Science*, 12(3), pp103-109, 1986.
4) Stock, J.H., Iliffe, T.M., and Williams, D.W., "The Concept 'anchialine' Reconsidered", *Stygologia*, 1(1/2), pp90-92, 1986.
5) Palmer, R.J., Warner, G.F., Chapman, P., and Trott, R.J., "Habitat Zonation in Underwater Caves in the Bahamas", *Proc Int Spelol Congr* (Barcelona), pp112-115, 1986.
6) Yager, J., "Remipedia, a New Class of Crustacea from a Marine Cave in the Bahamas", *J Crust Biol*, 1(3), pp328-333, 1981.
7) Hart, C.W., Manning, R.B., and Iliffe, T.M., "The Fauna of Atlantic Marine Caves; Evidence of Dispersal by Sea Floor Spreading While Maintaining Ties to Deep Waters", *Proc Biol Soc*, Washington, 98(1), pp288-292, 1985.
8) Palmer, R.J., "Conservation Problems in Underwater Cave Environments", *Proc Int Spel Congr*, 1987, pp84-86, 1987.

Cave diving & the HSE
1) *A Guide to the Diving Operations at Work Regulations 1981*, HSE Booklet HS(R)8, HMSO 1981.
2) *The Users Guide to The HSE Diving Regulations for Scientific Divers*, Underwater Association.

Fig. 75: A modern cave diver in the garb and equipment of an early Wookey Hole pioneer. Just a few decades, but great advances in technology and techniques.

GLOSSARY OF TERMS USED

ABLJ: Adjustable buoyancy life jacket.
Airbag: An inflatable device for raising objects underwater.
Ambient pressure: The pressure of the surrounding environment, at whatever depth or altitude the diver is.
Ammo Box: A metal box, formerly used to contain ammunition, commonly used to transport small items of equipment used in caving or cave diving. Waterproof to about 5m.
Atmosphere (At): Atmospheric pressure at surface or a multiple thereof - as in 4 ats = 4 x atmospheric pressure.
Backmounts: Breathing cylinders worn on a diver's back.
Backscatter: The reflection of light from material in suspension in the water.
BAR: Unit of measure equivalent to 10^5 newton per square metre (approximately one atmosphere).
BC: Acronym for buoyancy compensator.
BCRA: British Cave Research Association.
BDH Tube: A water-resistant plastic container often used to carry equipment through a cave.
Bends: Slang expression for decompression sickness.
Buddy bottle: A cylinder of breathing gas taken on a long dive for emergency use only.
Buddy diving: The practise of diving with a companion for safety reasons.
CMAS: Confederation Mondiale des Activites Subaquatiques (World Underwater Federation).
Composite tank: A breathing gas cylinder constructed by wrapping a metal cylinder with one of a variety of fibres to decrease overall weight.
Cyalume: A proprietary brand of chemical emergency light.
Demand valve: The device which reduces the pressure of the gas within the breathing cylinder to ambient pressure and enables the diver to breathe. (See also Regulator).
DIN: Deutsche Industrie Norme (German Industry Standard) - an internationally accepted standard of manufacture. When applied colloquially to cylinder taps and demand valve first stages, it indicates the screw-in linkage used to seal against pressures higher than 200 bar.
Dive computer: A waterproof computer with software which monitors and displays various aspects of a dive profile, eg depth, time and decompression.
Dive profile: The depth/time profile of a particular dive.
DPV: Diver propulsion vehicle (underwater scooter).
Dump valve: A colloquial term for the exhaust valve on a buoyancy compensator or a drysuit.
Dysbarism: A general term for all forms of decompression-related sickness.
Free dive: A short cave dive made without the use of breathing apparatus.
Full face mask: A diving mask with integral breathing regulator designed to cover the diver's entire face.

Halocline: The boundary between two layers of water of differing salinity.
Handed: Term describing whether equipment is constructed or worn with a particular side of use in mind - ie either right-handed or left-handed.
Heliox: A breathing gas composed of a mixture of helium and oxygen.
HSE: Health and Safety Executive.
Inflation valve: Press-button valve on drysuit or buoyancy compensator controlling gas injection under pressure into the suit/BC to adjust buoyancy.
Jump reel: Small reel, usually more manoeuvrable than a search reel, carried to bridge gaps in the line within an underwater cave.
Karst: Generic term for a limestone landscape displaying solutionally-induced features above and below ground.
Mixing zone: Zone of intermixture of two waters of different salinity or temperature.
Molefone: Proprietary device used to communicate through up to 100m of rock and/or water.
Nitrogen narcosis: Term used to describe the narcotic effects on a diver of nitrogen in a breathing mixture (eg air at pressures in excess of 2 bars).
Nitrox: A breathing gas composed of a mixture of nitrogen and oxygen. (Air is technically a nitrox mixture).
No-stop time: The limiting time at which a diver can stay at a particular depth without having to decompress.
Partial pressure: The percentage by volume of a particular molecular gas with a breathing mixture.
Phreas: The sub-water table part of a limestone aquifer.
Phreatic passage: Cave passage formed below the water table in a limestone aquifer.
P-Party rebreather: Early type of nitrox rebreather.
PTFE: Polytetrafluoroethylene - a lubricating plastic used in bearings, seatings and in tape form to provide a high-quality gas-tight seal.
Rebreather: A breathing apparatus which recycles all or part of a diver's gas supply, enabling him to extend it beyond the time limits imposed by open-circuit SCUBA (qv).
Redundancy: The concept of carrying enough life-support equipment to enable any one part to become redundant during a dive without endangering the diver's life.
Regulators: The American term for demand valves (qv).
Rescue dump: A supply depot within a cave or beyond a sump which contains food, medical and emergency supplies for use in an emergency.
Reverse gas diffusion: A problem caused by inert gas entering body tissues which are still disgorging the same or a denser inert gas from a previous dive, and thus not allowing the original decompression to take place at the predicted rate.
Rocket tube: An ex-services container which has a sealing O-ring and is waterproof to about 30m.
Scalloping: Solutional features on a cave wall which indicate direction (and, to a degree, speed) of current flow.
SCUBA: Self-contained underwater breathing apparatus.
Search reel: A small reel carried by cave divers to assist them with the recovery of lost line, or to keep them linked to the main line whilst making short forays away from it.

Sherpa: A caver who assists the cave diver by carrying equipment to the dive site.
Shotline: A line hung vertically from dive base, usually to enable a diver to attach equipment or to use as a marker for decompression stops.
Sidemounts: Breathing cylinders worn on the sides of the diver.
Silt out: A trans-Atlantic term used to describe zero visibility caused by disturbance of silt banks.
Snoopy loop: A small interlinking loop of rubber tyre inner tube and nylon cord, used to belay the diving line to rocks or flakes on the cave wall.
Solo diving: The practise of diving alone. Adequate equipment redundancy (qv), careful preparation and the relevant degree of experience can make this a safer procedure in particular underwater caves.
Squeeze: a) A tight constriction within a cave; b) A pinching effect on the body caused by inadequate inflation of a drysuit.
SRT: Single rope techniques - the use of a secured single rope with friction and clamp devices to descend and ascend vertical cave passages.
Stab jacket: Stabiliser jacket - a type of buoyancy compensator.
Stage dive: A dive involving the underwater porterage of one or more cylinders of breathing gas in addition to those actually worn by the diver.
Sump: A section of completely flooded cave passage.
Syphon: Alternative name for a sump (qv).
Tadpole: Nickname for an early type of ex-services breathing cylinder.
Tacklebag: A duffle-type bag used to haul equipment through cave passages.
Tank or Cylinder bands: The metal bands that hold the breathing gas cylinders to the diver's harness or back-pack.
Thermocline: Boundary layer between two layers of water of different temperatures.
Thirds Rule: The practise of using one-third of the total air supply carried by the diver for the inward journey, one-third for the return, leaving one-third for accidents or failure of the other breathing system.
Tissue saturation: The term used to describe the time or amount required of a particular gas to reach saturation point within human tissue.
Trap: Early name for a sump (qv).
Trimix: A breathing gas composed of three separate gases, usually oxygen, nitrogen and helium.
UIS: Union Internationale de Speleologie (International Speleological Union)
Vadose zone: The section of a limestone aquifer existing, or cave formed above the water table.
Vis: Visibility.
Wall-out: American cave diving term for a passage ending in a blank wall with no conceivable continuation.
Wings: A form of buoyancy compensator worn behind the diver.
Y-valve: A single cylinder valve which allows two separate demand valves to be fitted to one cylinder.

INDEX

A
A-clamps, 54, 43
ABLJ, 71
Accident analysis, 119
Air
  weight of, 71
Air consumption
  affect on buoyancy, 71
  result of stress, 17
Air margins, 102
  diver propulsion vehicles, 201
  for deep diving, 147
  for digging, 197
Airbells
  surveying problems, 194
  use of, 116
Air-lifts, 199
Airbags, 199
Alcohol
  effect on diving, 13
Altitude
  diving at, 149
Ammo box, 66
Apprehension, 14
Archaeological remains, 214
Archimedes Principle, 70

B
Back-scatter, 62
  affect on visibility, 76
  reduction of, 76
Base-fed line, 79, 110
  signal system, 79
Batteries
  non-rechargeable, 63
  rechargeable, 63
BDH Containers, 66
Belaying line
  silt control techniques, 78
Benjamin Cross-over Manifold, 55
Bicycle respirator, 5, 7
Biology, 215
Boat-handling, 207
Bottom walking, 6
Boyle's Law, 31, 146

British Sub-Aqua Club, 11
Buddy diving, 97, 210
  stress effect, 15
Buoyancy
  drysuit, 25
  in deep diving, 146
Buoyancy compensators
  ABLJ, 71
  deep diving, 146
  direct feed operation, 73
  diving without, 74
  oral inflation, 73
  stabiliser jacket, 72
  use for silt avoidance, 78
  wings, 71
Buoyancy control, 70
  factors affecting, 70
  saltwater, 71

C
Carbon dioxide
  toxicity of, 147
Carbon monoxide
  toxicity of, 148
Carrying equipment, 66
Cave Diving Group
  constitution, 238
  formation of, 7
  sections, 8
  sections, responsibility for training, 11
Cave fauna
  conservation of, 78
"Caves and Caving", 218
CDG Newsletter, 218
  secrecy file, 219
CDG Officials, 242
Central committee, 238
Charles's Law, 244
Climbing
  beyond sumps, 126
CMAS, 230
CMAS Speleological Commission, 221
Compass, 34
  magnetic problems, 34
Compressors, 63
  carbon monoxide build-up, 148
  on expeditions, 211
Conservation
  marine life, 207, 208

scientific aspects of, 217
  underwater caves, 214
Constrictions, 109, 116
Cyalumes, 63
Cylinders, 52
  back-mounting, 55
  care of, 53
  composite construction, 56
  corrosion of, 53
  cylinder bands, 58
  decanting between, 134
  high pressure, 56
  pitch hauling, 65
  side-mounting, 55
  sizes of, 52
  specifications, 52
  storage of, 53
  testing, 53
  threads, 54
  transport of, 65
  vertical hauling, 69
  volumetric content of, 52
Cylinder bands, 58
Cylinder valves, 54
  burst discs, 54
  dual manifold, 55
  protection of, 56
  Y-valve, 56

D
Dalton's Law, 147, 244
Decompression
  at altitude, 149
  buoyancy during, 146
  equipment for, 154
  on air, 150
  on expeditions, 213
  on mixed gas, 174
  repetitive diving, 153
  use of oxygen, 158
Decompression chambers
  on expeditions, 213
Decompression computers
  as depth gauge, 33
  at altitude, 150
  on repetitive dives, 154
  transport of, 164
Decompression diving
  in marine caves, 210
Decompression sickness, 119, 139, 146
  drug treatment, 143

265

Decompression sickness (cont)
  obtaining treatment, 144
  on expeditions, 213
  predisposing factors, 155
  therapeutic recompression, 141, 152
  use of oxygen, 143
Decompression tables, 151,154
  BS-AC, 156
  Buhlmann, 157
  use with dive computers, 164
Deep diving, 145, 210
  air margins, 174
  with DPV's, 203
Demand valve, 41
  A-clamp, 43
  attachment of, 49
  BC direct feed as, 73
  choosing a, 50
  configuration and performance, 42
  Din-fitting, 43
  DIN/A-clamp adaptors, 44
  double stage, 42
  dual hose, 42
  exhaust valve, 42
  first stage filter, 46
  first stage of, 45
  for deep diving, 147
  "handedness", 43
  high pressure leaks, 48
  hoses, 47
  long second stage hose, 49
  low pressure leaks, 48
  maintenance and repairs, 45
  maintenance tools, 48
  major servicing, 51
  O-rings, 46
  Octopus valve, 56
  2nd stage, 47
  2nd stage mouthpiece filter, 50
  spares, 48
  transport of, 66
  troubleshooting, 50
Depth
  stress effect, 16
Depth gauges, 31
  altitude compensation, 34
  altitude transport, 34
  calibration, 33, 34
  for altitude diving, 149

maximum depth indicator, 34
Descent Magazine, 218
Digging
  beyond sumps, 127
  techniques, 197
DIN-Fittings, 43, 54
  new high-pressure demand valves, 54
Distance
  stress effect, 16
Dive computers, 160
  use in caves, 164
Dive profile, 153
Dive timers, 36
Diver propulsion vehicles (DPVs)
  air margins for, 103
  use of, 201
Diving at altitude, 149
  depth gauges, 31
Diving slate, 34
Drop weights, 91
Drowning, 138
Drugs
  effect on diving, 13
Dry gloves, 26
Drysuits, 22
  adaption for cave diving, 27
  as buoyancy compensator, 72
  buoyancy, 23, 25
  buoyancy control, 70
  care and maintenance of, 26
  checking for leaks, 26
  crushed neoprene, 23
  deep diving, 146
  dressing, 24
  dump valve, 27
  expedition use, 211
  flooding of, 23
  foam neoprene, 23
  heliox diving, 174
  inflation valve, 27
  inversion in, 25, 74
  on long dives, 116
  rubber laminate, 23
  seals, 28
  underclothing, 26
  weighting for, 27
  zip lubrication, 24
Dual manifold, 55
  problems of, 104
Dump valves, 25, 27

E
Ear-clearing, 39
Ear-drums
  burst, 148
Electrolytic drinks, 20
Emergency kits
  contents of, 131
Emergency phone numbers, 243
Equipment, 20
  distribution, 37
  preparation of, 14
Equipment maintenance
  on expeditions, 213
Expeditions
  cave diving, 209, 210
  equipment, 210
  first aid, 213
  politics, 214
  sponsorship, 214
Explosives, 198
  use of, 127

F
Finning techniques
  silt control, 77
Fins, 28
  construction of, 30
  prevention of loss, 30
  taping buckles, 28
First aid, 135
  beyond sumps, 137
  emergency kits, 139
  dumps, 139
  emergency treatment, 129
  marine problems, 207
  on expeditions, 213
  training organisations, 133
Flying after diving, 150
Following lines, 94
Footwear, 28, 30
Free-diving, 112
Full face mask, 40, 50, 148
  for heliox, 176

G
Groundwater flow, 217
Guidelines, 98, 112, 154, 192, 211, 223

H
Halocline, 205, 214
Harnesses, 58